WOODTURNING DESIGN

MIKE DARLOW

Number 4 in Mike Darlow's Woodturning Series

Fox Chapel Publishing Co. Inc.

1970 Broad Street • East Petersburg, PA 17520 • www.foxchapelpublishing.com

Woodturning Design is the fourth book in Mike Darlow's woodturning series. The first three books in the series are *The Fundamentals of Woodturning*, *Woodturning Methods*, and *Woodturning Techniques*. The 7-hour instructional film covering the basics of woodturning, *The Practice of Woodturning*, is available as an NTSC two-DVD set in North America.

Distributed in North America by: Fox Chapel Publishing Company Inc., 1970 Broad Street, East Petersburg, PA 17520
Tel: (717) 560 4703   Fax: (717) 560 4702   www.foxchapelpublishing.com

Printed by H & Y Printing Limited, Hong Kong.

Darlow, Mike, 1943- .
    Woodturning techniques.

    Includes index.
        ISBN   1-56523-196-1

    1. Turning. 2. Woodwork. I. Title.

684.083

CONTENTS

ACKNOWLEDGEMENTS

I thank the people, companies, and organizations listed below for their advice and information; the supply of transparencies, photographs and scans; and for allowing me to photograph their work or items in their possession. Their contributions have been essential to the completion of this book.

I work in rural Australia where access to original books of earlier centuries is almost impossible. I thank the publishers of facsimile editions such as Dover Publications and Benjamin Blom for making these books widely accessible through facsimile, and for giving me permission to reproduce images from them.

I thank the staff at my local Moss Vale and Bowral branches of the Wingecarribee Shire Library, and at the State Library of New South Wales, for helping me to obtain reference books.

I am a self-publisher and I am only able to continue to publish this series because of the international sales. Over the past five years I have developed an excellent working relationship with Claire and Brian Davies of Stobart Davies in England; and Alan Giagnocavo, Peg Couch, and Shannon Flowers at Fox Chapel in America.

My greatest thanks go to my wife Aliki who has has become a demon editor and proofreader, and has allowed me to sometimes reschedule household duties. My sons Joshua and Samuel have also showed great tolerance.

Australia
Russell Brooks, Michael Cassidy, Mr and Mrs John Carroll, John Harris, Robyn Hawkins, Peter Herbert, Adrian Hunt, Michael Keighery, Ernie Newman, Howard Nicholson, Geoff O'Loughlin, Andrew Potocnik, Richard Raffan, John Rea, Fred Robjent, Rémi Verchot.

Georgia Hale, Art Gallery of South Australia; David McLaren, Bungendore Wood Works Gallery; Barry Connor, Connor Galleries; John Hawkins, J. B. Hawkins Antiques; Andrew Simpson, Simpsons Antiques; Alan Russell, Tudor House School; John Lane, The Village Pump Antiques.

Canada
Stephen Hogbin, Mike Hosaluk, Greg Payce, Frank Sudol.

England
John Ambrose, Paul Clare, John F. Edwards, Melvyn Firmager, Sir Ernst H. Gombrich, Ray Key, Jim Partridge, Roger Scruton, David Springett, Timothy Stokes, Robin Wood.

Jim Bright, The Leeds Museum Resource Centre (Temple Newsam House); Sylvia Crawley and Iain Harrison, Birmingham Museum and Art Gallery; M.F. Golding, Huntington Antiques; Dennis Harrington, Christ Church; The British Museum.

France
Gérard Bidou, Luc Caquineau, Christian Delhon, Jean-François Escoulen, Henri Groll, Jean-Luc Merigot.

Hubert Meyer, Sélestal Library.

Israel
Eli Abuhatzira.

Germany
Holger Graf, Peter Hromek, Georg Panz, Bernd Pfister, Rolf Steinert, Johannes Volmer, Hans Joachim Weissflog.

The Netherlands
Maria van Kesteren.

New Zealand
Graeme Priddle.

United States of America
Michael Brolly, Christian Burchard, J. Paul Fennell, R. Valen Frye, Dewey Garrett, Robyn Hunt, Bill Hunter, C. R. 'Skip' Johnson, Gary Johnson, Ron Kent, Michael Lambert, Simon Levy, Mark Lindquist, Steve Loar, Marlowe McGraw, Mike Mahoney, Johannes Michelsen, Rude Osolnik, Greg Payce, Michael Peterson, Jon Sauer, Merryll Saylan, Lincoln Seitzman, David Sengel, Wayne Shipman, Al Stirt.

Teresa Curran and Albert LeCoff, The Wood Turning Center; Alan Jutzi, The Huntington Library.

INTRODUCTION

This book aims to help you to design better by enabling you to increase your understanding and knowledge of design. To do this it has to make sense of design. I have been accused of writing like an engineer, and of putting information into pigeonholes. I plead guilty on both counts. I hope by these two means, and by describing the connections between the pigeonholes, to make design understandable to the majority of readers.

William Hogarth wrote on page 1 of the preface to his 1753 book *The Analysis of Beauty*: "It is no wonder that this subject [beauty] should have so long been thought inexplicable". The related subject of design is similarly difficult to explain which is why there has been far less written on woodturning design than on woodturning techniques. The nature of design also tempts writers to substitute obfuscation for expertise and wordiness for wisdom; and there is always the refuge of the breathless posturings beloved by decorator- and lifestyle-magazine journalists. I have tried to avoid these temptations, and instead follow Albert Einstein who said: "Everything should be made as simple as possible, but not simpler". My versions of "as simple as possible" seem to be more detailed than those of some other woodturning writers, and some of the regrettably dwindling band of reviewers have noted this. Fortunately, the feedback from readers of my four earlier books suggests that readers increasingly appreciate that:

1. There is little gain without effort—I have used *effort* rather than the cliché *pain* because if this book is painful to read, I have not done my job of presenting its contents properly.
2. It is unnecessary to fully understand and absorb a book in one sitting.
3. A reader can feel rewarded without finding the whole of a book directly relevant at the time he or she first reads it.

This book concentrates on the design of turned wooden objects rather than on designing for the essentially non-woodturning techniques which can be applied to woodturnings. Neither is this book:

1. A gallery of turnings to inspire you, or for you to copy.
2. A compendium of shapes.
3. A survey of historical woodturning designs.
4. A treatise on the geometry of shapes.

While the illustrated turnings will inevitably be treated somewhat as a gallery, they have been selected to illustrate the text. Not all have been selected because of their superior design. I encourage you to make your own judgments on the merits and any shortcomings of all the turnings shown.

The inclusion or omission of particular turnings or the work of a particular turner should not be taken to imply any judgments on my part. Many of the works displayed are by me, but are not labelled as such in the legend unless there could be confusion. Work by others is attributed wherever possible.

To restrain this book's length, I have not described each illustrated work's every association and nuance. Study and reflect on the works, it will be time well spent.

I do not have any formal training in the arts, design (except engineering design), philosophy, or psychology; a situation shared by many of my readers. I am convinced that a familiarity with all these areas is essential to a fuller understanding and enjoyment of woodturning design. While my coverage may be flawed, I hope that it will spur others to push into these hitherto no-go areas.

This book is the fourth in my woodturning series. Rather than repeat information from earlier books in the series in this book, I will refer you to the appropriate pages in *The Fundamentals of Woodturning*, *Woodturning Methods*, or *Woodturning Techniques*.

English lacks common (representing both sexes) pronouns such as those meaning *he or she*, and *his or hers*. Where there is not a suitable common word, I often use the usual masculine substitute, but intend no slight to the most welcome and growing number of female turning designers.

Mike Darlow, November, 2002.

KEY

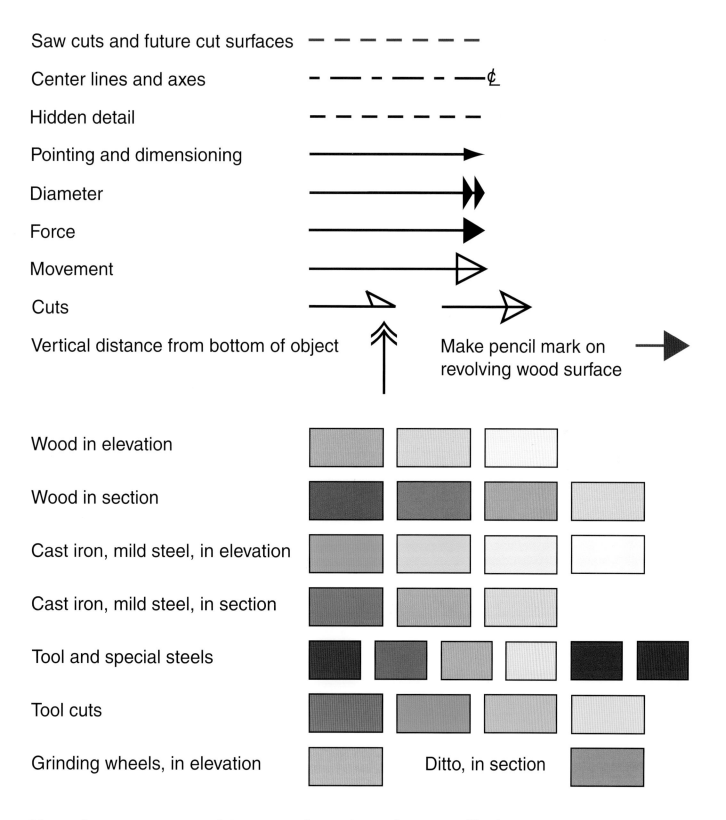

Saw cuts and future cut surfaces

Center lines and axes

Hidden detail

Pointing and dimensioning

Diameter

Force

Movement

Cuts

Vertical distance from bottom of object

Make pencil mark on revolving wood surface

Wood in elevation

Wood in section

Cast iron, mild steel, in elevation

Cast iron, mild steel, in section

Tool and special steels

Tool cuts

Grinding wheels, in elevation   Ditto, in section

Note, there may some departures from the colors specified.

Chapter One

THE DESIGN PROCESS

The challenge of woodturning design was well described by the first known writer on the subject, Charles Plumier (1646–1704), in his L'Art de Tourner first published in Latin and French in 1701:[1]

> To become a skillful turner, it is not sufficient just to thoroughly know the machines and the expert handling of the lathe tools. You must also understand the profile to give the best style to the workpiece. I call the best style that which gives pleasure to the eye and at first sight satisfies the spirit by its mere bearing and appearance.

What is "the best style"? Figure 1.1 shows a late twentieth-century example. How do you compare it with Plumier's ideal in figure 1.2? Plumier explains the difficulty, and its solution:

> It is quite difficult to explain this good [best] style and to establish some precise rules for it since it depends on the opinions and spirit of the people rather than on a fixed method. The eye alone must prescribe the rules and laws, as in the arts of painting and architecture where all the rules that have been advanced have never been known to shape the work in as pleasing a manner as those that are frequently conceived as a single idea or mere whim.

Plumier was referring above to the conflict between designing by conforming to rules and theories, and designing by intuition. The intuitive approach is summarized by the familiar "If it looks right, it is right". While I would add "but it could still probably be improved through a more formal design process", there is right in both camps.

The difficulties in designing described by Charles Plumier are real, and largely explain both the dearth of writing on woodturning design and the aversion to formal design among both those who turn "for fun" and even among professionals. However, to waste time turning failures just because you won't put in the necessary design effort strikes me as being neither enjoyable nor profitable. Perhaps a major reason for the popularity of bowl turning is the belief that you can produce a good bowl without having to do any formal design in advance. The wood is supposed to "speak" to you and thus empower you to free the wondrous bowl hidden within the unpromising blank—I may be deficient in the necessary spirituality, but wood doesn't speak to me all that often or all that clearly. Those woodturners who bypass formal design may also believe that:

1. They are not among that privileged minority born with designer genes.

2. Those not born with designer genes are doomed to design poorly.
3. Design is hard, boring, and unproductive work.

These beliefs are common, harmful, and wrong. They may stem at least in part from turners watching demonstrators produce beautiful turnings without apparently having done any prior design. What the audiences overlook is that the demonstrators have refined and memorized the designs of their demonstration turnings during many earlier occasions. Also, the turnings might have looked even better had the demonstrators formally designed the turnings and prepared gauges to use during their demonstrations beforehand.

While it is undoubtedly true that inborn design ability varies, we who are less gifted can and should continually produce good designs. I shall now reveal the secret of design success: it's WORK. If we all put as much effort into design as we put in on the lathe, there would be far less turned dross.

If the secret of good design is work, then it must also be sensibly directed work. That in turn demands commitment,

Figure 1.1 Three totemic sculptures turned in pecan and walnut between 1985 and 1987 by Mark Lindquist of Quincy, Florida; 6 ft (1.8 m) high. Photograph by Glenn Johnson.

Figure 1.2 A lidded urn ornamental-turning in "the best style", plate 65 from Plumier's *L'Art de Tourner*. Plumier wrote that this was one of several pieces which "seemed to me to possess enough good style to serve as models for those who wish to perfect themselves in the works of the lathe".[2] In my view however:

1. The wide, flat, bottom part of the main body lacks elegance and does not flow nicely into the stem.
2. The upper and lower narrow sections of the stem are too thin, and their beads and half beads all have approximately the same diameter which makes them visually boring. The central bun in the stem is an abrupt insertion.
3. The base plate is visually too thin. Its supporting bun feet are too high for the base plate shown.

What do you think?

and you will become more committed to designing better if your designs improve through an increasing understanding of the design process. This first chapter therefore introduces that process.

1.1 AN INTRODUCTION TO DESIGN

You should strive to produce well-designed woodturnings because:

1. Good design is a challenge. Once you cease to seek and answer challenges, it's time to pull down the coffin lid.
2. A poorly designed turning is a constant and irritating reminder to you and to others that you could have done better; and a needless waste of resources and of your turning abilities.
3. A poor design is less likely to sell, and may adversely affect your future sales.
4. While woodturnings are typically relatively unimportant items—a poorly designed woodturning will rarely be the cause of multiple deaths—a well-designed woodturning has the opposite effects to those listed in reasons 2 and 3, and improves the lives of all those who experience it, even if in modest and unconscious ways.

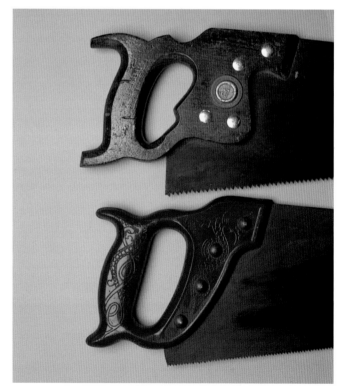

Figure 1.3 Handsaw handles. *Top*, the handle retains the redundant vestige of the hooks around which cords was once wound and then twisted to tension the blades of frame saws. *Bottom*, the vestige has finally gone.

We agree then that woodturning design is important. How do you go about it? The least-formal design process is sometimes called craft evolution. It can occur over centuries and involve many generations, or involve one craftsman over a relatively short time. J. Christopher Jones describes its characteristics thus:[3]

1. No formal drawings may have been made through the evolution of the design, nor may the reasons be known for design decisions taken in the past.
2. The form is modified over time according to the perceived successes and failures.
3. Discordant features can creep into the design; obsolete features can also be retained (figures 1.3 and 1.4).

While craft evolution will eventually result in an elegant and functional design, the process is too long and inefficient. Fortunately, woodturnings are relatively simple to design and can be adequately shown on simple plans, elevations, and sections, ideal for design-by-drawing.[4]

Design-by-drawing started with the scratching of lines onto rock or into the surface of soil. Construction drawings of temples and tombs from ancient Egypt are still extant. The essence of design-by-drawing is that you do your trials and make your mistakes on paper or similar rather than in the lathe. Therefore trialing by making models is an extension of design-by-drawing. But whether you use design-by-drawing or trial models, by taking a more disciplined approach to design you will achieve:

1. Better turnings.
2. More-efficient production.
3. Minimization of wasted time and material.
4. If you are a professional, more profit.
5. Greater creativity, individuality, and originality.

Few will argue against the first four benefits, but greater creativity resulting from more discipline! Surely this is a contradiction? No, the more disciplined approach:

1. Does not imply more-rigid thinking.

2. Allows more options to be trialed.
3. Is more likely to activate the subconscious processes which result in inspiration.
4. Still allows you to modify the design during turning if you find an earlier-unseen flaw in the wood or make a faulty cut. The modification is also more likely to be successful because you are clear about means and ends.

The full process for designing an object is outlined in figure 1.5. Where does design-by-drawing fit in? It's an integral part of the full process, and adds the qualification that design solutions are to be trialed and recorded on paper, pale wood or board, or on a computer screen. Design-by-drawing in combination with the figure 1.5 process encourage and enable you to:

1. Clearly define your intentions and any restraints.
2. Design and specify the turning, the manifestation of the intentions and restraints in 1. This specification should not be just physical because unless the turner (often you) is aware of the full intentions of the turning and how the design expresses them, he or she is less likely to fully and correctly manifest them in the turning.
3. Plan the production of the turning; the acquisition and allocation of materials, equipment, knowledge and skills.
4. Plan and optimize post-production factors such as packing, transport, exhibition, marketing, and sale.
5. Continually refine the design and review other decisions, including whether to continue, as you gain further knowledge.

Designing rarely follows the orderly linear process in the figure 1.5 flow chart. You might not start at the beginning; you may go down a cul-de-sac and have to double-back; you might take several stages forwards in parallel, or perform them in a cursory way; you may omit stages. I could discuss all the possible component actions of each stage separately, but this would lead to considerable repetition as some

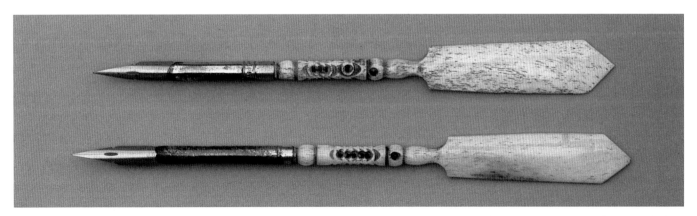

Figure 1.4 Bone-handled pens, late nineteenth century. The flat sections to the right of the turned sections recall the earlier quill pens.[5] Photographed courtesy of The Village Pump Antiques, Exeter, New South Wales, Australia.

component actions will be repeated in several stages, albeit with different emphases and to different levels of detail. This book will therefore follow the simplified linear path down the left of figure 1.5.

You are rarely the only person who is involved with one of your woodturning designs. Others who might be involved during the design, its production, and the subsequent life of the turning are:

1. The client, who may be:
    i.   The turner producing something for himself which he may keep, give away, destroy, or sell.
    ii. Someone who commissions a work.
    iii. A potential client or recipient. The designer will assess the needs, preferences, wealth, etc. of this client who may be a person or a group the designer knows; or be an imagined typical representative of a group, for example, a collector, or someone who buys at a market.
2. The turner, if he or she is not the designer.
3. Experiencers, all those who will come into contact with the turning, including: wholesalers, retailers, future owners, and those whose contact is less involved. "Experiencer" is not a mellifluous word, but its meaning is closest to the correct sense.

You and they can only become involved with your design and the resulting turning through mental processing, the subject of the next chapter.

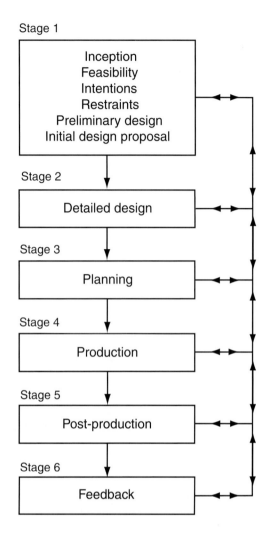

Figure 1.5 The woodturning design process.
The design process is often considered as separate from and preceding production, but in most cases it continues through and integrates with production, post-production, and feedback.

The preliminary design may be the first design drawn, or it may be a later, somewhat refined design. In either case it is to the state of refinement required for a decision to be taken on whether to proceed to detailed design; it is sometimes called an outline design because the details will usually not have been fully resolved. This preliminary design forms part of any initial design proposal which has to be submitted to a client for approval to proceed to the detailed design.

1.2 ENDNOTES

1. Charles Plumier, L'Art de Tourner (The Art of Turning), 2nd French ed. 1749, translated by Paul L. Ferraglio (Brooklyn, New York: Paul L. Ferraglio, 1975), p. 139. Plumier was an ecclesiastic (a member of the order of Minime), a botanist, an instrument maker, and an ornamental-turner. See Sydney George Abell, John Leggat, and Warren Greene Ogden, Jr., A Bibliography of the Art of Turning and Lathe and Machine Tool History, 3rd ed. (North Andover, Massachusetts: The Museum of Ornamental Turning, 1987), pp. 77–79. There is a biography of Plumier, Urban von Ign, Plumiers Leben und Schriften (Berlin: Verlag des Repertorums, 1920). I have not been able to locate a portrait of Plumier. If you know of one, I would be grateful for information.

2. Plumier, L'Art de Tourner, Paul L. Ferraglio, p. 178.

3. J. Christopher Jones, Design Methods (New York: John Wiley & Sons, 1970), pp. 15–20.

4. Jones, pp. 20–24.

5. A history of the pen is given in Joyce Irene Whalley, Writing Implements and Accessories (Newton Abbot: David & Charles, 1975).

Chapter Two

PERCEPTION

You cannot achieve a soundly based appreciation of beauty and design without some understanding of the mental processing involved. In this chapter I shall therefore attempt to explain how our minds work. Chapters 3 and 4 then discuss the history and today's understanding of the information, concepts, etc., we store in our memories and use in designing and in experiencing a design. This involves delving into philosophy, the logical analysis of underlying principles.

The areas discussed in this and chapters 3 and 4 were as alien to me as they may be to most readers before I started this book. Fear not because my task as an author is to make these areas understandable and relevant. The text I found most helpful was *The Sense of Order* (London: Phaidon Press, 1979) by Ernst H. Gombrich (figure 2.1).

2.1 HOW THE MIND PERCEIVES

An understanding of the workings of the mind has been built up over the centuries, most recently by cognitive psychologists who study how information is collected, processed, understood, and used. What is psychology? An American, William James, one of the founders of modern psychology, defined it in 1890 as "the science of mental life".[1]

In 1689 in his *Philosophical Essays Concerning Human Understanding*, John Locke proposed what Sir Karl Popper in his 1934 book *The Logic of Scientific Discovery* dubbed *the bucket theory of the mind*.[2] According to Locke the mind of a newborn baby is a *tabula rasa*, an empty slate.[3] This new mind then passively over time takes in information through the senses which allows it to build an impression of the world. Man thus has no innate (present at birth) ideas, and no teacher except his own experiences. While agreeing with Locke that knowledge is taken in through the senses, Popper proposed *the searchlight theory of the mind* which asserts that the mind of a newborn baby is neither empty nor passive, and is programmed to constantly scan and search its environment to answer "where?" and "what?". Illustrations of this are given in figures 2.2 and 2.3.

Popper's theory further asserts that our minds are programmed to suggest hypotheses based on sensed information, on information already stored in our memories, and on combinations based on both (figure 2.4). This happens when processing sensed information and during other mental processes such as reasoning. The information is assembled into an expectation sometimes called a *construction*, a *schema*, or a *conceptual set*, and the hypothesis

takes the form of "Does this expectation apply? Is this solution correct?". Our minds may then direct the senses to search for further information to test those hypotheses. For this to be possible there must be an expectation of regularity. Thus we are jolted by the exceptional, the unexpected, or a contrast between order and disorder. When however nothing is changing, the relevant sensors are switched off—for example, are you at present aware of the contact between your clothes and your skin? This process of repeated questioning on the basis of order, with order being defined by information held in memory, was christened *the sense of order* by Ernst Gombrich.

Figure 2.1 Professor Sir Ernst H. Gombrich. He was born in Vienna in 1909, moved to London in 1936, and died there in late 2001. His book *The Sense of Order* was my most important reference for *Woodturning Design*.

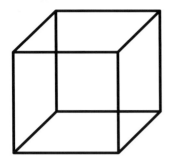

Figure 2.2 An illustration of Popper's searchlight theory of the mind, the Necker cube named for the Swiss physicist and mathematician Louis Necker (1730–1804). Although the drawing is just black lines in two dimensions, you perceive a three-dimensional cube. Look at the drawing for some seconds and the cube face which was at the front switches to the back. These faces then alternate as the mind attempts to make sense of an ambiguous drawing which has insufficient information to allow the mind to decide which way the cube is drawn.

Figure 2.4 An example of the use of conceptual knowledge given by Roger Scruton.[6] The top of this table is veneered in New Zealand native woods and made by Anton Seuffert of Auckland in about 1870. It creates an elliptical image on each of your retinas when you view it obliquely. However you perceive that the tabletop is circular because your memory contains the knowledge that similar images have resulted from viewing circular tabletops obliquely. Photographed courtesy of J. B. Hawkins Antiques, Moss Vale, New South Wales.

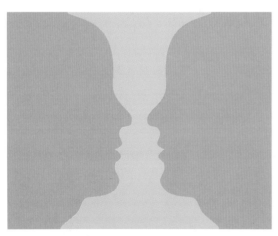

Figure 2.3   The face/goblet illusion.
     In his 1998 book *Visual Intelligence*[4] Donald Hoffman details the innate, active, rules-based process by which we make sense of what we see. Hoffman explains that this process interacts with and often precedes and drives our rational and emotional intelligences, and forwards constructions to them to use in further constructions. The rules described for making sense include those which cover how we distinguish an object from its surroundings, and how we distinguish what an object is. These rules are confounded by the inherent ambiguity of this illustration, first shown in a picture puzzle of 1795, and investigated in 1915 by Danish psychologist Edgar Rubin.[5]

9, 10, 11, 12, 13

G, F, E, D, C, 13

Figure 2.5 An illustration combining the senses of order and meaning. The ambiguous combinations of a vertical line and a squiggle at the right-hand ends of the two series are read as a *13* or a *B* according to whether numbers or letters precede them in the series.[7]

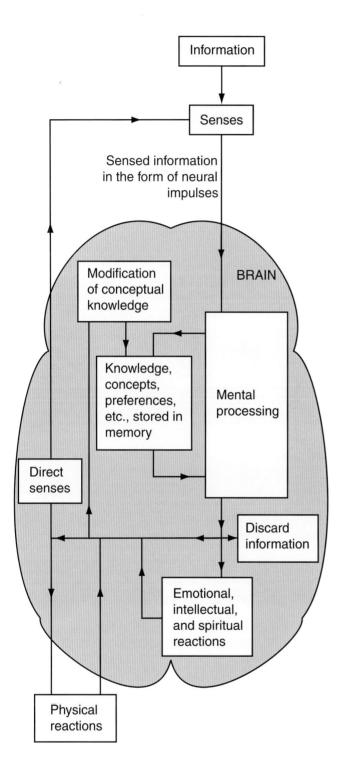

Figure 2.6 The processing of sensed information.
With sight, the initial information can be regarded as being two multicolored areas, one on each retina.

The area of a retina on which we can focus precisely, the *fovea centralis*, collects light from a circle subtending about 1°. If something of interest is noticed in the other part of the retinal images, the peripheral vision, we then direct our *fovea centralis* at it.

An example of our sense of order is forward matching. Gombrich quotes as an example descending a flight of steps. After going down the first few steps we do not need to pay attention again until the end of the flight. Forward matching, which is allied to our power to anticipate, also enables us to relate to pattern and rhythm.

Allied with the human sense of order is, Gombrich explains, *the sense of meaning*. Sensory input is processed by your mind (the software which runs on the hardware of your brain) not only according to the input's physical chacteristics, but also according to its meaning to the individual. Again, sensed information is questioned for meaning by comparing it with information relating to meaning stored in memory. Figure 2.5 shows a simple example.

Gombrich's senses of order and meaning are convenient names for the mental processing and memory stores which

Figure 2.7 Ornamental-turnings by Jon Sauer of Daly City, California. These scent bottles are 4 to 7 in. (100 to 175 mm) tall. Ornamental-turning is an area in which detail is actively sought and appreciated.

can be used in these connections. The process is explained in figure 2.6. Other writers have suggested graphic names for other useful combinations; for example, the philosopher Roger Scruton refers to the *sense of detail* (figures 2.7, 2.8, and 2.9).[8]

The knowledge, concepts, etc. you have stored and ordered in your long-term memory are called conceptual knowledge. This continually builds and changes, and influences your perceptions through time.

Perception is so quick and easy that it is thought to employ a rapidly accessible but not deep intelligence with a small knowledge base. Conception, the building of conceptual knowledge which is stored for future use in memory, is thought to be a slower, deeper process. However whether we have any innate aesthetic tastes on which to build, and if so, what they are and whether they are the same for all, has yet to be answered according to my reading. There is however a belief that we have a preference for convex, bulging forms.[9]

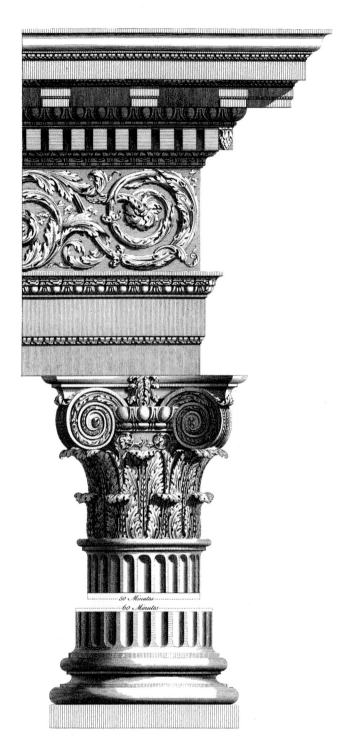

Figure 2.9 Detail in the Composite order pictured by William Chambers.[11] Reproduced courtesy of Benjamin Blom.

Spare a minute or two to savour the detail. Have we lost the ability and the desire to appreciate detail? or does our modern pace of life leave us less time to enjoy it? Are we also unable to believe that it is now possible to build to this level of detail, to input so much meticulous effort over a long period of time. Western man has never been more financially wealthy or more sensually impoverished.

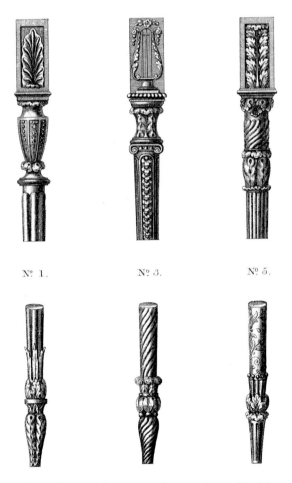

Nº 1.   Nº 3.   Nº 5.

Figure 2.8 Turned legs for pier and card tables showing a healthy level of carved detail.[10]
Reproduced courtesy of Dover Publications

MEMORY
It has been proposed that there are three types of memory:

1. *The sensory store* which receives information from the senses and holds it for about a second. During this time the information is separated into that which is irrelevant, which is then allowed to decay and is lost, and that which is relevant which is then passed to the short-term memory.
2. *The short-term memory* with limited capacity. Continuing to attend to, process, or rehearse that information transfers it to the long-term memory.
3. *The long-term memory* has a vast or perhaps unlimited capacity, and incorporates a complex encoding and retrieval system.

Memory is an important contributor to expertise. The expert has a wider range of existing solutions to problems in memory, and is therefore more able to respond quickly to a design problem by unconsciously selecting a likely one and putting the hypothesis "can I use this known solution?"

THINKING, REASONING, COMMUNICATING
Concepts are the building blocks that help us organize our thinking and responses; they are abstractions which simplify and summarize what we know, and they contain both general and specific information.

After practice, activities which once demanded careful thought become automatic, i.e. subconscious. Doing these automatic activities frees the mind for other activities; doing them consciously is disruptive.

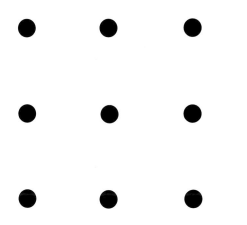

Figure 2.10 An illustration of creativity, the 9-dot problem.[12] The task is to connect all nine dots using four straight lines without lifting the pen from the paper. The solution is given on page 10. A clue: could this diagram have been the source of the cliché "thinking outside the square"?

Reasoning involves operating with information we have. There are three types of reasoning:

1. *Deductive* using logic.
2. *Inductive*, concluding on partial information or on probability.
3. *Dialectic*, evaluating conflicting points of view.

Reasoning uses information stored in memory. Using stored solutions is more efficient, but yields more predictable results. Creativity requires divergent thinking, not relying on solutions already stored in memory.

MOTIVATION AND EMOTIONS
Feelings are of two types: motivations which determine goals, and emotions which reflect feelings and organize our activities. Both galvanize us into action. Our feelings influence and are influenced by other mental processes.

2.1.1 OTHER MENTAL PROCESSES

I have described conceptual knowledge stored in memory. We have the ability to greatly increase that knowledge in desired areas. Our design ability is related to how creatively we can use that knowledge. Francis Galton suggested that creativity is related to an individual's ability to retrieve apparently irrational ideas, sift them, and use those selected constructively (figure 2.10).[13] It may be that the mental software which is concerned with creativity changes with experience, and that we can consciously improve our software. We can also design more effectively by allowing time for incubation and may be able to increase creativity by consciously using mental techniques such as lateral thinking and brainstorming.

INCUBATION
Incubation is an unconscious process which is by definition not instantaneous. You set your mind a problem, and your mind attempts to solve it by searching your conceptual knowledge, and by putting parts of that conceptual knowledge together in new ways. This subconscious processing can take a short time, hours, or days, and often results in the recall of something which you had forgotten but wanted to recall, or in a solution to a problem. Much of the mental processing associated with incubation takes place during deep sleep, and, according to Archimedes, in the bath. Incubation is valuable in facilitating intuition, the flashes of inspiration, the *Eurekas*.

LATERAL THINKING
The aim of lateral thinking is to produce ideas which are logical in hindsight. You have a perception of a design problem. Normally you process this problem logically using that perception and your conceptual knowledge to produce a solution. The purpose of lateral thinking is to provoke new

perceptions by such techniques as random juxtaposition and brainstorming.[14]

BRAINSTORMING
Brainstorming works best with a group. The idea is to provoke new perceptions by abandoning logical processing, and by striking sparks off one another. It is group provocation, a prelude to provide new starting points for logical thinking.

2.2 CONCLUSION

The present understanding of man's mental processing has taken about 2500 years to formulate. Some of the history of its formulation and the origins and development of concepts relating to design are described in the next chapter.

2.3 ENDNOTES

1. Gillian Butler and Freda McManus, Psychology: A Very Short Introduction (Oxford University Press: 1998), p.1. This book is an excellent introduction to the workings of the mind. I have used it extensively in writing this chapter.

2. Karl Raimund Popper was born in Vienna in 1902. He partly financed his study at the University of Vienna by working as a cabinetmaker, spent WWII teaching in New Zealand, and from 1946 was based in London. He was knighted in 1967, and died in 1994. Ref: The Great Philosophers from Socrates to Turing, ed. Ray Monk and Frederick Raphael (London: Weidenfeld & Nicholson, 2000), pp. 371–376.

3. Although credited to Locke, this term was first used by Thomas Aquinas. Ref: Bryan Magee, The Story of Philosophy (London: Dorling Kindersley, 1998), p. 59.

4. Donald D. Hoffman, Visual Intelligence (New York: W. W. Norton, 1998).

5. Hoffman, pp. 91–93.

6. Roger Scruton, Modern Philosophy (London: Sinclair-Stevenson, 1994), p. 329.

7. J.S. Bruner and A.L. Minturn studied this example of ambiguity, see Butler and Mcmanus, p. 20.

8. Roger Scruton, The Aesthetics of Architecture (Princeton, New Jersey: Princeton University Press, 1979), pp. 206–236.

9. Rudolf Arnheim, The Power of the Center: A Study of Composition in the Visual Arts (Berkeley: University of California Press, 1982), p. vii, and James Elkins, The Object Stares Back: On the Nature of Seeing (New York: Harcourt, Brace & Co, 1996), p. 125.

10. Thomas Sheraton, The Cabinet-Maker and Upholsterer's Drawing-Book (1791; reprint, New York: Dover Publications, 1972), plate 9.

11. William Chambers, A Treatise on the Decorative Part of Civil Architecture (1791; reprint New York, Benjamin Blom: 1968), opposite p. 57.

12. Butler and McManus, p. 51.

13. Editor Geoffrey Underwood, The Oxford Guide to the Mind (Oxford University Press, 2001), p. 219.

14. Edward de Bono, "Lateral Thinking," in The Oxford Guide to the Mind, editor Geoffrey Underwood, (Oxford University Press, 2001), p. 225–227.

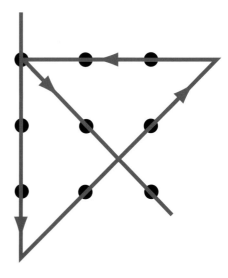

The solution to the 9-dot problem posed in figure 2.10.

Chapter Three

A HISTORY OF AESTHETICS

Designing is just one of the ways in which we connect with the world, make it a little better, and thus make life worthwhile and meaningful. The preceding chapter explained the role of conceptual knowledge, much of which has permeated into our memories unannounced. We may be unaware of its sources, its detail, or even of its presence.

Part of our conceptual knowledge concerns design and its consort beauty. This chapter concentrates on their history, and summarizes relevant writings in chronological order.[1] Ornamental-turners have written on design, but their focus has tended to be technical, and I have been unable to locate any historical writing on design by hand woodturners. Designing did not become a separate profession until the twentieth century, therefore most of the writings on design have been by philosophers and architects. The philosophical and architectural issues they raised are relevant to today's woodturners because woodturnings have always been intimately connected with the structures, contents, and the surroundings of buildings. Even when these issues and associated knowledge does not seem to be directly relevant to a particular design task, it will enrich both your designing and your experiencing of designs.

Through most of recorded history beauty was the all-encompassing aesthetic property and the focus of debate. This debate has centered on seven issues:[2]

1. Is beauty a physical property of things, and if so can the conditions for it be defined and created?
2. Is beauty only subjective, only a mental construct, and can it only be measured by the personal pleasure resulting from its perception?
3. Is the beauty of natural things distinct and different to the beauty of man-made things?
4. Is beauty connected with morality (right and wrong)? If so, is it the morality of the designed object or of its designers and makers which is relevant?
5. Is something beautiful if it fulfills its function? This raises the issue of spareness—if a design just fulfills the functional requirements, is it therefore beautiful?
6. Is there a relationship between the beauty of things and the processes used in their creation?
7. What is the proper relationship between ornament and structure, and how do they each contribute to the property of beauty?

Although the debates continue, beauty's role as an overall term declined through the eighteenth century. "Sublime" was among the first of an increasing number of other aesthetic terms which came into use. However the main factor causing the decline in importance of the term *beauty* was the introduction of the new term *aesthetic* by the German philosopher Alexander Gottlieb Baumgarten (1714–1762). He derived it from the Greek *aiesthesis*, having to do with the senses, and adapted it for the title of his two-volume *Aesthetica* (1750–58).[3] Through his book, Baumgarten established aesthetics (studies concerning art, its creative sources, its forms, and its effects) as a distinct form of inquiry. My history of this inquiry spans 2600 years, and is crudely split into three periods: ancient and medieval, Renaissance, and modern.

3.1 THE ANCIENT AND MEDIEVAL PERIOD

To put human life into context and give it meaning during this first period, thinkers had to reason to develop rational explanations which were not dependent on a broad and sound scientific knowledge base—there wasn't one, nor was there the means to create one. A simple illustration is that of how we see. One group of Greek philosophers, the atomists, believed that objects expelled material replicas of themselves in the form of thin films composed of atoms. These films entered the eye and caused vision by their impact. Thus vision was a form of touch. A different proposition by Plato was that light issued from the eye, a theory supposedly supported by the ability of nocturnal animals to see in the dark.[4] Such explanations became accepted as canons. This uncritical acceptance resulted in pressure to interpret subsequently discovered knowledge and conflicting concepts which were posited later in ways which were compatible with the canons. So entrenched became the explanations of the ancient, mainly Greek, philosophers and later the Christian churches, that as the means to test these canons gradually become available after the start of the Renaissance, the canons became a bar to the progress of understanding.

3.1.1 ANCIENT GREECE

In ancient Greece, woodturning was just one of the many specialized forms of skill such as painting, shoemaking, poetry, music, surgery, carpentry, and geometry. Each was a techne (Greek), or in Latin, an ars.[5] There was no separation of skills into the modern categories of fine art, decorative art, craft, etc. Philosophy (literally "the love of wisdom" from the Greek philein (love), and sophia (wisdom) was also a techne.

Philosophy is first recorded in the Greek empire in the sixth century B.C. The first philosophers broke with the past by:

1. Attempting to understand the world through reasoning alone (rationalism); rejecting religion, authority, and tradition.
2. Teaching others to reason. This encouraged independent thinking in place of a blind acceptance of the teachings of the teachers and others in authority.

The process was not restricted to Greece. The established beliefs and mythologies of other civilizations were being questioned during the same period by thinkers such as Siddhartha Gautama (Buddha) (563–483 B.C.) in India, Confucius (Kong Fuzi) (551–479 B.C.) in China, and Zarathustra (c. 628–c. 551 B.C.) in Persia. However, it is the teachings of five Greek philosophers which are most relevant to this aesthetic history.

XENOPHANES
Xenophanes was active late in the sixth century B.C. He stated that human knowledge is a human creation, and that man can never know whether his knowledge is true or not. From that time knowledge and its limitations were a major branch of philosophy now called epistemology.

PYTHAGORAS
Although it bears his name, Pythagoras (c. 570–c. 497 B.C.) did not discover the theorem for calculating the lengths of the sides of any right-angled triangle.[6] He was however among the earliest of the Greek philosophers to focus on human affairs, on morality, and on politics, as well as on the physical world. A mathematical genius, he believed that mathematics was an essential tool for understanding the world, and that numbers defined the basic order of things. Sir Isaac Newton (page 20) later demonstrated the partial truth of this view, partial because the behavioral aspects of life may never be describable mathematically. The Pythagoreans, followers of Pythagoras, also believed that harmony in music and the beauty of objects depended on numerical relationships. This view underpins the belief that there are rules of proportion, and remains strong even today.

SOCRATES
Socrates (470–399 B.C.), an Athenian, established dialectic, the seeking of truth by question and answer, as an important teaching method. He regarded beauty and other entities as having a universal and indestructible existence independent of time and place. Thus a beautiful object while in existence partakes of the timeless essence of true beauty. This conflicts with the modern view that beauty is solely a construct within the human mind.

Socrates chose suicide after being condemned to death

for corrupting the youth of Athens and not believing in its gods. The belief in gods, later in one God, and now often in no gods, did and would influence designers and the reactions of those who experienced designs.

The Sophists were philosophers connected with Socrates. Their arguments are surprisingly modern. They believed that the only beautiful thing is pleasure, and that an article is not beautiful in itself, but is deemed beautiful because it gives pleasure (what would later be called *aesthetic pleasure*).

PLATO
Plato (429–347 B.C.) was a pupil of Socrates. He later lived and taught in a house called The Academy. He was the earliest philosopher whose texts have survived. Plato borrowed from Pythagoras, and claimed that underlying the chaos of the material world was a mathematical order and reality not perceptible to the senses, but accessible and intelligible to the intellect. There were thus two worlds: the ever changing real world which we could sense, and another realm not in time and space which was permanent and in perfect order. Plato thus shared Socrates' view of beauty, calling its timeless existence *true beauty*; with true beauty being an *Ideal Form*. Humans were also of two worlds: the body, and the everlasting soul—this soul of Plato's later became an important concept of Christian religion. Plato held that life's main aim should be to penetrate to this underlying perfect world, and rehearse for death. The arts were undesirable because they seduced and distracted from this main aim.

Throughout antiquity mathematics and geometry were the bases for the design of major buildings. Things were beautiful not because they were pleasing to behold but because they conformed to the Ideal Form which was in this case a system of rules which governed harmony and relationships. Plato summarized the concept:

> If one were to separate from the arts the doctrine of numbers, measure, and harmony, little would be left but miserable remains . . . I do not mean by beauty of form such beauty as that of animals or pictures, which many would suppose to be my meaning. By beauty I mean, rather, straight lines and circles, and the plane or solid figures which are formed out of them by turning-lathes [figure 3.1] . . . These I affirm to be not only relatively beautiful, like other things, but they are eternally and absolutely beautiful, and they have peculiar [aesthetic] pleasures, quite unlike the pleasures of scratching.[7]

ARISTOTLE
Aristotle (384–322 B.C.) was sent to Athens to become a pupil of Plato, and in about 355 B.C. founded his own school, The Lyceum. He formulated logic. He rejected Plato's two worlds and believed there was only one, that which we could experience. The objects in this world were not just material,

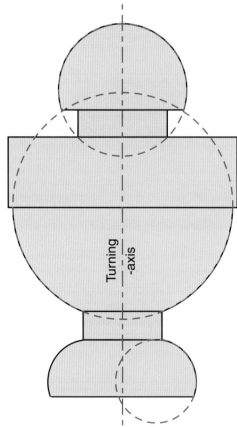

Figure 3.1 A Phileban solid, a caster, resulting from the rotation about a turning axis of two-dimensional shapes composed of straight lines and circular arcs. Such a solid is defined as beautiful by Plato, and termed Phileban because it is formed according to the quotation in Plato's dialogue *Philebus*.

they were put together with a unique form or structure, and it was this form which caused individual objects to be the things they were even when made of the same materials as different objects. For example, a dog and a cow are made from the same materials, but their structures differ.

Aristotle subdivided form into four *causes*:

1. *The material cause*: what it is made of.
2. *The efficient cause*: what makes it.
3. *The formal cause*: what gives it the shape by which it is identified.
4. *The final cause*: the ultimate reason for it.

Thus the four causes of a plant would be:

1. *Material*: stalk, leaves, flowers, and seeds—these could be broken down further into cellulose, etc.
2. *Efficient*: nutrients in the earth, water, light for photosynthesis.
3. *Formal*: its genetic makeup.
4. *Final*: to reproduce, to produce food, etc., and thus fit into the world biosystem.

In these causes Aristotle also succinctly described the task of design, to clarify and express these causes.

Plato and Aristotle were the archetypes of the two conflicting and continuing approaches to philosophy. Those who follow Plato believe that reasoning is more reliable than sensing. They hold that our sensed knowledge is secondary to concerns which cannot be sensed and are behind, beyond, or hidden, and only accessible through reasoning. In contrast, the *empiricist* view of Aristotle is that we should not accept explanations which deny the validity of the experiences that we are trying to explain. This approach was later refined into what we call *the scientific method* which recognizes that there can be conflict between directly-sensed information and scientific measurements.

3.1.2 ANCIENT ROME

Rome dominated the Greek city states from the last Macedonian War (171–168 B.C.). Although there were no Roman philosophers of note, a Roman wrote the only book on architecture to survive from ancient into Renaissance times. *De architectura libri decem* (*The Ten Books on Architecture*), was written by Marcus Vitruvius Pollio (born c. 84 B.C.) during the reign of Augustus (Emperor 28 B.C.–A.D. 14).[8]

3.1.3 THE MEDIEVAL PERIOD

The last western Roman Emperor Romulus Augustulus was deposed by the German king Odoacer in A.D. 476. The Christian church partially filled the vacuum, and for the next thousand years only ideas which were compatible with the church's teachings were permissible. Through the period, as in ancient Greece and Rome, beauty retained its wider meaning which combined aesthetically pleasing appearance with moral value and utility. An object could not be beautiful if it just gave aesthetic pleasure and had harmonious proportions; these two properties also had to conform to and support the object's purpose.

Another change was the division of the ancient category of skills (techne or ars). From about 150 B.C. the arts were divided into the *liberal* (intellectual and appropriate to the highborn and educated) and the *vulgar* (involving physical labor and payment). The liberal arts included grammar, rhetoric, dialectic, mathematics, and music theory. Woodturning was a vulgar art; so were painting, sculpture, architecture, and music performance. By the twelfth century the status of the vulgar arts had improved and they were being called *mechanical*.[9]

SAINT AUGUSTINE
St. Augustine of Hippo (354–430) is best known for admitting in his *Confessions* that "I cried out to the Lord, 'Lord, give me chastity and constancy—but not yet'". More importantly, he brought Plato's beliefs, particularly that of the soul, into the Christian church. He also accepted Plato's belief in the paramountcy of number. It was God-given because God was the origin of beauty, which was itself a product of measurement, number and harmony, and gave order to all things. Therefore beauty was expressed by, and was a product of, harmony and proportion, and this was true for all the arts including design and music.

THOMAS AQUINAS
Thomas Aquinas (1225–1274) further synthesized philosophy and Christianity, in particular the recently-discovered philosophy of Aristotle with the already Platonized Christianity. Aquinas argued that our knowledge was acquired through the senses and processed in our minds. There was nothing in the intellect which was not first in the senses. Thus the mind of a newborn child is a *tabula rasa* (an empty slate, a metaphor sometimes credited to John Locke (page 21)). This empiricist approach was conformable with the religious belief that the world was God's creation, and that the knowledge that might be gained was created by God. This approach would later be found inconvenient by both the Catholic and Protestant churches when challenged by Galileo who in 1632 presented new astronomical knowledge which contradicted the teaching of the churches and denied the special central position of the Earth and thus of man.

Aquinas also believed that utility was critical to beauty, and used as an example a saw made from glass. The saw would fail as a piece of art because it was useless, and for the same reason could not be beautiful.[10]

WILLIAM OF OCCAM
William of Occam (1285–1387) argued that in nature things which happened could have happened in other ways. Logical, orderly sequences did not necessarily apply. We must therefore observe what is, and reason about that. William was thus a promoter of empiricism (the school of philosophy which holds that knowledge is determined by sensory experience), and of what we now call the scientific method. He is best known for Occam's razor, his maxim that "It is vain to do with more than can be done with fewer".[11]

3.2   THE RENAISSANCE

The Renaissance is taken as the period in European history from about 1350 to 1600. Although the medieval division of the arts into liberal and mechanical continued, it came under increasing pressure. Musicians, painters, sculptors, architects, and writers believed that they deserved greater status and reward because their work was just as demanding as that categorized in the liberal arts. However, the vast majority of mechanical artists were not autonomous, but subservient employees or contractors dependent on patronage and commissions. It would not be until the middle of the eighteenth century that the fine arts became a separate and supposedly superior category.[12]

The Renaissance was a period of transition between the ancient and modern. The writings of Dante Aligheri (1265–1321) and Francesco Petrarca (Petrach) (1304–1374) spurred an interest in classical learning and a yearning to recapture the glory and prosperity of ancient Rome. (This is illustrated by Petrach's invention of the term Dark Ages for the years 476–800 during which there was no western emperor). As in ancient Greece and Rome, art was believed to depend on mathematics and geometry. This belief was based upon the revered texts of the ancient Greek philosophers, particularly those of Socrates and Plato. An interest in Roman architecture followed, and lead to the study of, and a veneration for, another ancient text, Vitruvius's De *architectura* (usually referred to as Vitruvius).

VITRUVIUS
Vitruvius had survived through about fifty-five later copies and recopies held in various European libraries (figure 3.2).[13] It was known during the medieval period, but did not spark much inquiry into architectural and design theory until the Renaissance.[14]

In the preface to the first of the ten books Vitruvius makes his pitch to the emperor Augustus: "I have drawn up definite rules to enable you, by observing them, to have personal knowledge of the quality both of existing buildings and of those which are yet to be constructed. For in the following books I have disclosed all the principles of the art".[15]

Although this claim is strong in hyperbole, the ideas Vitruvius put forward formed the basis for architectural

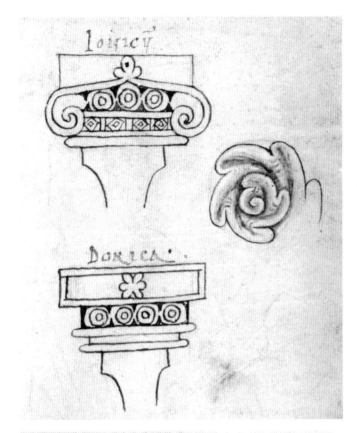

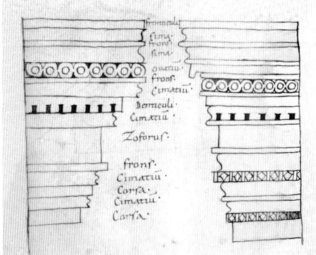

Figure 3.2 Two of the four pages of illustrations from the Vitruvius in Sélestat, France. (Illustrations supplied by Bibliothèque et Archives Municipale, Sélestat).The Sélestat copy, one of very few illustrated copies to survive, was probably made during A.D. 750–800.[16]

Vitruvius was first printed using movable type in 1486 after being compiled by the Veronese scholar Sulpicius da Veroli. The first printed and illustrated version was published in 1511 (figure 3.4). 1521 saw the publication of a version edited by Cesare Cesariano (1483–1543) and illustrated by Leonardo da Vinci.[17]

theory and argument until the nineteenth century. Vitruvius claimed that there were rules of architecture, but states in chapter I of Book II that humans were led on "by dint of observations made in their studies from vague and uncertain judgements to fixed rules of symmetry [proportion]". Although the rules had been derived arbitrarily by mere men, Vitruvius claimed that they were absolutely valid.

In chapter III of book I Vitruvius stated that buildings must be built with due reference to *firmitas* (durability and structural safety), *utilitas* (function), and *venustas* (beauty). Vitruvius divided beauty into three contributing parts:

Figure 3.3 *Left to right*, the Tuscan, Doric, Ionic, Corinthian, and Composite Roman orders pictured in the fourth book of the first English edition of 1611 of *The Five Books of Architecture* by Sebastiano Serlio. The five books were originally published singly in Venice and Paris between 1537 and 1547. They were first published together in 1584 in Venice. The first version of Vitruvius to show columns of different orders alongside for comparison was published by Cesare Cesariano in 1521. Reproduced courtesy of Dover Publications.

1. Proportion.
2. Artistry which demands *cogitatio* (painstaking effort) and *inventio* (the application of a lively intelligence).
3. The appropriate use of what we call the orders. An order is the column, optional pedestal, and superstructure unit of a temple colonnade decorated and proportioned according to one of the accepted modes. The orders were first systemized during the sixteenth century in Italy (figure 3.3). Vitruvius only specified proportions for the Roman Doric, Ionic, and Corinthian orders.

Vitruvius saw proportion not as an aesthetic concept, but as a numerical relationship. An object's beauty was determined by its numerical relationships, not by the modern measure of how much aesthetic pleasure results from experiencing it. In chapter I of book III Vitruvius elaborated, defining proportion in three ways:

1. As the relationships of the dimensions of the parts to each other.
2. As being based on a common module. Vitruvius specified three nose lengths, but the maximum diameter of the column shaft eventually became the norm for architectural designs which incorporated the orders.
3. By the correspondence of the proportions of a building and its parts to the proportions of the human body (anthropometric proportion).

By specifying that beauty was dependent on proportion, which was in turn dependent on both numerical relationships between the dimensions of parts, and on conformance to ratios derived from those of the proportions of the human body, Vitruvius dictated a dual concept of proportion which dominated architectural and design theory until the nineteenth century. The requirement of anthropometric proportion was reinforced by Vitruvius's personification of the orders in chapter I of book IV: "Thus the Doric column . . . began to exhibit the proportions, strength, and beauty of the body of a man". Similarly Vitruvius likened Ionic volutes to the "curly ringlets" of a matron and the shaft flutes to her robes; and the Corinthian was "an imitation of the slenderness of a maiden (figure 3.4)".

ALBERTI
Leon Battista Alberti (figure 3.5) wrote the first major Renaissance text on architectural theory. Called D*e re aedificatoria* (*The Ten Books of Architecture*) in tribute to Vitruvius, a first draft was presented to Pope Nicholas V in 1452.

Figure 3.4 Caryatides from the first illustrated printed edition of Vitruvius assembled by Fra Gioconda of Verona and published in Venice in 1511.
Fra Gioconda had not seen the caryatides on the porch of the Erektheion in Athens. Piranesi (figure 2.20, page 225) commented in 1761 that the stone maidens should not have such benign expressions when they were carrying such a heavy entablature (beam above), and that "satyrs, or sturdy rustics" would have been more appropriate.[18] Reproduced courtesy of Dover Publications.

Figure 3.5 Leon Battista Alberti (1404–1472) pictured in the frontispiece of the 1755 Leoni edition of *The Ten Books of Architecture*. Reproduced courtesy of Dover Publications.

However publication, in Latin, was delayed until 1485, thirteen years after Alberti's death. The first edition in Italian was published in 1546, and the first illustrated edition in 1550.[19]

Although greatly influenced by Vitruvius, Alberti had a much more systematic approach. He did not merely describe the triumvirate of durability and structural safety, function, and beauty, but inquired into them. He confirmed Vitruvius's tenets, particularly the importance of mathematical proportion to beauty which he defined in this connection as harmony. But while Alberti saw the importance of learning from proportion and number in nature, he did not ascribe to Vitruvius's dictum that all proportions needed to be related to those of the human body.

Alberti believed that buildings did not have to be strictly utilitarian, and should express human individuality. He stressed the superiority of Roman forms, but recommended they should be used with variety, and could be developed further "to produce something of our own invention".

For Vitruvius, ornament had been an explanation of structure or of its derivation. Alberti stipulated that ornament should be appropriate to the function and status of the building, but was applied, "an auxiliary Brightness and Improvement to Beauty".

Alberti defined a design drawing: "a firm and graceful pre-ordering of the Lines and Angles, conceived in the Mind, and contrived by an ingenious Artist".

Alberti's was essentially a book for patrons, and was initially unillustrated. Practicing architects wanted clear text and illustrations which they could copy and adapt (not much has changed). Such books were not long in arriving, and increasingly included measured drawings of extant Roman buildings, particularly of those which were considered the most beautiful. The accuracy of these drawings increased over the next two centuries. It also encouraged authors to become increasingly dogmatic when specifying their particular detailed proportions for the orders.

The most popular of these books ran to many editions, and were by: Sebastiano Serlio (1475–1554) published progressively from 1537; Jacopo Barozzi, known as Il Vignola (1507–1573) published in 1562; Andrea di Pietro della Gondola, nicknamed Palladio (1508–1580), published in 1570; and Vincenzo Scamozzi (1548–1616) published in 1615.

DURER
Although Alberti referred to a building as a body, he did not agree with the Vitruvian belief, almost universal among Renaissance writers, that the proportions of man are an essential basis of beauty. Albert Durer (1471–1528) between 1525 and 1528 produced three illustrated essays which attempted to confirm by analysis that beauty was indeed founded on rules, and did correspond to the proportions of the human body as extolled by Vitruvius in chapter I of book III. Here Vitruvius was echoing the earlier statement by Protagoras of Abdera (sixth century B.C.) that "Man is the

measure of all things, of existence of all things that are, and the nonexistence of all things that are not". In his manuscript *Speis der Maler* (1528) Durer commented:

> That master of the ancient world Vitruvius, architect of grandiose buildings in Rome, states that he who intends to build should conform to human beauty because the body conceals the arcane secrets of proportion. Hence, before discussing buildings, I intend to explain the form of a well-built man, and then a woman, a child, and a horse. In this way you will acquire an approximate measure of all the things you need. Heed first, therefore, what Vitruvius has written on the human body learned from great masters, painters and sculptors who earned great renown.[20]

While Durer evidently convinced himself of the validity of anthropometric proportion, through the Renaissance and afterwards the belief gradually received less prominence, and became widely ignored. It was however resurrected by Le Corbusier in 1950 in his concept of The Modular Man.

3.3   THE MODERN PERIOD

The Renaissance writers on architectural theory saw architecture as what we would call a science. However the modern concept of a science and the scientific-method approach to knowledge did not flower until the end of the seventeenth century. The transition from reasoning within and from prescribed ancient canons to the scientific approach began in astronomy. This a field in which the motions are large, slow, and regular, and could therefore be measured with reasonable accuracy.[21]

This period also saw the separation of what we now call the fine arts. This process started in about 1630 and took two centuries, but even by the early 1770s Johann Georg Sulzer (1720–79) was able to classify architecture as a fine art.[22] It was also during this period that national academies, museums, and art galleries first came into existence. Another critical development was that of a market in art which gradually overtook patronage as the major source of artists' incomes.[23]

3.3.1   THE BIRTH OF SCIENCE

COPERNICUS
The Ptolemaic system, named after the Alexandrian astronomer Claudius Ptolemy of the second century A.D., put the Earth as the center of the Universe with the planets and stars moving in circular paths at constant speeds around it. Nicholaus Copernicus (1473–1543), a Polish churchman, saw that the discrepancies in the observed paths of the planets could be explained if the Sun, not the Earth, was at

the center of the planets' orbits. Copernicus knew that this view would cause trouble within the church because it conflicted with the church's teaching and the statement in Psalm 93 "Thou [God] hast fixed the Earth immovable and firm". Copernicus therefore ensured that the publication of

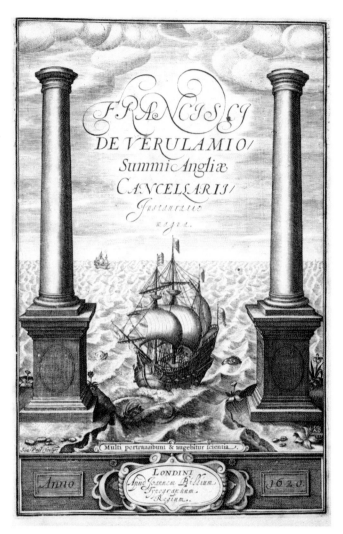

Figure 3.6 The title page from Sir Francis Bacon's *Novum Organum* (1620).
The translation of the Latin motto beneath the ship is "Many will pass through to multiply and enrich science". The illustration is a metaphor for science freeing itself from the traditional boundaries. The gateway is the legendary Pillars of Hercules, commonly applied to the Straits of Gibraltar, which marked the limits of human habitation. The ocean beyond the pillars is however not empty because somewhere distant is the Utopian island state described by Bacon in his novel *The New Atlantis*, where the goals of "Instauratio Magna" (Great Innovation) are implemented. The illustration also alludes to the role that navigation was playing in the advancement of scientific knowledge.[24] Reproduced by permission of The Huntington Library, San Marino, California.

his beliefs in *On the Revolutions of the Celestial Spheres* was delayed until the year of his death. His teaching was condemned by the Church and such notables as Martin Luther and Robert Calvin because it challenged both the Bible and the wisdom of the supreme intellects of the ancients. Opponents argued that Copernicus could not be correct because the whole of established knowledge and authority would be open to doubt, and because the Earth and man would then be far less important to God. The teaching of Aquinas that all knowledge came from God was conveniently ignored.

KEPLER
Astronomers were seconded to refute Copernicus. Danish astronomer Tycho Brahe (1546–1601) was the most notable, building an observatory with huge sextants and quadrants. (The telescope was not invented until shortly before 1608). His observations were passed to his assistant, the German astronomer Johannes Kepler (1571–1630). In *New Astronomy* (1609) and *Harmonies of the World* (1619), Kepler demonstrated that the observations were best explained if the planets orbited the Sun in elliptical orbits and at varying speeds. This finding increased the attack on the church's law.

Kepler in 1604 was also the first to appreciate that the eye worked by focussing light onto the retina, thus further undermining the authority of the ancients.

BACON
Another who promoted the freedom to seek truth unrestricted by the teachings of the church was Sir Francis Bacon (1561–1626). Fortunately the intellectual climate was less repressive in England.

Bacon was a courtier and held several important offices of state including Lord Chancellor. He was fascinated by science (then called natural philosophy), and promoted it strongly. He saw that science could give man power over nature and enable man to increase his prosperity. Bacon even died pursuing science, from a chill caught after leaving his carriage to further his investigation of food preservation by stuffing a dead fowl with snow.[25] (Aptly, the American who developed frozen food and first sold it in 1929 was named Clarence Birdseye (1886–1956)).

Bacon's major philosophical text, *Novum Organum* (figure 3.6), was titled in answer to Aristotle's *Organon*. Bacon argued that you cannot understand nature using the deductive logic of Aristotle, by arguing from abstract general principles (figure 3.7). Bacon also challenged the tendency, allied to the deductive method, to blindly accept classical traditions and church teachings. Instead, to advance knowledge you must make controlled observations to create a mass of reliable recorded data. Analyzing this data then enabled hypotheses to be drawn, which could in turn lead to the inductive generalizations we call natural laws.

Bacon stressed the need for science to be taught and studied. He warned against ignoring observations which might negate tentative hypotheses. He also warned against "idols", distortions which we might introduce because we were human. These included our tendencies to place total reliability on what we sense, to color our judgements by our feelings and expectations, to confuse language with reality, and to be influenced by others' unfounded views.

3.3.2 THE ENLIGHTENMENT

Science-based discoveries of natural laws and of explanations of natural phenomena began to be made in the seventeenth century. These sometimes conflicted with religious teachings. A few thinkers such as Hume became atheists, but the majority sought a compatibility between religion and inductive science. Was human destiny entirely controllable by man within the context of natural forces, the system of government, and traditions? Or was there a supreme power and/or other forces not necessarily of time and space? and if so, how should man relate to them? On the political level, the divine right of kings and the birthrights accorded to the aristocracy were challenged by republicanism, notably in Charles-Louis de Montesquieu's *Spirit of the Laws* (1748).

In architecture the teachings of the ancients, particularly those of Vitruvius, were questioned, and reasons and evidence were sought to explain beauty and man's reactions to it.

GALILEO
Galileo Galilei (1564–1642) was deeply religious, and wanted to understand how God ordered the world. He was the first to draw together mathematics, physics, and astronomy. He overtly challenged the Catholic Church with his findings, and thereby incurred its wrath. While not rejecting the Greek philosophical method of seeking to understand the world through logic and reason, he saw that the conclusions needed to be tested through measurement and experiment as far as the technology of the day allowed. Leading by example, Galileo overturned the accepted wisdom that denser bodies fell faster than less dense bodies. He also experimented with pendulums (timing them with his pulse) in about 1582. This lead him to design the first pendulum clock in 1641, although proof of this was not discovered until about eighty years later when his design was discovered among sheets of butchers wrapping paper. Meanwhile the application of pendulum clocks had been solved by the Dutch scientist Christian Huygens (1629–1695), and first applied in 1657.[26]

In 1609 Galileo learned of the invention of the telescope in Holland. He built a more powerful version, and published his observations in *The Story Messenger*. He described the Moon's surface as rough, not smooth as had been supposed. He also detailed the spots on the Sun, and reported four hitherto unknown planets, satellites of Jupiter, which strengthened the evidence for Copernicus's heliocentric (that the planets orbit the Sun, not the Earth) theory.

In *Dialogue on the Two Chief World Systems—Ptolemaic and Copernican* (1632) Galileo argued for Copernicus's discovery, but not for Kepler's because Galileo did not believe that planets had elliptical orbits. The book was brought to the attention of the Inquisition which had been founded by Pope Gregory IX in 1233 to seek out and destroy heresy. During the thirteenth and fourteenth centuries the Inquisition had been successful, but from the sixteenth century its efforts tended to strengthen rather than stifle dissent, and it became less confident. Therefore after his trial, Galileo, being that rarity a celebrity scientist, was allowed to publicly recant, and was then only committed to permanent house arrest.

The church was not being as malevolent as is popularly supposed by bringing Galileo before the Inquisition. His book was interpreted as a statement, not merely a hypothesis, and Galileo was not able to prove his statement. The issue was also in an area which the church had long seen as God's preserve.

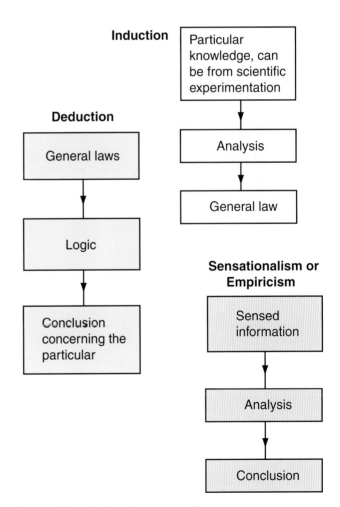

Figure 3.7 Deduction, induction, and sensationalism also called empiricism.

DESCARTES

René Descartes (1596–1650) was born in France and later settled in Holland because it permitted greater freedom of expression. His publications on mathematics and philosophy between 1629 and 1649 were hugely important. He invented coordinate geometry, and the graph—hence the *Cartesian* coordinates, sometimes called the *x and y axes*. He believed that the process of deduction could be applied outside the domain of mathematics. In deduction you proceed from general premises, which are so simple as to be certain, by logical simple steps, each so simple as to again be certain, to conclusions that are neither simple nor obvious (figure 3.7). What made deduction reliable outside mathematics was that God was perfect and would not therefore want to deceive mankind. Descartes' promotion of deduction lead to *rationalism*, the belief that sensed information is unreliable, and that deductive reasoning is the superior path to greater knowledge.

Figure 3.8 Directional ornament on swash-turned balusters in the Museum fur Kunsthandwerk, Berlin. Swash turning is first described in Joseph Moxon's *Mechanick Exercises* published in 1678. For a description of swash turning see *Woodturning Methods,* pages 57 to 58.

This photograph first appeared in Rolf Steinert, *Drechseln in Holz* (Leipzig: Fachbuchverlag Leipzig, 1993), p. 349, and is reproduced by permission of Rolf Steinert. Photograph by Christoph Georgi, Schneeberg.

CARAMUEL

Juan Caramuel de Lobkowitz (1606–1682) in 1678 specified that the gradients of staircases should be taken into account when ornamenting their balusters (figure 3.8).

NEWTON

Sir Isaac Newton (1642–1727) was, like Bacon, strongly religious. He was among the earliest to use the scientific method of performing experiments to test hypotheses and theories. He believed that no idea had worth unless it had been proved by experiment, and believed in and

Figure 3.9 The five Roman orders, plate I of Perrault's *Ordonnance for the Five Kinds of Columns after the Method of the Ancients*.

Perrault believed that his rules for the orders could be superseded by superior rules in the future, and were but a stage in a continuous development and ever-increasing rationalization. Modern architecture was therefore superior because it incorporated the accumulated experience of the past.

Perrault cited the small differences between the proportions of extant ancient columns and between the proportions recommended by earlier writers as evidence that the proportions which give beauty are not fixed.

demonstrated the power of mathematics to help in understanding. In *Principia Mathematica* (1687) he proved through his discovery of gravity, and the Inverse Square Law which quantified it, that the planets moved around the Sun as Copernicus had described, and at changing velocities in elliptical orbits as shown by Kepler. Before Newton observations had shown what the planetary motions were, but until Newton's discovery and quantification of gravity there was no proof, no explanation, and no understanding; hence Galileo's vulnerability before the Inquisition. Newton further showed that natural laws were generally applicable, on Earth and elsewhere. This undermined the belief that life was at the whim of God, and that humankind and the Earth were special.

PERRAULT

The French excel in bizarre deaths, and Claude Perrault's in 1688 from an infection contracted through a cut sustained while dissecting a camel is an excellent example.[27] Claude was born in 1613 in Paris. He and two of his four brothers, Charles and Nicholas, were prominent in intellectual society during the reign of Louis XIV. Charles is chiefly remembered for collecting and publishing fairy stories including "Little Red Riding Hood", "The Sleeping Beauty", and "Puss in Boots".

Claude Perrault was trained in medicine. He may have met John Locke (figure 3.10) during Locke's sojourn in France from 1675 to 1679. He certainly supported Locke's empiricism.

In 1664 Perrault was commissioned to make a new translation of Vitruvius which was published with commentary in 1673, and in an enlarged and revised edition in 1684. In 1683 he published his *Ordonnance for the Five Kinds of Columns after the Method of the Ancients* (figure 3.9). In it Perrault proposed two criteria of aesthetic judgement:

1. *Positive beauty*, governing fitness for use, soundness of construction, and durability.
2. *Arbitrary beauty*, essentially artistic beauty.

Perrault elevated fitness to a principal requirement of beauty. He also stressed that judgements on artistic beauty were influenced by what was customary.

Perrault accepted that "The Ancients rightly believed that the proportional rules that give buildings their beauty were based on the proportions of the human body", but that "different rules are determined by the different intentions to make a building more massive or more delicate".[28] He agreed with Vitruvius that proportions resulted from custom and tradition, but did not agree that they were then correct for all time. Neither did he believe that there were specific proportions which were beautiful because they conformed to those that "nature has established", such as musical harmony. Perrault also rejected the Vitruvian implicit promotion of symmetry based on the fact that the body's left side mirrors its right. Instead Perrault viewed symmetry

as an essential component of positive beauty. Perrault considered proportion and the ratios between dimensions to be arbitrary beauty.

Although attacked by the architectural establishment, Perrault's ideas permeated into contemporary thought. By 1693 a *Dictionnaire d'architecture* was able to define proportion as "the appropriateness of the dimensions of the members in each part of a building, and the relationship of the parts to the whole". Appropriateness, and not just of dimensions, is a concept which I will discuss in the next chapter.

LOCKE

The reaction against the deductive-based rationalism of Descartes was called empiricism or sensationalism (figure 3.7), and was lead by John Locke (figure 3.10). His 1689 *Philosophical Essays Concerning Human Understanding* advanced the following ideas:

1. The mind of a newborn child is blank, a tabula rasa; it has no innate ideas.
2. Ideas enter through the senses, or are generated by reflection.

Figure 3.10 John Locke (1632–1704), English philosopher, painted by Sir Godfrey Kneller. Locke promoted what Karl Popper later called the bucket theory of the mind (page 6). Illustration supplied by Christ Church, Oxford.

3. The mind is able to combine simple ideas into new, complex ideas, and to generalize from experience.
4. The knowledge we derive from sensed input is not necessarily correct, and is therefore merely probable.

Locke's writings promoted new thinking on how architecture conveyed meaning, and on how designers could manipulate that meaning. The earliest resulting treatises were *Characteristics* (1711) by the third earl of Shaftesbury, and the 1712 essays *Pleasures of the Imagination* by Joseph Addison. In *Characteristics*, Shaftesbury only differentiated between the sensing of beauty and ugliness. Addison promoted a greater range of aesthetic adjectives including: great, novel, new, uncommon, and strange. His sensationalism lead to the hypothesis that architectural meaning was based on correspondences between man-made and natural forms; and that it affected the emotions, thoughts and even morals as much as, if not more than, literature and the fine arts. After 1750 the range of aesthetic categories broadened to include the *sublime* and the *picturesque*.

PLUMIER

Plumier was a member of a Catholic order and of the French intellectual elite. His 1701 statement quoted on page 1 that beauty depends not on precise rules or a fixed method of design, but on the "opinions and spirit of the people" demonstrates that there was significant acceptance of the subjective nature of beauty by the end of the seventeenth century. This acceptance was well before Hume's and Kant's philosophical explanations of the subjective nature of aesthetic judgements (page 28).

FRÉMIN

In 1702, Michel de Frémin, a Parisian treasury official, published a layman's commentary on architecture. He saw function as the most important contributor to beauty, and demoted aesthetic consideration. Ornament was purely additive, and its design should be subordinate to function, "the purpose for which the building is intended".

DE CORDEMOY

Abbé Jean-Louis De Cordemoy (1651–1722) in 1706 argued for a pure architecture based on the antique in which structural members were truly structural. This architecture was to be cleansed of all later excrescences such as engaged columns. (An engaged column is built into a wall so that only about half of the shaft, base, and capital project).

LE CLERK

Sébastien Le Clerk in a treatise of 1714 dismissed proportion as a science, "it [proportion] is not to be understood as a purely rational relationship in the manner of geometry, but rather a fitness of the parts founded in the good taste of the architect". He rejected the validity of taste dictated by academies and other would-be tastemakers. He also disagreed with Perrault's concept that beauty resulting from proportion is determined by tradition and custom; instead arguing that the true criterion of beauty is the pleasure resulting from sensory perception.

BOFFRAND

Germain Boffrand (1667–1754) was a successful practicing architect who published his *Livre d'architecture* in 1745. He warned that if beauty were judged subjectively, there was a danger that fashion would dominate and lead to the degeneration of design. Hence the importance of adhering to principles of architecture to ensure a *noble simplicité*. He also proposed that buildings should express (communicate) the characters of their occupants and functions by their designs and furnishings.

BRISEUX

Charles-Étienne Briseux (1660–1754) in a work published in 1752 supported the ancient idea of proportion, that nature prescribes the harmonious proportions common to music and architecture. He wrote that the sensed effects of proportion are the same on everyone, but that individual appreciation varies because of individual knowledge, intellect, and physiological disposition.

BAUMGARTEN

In his *Aesthetica* (1750–58) Alexander Gottlieb Baumgarten defined aesthetics as "the science of the beautiful", and stressed that rules governed beauty. This belief in rules was later denied by both Hume and Kant (page 28), and is now the minority view.

NEOCLASSICISM

Neoclassicism was the dominant architectural and decorative style in Europe in the middle of the eighteenth century, but was not considered as just a further step in the development of Roman architecture which had restarted in the Renaissance. It was instead regarded as resulting from the fundamental Enlightenment investigations into the bases of architectural form through philosophical thought, free of the shackles of tradition, church dogma, and myth. These investigations also included the accurate, Baconian measurement of ancient sources.

The rise of neoclassicism was also spurred by the discovery of two Roman cities which had been buried by an eruption of Vesuvius in A.D. 79. Excavations began in Herculaneum in 1709, and in Pompeii in 1748, and enabled accurate observations of the Roman decorative arts.

Greek architecture was barely known in Europe until the middle of the eighteenth century because most of the remains had been inaccessible within the Ottoman empire. Even those at Paestum near Naples were forgotten in a swamp, and assumed to be Roman. The first book to detail ancient Greek architecture was Julien David Leroy's 1758

Ruins of the Most Beautiful Monuments of Greece. It beat to the market *Antiquities of Athens*, published in four volumes between 1762 and 1818) by James Stuart (1713–1788) and Nicholas Revett (1720–1804). These books sparked controversies including: was Greek architecture pure and Roman architecture not? which was superior, Roman or Greek architecture? and, could studying ancient buildings help in the quest for a modern architecture?

The interest in Roman architecture during the Renaissance had been connected with a belief that its adoption would help to bring ancient-Rome-like success to a nation. Similarly, Enlightenment thinkers believed that correctly-designed buildings stimulated socially and morally enlightened societies by renewing the social and moral spirits that the ancient Greek and Roman civilizations were assumed to have possessed.

HOGARTH

English painter and engraver William Hogarth (figure 3.11) aimed his *The Analysis of Beauty* (1753) at artists and connoisseurs.[29] A more practical text than most of the period, it is relevant to woodturning because it was accompanied by two large prints, the first of which (figure 3.12) included pictures of turnings among its explanatory border illustrations.

Hogarth insisted that aesthetic judgements should be made according to what appealed to the eye, "by common observation". In the introduction to *The Analysis of Beauty*, Hogarth recommended that an important part of perceiving is to imagine "every object . . . to have its inward contents scooped out so nicely, as to have nothing of it left but a thin shell". While the value of this "conceit" is unclear for solid objects, it is essential to woodurners when hollowing.

Hogarth dismissed the "blind veneration that generally is paid to antiquity" which had become "a sort of religious esteem". For Hogarth, ancient statuary was often admirable not because of its sources, but because it had serpentine lines (figures 3.13 and 3.14). An absence of serpentine lines resulted in ugliness. Hogarth used as an example the unfortunate toad which was "totally void of this waving line". (There is however a toad-back molding which incorporates two serpentine lines shown on page 145). Allan Ramsay, a portraitist of philosopher David Hume, countered Hogarth's example of the toad. Ramsay opined in his 1755 *Essay on Taste* that beauty depended not on intrinsic qualities but to a great extent on convention: "It hardly admits of a doubt, that a blooming she-toad is the most beautiful sight in the creation of all the crawling young gentlemen of her acquaintance".

At the end of his introduction Hogarth explained that there were six "fundamental principles" intrinsic to beauty, which "please and entertain the eye . . . mutually correcting and restraining each other occasionally". These principles, to each of which Hogarth devotes a chapter, are:

1. *Fitness*, which "is of the greatest consequence to the beauty of the whole". Fitness encompassed function, adequate strength, stability, appropriate dimensions and proportions, and the appropriate arrangement of parts. Hogarth illustrates this with candlesticks (figure 3.15), and a parsley leaf (figure 3.16). He used the twisted column as an example of a form which compromised strength for ornament and was therefore not fit (figure 3.17). He summarizes the arrangements of parts by noting the effects of distance (figure 3.18); and then by

Figure 3.11 **William Hogarth** (1697–1764).

Figure 3.12 **Plate 1 of *The Analysis of Beauty*.**

comparing the sides of stove-grates (figure 3.19), and again candlesticks (figure 3.20).

2. *Variety*. Insufficient variety produces monotony; too much and "the eye is glutted". One example of good variety is "gradual lessening". By this principle a cone is superior to a cylinder. To Hogarth true beauty is the active discovery of variety, but the variety must be "composed", not "uncomposed" which produces "confusion and deformity".

3. *Uniformity*, which included regularity and symmetry. Hogarth believed that uniformity was usually a dictate of fitness rather than an essential part of beauty.

4. *Simplicity*, which "without variety is wholly insipid". Therefore the outline of an egg is preferable to an ellipse, which is in turn preferable to a circle.

5. *Intricacy*. "Pursuing is the business of our lives . . . [and] gives pleasure." Here Hogarth takes his theme from Locke's metaphor at the beginning of *Philosophical Essays Concerning Human Understanding*: "The mind's searches after truth are a sort of hawking and hunting, wherein the very pursuit makes a great part of the pleasure". Thus Hogarth's view of intricacy is a precursor of Popper's searchlight theory of the mind introduced on page 5, and is confirmed by the "enjoyment in winding walks, and serpentine rivers".

6. *Quantity* is large size or massing. It "adds greatness to grace", but in excess is clumsy or ridiculous. "Nevertheless custom and fashion will, in length of time, reconcile almost every absurdity whatever, to the eye, or make it over-look'd."

The idea that function could be an important contributor to beauty was not a product of the Enlightenment or of medieval thinkers; it was much earlier. For example, the Irish bishop and philosopher George Berkeley (1685-1752), after whom the Californian university city is named, had copied into his book *Alciphron* (1732) a dialogue involving Socrates first reported by the Greek historian Xenophon (431–c. 350 B.C.). Included in the dialogue is: "'Can a dungbasket then,' said Aristippos, 'be a beautiful thing?' 'Undoubtedly,' answered Socrates, 'and a shield of gold may be a vile thing considered as a shield; the former being adapted to its proper use, and this not'". Hogarth was familiar with this passage and refers to it in his preface. However in chapter I on fitness, Hogarth instead adapts a passage from David Hume's *Enquiry concerning the Principles of Morals* (1751) as follows:

Thus though a building were ever so large, the steps of the stairs, the seats of the windows, must be continued of their usual heights, or they would lose their beauty and their fitness; and in shipbuilding the dimensions of every part are confined and regulated by fitness for sailing. When a vessel sails well, the sailors always call her a beauty, the two ideas have such a connection.[30]

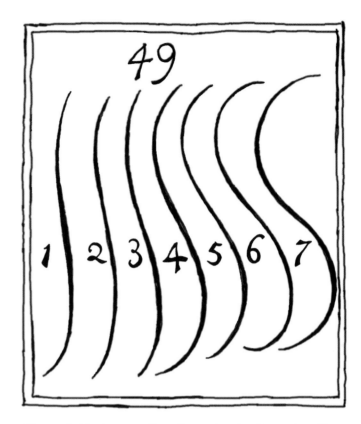

Figure 3.13 **Serpentine lines,** border illustration *49* from plate I of *The Analysis of Beauty*. Line *4* is the ideal, the *Line of Beauty*. Lines *3*, *2*, and *1* are progressively meaner; *5*, *6*, and *7* as they bulge more become "gross and clumsy". The beauty of serpentine lines was later confirmed by John Ruskin in *The Stones of Venice* (1851 and 1853) (pages 31–33).

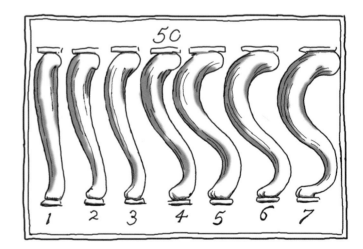

Figure 3.14 **Serpentine lines applied to chair legs,** border illustration *50* from plate I of *The Analysis of Beauty*. According to Hogarth, leg *4* follows the Line of Beauty and is therefore the most beautiful—I find leg *4* too bandy, and legs *2* and *3* superior.

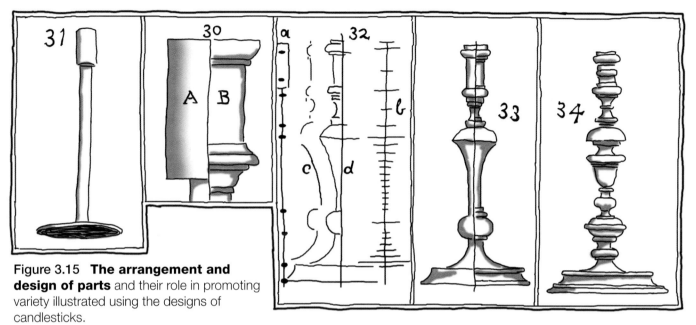

Figure 3.15 The arrangement and design of parts and their role in promoting variety illustrated using the designs of candlesticks.

Illustration *31*, shows a candlestick at almost its most basic.

Illustration *30*. A, *left*, shows a basic socket. B, *right*, shows a socket with greater variety. The depth and diameter of the vertical hole which houses the bottom part of the candle is a matter of fitness, as are the total height of the candlestick and the diameter of its base.

Illustration *32*. Drawing *a* demonstrates how the vertical lengths of the various parts should be varied from one another, and that one part should always be longer than the rest. Drawing *b* shows that the diameters of the parts should be varied. Join all the horizontal lines in drawing *b* with different curves and straight lines (drawing *c*), "and you have the candlestick" in drawing *d* and illustration *33*. Two styles of the same candlestick are shown in illustration *33*, that on the right being more ornate.

Illustration *34*. This candlestick "appears crowded" having been divided into a much greater number of parts. It "wants distinctness of form on a near view, and loses the effect of variety at a distance".

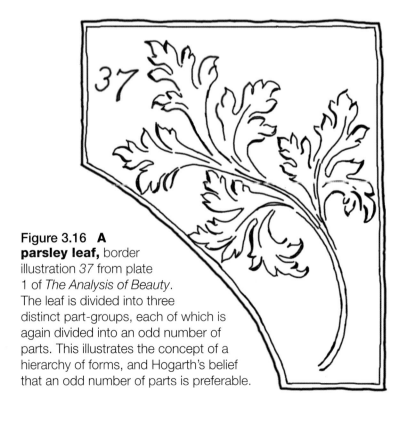

Figure 3.16 A parsley leaf, border illustration *37* from plate 1 of *The Analysis of Beauty*. The leaf is divided into three distinct part-groups, each of which is again divided into an odd number of parts. This illustrates the concept of a hierarchy of forms, and Hogarth's belief that an odd number of parts is preferable.

Figure 3.17 A twisted column, a form which was "undoubtedly ornamental" but lacked fitness and displeased because it conveyed "an idea of weakness" when supporting a load. Photographed courtesy of The Village Pump Antiques, Exeter, New South Wales.

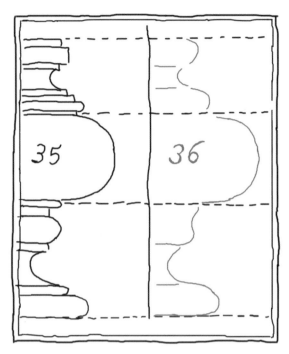

Figure 3.18 **Distinctness of parts to avoid visual confusion.** Hogarth explains that adjacent parts when seen in close-up need to fall into groups (part-groups), here separated by the dotted lines. He also stressed that some of the parts should be bold enough to stand alone. Thus form *35* retains design clarity even when viewed from afar as form *36* demonstrates.

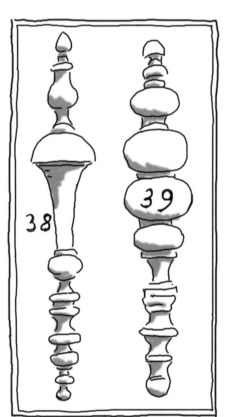

Figure 3.19 **"The art of composing well is no more than the art of varying well"** demonstrated by the parts of stove-grates shown in border illustrations *38* and *39* from plate 1 of *The Analysis of Beauty*. Both turnings have the same number of parts, yet design *38* has far greater distinction because its parts are varied in their sizes, shapes, and placements.

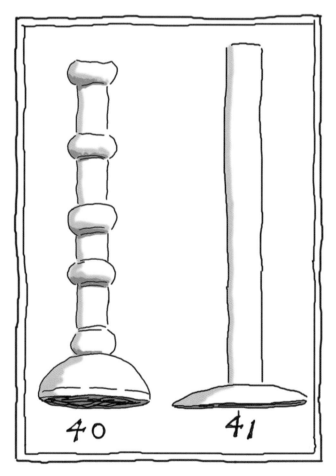

Figure 3.20 **Variety.** Candlestick *40* has little variety, and in Hogarth's view "would be better to be quite plain [like candlestick *41*] than with such poor attempts at ornament".

Hogarth recognized that after satisfying the concerns of function and proportion, a lot of choice was left. This choice was that of a style. Hogarth was against the domination of one style (in English architecture then the neoclassical Palladian), and early in believing that buildings with different functions "might be built more in distinct characters than they are, by contriving orders suitable to each [function]". Hogarth was thus not averse to Gothic, Chinese, or other styles, but recommended that they be improved by the application of his design principles.

Hogarth's book met with limited contemporary success, but his concept of parts was to prove influential in the twentieth century as will be described in chapter 7.

LAUGIER

Abbé Marc-Antoine Laugier (1713–1769) in the second 1755 edition of his *Essay on Architecture* pictured a primitive hut built using the three essential and "natural" (unaffected) structural elements: the column, the beam, and the sloping rafter. Laugier proposed that the logic of the allegorical primitive hut's construction should guide designers, "Let us keep to the simple and the natural, it is the only road to beauty". Thus reason, not tradition and rules, should govern design. Laugier's reason was however based on the construction of a building rather than on a building's intended purpose.

BURKE

Edmund Burke (1729–1797) was born in Ireland, and became a notable Whig member of the House of Commons and political theorist. His unillustrated *A Philosophical Enquiry into the Origin of our Ideas of the Sublime and Beautiful* (1757) (figure 3.21) was far more successful in its day than Hogarth's book. Burke's book is concerned with the responses of the human mind to aesthetic and emotive objects and experiences, themes which suggest that if it were published today it would be better titled *A Psychological Enquiry* . . .

The sublime was a hot topic of the day, and, whether natural or man-made, created in the mind emotions such as awe or veneration. These emotions were, Burke explained, close to fear and terror. Therefore in architecture only magnificent, spectacular, or huge buildings are likely to be sublime.

Burke's other arguments include the notions that:

1. "Taste [is] no more than that faculty, or those faculties of the mind which are affected with, or form a judgement of the works of imagination and the elegant arts . . . Taste (whatever it is) is improved exactly as we improve our judgement, by extending our knowledge, by a steady attention to our object, and by frequent exercise [of it]." Individual taste is affected in its ability to discern by the "degree of natural sensibility, or from a closer and longer attention to the object", and in badness or goodness by judgement.

2. "Beauty demands no assistance from our reasoning." Nor does Burke believe that functionality is "the cause of beauty, or indeed beauty itself". Similarly, neither virtue, nor mathematical or anthropometric proportion affected beauty: "I have great reason to doubt, whether beauty be at all an idea belonging to proportion".

3. Beauty is associated with the sensible qualities of smallness, smoothness, delicacy, clean but not strong colors, and an absence of angular variation but a presence of smooth variation.

4. "Imagination is incapable of producing anything absolutely new; it can only vary the disposition of those ideas which it has received from the senses."

5. Elegance is beauty with regularity.

6. Delight requires that the senses "must be shaken and worked to a proper degree", and lies between monotony and confusion.

A

Philosophical Enquiry

INTO THE

ORIGIN of our IDEAS

OF THE

SUBLIME

AND

BEAUTIFUL.

LONDON:

Printed for R. and J. DODSLEY, in Pall-mall.

M DCC LVII.

Figure 3.21 The title page of a 1757 copy of Edmund Burke's book.[31]

7. That which is "far from being compleatly fashioned" (unfinished) affords "a more agreeable sensation than the full grown [finished]; because the imagination is entertained with the promise of something more. . . . Perfection is not the cause of beauty".

8. "Another source of greatness is difficulty. When any work seems to have required immense force and labor to effect it, the idea is grand. . . . Rudeness . . . increases this cause of grandeur, as it excludes the idea of art and contrivance." This theme has interestingly been turned on its head by turners who intentionally strive for art through rudeness (figure 3.22).

LODOLI

The teachings of Franciscan priest Carlo Lodoli (1690–1761) were published first in 1757. According to pupil Francesco Algarotti, Lodoli wished to abolish ornament because it was without function, an affectation and a falsity. Lodoli's functionalism was however based not on building use, but on *truth to material*—the concept that differences in material dictate differences in form.

Figure 3.22 Intentional rudeness, *Unsung Bowl Ascending* by Mark Lindquist of Quincy, Florida. According to Edmund Burke, "Rudeness . . . excludes the idea of art and contrivance". Perfection was the only conceivable focus for both art and craft in Europe in the middle of the eighteenth century.

The bowl is spalted maple; 16 in. high x 18 in. dia. (400 x 450 mm); and is in the collection of Mrs Edmund J. Kahn. Photograph by Paul Avis.

HUME AND KANT

Mental processing, including that done with our senses of order, meaning, and detail, can result in a distinct form of human experience known as aesthetic which is common to the appreciation of art and beauty, both natural and man-made. (According to modern research this aesthetic sense may have evolved to help choose a mate and retain the interest of that mate during the long-term monogamous relationship needed to bring up children successfully). This aesthetic form of experience is pleasurable and contemplative, and releases us from the practical concerns of life. Our present views of aesthetics (the understanding of this form of experience) are largely based on two eighteenth-century texts: Hume's *Of the Standard of Taste* (1757), and Kant's *The Critique of Aesthetic Judgement* (1790). David Hume (1711–1776) was born and lived for most of his life in Edinburgh. Immanuel Kant (1724–1804) rarely left Konigsberg in East Prussia.[32] Both claimed that:

1. Aesthetic judgement is a felt response to the object which presupposes taste (the mental faculties employed in aesthetic judgement).
2. Aesthetic qualities are subjective.
3. There are no, and could be no, rules or criteria for aesthetic judgements, and there are no principles or standards of taste.
4. Kant stressed that what we can apprehend with our faculties is not necessarily all that exists. That which exists but cannot be experienced Kant called "transcendental".

Before Hume and Kant it was commonly thought that rules must exist which determined whether something was beautiful, but that these rules had not yet been exactly defined because they were difficult to discover. Such aesthetic rules would enable aesthetic judgements to be made on the basis of an object's relevant non-aesthetic properties. Such a rule might be: if the ratio of height to width lies between certain values, the object is beautiful. While it is now widely held that rules concerning the non-aesthetic properties of an object cannot be used as a basis for aesthetic conclusions, the absence of rules does not prevent generalizations (guidelines) on non-aesthetic properties being worthwhile in particular circumstances.

The system of perception propounded by Hume and Kant in which the non-aesthetic properties are sensed and perceived, but the aesthetic response is over and above, is called *aesthetic subjectivism*. If unqualified aesthetic subjectivism existed, everyone could have different views, but assuming that most people's mental processors are similar, and they have similar experiences, common sense suggests that the subjectivism will be restrained.

BLONDEL

The lectures of Jacques-François Blondel (1705–1774) were published between 1771 and 1777. They introduced the concept of inventing particular styles for buildings with particular functions by dividing traditional architectures into parts which could be modified as needed, and then recomposed into new styles.

LE CAMUS
Nicolas Le Camus de Mézières in 1780 described the concept of proportion not in terms of ratios of lengths, but as a harmony of masses.

RELIGIONS AND CHURCHES
In 1774 Ann Lee arrived in America and started the "shaking Quakers". Their craft work reflected their beliefs that to make a thing well was an act of prayer, and that anything which was not useful should be eliminated. Shaker woodwork is but one example of the effects that religious beliefs and teachings can have on design. Other religions and churches believe that:

1. Ornament and decoration demonstrate the human preparedness to sacrifice for and glorify a deity. This is the attitude of the Catholic and Orthodox churches.
2. Only specific types of ornament and decoration are wrong. The Qur'ān does not comment on the representation of living things, but from the eighth century such representations were prohibited. The Muslim theological explanation was that any representation competed with God because he alone can create living things. Due to the prohibition, imagery was replaced with calligraphy, and calligraphy was developed into an art (figure 3.23).
3. All ornament and decoration is wrong, a distraction to sincere worship. This attitude, adopted by some Protestant churches, is similar to Plato's (page 12).

MORITZ
Karl Philipp Moritz (1756–1793) posited in 1793 that the justification for ornament is educative. It should "delight

Figure 3.23 Moresque ornament. This Arabic inscription from the Alhambra reads, "There is no conqueror but God". Illustration from page 66 of *The Grammar of Ornament (1856)* by Owen Jones.

the soul through the eye and imperceptibly influence the refinement of taste and cultivation of the spirit" through "indicating and describing the essence of what is ornamented, so that we as it were recognize it and find it again in the ornament".

Moritz was psychologically aware as his comments on the orders demonstrate (figure 6.26, page 130). He appreciated that grandeur and the sublime can result from uniformity and repetition.

GOETHE
In 1795 Johann Wolfgang von Goethe (1749–1832), author of the drama *Faust*, rejected the beliefs that beauty flowed from truth to material and functionalism: "As long as only the immediate function was envisaged, and materials were allowed to control what was built rather than to be controlled, no art was possible . . ."

3.3.3 THE NINETEENTH CENTURY

The nineteenth century was marked by huge increases in populations (that of Europe more than doubled), and by the flowering of the Industrial Revolution. New and bigger buildings were needed, and an increasing number of specialized functions had to be served.

A feature of the nineteenth century was a new consciousness that there had been a history of design styles, each particular to a certain time and place. Neoclassicism dominated building design until about 1835, but earlier, in around 1770, the picturesque and the sublime had become dominant in garden design. The design choices expanded through Napoleon's expedition to Egypt in 1798, the artifacts and knowledge of distant places gained through the trading companies such as the East India Company, and through expeditions of conquest and subjugation. There were three consequences:

1. Different styles came to be preferred for different building uses: law courts and prisons were Greek Doric, and cemeteries Egyptian. Perhaps the most common application of *associative symbolism* was the use of Gothic styles for churches.
2. The desire by the designers of individual nations for a modern design style particular to each nation.
3. The need by those with pretensions to design expertise and scholarship to provide solid grounds for their choice of design style—it was irresponsible to decide on a whim.

The grounds for the choice of a style, national or otherwise, included: religion, morality, the good of society, structural clarity, cost, function, truth to material, and historical purity. Thus the newly discovered Greek architecture was beautiful because it was ancient, and had not been debased by later Roman influences. This did not stop it being despised by William Chambers (1723–96) in his 1759 *A Treatise on Civil Architecture*: "How distant the Grecians were from perfection in proportions, in any part of profiling, and other parts of the detail".[33]

The discovery of foreign styles of design was matched by discoveries in science and technology. The cost of iron, and, in the latter half of the century, of steel, dropped sufficiently to allow their increasing use in building construction. Would these new materials catalyze a new architecture? Material does not define form, and the new materials were better suited for shaping into any form and surface than were wood and masonry. The concept of truth to material became a subject for debate.

DURAND

In *Précis des leçons d'architecture* (1802) Jean-Nicholas-Louis Durand (1760–1834) proposed a rationalized system of design based on:

1. A grid for plans and elevations. Volumes were derived from these rather than the contrary.
2. A concentration on the arrangement of parts rather than on the design of the parts.
3. Minimizing cost.
4. A reduced, austere architectural vocabulary in which ornament was superfluous, and forms depended on the properties of materials and their efficient use.

Following this design approach would, according to Durand, automatically lead to beauty.

Friedrich Oettingen-Wallerstein in a pamphlet of 1835 extended Durand's concept of minimizing cost by demonstrating that construction would be cheaper if you designed for a specified building life. Now that much of what we buy is designed to comply with this concept, we could ask "cheaper for whom?"

PUGIN

Augustus Welby Northmore Pugin (1812–1852) was a designer, architect, and theorist.[34] He was the first of four important British nineteenth-century contributors to the theory of the decorative arts; the others were Ruskin, Morris, and Owen Jones.

Pugin started a business designing and making furniture in 1829, but it went bankrupt after only two years. In 1835 he converted from lax Protestant to fervent Catholic.

In 1836 Pugin published his best-known book *Contrasts: or, a parallel between the noble edifices of the fourteenth and fifteenth centuries, and similar buildings of the present day; shewing the present decay of taste.* This book contrasted the predominantly Greek-revival architecture of his own time and its attendant social ills with the splendid architecture and supposed social harmony of four centuries earlier. Pugin argued that the state of society and the state of its architecture were linked. Thus the decline of design and architecture from medieval times was caused by the rise of Protestantism. The revival of pagan classicism had also contributed to the decline by eroding morality and bringing on the excesses and evils of capitalism. In contrast "The [Roman Catholic] Church was the great and never failing school in which all the great artists of the days of faith were formed".

Pugin was more than a powerful promoter of Gothic historicism, he saw Gothic as the ideal modern style because of its beauty and its functionality. As an example in *On Metalwork* (1841), he contrasted the Gothic face-mounted hinge which was both beautiful and secure (figure 3.24), against the edge-mounted butt hinge which was hidden and from which a door was easily torn.

Pugin's promotion of Gothic also lead him to condemn:

1. The interchangeability of ecclesiastical and secular forms.
2. The confusion of decoration and structure. Pugin opens *The True Principles of Pointed or Christian Architecture* (1841)

Figure 3.24 Beautiful and secure face-mounted hinges on the west door into St. Francis Xavier's Catholic church, Berrima, New South Wales. This church was designed by A. W. N. Pugin, and built in about 1849.

by stating "The two great rules for design": "there should be no features about a building which are not necessary for convenience, construction, or propriety", and "all ornament should consist of the enrichment of the essential construction". The use of "true" in the manifesto's title was deliberate. To design otherwise was deceptive. A moral stricture was also contained within the first of the two rules by the use of "propriety" which for Pugin meant the kinds of buildings society should have were it to return to the Catholicism and the social harmony of the Gothic period.

3. The distortion of scale and purpose in the then popular picturesque Gothic.[35]
4. The adoption of styles instead of their generation.
5. The contemporary "disguising instead of beautifying articles of utility".
6. Irrationality: for example, shaded wallpapers in which a two-dimension design masquerades as a three-dimensional arrangement. Pugin stressed in *Floriated ornament* (1849) that leaves or flowers should be "drawn out or extended so as to display their geometrical forms on a flat surface".
7. The "deception" of disguising materials: for example, cast iron is "disguised by paint, either as stone, wood, or marble". "Cheap deceptions of magnificence encourage persons to assume a semblance of decoration far beyond either their means or their station." Pugin promoted forms which were "admirably suited to the material", but avoided clarifying the concept. The repetitive casting of iron was "subversive of . . . variety and imagination".
8. The narrowing of the craftsmans' vocabulary of skills which was resulting from the spread of machinery.[36]

The Gothic ideals were not only the preserve of Roman Catholicism; the Ecclesiologists, an Anglican group concerned with church architecture active between 1840 and 1870, promoted the massiveness and simplicity of thirteenth-century Gothic. They also favored structural polychromy, the use of color to clarify and define structure. This aid to design clarity has been unfortunately neglected by some of today's turners of vessels conglutinated from many pieces of differently-colored woods. In such vessels there is often little or no relation between the colored bands and the form; and the definition of parts such as the neck, body, and base through turning moldings on their forms has also been neglected.

SCHINKEL
Karl Friedrich Schinkel (1781–1841), the leading Prussian neoclassical architect, lamented in 1841, "Each period has its own architectural style, why haven't we established our own?" It had been realized that there had been a historical progression of styles. Hence the demand for one for the nineteenth century.

Schinkel defined the task of architecture as "to make something practical, useful and functional into something beautiful", a definition akin to John Ruskin's differentiation of architecture from building. Schinkel also advocated visible structure: "All the essential structural elements of a building must remain visible: as soon as basic parts of the construction are concealed, the entire train of thought is lost. Such concealment leads at once to falsehood. . . ."

SEMPER
Gottfried Semper (1803–1879) was an important German design theorist. Semper lectured extensively, and promoted many ideas which we now take for granted, including:

1. That modern man has lost the design innocence which resulted in symmetry and repetition, and has had to replace it with rationalism.
2. Making a virtue of necessity. For example, North American Indian clothing was made by stitching together pieces of leather. The stitching was used as a decoration rather than being hidden, and the pieces of leather were trimmed and arranged to make a pattern.
3. Using materials in structurally sound, functionally sensible, and natural ways. Semper regarded wood bending as unnatural and violent despite its use by the Thonet company to produce chairs which were strong, light, and attractive.

Although he is associated with functionalism, Semper's was not a functionalism stripped of decoration. He wanted decoration to have purpose. He offered as an example personal ornament which could accentuate movement (a flowing skirt), accentuate a form by encircling it (a belt), or accentuate a directional dimension (hair piled high on the head).

RUSKIN
John Ruskin (1819–1900) was a prolific writer and speaker on the arts and architecture. He was enormously perceptive, although not always objective, and, like Pugin, had an exceptionally strong sense of detail. The two agreed on many aspects of design, although both tended to polarize their arguments. Ruskin also sought to differentiate his theories from, and even belittle, those of the earlier Pugin. Ruskin wrote two sermonic books on architecture: *The Seven Lamps of Architecture* (1849), the most relevant here, and *The Stones of Venice* (1851–1853).[37] In these books Ruskin makes the following points:

1. The "chief of all purposes" was "the pleasing of God". Ruskin was as fervent an Anglican as Pugin was a Roman Catholic.
2. Designs fell "into two broad classes" akin to the sublime and the beautiful. The sublime-like was an original expression of the human mind, "an understanding of the dominion . . . vested in man". The beautiful was

"imitated from natural forms" and was "a just and humble veneration for the works of God".

Ruskin attempted to clarify his concept of "natural forms". They were not "limited . . . to imitative forms . . . only it is out of the power of man to conceive beauty without her [nature's] aid. . . . All beautiful lines are adaptations of those which are commonest in the external creation". Figure 3.25 shows natural "beautiful lines" drawn by Ruskin.

3. "Noble ornamentation" is "the expression of man's delight in God's work". "Ignoble ornamentation" is "the expression of man's delight in his own [work]". While Ruskin singles out a column in the Place Vendome as ignoble, he could equally have tilted at the capital invented by Hogarth shown in figure 3.26.

4. Ruskin scorned "Architectural Deceits": "the suggestion . . . of structure or support, other than the true one . . . the painting of surfaces to represent some other material . . . or the deceptive representation of sculptured ornament upon them", and "the use of cast or machine-made ornaments of any kind". However gilding "in architecture is no deceit, because it is therein not understood for gold".

5. Ruskin considered ornament as separate from structure, while Pugin saw ornament's role as to enrich structure. For Ruskin, as later for Morris, man-made objects reflected the state of the society in which they were made because this largely governed the mode of production: "I believe the right question to ask, respecting all ornaments, is simply this: 'Was it done with enjoyment?'" Machine-work or work done by men working as machines was cold and lifeless. "It is not coarse cutting, it is not blunt cutting, that is necessarily bad; but it is *cold* cutting—the look of equal trouble everywhere. . . . The chill is more likely, indeed, to show itself in finished work . . ."

Not surprisingly Ruskin didn't like lathes: "if completeness is thought to be vested in polish, and to be attainable by help of sand paper, we may as well give the work to the engine lathe at once".

Ruskin also stressed that the appropriate finish was not just a reflection of a workman's happiness and autonomy: "*right* finish is simply the full rendering of the intended impression . . . and it is oftener got by rough than fine handling". Similarly, "sculpture is not the mere cutting of the form; it is the cutting of the effect of it".

6. Ruskin stressed that only areas which would be seen in repose should be decorated. Do not "decorate things belonging to purposes of active and occupied life. Wherever you can rest, there decorate". An allied abhorrence was "trying to disguise disagreeable necessities by some form of sudden decoration". He cited ventilation outlets which imitated roses.

7. Ruskin largely agreed with Hogarth on proportion. For

Ruskin proportion could not exist between "equal things [or parts]. They can have symmetry only. . . . Have one large thing and several smaller things (Ruskin specifies a minimum total of three), or one principal thing [part] and several inferior things [parts], and bind them well together". Ruskin notes that symmetry should only be used when the object is divided by vertical planes; and that divisions by horizontal planes are the province of proportion, and should not be equal in height.

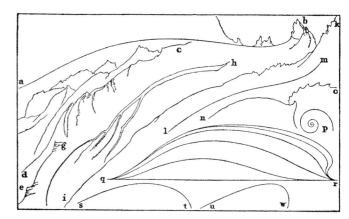

Figure 3.25 **"Lines from natural forms"** drawn by John Ruskin directly from nature, Fig. XVI from *The Stones of Venice*. "Almost all these lines are expressive of action or *force* of some kind, while the circle is a line of limitation or support." Ruskin's favorite is *ab*, the curve of a glacier, and resembles, like *mn*, Hogarth's serpentine lines shown in figure 3.13 on page 24.

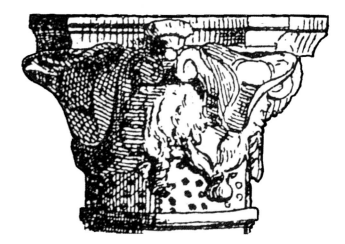

Figure 3.26 **An "ignoble" capital** to Ruskin, but to its designer William Hogarth "A capital composed of the aukward and confin'd forms of hats and periwigs . . . in a skilful hand might be made to have some beauty".[38] This capital is pictured in plate 1 of *The Analysis of Beauty*.

8. Ruskin praised "art which proceeds from an individual mind, working through instruments which assist, but do not supersede, the muscular action of the human hand, upon the materials which most tenderly receive, and most securely retain, the impressions of such human labour". He criticised industrial production because it removed "the value of the appearance of labour upon architecture" and suppressed the "living spirit" of the workman.

9. Ruskin opposed machines and new materials except for engineering uses such as railways. "All cast and machine work is bad . . . and dishonest. . . . Metals may be used as a *cement* [fastenings], but not as a *support*."

10. Ruskin opposed the more interventionist restoration advocated by Viollet-le-Duc (pages 34 and 35). Ruskin supported conservation, not restoration. The "picturesque elements" of weathering and the patina should not be scraped away. "It is impossible . . . to restore anything that has ever been great or beautiful. . . . We have no right whatever to touch [the buildings of past times]. They are not ours. They belong partly to those who built them, and partly to all the generations of mankind who are to follow us. . . . A building cannot be considered in its prime until four or five centuries have passed over it."

11. Ruskin had no truck with those who desired a nineteenth-century style: "We want no new style of architecture. . . . But we want *some* style. . . . Originality . . . does not depend on invention". It comes from the "inevitable, uncalculated, and brilliant consequences of an effort to express".

SKIDMORE

In an 1854 lecture the ironmaster F. A. Skidmore argued that iron, and by implication all metals, could be worked into a formal language of their own, finer and more delicate than that of stone, and into the natural forms Ruskin upheld as guarantors of truth in art.

JAPANESE INFLUENCE

In 1853 and 1854, U.S. naval officer Commodore Mathew Calbraith Perry headed an expedition which forced Japan to enter into trade and diplomatic relations with the West after two centuries of isolation. This lead to exhibitions of Japanese objects in London in 1854 and 1862. Irregular tea bowls were exhibited which harmoniously combined simplicity, beauty, and even the nobleness of poverty. This quality, called *shibui* in Japanese, enshrined both Ruskin's happy-workman concept and Burke's romantic idea that art is suggestion. [39]

VIOLLET-LE-DUC

Hanno-Walter Kruft calls Eugène-Emmanuel Viollet-le-Duc (1814–1879) "a backward-looking visionary". Viollet-le-Duc was the leading French architectural theorist of the nineteenth century, and wrote seven books on architecture, some which were multivolumed. The best known, *Entretiens sur l'architecture* (*Discourses on Architecture*), was published in two volumes, the first in 1863 and the second in 1872. [40]

Viollet-le-Duc admired French Gothic cathedrals which he saw as structures which had been rationally designed to fulfill the Church's liturgical requirements. However Viollet-le-Duc was not a medievalist, and wanted contemporary architecture to move forwards through applying Gothic rational principles. He was excited by the possibilities associated with new materials, particularly glass, iron, and steel, which were then in their infancy as significant structural materials. For example, the rolled sections which are the basis for much of the recent and current use of steel were just being introduced. Hence Viollet-le-Duc's statement in *Discourses*, XII, "We have not seriously considered how to make the best use of the material [iron] by giving it forms appropriate to its nature". Although Viollet-le-Duc's writings inspired later architects, notably the American Louis Henry Sullivan (page 37), Viollet-le-Duc ignored the communicative design rationale of meaning which became the basis of postmodernism, the dominant style in the 1970s and 1980s.

Viollet-le-Duc stressed that the plans of a building should be designed to efficiently fulfill the building's functions. Only after the plans were completed should the facades, which should conform to the plans, be designed. This process resulted in asymmetrical elevations and irregular massing, and is essentially the reverse of that used in classical architecture. The result was also likely to be attractive because it was rational; it would not necessarily be beautiful, although rationality was an essential component of beauty.

The structure of a building should also be dictated by the building's plan and purpose, and be as simple as possible. The materials selected should be the best suited, and should be used in a manner consonant with their inherent qualities. "We should not continue to employ those [traditional] forms [for example, the bulky wooden structures which had to be designed to accommodate wood's differential movement], but should try to discover others that harmonize with the properties of" the new materials as they are brought into use. This moral attitude to materials paralleled Ruskin's in *The Seven Lamps of Architecture*. Viollet-le-Duc also believed that materials should be employed honestly, and not in ways which imitated other materials or imitated the methods in which other materials were traditionally employed.

Viollet-le-Duc wrote in *Discourses*, XVI that there had been three distinct approaches to ornament:

1. That used in ancient Egypt "Deriving . . . from the objects and materials employed in building".

2. Roman, in which ornament was regarded "only as a decorative accessory, without any connection with [the] structure", designed to "dazzle, to astonish" and "of no

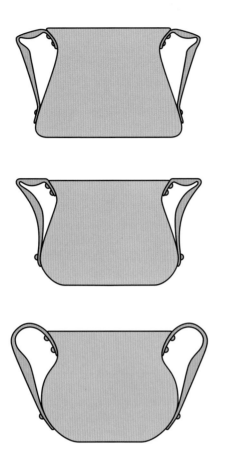

Figure 3.27 The progress and decay of style, three copper vessels whose forms Viollet-le-Duc used to illustrate the concept in *Discourses, VI*.

Top, the primitive form of vessel, has "a flat circular bottom so that it may stand firm when full", is necked to "hinder the liquid from spilling", and "widens out suddenly at the edge to facilitate pouring". The handles, which are attached with rivets, do not project above the rim and thereby allow the vessel to be inverted and drained dry. The top vessel thus has style because:

1. It "Exactly indicates its purpose".
2. It "Is fashioned in accordance with the material employed and the means of fabrication suited to the material".
3. Its "form is suited to the material of which the utensil is made, and the use for which it is intended".

Middle, this vessel has a developed form. Succeeding coppersmiths altered the body that had been hitherto been regarded as perfect to attract purchasers by the distinction of novelty.

Bottom, this vessel has a decadent form. The last coppersmith "having lost sight of the principle, bids adieu to reason and follows caprice alone", resulting in a vessel which is less stable, cannot be inverted without damaging the handles, and is therefore "deprived . . . of its proper style".

concern to them whether the ornamentation suited the material made use of or not". For Viollet-le-Duc, Roman ornament possessed neither fitness nor clearness.
3. The medieval approach in which ornament "forms part of . . . and even . . . accentuate[s] the construction".

Thus for Viollet-le-Duc, ornament, while indispensable, should be:

1. Subordinate to the composition of the object as a whole.
2. Applied to structurally significant locations.
3. Appropriate to the material and designed so as not to weaken it.

Viollet-le-Duc wrote extensively on style which he defined as "the effort of the active imagination regulated by reason". Whether that style became a period style was a separate question. Viollet-le-Duc also described three stages in the development and fashion-driven decay of style where there was no progress in the technical means to express that style (figure 3.27). Viollet-le-Duc recognized that style, which is "the presentation of ideas in a palpable form, in a defin-ite embodiment", must progress as the means to express the ideas progress, and that designers should also drive that progress. He cited the "hundred-gun ship of war, rigged as a sailing vessel" which appeared beautiful because it was "so perfectly adapted to [its] purpose", but had been superseded by the steamship. Therefore if a sailing warship had been built in say 1870, it could not be beautiful "on the principle just now cited". Viollet-le-Duc did not clarify whether a sailing ship built in 1770 would, if perfectly maintained, still be beautiful a century later because it fulfilled its purpose when built despite it being obsolete in 1870.

Viollet-le-Duc warned of the destructive power of tradition. He noted the paradox between the latest furniture-making machines which were in a modern style, and their use in making furniture which imitated earlier period styles. In many of today's furniture factories the same situation reigns.

In 1844 Viollet-le-Duc was commissioned to restore the Gothic cathedral of Notre-Dame de Paris. Building restoration was a new phenomenon in the nineteenth century. Viollet-le-Duc advocated a flexible approach based on scholarship. He was alive to the problems which result from the alterations and additions made over the years (figure 3.28). Also, the lack of perfect knowledge of a building's history rendered hard-and-fast rules such as "only repair what there is" or "return the building to its earliest state" foolish. Viollet-le-Duc stressed that any part which was replaced "should be replaced with better materials, and in a stronger and more perfect way". He also stressed that contemporary utility should be considered. "To restore a building is not to repair or rebuild it but to re-establish it in a state of entirety which might never have existed at any

Figure 3.28 Conserve or restore? A seventeenth-century turned armchair in the collection of the Museum of Welsh Life, Cardiff. The casters were put on during the second half of the twentieth century by a previous owner, and their presence raises two restoration/conservation questions:

1. Should the casters be removed although they form part of the chair's history? Should the recentness of the fitting of the casters influence the decision?
2. If it were decided to remove the castors, and if the legs were shortened when the castors were originally fitted, should the legs be restored to their original lengths? If so, should the new leg extensions be finished to match the rest of the chair, or should their newness be left obvious?

There are no correct answers to these questions, illustrating Viollet-le-Duc's belief that each case needs to be considered on its merits. A factor which is often relevant in determining the scope of conservation/restoration work is whether an object will be a display or museum piece and be unused, or whether it will be used in the future and if so in what ways.

Illustration supplied by the Museum of Welsh Life.

given moment". His approach to restoration was far more interventionist than that promoted by John Ruskin and William Morris.

Viollet-le-Duc claimed that structural efficiency should be the basis for a nineteenth-century style. Instead cost was often the arbiter, aided by the postulate that utilitarian means undecorated. Viollet-le-Duc also promoted the hypothesis that the medieval cathedrals had a perfect structure in which every element contributed to the equilibrium, and in which material was at a daring, reasoned, minimum. In short the perfect harmony between means and ends. Not only was he a prophet for the Gothic Revival, he saw that the spirit of the thirteenth-century, medieval-cathedral designers was what was needed to use "the abundance of means and materials" which were becoming available. Classical design was to Viollet-le-Duc, as it was to Ruskin, a form of slavery of the human spirit.

JONES
Owen Jones (1809–1874) lists thirty-seven propositions "in the arrangement of form and colour" at the beginning of his 1856 *The Grammar of Ornament*. What was notable about the book was the display in colour of many styles of ornament and decoration from different cultures at different times. Jones praised in particular Moorish design, "Every principle which we can derive from the study of the ornamental art of any other people is not only ever present here, but was by the Moors more universally and truly obeyed".[41]

MORRIS
William Morris (1834–1896) had two passions: "to produce beautiful things", and "a hatred of modern civilization".[42] Blessed with a romantic imagination, he was greatly influenced by the Scottish historian and essayist Thomas Carlyle and by John Ruskin to detest the evils of the Victorian age: its clutter of fussy, mass-produced perfection; and labor which was joyless because it was repetitive, machine-governed, and isolated from the rest of the production process including the design. While Karl Marx saw work as a setting for political struggle, Morris saw creative work as the end, not a means to an end.[43]

Morris was not only a thinker, he was a doer, and fought a spirited rearguard action against mass production. With a brotherhood of like-minded artists, a mathematician, and a surveyor, he set up the company in 1861 which became Morris & Co. in 1875. It operated under supposedly idyllic medieval lines, applying the ideals of honesty, handwork, truth to material, and non-illusionistic pattern to a wide range of products. These including tapestries, wallpaper, stained glass, and furniture, and were designed by Morris, Philip Webb, and Edward Burne-Jones. Although the influence of the medieval aesthetic was undeniable, these were fresh, uncluttered designs(at least to the nineteenth-century eye). Morris believed that art should be affordable to all. In practice only part of Morris & Co's production was (figure 3.29). The cumulative effect of Morris & Co's simpler designs, sympathetic use of natural and local materials, and craftsmanship, did much to bring about the Arts and Crafts movement, the ethos of which remains influential today.

Morris's attitude to machinery is detailed in his essay "The Revival of Handicraft" (1888).[44] Morris stated that during the medieval period there was "little or no division of labor, and what machinery was used was . . . a help to the workman's hand labor and not a supplanter of it". Morris distinguished two arts: that input by the workman, and that input by the designer. The presence of the former was creating a demand for handmade goods, even if they were unornamented. Was this "a mere reactionary sentiment" or a "real coming change", a revolt against "the system of machine production". Morris saw several bars to the revolt he desired including the consumer's ignorance of production and loss of "due sympathy with the life of the workshop", and the capitalist masters' dictation to the market of what would be manufactured for sale. Would the situation "evolve itself into a fresh period of machinery more independent of human labour than anything we can conceive of now, or would it develop its contradictory in the shape of a new and improved period of production by handicraft?" Morris hoped for the latter because machine production was ugly, was degrading public taste, was "altogether an evil". There were, however, limited short-term benefits: "production by machinery . . . as an instrument for forcing on us better conditions of life . . . has been, and for some time yet will be, indispensable." Morris was not without hope. The revival of handicraft and with it beauty and pleasure in one's work was possible if society became socialist.

Morris poo-pooed the notion that ugliness was desirable because it highlighted beauty; he was also against the conscious "production of beauty for beauty's sake" because it resulted in "affectation and effeminacy". For Morris, beauty was a by-product of the conscious effort "to produce great works for the glory of the City".

Morris came to detest restoration as artificial, and in

Figure 3.29 Affordable furniture by Morris & Co. *Left*, a Sussex armchair, and *right*, a Rossetti armchair. Both chairs were made in about 1868. Morris regarded these and similar chairs as among his most important contributions to decor because of their affordability. Photograph supplied by the Art Gallery of South Australia, Adelaide.

1877 founded with colleagues the Society for the Protection of Ancient Buildings. By that time "protection" had come to mean to Morris doing no more than the minimum to keep the building in sound order, using, where repairs were necessary, ancient materials. Morris agreed with Ruskin, not Viollet-le-Duc. The Society argued that "antiquity was a finite resource which could only be managed", and that modern liturgical fashions did not justify alterations to medieval churches. These beliefs were part of an attack on historicism and the belief, particularly associated with the Gothic (or Gothick) revival, that conjectural restorations, alterations and additions based on archeology and quasi-science "made a church more ancient". Morris did not see protection (conservation) and a respect for the past as enemies of design progress.

NIETZSCHE
The German philosopher Friedrich Nietzsche (1844–1900) believed that truth was a mere cultural necessity, and that value could only be measured terms of greatness and excellence. In his 1874 *The Use and Abuse of History* he criticised historicism because it undermined will and turned man "into a restless, dilettante spectator".

HILDEBRAND
Adolf von Hildebrand in an 1899 essay "*Hand Work—Machine Work*" discussed the distinction between an experiencer's perception of a finished creative work and the process used to create it: "The true enjoyment of art resides in the contagious power that passes from what the human organ has imprinted in the work to the visual organs of the viewer, making him an active participant". Machine-made objects could not possess and could not therefore pass this "contagious power".

CHOISY
Auguste Choisy (1841–1909) was trained as an engineer. Not surprisingly in his *Histoire de l'architectre* (1899) he saw the whole history of architecture as reflecting developments in technology.

Choisy saw a module as essential for sound planning, and explained that proportion could not be a system of fixed rules because some dimensions were variable and some were fixed or only variable within limits. In a building examples of fixed dimensions are the heights of handrails, and the dimensions of the risers and goings of steps—this echoes Hogarth's writing on fitness described on page 24.

3.3.4 TWENTIETH CENTURY

During the nineteenth century the architectural focus was on style, particularly on the searches for national styles. For much of the twentieth century architecture and design were supposedly allied to the political cause of socialism.

Socialism's doctrine was international cooperation, and its style was modernism.

The twentieth century brought a host of technological inventions: synthetic glues, plastics, new metals, tubing, extrusion, and sheet glass and board products in large sizes. Modernism sought to exploit these advances to create new design vocabularies freed of expensive and debasing ornament. These vocabularies could in turn be used to improve the lot of the common man through creating cheaper and more functional buildings and objects. The common man was not wholehearted in his acceptance of what was deemed good for him, and historicism and even what was derided as *kitsch* continued to be popular.

Modernism spawned the new decorative style of the interwar period, art deco, a name taken from the title of the first major decorative arts exhibition after World War I held in Paris in 1925, L'*Exposition Internationale des Arts Décoratifs et Industriels Modernes*. Art deco utilized dramatic (and not always inexpensive) materials in simple geometric forms and patterns.

Eventually there was a reaction (postmodernism) against the austerity and lack of humanity of functionalism, although modernism's economic imperative continued and strengthens. The ideals of modernism have been overtaken, and it is now regarded as just another style, rather than the elimination of style and the synthesis of design and social good.

In the arts after World War II concept became idolized and workmanship was debased. Fortunately it was realized that a concept is worthless unless it can be manifested, that an adequate manifestation cannot always be produced by a contractor or employee, and that workmanship is not necessarily drudgery. Not only can workmanship be rewarding and fun, it is intimately connected with designing, and feeds back into and enriches designing.

SULLIVAN
Louis Henry Sullivan (1856–1924) was the best-known architect of the Chicago School. In his autobiography (1923) he states "a formula he [Sullivan] had evolved, through long contemplation of living things, namely that *form follows function*".[45] Sullivan's was not however a material- and structure-based functionalism; it was instead the sum of the relevant natural, social, and intellectual human needs. Sullivan's functionalism was similar to Viollet-le-Duc's.

VAN DER ROHE
The Bauhaus in Germany and the Vkhutemas in Moscow were design schools which were hugely important to the development and expansion of modernism through their training of architects and designers. Ludwig Mies van der Rohe (1886–1969) was director of the Bauhaus from 1930 to 1933. Its closure by the Nazis in 1933 warned that modernism was not compatible with Hitler's desired neoclassical monumentalism. Like several of his colleagues, van der Rohe

Figure 3.30 Postmodern design, mugs cast from turned wooden patterns based on a tin can and a Styrofoam cup. The angels wings recall medieval and Renaissance images. Designer and potter, Michael Keighery of Newtown, Sydney.

moved to America shortly before World War II. There he went to the Illinois Institute of Technology at Chicago. He coined the modernist formula "less is more".[46]

POSTMODERNISM

The most recent style of significance, postmodernism, was a reaction against the "ice-cold world of robots". This phrase was used by the German philosopher Ernst Block (1885–1977) in the first major attack against modernism in the mid-1950s. The better known but later response by American Robert Venturi (b. 1925) in 1966 in *Complexity and Contradiction in Architecture* countered van der Rohe's phrase with "less is a bore". Venturi's 1972 book *Learning from Las Vegas* called for a return of symbolism, eclecticism, and historicism, for ornament which has meaning:

> Allusion and comment, on the past or present or our great commonplace or old clichés, and inclusion of the everyday in the environment, sacred and profane—these are what is lacking in present day Modern architecture.[47]

Postmodernism generally resulted in the addition of playful ornament to a modernist core, and provided a climate for a more overt and adventurous use of engineering. However, despite the world being wealthier than ever before, economic functionalism, often in alliance with the degraded and passive tastes which had appalled Morris, continue to rule

design, and dictate a lessening of the use of solid wood and woodturning.

3.4 SUMMARY

The preceding part of this chapter has roughly traced the development of design theory. The summary below demonstrates how views have and continue to conflict.

Beauty:

1. Depends on number, especially on the closeness of the proportions of the object and its parts to those in musical harmony—Pythagoras, Plato, Vitruvius, St. Augustine, Baumgarten.
2. Consists of partaking of true or ideal beauty which is outside time and space—Socrates, Plato.
3. Is a felt response—the Sophists, Le Clerk, Briseux, Hume, Kant.
4. Is concerned with moral values—Ruskin.
5. Depends on utility—Aquinas, Perrault, Frémin, Hogarth.
6. Depends on artistry—Vitruvius, Perrault.
7. Depends on conformance to a module—Vitruvius.
8. Is related to the proportions of the human body—Vitruvius, Durer, Perrault.

9. Requires variety—Alberti, Hogarth.
10. Is based on what is or was customary—Perrault, Plumier, Ramsay.
11. Must be based on nature—Ruskin.
12. Depends on the presence of serpentine lines—Hogarth.
13. Is characterized by smoothness, delicacy, etc.—Hogarth, Burke.
14. Is related to economy—Durand.
15. Is the manifestation of functionalism—Frémin, Durand.
16. Depends on the appropriate arrangement of parts—Hogarth.

Ornament should:

1. Explain the structure or its derivation—Vitruvius, Pugin.
2. Be separated from the structure—Ruskin.
3. Be appropriate—Alberti.
4. Be applied—Alberti.
5. Be functional—Frémin.
6. Be abolished—Lodoli, Durand.
7. Be educative—Moritz.
8. Not be deceptive—Pugin, Ruskin.
9. Accentuate dimensions and movement—Semper.
10. Be done with enjoyment—Ruskin.
11. Be based on nature—Ruskin.
12. Not represent living things—Muslim belief.
13. Be allusive—Venturi.

Restoration should:

1. Be restricted to conserving what is extant—Ruskin, Morris.
2. Be decided on merits, one being that compatibility with present-day use requirements overrides conservation—Viollet-le-Duc.

Such conflicting views and differences of emphasis prevented the development of a unified design methodology. A fresh approach was needed, and from the second half of the nineteenth century it was hoped that a scientific basis for aesthetic judgement could be developed through exploring the psychology of form using techniques allied to medical research. This resulted by 1890 in the formulation of *Gestalt* (a German word meaning approximately "put together") psychology. Gestalt psychology promotes analysis from above down, from the whole down to the characteristics of a form's constituent parts. It stresses that the preferred shape, position, and function for each part is not deducible by analyzing the parts in isolation.[48] It is an approach I shall follow in later chapters.

Research and thinking by philosophers, psychologists and others continued during the twentieth century, and was introduced in chapter 2. In the next chapter I shall apply this research and thinking and ideas originating in earlier times to clarify concepts important to woodturning design.

3.5 ENDNOTES

Full endnotes for this chapter would occupy almost as many pages as the main text. I have therefore given details of those books which I have referred to extensively (all of which are fully indexed) and where I have used them. I have given conventional endnotes for those books which I have used in specific and limited areas.

1. Most of the information in sections 3.1, 3.2, and the early part of 3.3 is extracted from general texts on the history of philosophy, especially: Christoph Delius and others, *The Story of Philosophy from Antiquity to the Present* (Cologne, Germany: Konemann, 2000); Anthony Kenny, ed., *The Oxford Illustrated History of Western Philosophy* (Oxford University Press, 1994); Bryan Magee, *The Story of Philosophy* (London: Dorling Kindersley, 1998); and Martyn Oliver, *Philosophy* (London: Hamlyn, 1997).
2. Michael Kelly, editor in chief, *Encyclopedia of Aesthetics*, vol 1 (Oxford University Press, 1998), p. 239.
3. Larry Shiner, *The Invention of Art* (Chicago: The University of Chicago Press, 2001), p. 146.
4. Donald D. Hoffman, *Visual Intelligence* (New York: W. W. Norton, 1998), p. 65.
5. Shiner, pp. 19–20.
6. The theorem had been used by the Babylonians 1000 years before Pythagoras was born. Richard Mankiewicz, *The Story of Mathematics* (London: Cassell & Co, 2000), p.12.
7. Robert Maynard Hutchins, ed. in chief, *Great Books of the Western World*, vol. 7 Plato (Chicago: Encyclopaedia Britannica, 1952), pp. 630–631.
8. Hanno-Walter Kruft, A *History of Architectural Theory from Vitruvius to the Present* (New York: Princeton Architectural Press, 1994), pp. 23–24.
9. Shiner, pp. 22, 28-30.
10. Shiner, p. 34.
11. Oliver, p. 53.
12. Shiner, p. 75–77.
13. Ostwald Mathias Ungers, "Ordo, fondo et mensura: the Criteria of Architecture," Henry A. Millon, ed., *Italian Renaissance Architecture from Brunelleschi to Michelangelo* (London: Thames and Hudson, 1994), p. 308.
14. Kruft gives an excellent summary of Vitruvius on pages 21–29. Several books on Vitruvius and several translations of Vitruvius are available including: Marcus Vitruvius Pollio, *The Ten Books on Architecture*, trans. Morris Hicky Morgan (1914; reprint, New York: Dover Publications, 1969); and Frank Granger, ed. and trans., *Vitruvius on Architecture*, 2 vols. (Cambridge, Massachusetts: Harvard University Press, 1931).
15. Morgan, p. 4.

16. A discussion of the illustrated copies is given in Gustina Scaglia, "A Translation of Vitruvius and Copies of Late Antique Drawings In Buonaccorso Ghiberti's Zibaldone," *Transactions of the American Philosophical Society* 69, part 1, (February 1979): 10–15.

17. Ungers, pp. 308–309.

18. Kruft, p. 200.

19. The most accessible current version is Leon Battista Alberti, *The Ten Books of Architecture* (1755 Leoni Edition; reprint, New York: Dover Publications, 1986), publisher's note.

20. Ungers, p. 309.

21. The general references for section 3.3 are the philosophy books listed in endnote 1, Kruft, and Gombrich. Also: Barry Bergdoll, *European Architecture 1750–1890* (Oxford University Press, 2000); James Stevens Curl, *Georgian Architecture* (Newton Abbot, England: David & Charles, 1993); and Claude Mignot, *Architecture of the 19th Century* (Fribourg, Germany: 1983).

22. Kruft, p. 189.

23. Shiner, pp. 99–129.

24. Christoph Delius and others, The Story of *Philosophy from Antiquity to the Present* (Cologne, Germany: Konemann, 2000),p.35; Anthony Kenny, ed., *The Oxford Illustrated History of Western Philosophy* (Oxford University Press, 1994), p.108; and Frank N. Magill, ed., *Masterpieces of World Philosophy* (New York: HarperCollins), pp. 216–223.

25. Edward de Bono, *The Greatest Thinkers* (London: George Weidenfield and Nicolson, 1976), pp. 94–95.

26. Eric Bruton, *Clocks & Watches* (Felton, Middlesex: Hamlyn Publishing Group, 1968), pp. 63–65.

27. Claude Perrault, *Introduction to Ordonnance for the Five Kinds of Columns After the Method of the Ancients* (1683; reprint Santa Monica, California: The Getty Center, 1993). The book includes an extensive introduction by Alberto Pérez-Gómez.

28. Perrault, p. 47.

29. At least one modern edition is available: William Hogarth, *The Analysis of Beauty* (1753; reprint, New Haven, Connecticut: Yale Univeristy Press, 1997). Ronald Paulson has written an extensive introduction and notes to this edition which have been of great value.

30. Jack Lindsay, *Hogarth: His Art and His World* (London: Hart-Davis, MacGibbon, 1977), p. 179.

31. Edmund Burke, A *Philosophical Enquiry* (1757; reprint, Oxford University Press, 1990).

32. Sebastian Gardner, "Aesthetics," A.C. Grayling, ed., *Philosophy; A Guide Through The Subject* (Oxford University Press, 1995), p. 599.

33. William Chambers, A *Treatise on the Decorative Part of Civil Architecture* (1791; reprint, New York: Benjamin Blom, 1968), p. 19.

34. My main reference was *Pugin: a Gothic Passion*, ed. Paul Atterbury and Clive Wainwright (New Haven, Connecticut: Yale University Press, 1994).

35. J. Mordaunt Crook, *The Dilemma of Style* (London: John Murray, 1987), p. 44.

36. Crook, p. 53.

37. Easily accessible reprints include: John Ruskin, *The Seven Lamps of Architecture* (1880 2nd ed; reprint, New York: Dover Publications, 1989); and John Ruskin, *The Stones of Venice*, ed. J. G. Links (1853; reprint, London: Penguin Books, 2001).

38. Hogarth, p. 46.

39. Bernard Leach, A *Potter's Book* (London: Faber & Faber, 1960), pp. 8–9; Soetsu Yanagi, *The Unknown Craftsman*, rev. ed. (Tokyo: Kodansha International, 1989), pp. 120–121.

40. For this section I have mainly used M. F. Hearn, ed., *The Architectural Theory of Viollet-le-Duc* (Cambridge, Massachusetts: The MIT Press, 1990), and have leant heavily on Professor Hearn's commentaries.

41. Owen Jones, *The Grammar of Ornament* (1856; reprint, London: Studio Editions, 1986), p. 66.

42. John Burdick, *William Morris Redesigning the World* (New York: Todtri Productions, 1997), p. 4.

Collections of Morris's works are widely held. There is also a William Morris Gallery in Forest Road, Walthamstow, London.

43. Parry p. 366

44. William Morris, *Architecture Industry & Wealth* (London: Longmans, Green, 1902), pp. 214–227.

45. The association of the words form and function was hardly new. P. Rioux de Maillou wrote in 1895, "The principle of the relationship between form and function, as a basis for beauty, had been utterly vindicated by the facts". Isabelle Frank, ed., *The Theory of decorative Art*, (New Haven: Yale University Press, 2000), p. 188.

46. The phrase was coined by poet Robert Browning in his 1855 poem "Andrea del Sarto". See James Trilling, *The Language of Ornament* (London: Thames and Hudson, 2001), p. 14–15.

49. Robert Venturi, Denise Scott Brown, and Steven Izenour, *Learning from Las Vegas* (Cambridge, Mass:), p. 53.

50. The major modern book on Gestalt aesthetics is Rudolf Arnheim, *Art and Visual Perception*, rev. ed. (Berkeley: University of California Press, 1974).

Chapter Four

DESIGN CONCEPTS AND ISSUES

In the preceding chapter I outlined a history of design concepts. In this chapter I discuss how some of these concepts are understood today. I also discuss some of the issues which have arisen from these concepts. The discussions are grouped under four loose headings:

1. The modern meanings of the aesthetic terms beauty, imitation and representation, expression, artifice, bizarreness, functionalism, proportion, detail, appropriateness, and realization.
2. Concepts which may influence the way we perceive turnings: whether they are art or craft, fashion, style, historicism, and truth to material.
3. Workmanship and deskilling, concepts concerned with the production of a turning.
4. Concepts concerned with morality in design: forgery, conservation and restoration, plagiarism, and reproduction.

These discussions lay the groundwork for the design advice and analysis covered in later chapters.

Figure 4.1 The modern, restricted meaning of beauty is "smooth, quietly colored, perfect, cool, refined". Edmund Burke was among the most influential promoters of this meaning (page 27).

The stem of this cup is separate and a push-fit onto a short, cylindrical base turned on the bottom of the cup. The cup can thus also be displayed without the stem.

4.1 MODERN AESTHETIC MEANINGS

I found Roger Scruton's *The Aesthetics of Architecture* invaluable when writing this first section.[1] Many of the thoughts are his although I have not always put them within quotation marks. Other sources are listed in the endnotes.

4.1.1 BEAUTY

Beauty was the only, or at least the major, aesthetic quality for the ancients and for Renaissance designers. It was also associated with goodness and truth. "Beautiful" is now just one of many adjectives used to describe different aesthetic qualities (figure 4.1), or is an overall term meaning "aesthetically commendable".[2] A thought-provoking definition of beauty is George Santayana's "pleasure regarded as the quality of a thing".[3]

Beauty is not consequential, an inevitable result of solving design problems well or of designing purely functionally; nor is beauty an unpursuable by-product, something which occurs or does not according to factors which you cannot influence. Beauty is an indefinable and insufficient aim. Beauty is not an absolute; there are degrees of beauty; even ugly turnings can have beautiful details. Many factors, not just the narrow concept of beauty, can combine to make a turning successful to both its designer and to others who may experience it.

4.1.2 IMITATION AND REPRESENTATION

I shall discuss expression on pages 43 and 44. Expression's role in creation was largely ignored until the end of the nineteenth century. Before then a work of art or craft was thought to be either an imitation or a representation of its subject. Scruton describes an imitation as merely a strong resemblance or reference to something (figure 4.2). An imitation can also be reminiscence of something such as an object or an event. An imitation only becomes representational when you have to know more than just what the thing imitated looks like (figures 4.3 and 4.4). A representation thus incorporates its designer's thoughts or knowledge about a subject, and an experiencer has to think about and grasp these thoughts to understand the representation.[4] For this, the experiencer's knowledge of the representation does not have to be identical to the designer's, but it has to be adequate.

Figure 4.2 **An imitative bowl** exploiting form, the pinkness of New Zealand beech, and the flesh color of paperbark.

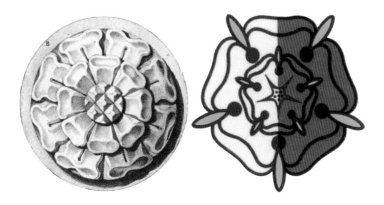

Figure 4.3 **Imitative and representational rosettes.**

Left, a drawing of a medieval wooden boss by Augustus Charles Pugin (1762–1832), father of A. W. N. Pugin.[5] Pugin's drawing imitates the boss. The boss in turn imitates a flower, it does not represent or say anything about the flower which requires other than recognition.

Right, the emblem of Tudor House School, Moss Vale, New South Wales. This rosette's representation is only understood by those who realize that the white and red colors refer to the English Wars of the Roses (1455–1485) between the Houses of Lancaster (red) and York (white). The Tudor rose, was adopted as a badge by Henry Tudor after he defeated the Yorkist king Richard III at Bosworth Field in 1485. Henry VII reigned until 1509.

Figure 4.4 **A representation** of the destruction and cleansing of fire, and the ability of eucalyptus trees to regenerate after being burnt. Andrew Potocnik of MacLeod West, Victoria, Australia, titled this work *Ash Wednesday* after a particularly serious bushfire in Victoria on the first day of Lent, 1983, in which 72 people died. It is 26 in. (650 mm) high.

4.1.3 EXPRESSION

William Wordsworth defined poetry as "the spontaneous overflow of powerful feelings". This romantic view that human creation stems from the expression of feelings (emotions) was first formalized into the expression theory of art by Benedetto Croce (1866–1952). Expression is not restricted to art. If while you draw during design-by-drawing. you experience emotion, you are expressing. R. G. Collingwood's thoughts on expression in his 1938 book *The Principles of* Art remain influential, and in summary say:[6]

1. Artistic expression is a special form of self-expression.
2. Through expressing the artist seeks relief from the pressure of feeling, and may also be seeking understanding from present or future experiencers.
3. The work created "incorporates" the artist's state of mind in a way similar to that in which smiles and grimaces both display and are inseparable from certain mental activities.

Scruton also summarized Collingwood: "Expression is not finding the symbol for a subjective feeling, as of coming to know, through the act of expression, just what the feeling is".[7] In this artistic expression, the degree of emotional takeover is almost total until the artist suddenly comes to realize that he or she has been expressing. Artistic expression is therefore unconscious. It is at one end of a spectrum in which, as the proportion of expression which is artistic declines, that which is conscious increases until *it* is total. Conscious expression is also an expression of emotions, but of emotions of which the person is already conscious. When you manifest an emotion of which you are conscious, you do it "on purpose", and this for Collingwood is associated with craft. This distinction between art and craft based on the presence or absence of artistic (unconscious) expression is now widely rejected. Further, emotional expression, whether conscious or unconscious, is now regarded as contributing to aesthetic value, and is able to be displayed by an object.

Is emotional expression possible in woodturning? I believe it is. Turners can manipulate turning tools with emotion, both conscious and unconscious, during turning. The rapid rotation of the workpiece may blur the result of any expressive tool manipulation, but it does not deny it. Nor is emotion only recorded through the manipulation of tools (figure 4.5); it can be expressed in the design. Perhaps the emotions most commonly expressed in woodturning are a love of wood and a love of skill (figure 4.6), but, as many turners know, while an expressive object can express its designer's emotions, it will not necessarily evoke the same emotions in an experiencer.

The concepts of imitation, representation and expression cannot be clearly separated or defined (figure 4.7). This truth applies to most terms used in design, including that discussed next, artifice.

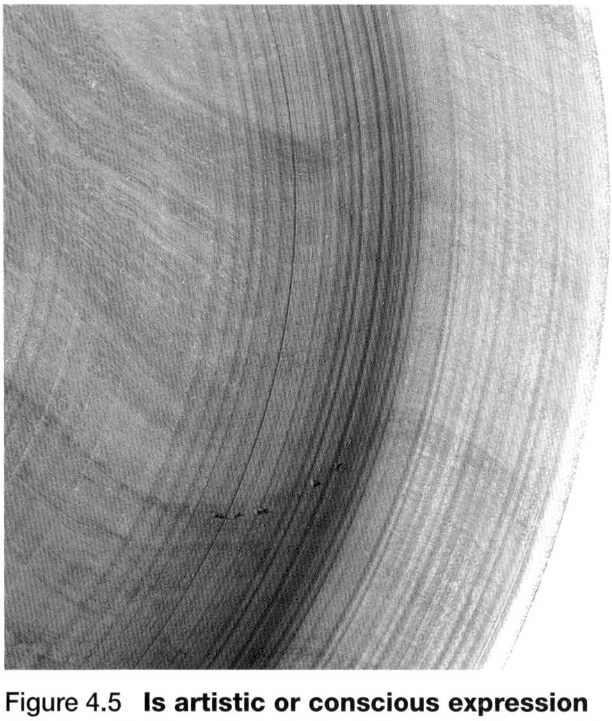

Figure 4.5 Is artistic or conscious expression dominant? It is unlikely that artistic expression could have been sustained during the long duration of care and control needed to turn the whole surface of this 18 in. (450 mm) diameter jarrah (*Eucalyptus marginata*) platter.

Figure 4.6 A conscious expression and demonstration of skill. A nest of nine bowls from the one jarrah burl by Mike Mahoney of Orem, Utah. The largest bowl is 8 in. high x 13 in. dia. (200 mm x 325 mm).

Figure 4.7 Movement expressed and imitated in *Java Jig* by Michael Lambert of Santa Cruz, California. The movement expressed in these pieces is greater than can be expressed in woodturning (pages 111 and 112), but shows the possibilities.

The ogee forms of the round bodies express movement which is accentuated by the angularity of the arm-resembling spouts and handles. Other expressive features are the tilts of the rims and lids, and the lifts of the bases which recall the lift of a dancer's skirt, heel or toe. These features have often been used in animated cartoons.

4.1.4 ARTIFICE

An artifice is "a crafty (an unfortunate choice of word) device or expedient." Artifice is not restricted to art, and implies something contrived to gain an end. In turning, the term is most often applied to the designing of works to conform to market requirements. Production turners of balusters and other functional items adapt their designs to market requirements, but their work is not usually regarded as artifice. Perhaps the key to the distinction is expression. If so, artifice is the imitation of emotional, particularly artistic, expression in an object to aid that object's sale.

From about 1970 there has been a strong focus on developing the concept of, and a market for, art turnings. A motivation for some turners has been that "objects that are sold on aesthetic grounds are not subject to competition by price".[8] While this statement is untrue, prices for art are less comparable, and are therefore less governed by competition. With all turners now aware of the benefits in both status and money which apparently flow when their work is perceived by the market to be art, can much art turning be free of some degree of artifice? and is artifice a heinous crime anyway?

How does an experiencer differentiate emotional expression from artifice, and apportion values? Judgements

Figure 4.8 Artifice or emotional expression? The chainsawn rim surface was produced by a forestry worker who gave no thought to whether the surface would be retained as a finished surface or not. The subsequent decision to retain the surface in the completed bowl could result from:

1. A decision to incorporate the "found" surface's aesthetic qualities into the platter.
2. An artifice, an attempt to imply that the chainsawn surface was intentionally designed and then produced.

have to be subjective because few creators will publicly admit to artifice; nor do I intend to imply that any work pictured in this book results from artifice. To illustrate the term I have used a bowl I designed and turned (figure 4.8).

4.1.5 BIZARRENESS

A form or ornament can be an imitation, but that imitation does not need not be faithful or even reasonably faithful to the appearance of the subject. Without becoming a representation, an imitation can be so distorted that it becomes grotesque or bizarre.

"Bizarre", from the Basque word *bizar* for beard, means strange or odd. Julien-David Le Roy (1724–1803) was among the first to use bizarre in the design context. In 1758 he applied it to members not having structural justification.[9] The adjective "bizarre" is now applied to:

1. Something which is simply odd or unusual in form (figures 4.9, 4.10, and 4.11).
2. Something which seems to have meaning, but the meaning is hidden from the experiencer (figure 4.12). The assignation of the term bizarre by an experiencer can result from frustration, or be an admission of inadequacy by the experiencer. A common cause seems to be the difficulty of communication between those who might be classed as spiritual and those who might be classed as "having their feet on the ground".

A judgement that an object is bizarre is subjective, and may be positive or a negative. It is often negative when the form of the object implies meaning, but the experiencer judges that there is none or that it is trite. Such bizarreness can occur when a designer without inspiration is determined to demonstrate originality.

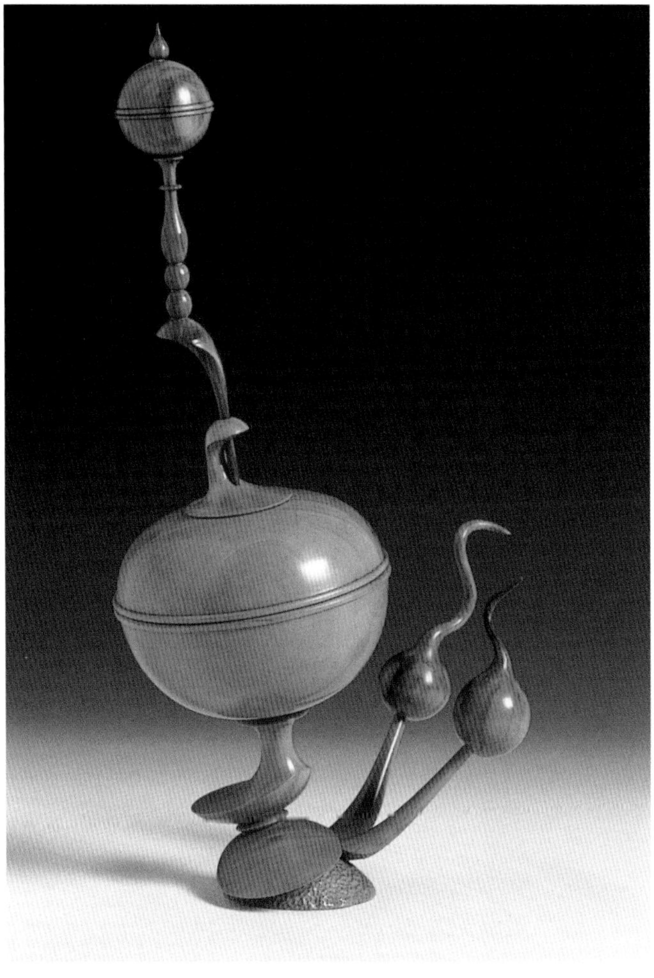

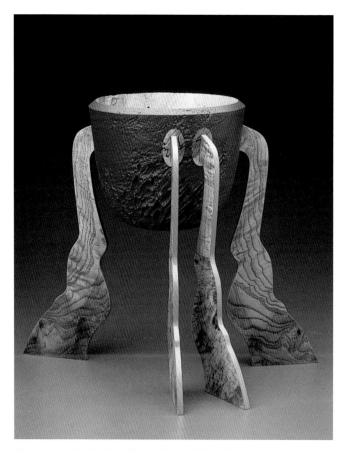

Figure 4.9 Positive bizarreness due to unorthodox form, *Mutation* by Jean-François Escoulen of Puy St. Martin, France. This box demonstrates the instability which is a major and bizarre feature of Escoulen's boxes. It is 12 in. (300 mm) high, and made from Pernambuco and green ebony.

Figure 4.10 *Falls River Bowl* (1986) by Steve Loar of Warsaw, New York. A powerful, novel, form, 15 in. (375 mm) high. The shape of the legs and the figure of the outer veneer of the plywood suggest flowing water. Photograph by Jamey Stillings.

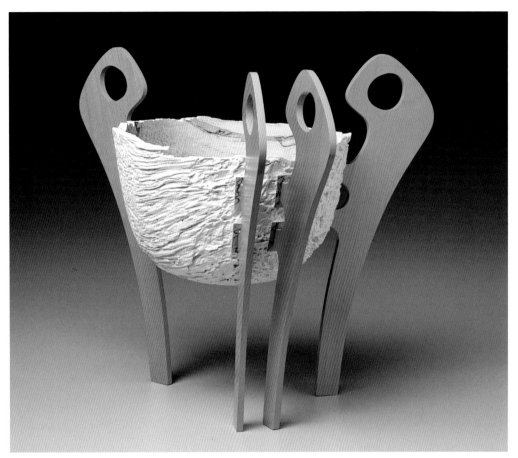

Figure 4.11 *Bowl for the Coastal Tribes* **by Steve Loar,** 1985, 13 in. (325 mm) high. Another example of the positively bizarre. The plywood legs ceremonially present the spalted maple bowl and seem to combine an echo of Salvador Dali and the profile of a primitive amphibian. Collection of David Ellsworth. Photograph by Jamey Stillings.

Figure 4.12 *Don't Stand So Close To Me* **by Steve Loar,** 1993, 12 in. (300 mm) high. My reaction to this work was that it was bizarre both because of its unusual form and because I was unable to understand what it represented. I was, however, confident that it did represent something. I later discovered that this work is titled after a song by the rock group Police, and is about a teacher fighting his sexual attraction to a student.

Steve Loar wrote of this work: "I have been selecting songs which conjure up images of relationships, moods, colors, and textures; then using the lyrics to choreograph the scene. The challenges were many, but foremost was the task of creating a composition which was intriguing to the viewers, and would then allow them to interpret a story of their own, whether or not they knew the song/lyrics. And to do all of this in 360 degrees!"[10]

Collection of Fleur Bresler.

4.1.6 FUNCTIONALISM

Functionalism is the theory that true beauty results from adapting form to function. The theory does not deny aesthetic value, arguing that aesthetic experience is an experience of "function as it appears".[11] Its proponents also argue that functionalism is rational and is therefore a superior aesthetic theory to those which permit irrational ornament. This "form follows function", "less is more" aesthetic, although associated with the modernist movement of the twentieth century, was foreshadowed long before by the Roman orator, statesman, and philosophical writer Marcus Tullius Cicero (106–43 B.C.) who wrote:

> In a ship, what is so indispensable as the sides, the hold, the bow, the stern, the yards, the sails, and the mast? Yet they all have such a graceful appearance that they appear to have been invented not only for the purpose of safety but also for the sake of giving pleasure.

Would a Cicero of today say the same of a corrugated-iron shed, that modern paragon of functionalism, economy, and structural honesty?

The narrow view of functionalism which defines function as the "use for which the object is designed" would not have been supported by two of its supposedly major proponents, Viollet-le-Duc (pages 33–34) and Sullivan (page 37). Both had a much wider definition of function (page 37); neither sought the abolition of ornament.

True functionalism should be regarded as an anathema by hand woodturners. If it were implemented, woodturning would mostly involve turning dowelling (figure 4.13) and square-edged disks. If economic functionalism ruled, woodturning would almost disappear because most woodturnings would be replaced by pieces of wood with flat faces square to one another. Why hasn't this happened? I believe because of the human need to relate to man-made objects which I discuss later in this chapter.

4.1.7 PROPORTION

There is an entrenched belief that an object's beauty is related to its overall proportions. The grounds for this belief include:

1. That there is a correlation between mathematically nice proportions and beauty. This ground derives from Pythagoras (page 12). Thus the Golden proportion (figures 4.14 and 4.15) and the Fibonacci series (figure 4.15) each enjoy a unique mathematical nicety, and are therefore presumed to guarantee beauty. Another mathematically nice and therefore favored proportion is the 3:4:5 of a particular right-angled triangle.
2. That there are "Ideal" proportions, and that beauty results if an object's overall proportions conform to these Ideals. The Ideal proportions of Socrates and Plato also happen to be mathematically nice.
3. That there are proportions which are superior because they occur in nature. Notable examples are: the proportions underlying musical harmony which supposedly guarantee visual harmony in objects, and those of the human body, extolled by Vitruvius. Simpler proportions, such as the ratios of overall length to width of certain natural species, are also promoted as important. A modern supporter of this belief is Gyorgy Doczi who in his book The Power of Limits illustrates that certain proportions and profiles occur in both nature and in beautiful man-made objects.[12] Again and conveniently, the superior natural proportions are typically mathematically nice.
4. That experiencing objects having favored proportions produces more aesthetic pleasure. This ground is

Figure 4.13 Dowelling used in a factory produced chair. The economic functionalism is softened by the rush seat and the clear-finished beech frame which are intended to give a "country" flavor.

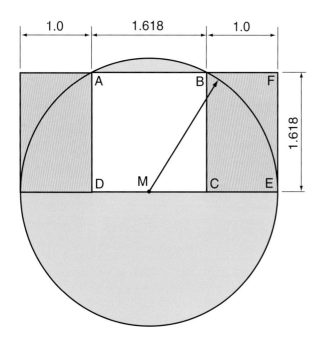

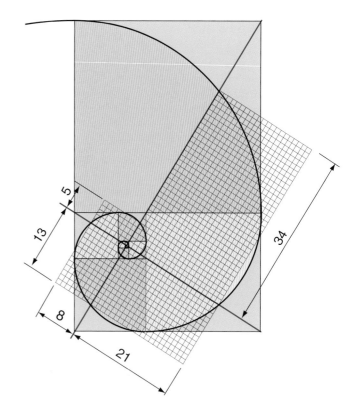

Figure 4.14 The *Golden rectangle* AFED was discovered by Euclid, a Greek mathematician who taught in Alexandria in about 300 B.C. during the reign of Ptolemy I Soter. Euclid is best known for his treatise on geometry *Elements.*

ABCD is the square which fits exactly within a semicircle. M is the midpoint of DC, and the center of the circle.

DC:CE = FE:CE = DE:FE = 1.618:1 = 1:0.618

where 1.618:1 and 1:0.618 are called the *Golden ratio* or *Golden mean*.

A Golden rectangle has the property that if divided into a square and a rectangle, that rectangle is a Golden rectangle. This smaller Golden rectangle can in turn be divided into a square and a still smaller Golden rectangle, etc., etc. This unique property called *reciprocity* can be used to build a logarithmic spiral by working towards its center, or from its center (see figures 4.15 and 7.??). The Golden ratio is also associated with the Fibonacci series (figure 4.15) and the regular pentagram

Figure 4.15 The Fibonacci series used to draw a logarithmic spiral.

Leonardo Fibonacci of Pisa (c. 1170 – c. 1230) introduced the series in *Liber abaci* published in 1202. Fibonacci developed it through solving the recreational problem "How many pairs of rabbits can be produced from a single pair if it is assumed that every month each pair begets a new pair which from the second month becomes productive?" Each number in the series is the number of pairs of rabbits at the beginning of the corresponding month. (The accuracy of Fibonacci's series is attested by the holes in our lawn and our stripped vegetable garden).

The series starts:

1, 1, 2, 3, 5, 8, 13, 21, 34, 55, 89, 144, . . .

Each number is the sum of the preceding two. Also the ratio of one number to that which precedes it tends towards the Golden ratio 1.618:1 as the lateness of the number increases.

Despite the fame of the Fibonacci series, there does not seem to be much application to woodturning design for several numbers of the series in order.

considered modern, but originated with the Sophists (page 12).

5. The belief that some people have superior design appreciation (taste), and that those with inferior taste would design more beautiful objects if they were to follow the recommendations of such tastemakers. To validate their recommendations, tastemakers have often relied on the measurement of personally selected historical examples.

6. "Scientific" experiment. For example, Doczi quotes 1876 research showing that people preferred rectangles with sides lengths in the Golden ratio.[13] A similar experiment, said to have been carried out by the Greek philosopher-mathematician Eudoxus (c. 408–c. 355 B.C.), showed that people felt that the most pleasing division of Eudoxus's walking stick was also in the Golden ratio. A division in the center was boring, more extreme divisions than that of the Golden ratio lacked balance and harmony.[14]

None of the above six grounds which purport to show a correspondence between overall proportions and beauty *demand* that we accurately determine the overall proportions of an object as we look at it. In my view the probability that we measure overall proportions during perception is low. Figure 4.16 suggests that for most objects there is no logical placement for a proportion-defining rectangle, and that such a rectangle is an artificial, arbitrary, and largely meaningless construct. Further, even for objects which are suited to the accurate measurement of proportion, our ability to do so is limited, and is even less likely to be accurate when the object is not viewed in elevation (figures 4.17 and 4.18).

Other factors which lessen the likelihood of a correlation between overall proportion and beauty include:

1. That, as illustrated with the man-made objects in figure 4.16, many confirmations that natural objects conform to favored proportions are merely a result of judiciously choosing where to measure from and to. They also result from choosing particular specimens, because just as with people, the proportions of different specimens of the same species vary. If there aren't any fixed proportions for beautiful natural objects, there cannot be any natural-proportion-based rules to guarantee beautiful man-made objects

2. The challenge to the worth of the proportions promoted by tastemakers by Claude Perrault in his *Ordonnance* (page 21). He noted that different authors on the column orders specified slightly different proportions. This proved to him that there weren't any laws of exact proportion except, strangely, the Vitruvian concept of anthropometric proportion.

3. That continual promotions of the same overall proportions by tastemakers combine to establish customary overall proportions, and that these in turn influence the proportions which are regarded as beautiful. If the mind is jolted by the unexpected as posited by Popper (page 5), an abundance of man-made objects with the same previously-unusual proportions will render such proportions less unusual, perhaps even customary. How far is beautiful a reflection of customary proportion rather than being related to certain unchanging proportions?

Figure 4.16 Choosing where to measure proportions. The overlaid cyan Golden rectangles confirm that all the turnings "have" the Golden proportion. The choice of where to measure dimensions to confirm the Golden proportions varies in its arbitrariness. For example, with the teardrop form, *right*, is it logical to assume that the top of the rectangle should run through the very top of the long taper.

4. The doubt that some of the "scientific" experiments concerning proportion are valid. I do not claim that my own experiments in figures 4.16 to 4.20 have scientific rigor, but point out that to prove a theory there cannot be any exceptions, while a theory is disproved by only one exception.

5. Is a system of proportion defined in terms of lengths and diameters the only one and the ideal? What about areas in elevation? or the masses (volumes) proposed by Le Camus (page 29)? Should the system also take into account lever arms from the centers of such areas and volumes from some neutral axis? The problems of determining useful rules from the simplest-possible system based on lengths has proved impossible. To be able to define rules based on more complex properties would be even more unlikely.

6. The inability of man to develop any laws connecting overall proportion and beauty. Charles-Étienne Briseux in 1752 defined the dilemma of believers in rules of proportion (I assume seriously because he agreed with them): "It is true that it has not so far been possible to determine unalterable [proportions], but all authors are agreed on the necessity of adhering to them".[15]

7. The lack of a significant difference in beauty between objects which have favored overall proportions and those which don't (figures 4.19 and 4.20).

8. That if the application of favored proportions were valid, it would lead to predictability and repress innovative design.

An awareness of such factors is not new, nor therefore is the belief that there aren't any laws which connect proportion and beauty. For example, in 1757 in A *Philosophical Enquiry* Edmund Burke wrote:

Beauty is no idea belonging to mensuration; nor has it any thing to do with calculation and geometry. If it had,

Figure 4.17 Judging proportions. When viewing objects ideally in elevation, can you assess the ratios of height to diameter? If you cannot even for these simple cylinders, the eye cannot establish the exact overall proportions of any form. (The ratios are given at the end of the endnotes).

Figure 4.19 The correlation between beauty, overall proportion, and the Golden ratio. Which box conforms to the Golden ratio? (Answer at the end of endnotes) Which is the most beautiful?

If you judge that all five boxes are similar in beauty, is that because:

1. The boxes which do not conform to the Golden ratio are perceived as approximating to it, and are therefore similarly beautiful.

2. The other boxes have proportions which are different but equally unique, and overall proportion has little or nothing to do with beauty.

The overall proportion of an isolated object may be irrelevant to beauty because it does not relate to anything else, because it "looks outwards". In contrast, the proportions of parts seem to have much more relevance to beauty because they relate "internally", to one another. This proposition is supported by Ruskin's statement "Proportion is between three terms at *least*".[16] However I shall also discuss proportion between two parts.

Overall proportions are however relevant when separate objects are viewed as components or sets (figure 4.21), perhaps because components' overall proportions then become, in a sense, internal.

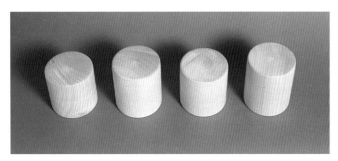

Figure 4.18 Judging proportions when viewing non-ideally. These cylinders are photographed using a camera lens with approximately the same focal length as that of the human eye. Can you identify the cylinders' overall proportions? I suggest that accurate judging of proportion becomes even less likely when an object is viewed in other than elevation. (The ratios are given at the end of the endnotes).

Figure 4.20 Applying the Golden ratio.
In this box the ratio 1.618:1 applies to four pairs of dimensions: the box diameter to the box height, the height of the exposed part of the base to the height of the lid, the height of the cylindrical part of the lid to the height of its beaded part, and the height of the larger bead to the smaller bead. Does this multiple conformance to the Golden ratio ensure extraordinary beauty? I suggest not.

Figure 4.21 Overall proportions of objects in sets.
   Left to right, these *Cessolis* chessmen have ratios of height to diameter of: 1.27:1, 1.55:1, 1.73:1, 2.00:1, 2.37:1, and 2.52:1. These proportions do not have any mathematical connection or nicety, but approximate to those of the Staunton design which is used for major tournaments. I suggest that there is little difference between the beauty of the individual pieces

   This chess set is named after Jacobus de Cessolis who published a sermon "on the customs of men and their noble actions with reference to the game of chess" in about A.D. 1300.[17] In this set's design:

1. The saw cut of the Staunton bishop is retained, but is enlarged and vertical, and resembles a bishop designed by Jörn Pfab of Hamburg shown in *Arts and Crafts of Hamburg and Northern Germany* (Hyogo Prefectural Museum of Modern Art, Kobe, Japan, 1985), plate 370.
2. The Cessolis knight with the hole drilled through also resembles the knight from the same Jörn Pfab set, and creates the representation of a horse's head or of a medieval knight's visored helmet. The hole is drilled into the square cross section knight blank before turning.
3. The tops of the king and queen have the same, and therefore mating, curvatures, and echo the Staunton king's crown and queen's coronet.

Figure 4.22 Perfect and imperfect spheres. The first and overriding judgement we make when a form or part is close to a sphere, cylinder, or cone is whether the form conforms exactly to that of a perfect sphere, cylinder, or cone. Here one form attracts attention (jolts) because it is not truly spherical.

Figure 4.23 Spherical conformance. A Cuban mahogany, 10 in. (250 mm) diameter sphere from Christian Burchard's *Old Earth Series*. Christian lives in Ashland, Oregon.

Were this turning perceptibly not quite spherical, it would be judged unsuccessful no matter how beautiful the wood, the ornament, or the finishing.

we might then point out some certain measures which we could demonstrate to be beautiful, either as simply considered, or as related to others; and we could call in those natural objects, for whose beauty we have no voucher but the sense, to this happy standard, and confirm the voice of our passions by the determination of our reason.[18]

Although the validity of rules of overall proportion is at best doubtful, we are jolted by imperfections in the simplest regular shapes and volumes such as a straight lines, squares, circles, and spheres. Therefore forms which are close to regular forms are judged to a major extent not on their beauty, but on their departures from the relevant geometrical ideals (figures 4.22 and 4.23).

If beauty does not depend on overall proportion, what does it depend on? There have been two main approaches:

1. That beauty was the by-product of, or was the same as, non-aesthetic factors such as function or the presence of overt signs of human involvement such as tool marks.
2. That beauty resulted from certain shapings and arrangements of parts.

The second approach is surely the more promising. Associated with it is the concept of delight, a lively form of beauty which joins harmony with variety. Owen Jones postulated in Proposition 9 of *The Grammar of Ornament* that "Those proportions will be most beautiful which it will be most difficult for the eye to detect". This proposition is similar to Edmund Burke's belief that pleasure in perception derives from the right mean between monotony and confusion. Thus ordinary things drop below the threshold of our awareness, whereas an object which demands too much sensing and understanding at the one time causes mental overload, and the mind moves on to something less demanding. There is a connection here to Popper's searchlight theory of the mind (page 5).

Clearly the concept of delight has little or no connection to the proportion of overall height to maximum diameter of a turning, although it may have some to the relative proportions of objects which are viewed together or form a set (figure 4.21). There is however a connection between delight and the *internal* proportions of objects, the proportions of different parts and their positions relative to one another. Hogarth's examples of the "art of composing well" shown on pages 25 and 26 are remarkable examples of this. He does not promote his examples as laws, but does warn that "all deviations from [the principles] will produce the contrary". Nor does he specify particular proportions. While he held the modern majority view that there aren't any laws of proportion, he believed that there can be qualitative guidelines for proportion. (I describe guidelines founded on Hogarth's principles on pages 168 to 171). This view also conforms to the view of Hume and Kant that there are standards of taste, that beauty is not solely subjective.

In *The Aesthetics of Architecture* Roger Scruton discusses detail, a concept related to but more developed than that of delight. He notes that a poor composition of lively, sympathetic, and intelligible parts will be preferred to a form with supposedly perfect proportions but ugly details.[19] Thus good proportion is exhibited by an object "whose parts—judged in terms of their shape and size rather than in terms of their ornamentation—provide adequate visual reason for one another".[20] For Scruton, "there is no true concept of proportion which can be divorced from that of the details which embody it".[21]

4.1.8 DETAIL

To discuss detail clearly in this and later sections, I must first define five terms:

Form is the shape considered apart from size, color, material, or meaning. The surface textures are part of the form, but are generally considered separately. The form of an object includes the volumes of any ornament.

Ornament is three-dimensional. Although it includes linear moldings, moldings tend to be put in a separate category. Ornament is discussed in chapter 6, pages 117 to 122.

Moldings are three-dimensional and linear, and usually run along or around a turning, or helically. They are not structural, are generally ornamental or ornamental and functional, but can be purely functional like a drip groove. Moldings are often used to define and emphasize structure or boundaries. Moldings are discussed at length in chapter 6, pages 122 to 148.

Decoration is two-dimensional detail, and is commonly painted. If you select wood for its surface colors and patterns you are not applying decoration in the conventional sense, but you have an intention to decorate. Is texture ornament or decoration? I have arbitrarily included it with the latter.

Details are small parts which have intrinsic form and meaning. You can therefore conceptually isolate and study a detail. Joints, fastenings, and connections are common areas for detail. Ornaments, moldings, and decorations are particular types of detail. Ten further factors concerning details are discussed below:

1. Common details were often solutions to practical problems such as the need to weatherproof or the need to allow for wood shrinkage and expansion. Other details were developed to solve aesthetic problems. The existence of such practical and aesthetic problems has

first to be realized and defined by the designer, otherwise there is no need for a solution. Thus an important part of designing is the perception of problems which others less perceptive either do not appreciate or cannot define.
2. Detail can be the main area of design freedom left for a designer (figure 4.24). Other design variables may be prescribed by situation, function, economy, or the client.
3. Detail can result from or exhibit an object's method of production. The available methods for creating forms are casting, modelling (formed by manual or mechanical deformation of the material in a plastic state), carving (which includes woodturning), and assembling.
4. Our response to a detail may be inseparable from our perception of its method of production. A man-made

Figure 4.24 Eggcups without and with detail. The details of the right-hand eggcup were at my whim, because they barely improve functionality, there wasn't an outside client, and cost was unimportant; they do however have design logic:

1. The edge roll strengthens the rim, provides a small funnel which aids seating the egg into the cup, and provides a visual termination to the upward flow of the cup. The fillet and congee adjacent to the edge roll provide a defined but gentle transition between the edge roll and the cup body.
2. The center fillet is taller than the other two and signifies a separateness between the cup and its supporting structure, the base. Fillets can be used to add crispness, or if wide to signify separation into parts.
3. The bottom fillet is narrow to add crispness without strongly separating the ogee into a scotia and a torus.
4. The torus molding on the base echoes the rim's edge roll, gives a visual impression of supporting, and avoids a sharp edge which could be easily damaged or do damage.

object is, Scruton explains, "the memorial of an activity".[22] Does an experiencer's perception that something is handmade give more pleasure than if it were perceived as machine made? If "yes", it is likely that we respond most sympathetically to details which exhibit the most expressive and direct human involvement. It is also likely that our perceiving involves an empathy with, perhaps even a sympathetic inclusion in, the actual process. Thus many prefer a carved surface to a cast one, even a cast one for which the mold was left with overt tool marks. However this preference does not always hold: overt hand workmanship is inappropriate in many situations, and some experiencers are able to differentiate good workmanship from incompetent, and perhaps even artifice from true expression.

We must however have knowledge of the process to feel empathy or inclusion. The gradual elimination of woodwork and metalwork from secondary school education is surely lessening students' abilities to perceive methods of production, to empathize with them, and to differentiate between materials. This growing lack of familiarity with hand making must change public taste. A symptom is the replacement of the consumers' confidence in their own judgement by a consumer dependence on brands.

As modern man loses his familiarity with hand making, is he also losing his sense of detail? The belief that he is is not a recent phenomenon. Viennese architect Otto Wagner (1841–1918) wrote in *Moderne Architektur* (1895) that man's ability to perceive had changed and should be taken into account by architects:

> The modern eye has lost a feeling for small and intimate scale, and accustomed itself to less varied images, to longer straight lines, to more extensive areas, to larger masses . . .[23]

If Wagner is correct, the likely reasons are that we live faster and have less time to contemplate detail, and have less active involvement in, and knowledge of, the creation of detail. Alternatively, we may be focussing our sense of detail elsewhere or more widely among the ever-increasing range of aesthetic choices, for example, in selecting computer games.

5. A detail can be enjoyed for itself, but is best understood in terms of its contribution to the turned object which should be positive not negative. Good details improve good forms and distract from bad forms. Poor details drag down good forms.

6. Details can be applied to a form separately or in combination. When separately there should be an adequate visual connection between the form and the detail. When details are applied in combination, each detail should provide an adequate visual reason for those adjacent.

7. Details may be composed of smaller details which in turn can be composed of smaller details, etc. Many theorists have described this hierarchical concept, notably Hogarth through his parsley leaf (page 25). Conversely, form builds through the progressive aggregation of detail.

8. The designs of details and the principles on which they are organized defines the style.

9. It is not necessarily true that deleting the ornament from an object lessens an experiencer's aesthetic enjoyment of the object. Where the detail is confused, lessening it may heighten aesthetic enjoyment.

10. The absence of detail causes one's sense of detail to search for smaller-scale detail such as surface texture. Thus even the tiniest blemish is a major distraction to the otherwise perfect surface of a large plane.

The ten factors above describe detail, but how do we judge detail? Roger Scruton advocates the criterion of appropriateness promoted by Claude Perrault. Perrault stated that the criterion of appropriateness should be applied to "the dimensions of the members in each part of a building, and the relationship of the parts to the whole". It can and should be applied to all the variables of a design.

We might judge detail using appropriateness as our criterion, but what do we judge it with? And why? Our sympathy with detail is a response to what Roger Scruton calls "the sense of detail", a concept introduced on page 8. This sense of detail, like Gombrich's senses of order and meaning (pages 5 and 7), is a useful construct for a mental capability which is not a separate and definable entity within the brain. This sense of detail is "an indispensable component in aesthetic attention, being fundamental both to the elementary art of aesthetic choice and also to the sophisticated process of critical reflection". It also forms "a connection between aesthetic and practical judgement".

You are born with a sense of detail which is unique to you. In some this innate sense is strong, in others less so. It strengthens if you take an active interest in detail. Your sense of detail at any time during your life also reflects your past exposure, both active and passive, to details. This exposure in turn reflects what was customary in the cultures you have experienced. Although each person's sense of detail is unique, there is some general agreement on what is appropriate, although the amount and the substance of the agreement vary between any two individuals.

4.1.9 APPROPRIATENESS

Alberti considered that "beauty resided in a harmony of parts, fitted together in such a way that nothing could be added, diminished or altered but for the worse".[24] This lofty description of what appropriate means has been further fleshed in statements by Roger Scruton in pages 222 to 232 of *The Aesthetics of Architecture*:

1. Often "the principal exercise of aesthetic judgement" is "the apt and telling choice of parts, . . . the search for an organizing principle, for an order implicit in detail, [which] leads automatically to the development of style".
2. Appropriateness is central to aesthetic judgement, "the existence of one part provides a reason for the existence

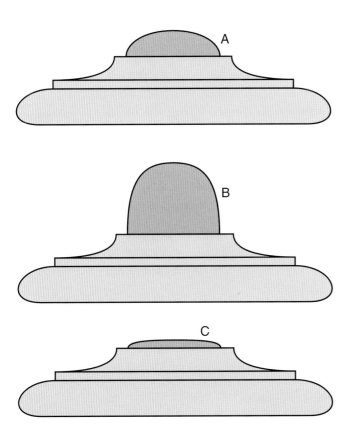

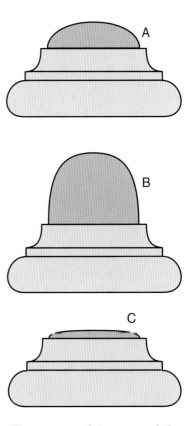

of another, . . . the process of reasoned 'fitting together.'"
3. Appropriate is not the means to an end nor just the "'Optimal solution'" to aims. This solution approach involves the "arbitrary limitation of the problem it is supposed to solve".
4. Appropriate is not only an aesthetic concept, it may relate to cost, function, meaning, morality, etc. "The pursuit of the appropriate appearance is an eliminable part of knowing what to do, in those activities for which, because of their complexity, no single aim can be enunciated."
5. Appropriateness is "the natural fittingness of part to part, of an achieved articulation. . . . The correspondence of part with part is also a correspondence of" the design with the designer and experiencer. Figures 4.25 and 4.26 demonstrate this.

I hope that these statements have given you a feeling of what appropriate means. They also imply that the design process cannot be precisely defined or described because much is intuitive and arbitrary.

Figure 4.25 The appropriateness of a pellet. The drawings are elevations of turned patera; the pellets are shaded darker.

Pellet *A* looks appropriate; pellets *B* and *C* do not. To say "I feel that pellet *B* is too tall" is sufficient. Say "Pellet *B* is too tall in proportion . . ." and there is an implication that you know both what the proportion should be quantitatively, and what it should be related to. You might be able to derive a rule such as "the height of a pellet on a patera shall be a certain percentage of the total height of the patera", but such a simple rule would be too narrow in its application to be worthwhile. Similarly a rule with wider application would be so complicated and hedged with qualifications that it also would not be worthwhile.

This figure inevitably reflects my own sense of detail. It is not a sense which I claim is superior to anyone else's. Perhaps some readers judge that pellets *B* or *C* are more appropriate than pellet *A*.

Figure 4.26 The appropriateness of the same pellets when parts of smaller patera. Pellet *B* now looks much more appropriate. This suggests that pellet *B* in the preceding diagram was not just too high in proportion to the height of the parts below, but that diameters and probably other properties are also relevant.

4.1.10 FEELING AND REASONING

In the next chapter I discuss how you clarify the intentions which your design should fulfill. You define intentions to some extent intuitively, and then attempt to judge their relevance by reason. Similarly, you guess (a crisp word meaning "produce by subconscious means, by intuition") a design solution which meets certain intentions, and then judge it by reasoning. You can only reason (rationalize) after the intuition. Similarly, when you experience a turning you first feel. You might feel that it is ugly, or unstable, or . . . Only then, if you or others require it, do you attempt to justify your feelings by reason. If you cannot explain by reason, you have to fall back on statements such as "it looks right" or "that's the way I feel". Such statements are often dismissed as idiotic mouthings. I think that it is entirely understandable that you cannot rationalize feelings which have arisen from your subconscious. Likewise, an inability to describe feelings other than vaguely does not destroy their validity.

Through designing, acquiring design knowledge, analyzing your felt reactions, and giving time and commitment to these activities, you will develop your taste. Do these things receptively, rather than merely to confirm your existing prejudices, and you will become more discerning, and more able to argue for your taste. Design will also become a more important part of your life.

4.1.11 SELF-REALIZATION

Each of us is conscious that we are part of a world, both now, and of the past and in the future. Your relationship with a design or a turning, however minor, contributes to that wider consciousness. Roger Scruton calls the building of relationships which contribute to your sense of being part of the world, to your sense of being human, *self-realization*.

There is general agreement that aesthetic judgement is subjective, dependent on your individual taste. Yet it is also partially objective because you and/or others will want you to justify your taste and judgements through presenting reasons which you and others will find valid. You desire to confirm the validity of your judgement (which is felt) in terms of the appropriateness or inappropriateness of the object. There is pressure that intuition be publicly intelligible.

When you design a very simple object totally prescribed by function and economy, such as a sewing needle, your design freedoms are limited. You have the problem when designing other objects that there are a large, usually infinite number, of designs which will do the job. Many of the differences between design alternatives are minor, but they still require you to unconsciously accept them, or consciously choose between them. In designing, therefore, you extract choices from a chaos of functionally- and economically-equivalent alternatives. This extraction is done subconsciously, and then assessed rationally. The

subconscious surely takes self-realization into account when extracting its choice.

Georg Wilhelm Friedrich Hegel (1770–1831), a professor of philosophy at Berlin University, is particularly associated with the concept of self-realization. He defined it as the activity of creating and engaging in a public world, and of coming to experience oneself as part of such a world. Thus happiness is the realization of self in the context of the human world. Humans are not mere bundles of desires. The satisfaction of a desire is not the satisfaction of a person. We do not merely have desires, we know that we have them, and, in knowing that we have them we attempt to achieve an understanding of their origin and value. Although done in the present, this attempt to achieve understanding is not concerned just with the present. The sense of one's own continuity in time is important in self-discovery.

Aesthetic judgement is an indispensable factor in everyday life and in self-discovery. The designer and the experiencer both see the object as part of their interaction with the world. A purely functional object only addresses desires. It does not answer to the aesthetic sense, to the self-realization of the individual, but only to his gratification, and cannot therefore be fully satisfying. To be fully satisfying objects must have expression, must allow or promote self-realization.

The aesthetic sense does not therefore merely judge, say, beauty in its narrow sense. A judgement of beauty incorporates judgements on aspects which can be rationalized such as economy and function, and on concepts which resist rationalization such as appropriateness and self-realization through the object. To relate with something you must have some previous knowledge of it to know what it is, or it must relate to something which you already know. If that relationship is felt to be positive, what you have judged you can term appropriate.

4.1.12 SUCCESSIVE REFINEMENT

An important part of determining what is appropriate in a design is the "WORK" which I revealed on page I as the secret of design success. Much of this work in design-by-drawing is successive refinement. Alberti described successive refinement well, and stressed the importance of seeking other opinions and of allowing incubation time:

> Thoroughly consider the whole Design yourself, and take the advice of Men of Skill upon it . . . Examine every minute Part of your future Structure eight, nine, ten Times over, and again, after different Intermissions of Times; till there be not the least Member from the Foundation to the Roof of your whole Building, within or without, great or small, but what you have thoroughly and long weighed and considered, and determined of what Materials it shall be made, where placed, in what

Order and Proportions, and to what it shall answer and bear relation.[25]

Figures 4.27 to 4.29 illustrate the role of successive refinement in a simple design task, and figure 4.29 confirms that there are an infinite number of functionally- and economically-equivalent alternative forms for even a simple peg. The detailed description of the process of designing starts in chapter 5, but before that there are further concepts and issues I wish to discuss.

Figure 4.28 **Pegs turned to detailed design *I* on the next page.**

Stage 1

| Inception |
| Feasibility |
| Intentions |
| Restraints |
| Preliminary design |
| Initial design proposal |

Stage 2

| Detailed design |

Stage 3

| Planning |

Stage 4

| Production |

Stage 5

| Post-production |

Stage 6

| Feedback |

A "request" from my wife for a row of pegs on which to hang coats, hats, and bags.

No feasibility study is ever necessary for a request from my wife.

Adequately defined by my wife's request.

None of note.

Such pegs have been made by turners for centuries, although the form I chose is associated with the Shakers. After deciding on the length of the projection and the shape and maximum diameter of the mushroom using a combination of functional inputs and arbitrary judgements, the designs of the bead, fillet, tapering neck, and mushroom knob were provided by my conceptual memory. A rough sketch was made (the preliminary design) and submitted with information on the timber, the finishing, the positioning of the pegs, and the timing. This initial design proposal was approved by my wife.

The longest part of the design task. Figure 4.29 shows only a few of the infinite number of possible forms which conform to the preliminary design's chosen length of projection, maximum diameter, and approximate form. Rather than produce multiple variations at random as shown in figure 4.29, you would successively refine your initial design to more quickly determine the most appropriate detailed design.

In some instances your preliminary design will not yield an acceptable and appropriate detailed design. You would then modify the preliminary design, or backtrack further into stage 1.

Figure 4.27 **Realizing stages 1 and 2 of designing the pegs shown in figure 4.28.**

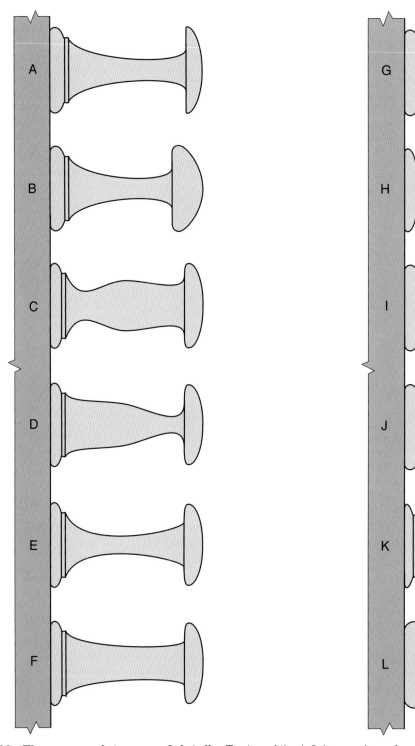

Figure 4.29 The appropriateness of details. Twelve of the infinite number of possible designs of Shaker-style peg illustrated on page 133 of *The Fundamentals of Woodturning*. Most of the designs show some inappropriateness with *I* being in my view the best. Study them and try to rationalize your feelings about the different details. While the narrowing of the neck at the left-hand end in *C* is structurally unsound, most judgements will be of the sort "that looks too big" or "I feel that that detail is too sharp". Such explanations may seem inadequate in an age when scientific proof is expected, but they are valid, and as good as we are going to get for most instances. Underlying them though is the perennial question of how we make judgements of appropriateness: do we have an innate sense of detail? (I believe yes, but that it varies between individuals), and how much do the software of the senses and the stored conceptual data change due to education and our observations of what is customary?

4.2 CONCEPTS WHICH INFLUENCE OUR PERCEPTIONS

In judging an object we are influenced by our understandings, by our prejudices. We classify the object, and that classification then influences other judgements. This section discusses some of the classifications which are relevant in woodturning.

4.2.1 ART OR CRAFT?

The definitions of, and the differences between art and craft have been discussed ad nauseam and without worthwhile conclusions. General differentiation based on the materials and techniques used, or whether concept or workmanship is dominant, or on other factors has failed because so many examples do not conform (figure 4.30).

Woodturning is not easily categorized. It lies somewhere at the conjunction of art, craft, and manufacturing, with

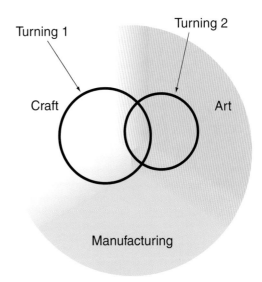

Figure 4.31 The conjunction of art, craft, and manufacturing. The absolute quantities of each do not have to total equally for all turnings (not that you can accurately measure these quantities).

Figure 4.30 Craft or art? *Kosima*, two charred, dyed, and painted ash rice bowls by Merryll Saylan of San Rafael, California. The pine boxes frame and thereby further emphasize that these bowls can, perhaps should, be regarded as other than utilitarian pieces. The boxes are 7 in. high x 9 in. wide x 8.5 in. deep (180 mm x 230 mm x 220 mm).

different examples lying in different positions about the conjunction (figure 4.31).

The classification of a turning as an example of art, craft, or manufacture affects its monetary value. I shall not here discuss value except to say that the price paid is our only quantitative measure of it, and a very inaccurate one.

A perceived difference between art and craft concerns quantity. Manufacturing is often concerned with huge quantities, craft permits batch production , but an essence of art works is that each is unique. Informed collectors tend to want new work not copies of earlier works. Art turners are therefore under pressure to continually develop their turning designs, even if in some instances the new is less convincing than the old.

Another classification issue is whether the category of turning should be limited. Some pieces displayed in turning shows seem never to have been near a lathe. Is an object which was roughed on a lathe but after subsequent working retains no turned surface still a turning? My view is that we should be inclusive rather than exclusive because any attempt to set thresholds will prove futile and divisive. However, where judging is involved and the object is in a woodturning category, only the extant woodturning content and its contribution to the whole object should be considered by the judges.

4.2.2   FASHION

C. Percier and P. L. F. Fontaine in *Recueil de décorations intérieures* (1812) stated that there is no intrinsic difference between style and fashion, and gave three reasons why fashion changes:

1. The psychological desire for change.
2. The desire of consumers of fashion to create an impression, to show that they know what is in fashion and can afford it.
3. The commercial advantage which producers and sellers gain from rapid obsolescence on stylistic grounds. (These stylistic changes are also designed to exploit technological changes and changes in labor and material availabilities and costs).

They summarized their beliefs thus: "Things are not desired because they are found to be beautiful; they are found to be beautiful because they are desired". An extension of this is the desirability of the works of fashionable artists and craftspeople almost irrespective their qualities as perceived by the hoi polloi, "a shift from the product to the producer as the object of aesthetic response".[26]

The three reasons for the power of fashion remain valid. Ordinary is judged through our sense of meaning as being unworthy of one of Popper's jolts (page 5), but we can jolt others by creating or being seen to appreciate the new and extraordinary. Fashion shows, and their equivalents outside couture, are therefore intended to reveal the new and extraordinary, both to potential buyers and to the admirers of buyers. There is pressure not to delay your purchase because today's extraordinary is tomorrow's passé. But there are also restraints. In behavior, the restraint is the social stigma which results if you do not to conform to the social norms, although what these are depends on which section of society you identify with. In design generally the main restraints are economy plus the Vitruvian triumvirate of safety and durability, function, and beauty. In art, where these factors have little relevance, the likelihood that the future resale value will be much below the present purchase price can restrain all but the boldest collectors.

4.2.3   THE ART MARKET FOR WOODTURNINGS

A phenomenon of the last quarter of the twentieth century was the growth of a market for both high-quality and "high" craft (figure 4.32). (This market was distinct from the growth in craft markets which also took place during the same period). The market for high craft was and remains a market for art drawn from wider and less-expensive categories than fine-art paintings and sculpture. What this new market sought to eliminate was the artificial distinction between art and craft based on material and process. What it sought to harden was the perceptual distinction between art and craft based on concept, function, and number. Collectors were encouraged to believe that craft exhibited workmanship, and was low status, functional, made in batches, and without the higher dimension of concept. In

Figure 4.32   A retail outlet for both functional and art woodwork. The Bungendore Wood Works Gallery near Canberra, Australia, promotes and sells high-quality woodwork to collectors and to the public.

contrast, art was high status, was concept manifested, was not functional, and was indifferent to workmanship. Further, each art object was an individual creation, and was therefore unique and "rare". The new art market for craft to which woodturners were among the later aspirants bestowed real benefits on turners: higher prices, greater status, more autonomy, more scope. The art market for woodturnings attracted and was partly created by those turners who considered themselves artists in a medium which the fine-art market had yet to accept. The potential economic benefits also attracted a wider range of turners.

North America provided the best conditions for growth for an art market for woodturnings: surplus wealth, favorable tax laws, and a tradition of collecting and donating collections (figure 4.33). North America's wealth was based upon new products in a New World and was more receptive than the conservative "old money" in Europe.

The art market for woodturnings is like other markets, it is sustained by perceived value and by the promise of that value increasing. Unlike markets based on utility, art-based markets have the fundamental attraction to new entrants that those who have already bought have a vested interest in continuing to buy to prevent a collapse in the value of the works which they already hold. It is a wonderful self-sustaining mechanism which will only collapse if there is a prolonged world depression or major social revolution. It is a mechanism in which collectors and turners both gain. Now that Nietzscher's world in which morality bows before will

is with us, and the Gordon Gecko creed "greed is good" is fact, why shouldn't turners join the grab for the spoils? "A fair day's work for a fair day's pay" was ineffective once the lower orders saw that they could also be capitalists. The only loser is the obsolete concept of integrity, and that doesn't appear on your bank statement.

Peter Dormer, a British commentator on the decorative arts, is one who doesn't accept the wonder of an uninhibited art market for craft:[27]

> A combination of postmodern excess and an ambition to be seen as an artist has tempted many a contemporary craftsperson into some highly skilled work of exaggerated design, size and complexity and hugely inflated prices. This phenomenon is most widespread in America, where there are more rich men and women prepared to buy the work for their new craft-art collections. The collections are frequently appalling and are, in essence, handicrafts gone to fat. Nothing in art or design or architecture or craft is more foolish than the sight of modest ideas ballooning and buffeting on the thermals of rich ignorance . . . Among those with a vested interest in craft there has been too much reluctance to admit that the world of craft is a world of modest ideas with a straightforward, commonplace vocabulary of familiar and functional forms which can be used purely decoratively. No pot or chair or table or glass vase can stand translation into a monument. The inherent modesty of craft is its strength.

Implicit in Dormer's stance is a demand that craft remains corralled within its traditional boundaries, and that craftspeople reject the rewards of artifice. Woodturners have rejected Dormer's stricture, and rightly. In addition to greater status and income, art turning has promoted a greater interest in turning, new techniques and equipment, and an exploration of new and worthwhile design areas.

Is Dormer also warning of a collapse in demand and prices? I have explained that the market cannot allow more than a minor and temporary adjustment, but harder times will come for some turners if collectors' tastes mature. Too many collectors lack knowledge and confidence, and their desire to create an impression leaves them vulnerable. Did the organizer of a show for American woodturning collectors exclude functional and humorous turnings to benefit the collectors? Fortunately, the growth of a market for collectors has been generally positive; it has encouraged much true creativity. If functional turners have felt that their merits have been overshadowed, the solution is in their hands.

Figure 4.33 Books on collections. Owen Evan-Thomas's book was self-published in 1932. Edward H. Pinto's *Treen and Other Wooden Bygones* (1969) remains the standard reference on treen. His collection is now housed at the Birmingham Museum and Art Gallery in England. The books on the Wornick and Mason private collections were published in 1996 and 2000 respectively to coincide with public exhibitions of the collections. Such exhibitions publicly validate and recognize the tastes and foresights of the subject collectors.

| Elizabethan (1558–1603) | Chippendale (c. 1754) | Sheraton (c. 1791) | Victorian (c. 1853) |

Figure 4.34 Four styles of English bedpost which are defined by their details.[28]

Elizabethan: a turned section surmounts a classically inspired pedestal. The turning is massive with deep coves and bold carvings. At the top is another classical detail, an Ionic capital.

Chippendale: a vestigial plinth supports an elongated classical column which in the left-hand post is annulated.

Sheraton: the plinth has disappeared. The stretched column shaft is shorter, but surmounts a vase or urn form. There is extensive, finely detailed, low-relief carving.

Victorian: the turned section has returned to the plain column of the Chippendale style, but the column shaft is now supported on a large bulb.

Illustrations of Chippendale, Sheraton, and Victorian bedposts reproduced courtesy of Dover Publications.

4.2.3 STYLE

Style is vitally important. Today's fashion, food, and interior-design magazines tell us so. Percier's and Fontaine's contention that style and fashion are intrinsically the same does not hold today. A fashion is a style which is widespread at a particular time. You do not think of an individual having a fashion, whereas style can be applied to an individual. There are also general styles associated during a period with a group, or a region. If a fashion continues to be used or referred to long after the peak of its popularity, it becomes a style. In the late 1920s and 1930s art deco was the fashion, now it is a style and doesn't need to be qualified with dates.

It is important for the jobbing turner to be familiar with, and able to design in any of, the turning styles a client may want. An established style is an already ordered and appropriate system of details and their arrangement. Therefore specifying or choosing an established style completes much of the design task, and usually leaves only the final refining to be done. If, however, you are an art turner, you will want to develop a style which is recognizably your own, promote it as your own, keep it for your exclusive use, and extend its useful life by continually refashioning it.

The identity of a particular style, whether general or individual, has much to do with the repetition of particular forms, ornament, and decoration (figure 4.34). Other related factors which can also be significant to the identity of an individual style are:

1. The concentration on objects of particular types and/or with particular functions tends, perhaps wrongly, to be a stylistic signature (figure 4.35).
2. The repetition of particular categories of meaning (figure 4.36).
3. The material or combination of materials and components used (figure 4.37).
4. The techniques or equipment used (figure 4.38).

The characteristic of styles and fashions is that their popularity varies. There are usually three stages in the life of a style: youth, in which the style is being worked out and becomes accepted; maturity, in which it becomes widely accepted; and decline as people become bored by it. The decline is also often accompanied by extremism, by excessive exaggeration of the style's particular features, to keep the style alive. The decline may result in the disappearance of the style, or in its continued use at a lower and usually varying level. Styles can be resurrected unchanged; or resurrected in modified, updated, or parodied versions.

The characteristics of a style "date" it to the time when it was fashionable. These characteristics may be appropriate in later times, but being unfashionable, are often used to damn the designs of the later objects which have them. *Historicism* is a dirty word to some.

Figure 4.35 Functional, ornamented lace bobbins are a specialty of David Springett of Rugby, England. He has also written two books on lace bobbins.[29]

Figure 4.36 Satirizing function. This goblet is one of a series of woodturnings by David Sengel of Boone, North Carolina, which use applied rose thorns to debunk the seriousness of function. Ebonized pear, 7 in. x 3 in. dia. (180 mm x 75 mm). Photograph by Michael Siede.

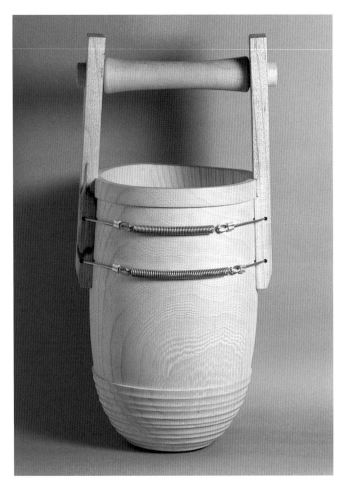

Figure 4.37 Bucket, one of a series of vessels exploring applications for stainless-steel wire and springs.

Figure 4.38 An example of the pictorial piercing technique associated with Frank Sudol of Paddockwood, Saskatchewan, Canada. He also favors tall cylindrical forms, a second factor defining the Sudol style. *Serengeti II* is turned in birch, and is 31 in. high x 10 in. dia. (790 mm x 250 mm).

4.2.4 HISTORICISM

Historicism is related to terms such as *contextualism*, *eclecticism*, and *revivalism*. Historicism has three related meanings, the first being used most often:[30]

1. The use of earlier designs and design elements and concepts in later designs (figure 4.39).
2. Producing using a historical and obsolete method (figure 4.40).
3. That each region in each age has a distinct culture, and that part of that culture is its contemporary design. A region's contemporary design in each age reflect the region's society, culture, technology, and available materials at that time, and should therefore be judged according to these factors.

Historicism is part of the cause of the schism between some of those who believe that they turn art, or who aim to turn art, and other turners who produce functional items, often in traditional styles. This schism harks back to Hegel (page 56) who in Berlin during the 1820s gave public lectures on aesthetics. They were published in book form in 1835. In his lectures Hegel opined that the character of a society and its prime mover during an epoch is essentially its spirit. This spirit, Hegel said, is embodied in the style of the epoch's cultural products. Therefore the style of an epoch's cultural products is the authentic manifestation of its spirit. The converse also applies, and through design the spirit of an age can be manipulated. Designers therefore have a duty to design and thereby manipulate their society's spirit for the good of that society. (A similar belief contributed to the revival of ancient-Roman architecture during the Renaissance. The revival was expected to contribute to a restoration of the prosperity and power that had been enjoyed during Roman times).

Hegel's belief was rejected by Karl Marx (1818–1883). Marx believed that material conditions and economic relations governed society, or could be said to be its spirit.[31] Yet the Hegelian view remains powerful. Art turners thus see themselves as leaders. Claude-Henri de Saint-Simon (1760–1825) wanted artists to be visionaries, leading society from the front, to be avant-garde, literally the front part of the army.[32] Some art turners therefore regard turners working in traditional styles as consciously or unconsciously working to reverse forward progress. These same art turners conveniently tend to overlook that they may be replicating bowl and other vessel shapes which have been in continual production since the Bronze Age. Nor is the intolerance one-sided. Some traditional turners choose to ignore or reject the new methods and markets developed by the art turners.

It was realized during the nineteenth century that through history there had been a succession of styles, each particular to a certain time in a certain region. Modern communications are rapidly dissolving such regional stylistic differences. The resulting contemporary international woodturning style is, however, far from homogeneous and tends to be a combination of the most-desired contemporary individual styles. It is also continuously changing.

Is there a duty for today's woodturners to work in this contemporary international style rather than in one from the past? My answer is not a simple "yes" or "no":

1. Any individual turner does not have a duty to turn in any particular style. The idea of improving society through turning is presumptuous; for architecture it may be less so.
2. Although the style of turning of one or a few individuals has negligible national, still less international, effects

Figure 4.39 A chair with details based on those of ancient Egyptian stools found at Thebes (see figure 12.1 for Thebes' location).[33] The details are the dished seat, the diagonal spindles, and the ring-turned elongated reels which form the bottom parts of the legs.

This chair's designer, William Holman Hunt (1827–1910), was an important English Pre-Raphaelite painter. Photograph supplied by the Art Gallery of South Australia, Adelaide.

Figure 4.40 An obsolete turning method? Robin Wood, professional pole-lathe turner of Derbyshire, England, and a nest of his bowls.

Robin argues that he makes a positive contribution to woodturning and to society:[34]

1. He has made an archeological contribution through preserving and researching knowledge on a once important manufacturing technique and its products.
2. Because his method is seen and promoted as ancient, the public has become more willing to appreciate warped, rippled, and unsanded woodware. In an age when smoothness is the norm, the surprising pleasure of roughness can awaken lost sensibilities.
3. His "specialist archaeological replicas" enable people to enjoy "a piece of history".

The opposing arguments include:

1. Robin is a distraction from, even a brake, to social fulfillment through increasing economic rationalism.
2. Society would gain if Robin's talents were employed elsewhere.
3. An electrically-powered hand lathe is more efficient, and its use does not prevent turnings being left unsanded and with a similar off-the-tool roughness.

on society, were a majority of turners to follow one style, there would tend to be stylistic stagnation. Notice, I specified one style, not an earlier or antique style, because there is no logical cutoff between present and earlier styles. Whether you copy the style of an avant-garde piece posted on the World Wide Web seconds before or copy that of a piece turned centuries ago, you are copying something from the past. What is desirable is that most turners seek to advance their designing. Is it more desirable that they seek to advance it from a recent style base than from an older style base? In my view "no", except that the recent style base is more likely to incorporate features which relate to today's society and conditions.

3. You may hold the view that the most beautiful turnings were those of, say, the eighteenth century. Your desire to design in that style may then be a purely aesthetic decision. To criticize your decision on moral, Hegelian grounds assumes that you and society would be benefit if you designed turnings in a style which you believed was less beautiful.

4. Antique or other styles may be appropriate for some situations. They may be dictated by a client, or required to match or complement existing objects and surroundings.

5. Woodturning has essentially changed little in 3000 years, and woodturnings are relatively simple objects. There are unlikely to be dramatic undiscovered design solutions to those functions which woodturnings have satisfied for an appreciable time unless the underlying restraints can be jettisoned. Without such jettisoning, different styles are just differences in ornament, and today's style is often just a watered-down historical style in which, for example, the fillets and small moldings are omitted. This does not seem to be an adequate response either ethically, or aesthetically. Nor is it preferable to continuing to replicate the best of the earlier styles.

6. Big steps in design progress usually result from discoveries and advances which introduce new functions, new materials, or new processes for working materials. In woodturning new functions are rare, wood remains the same, and woodturning methods remain essentially unchanged. This stasis is why turning is increasingly demoted to a secondary technique in art woodturning.

7. Many professional turners cannot afford to refuse work. They see having to accept jobs which some would regard as mundane as part of the reality of work. Therefore if a client specifies or the market seeks historicism, turners will produce it. The customers' motive may be a mixture of aesthetic preference and nostalgic sentiment about the past rather than a conscious belief that the use of an earlier style will cause positive change. However, is the continuing popularity of antique styles in apartments in multistory buildings throughout the world a major blight? Surely not. It might also improve the manners and give a feeling of permanence to apartment dwellers, a small confirmation of Hegel's spirit.

To summarize, the only serious objection to historicism in woodturning is that it can impede design progress and prop up design laziness. However, as I have noted, historicism does not have to be the accurate replication of complete turnings. Historical styling and details can be used in:

1. New, but historically feasible, even if sometimes unlikely, pieces (figures 4.39, 4.41 and 4.42). The proportion of exact replication can vary enormously, and historical elements can be adapted rather than be copied.

2. Designs which could not have been produced contemporaneously. The use of electricity for lighting and the resulting need for electric lamps commenced long after the Japanese candlesticks which inspired figure 4.43 came into use. Another often-quoted example is the Queen Anne television cabinet. It serves a new function, and uses a recently developed material, veneered plywood or similar, for the carcase.

3. Designs which parody and/or distort (figure 4.36). This was a major force in the late twentieth-century style post-modernism. Criticized as nihilistic, narcissistic, and self-indulgent by some, to others this style is fun.

I hope that I have shown that historicism can be a creative contributor to design progress. Indeed, design progress is impossible without building on the past.

Figure 4.41 A contradiction of historicism, a vessel more rendolent of *archeologism* than historicism, by Jim Partridge of Oswestry, England. The charred surface of the burr oak is ambiguous, both modern and ancient; the form is modern but primitive.

Made in 1987, this bowl from the *Blood Vessel Series* is 6 in. (150 mm) high. Photograph supplied by The Wood Turning Center, Philadelphia.

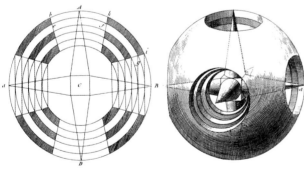

Figure 4.42 ***Top*, a synthesis of historicism and modern design.** *Woodturning Virus* by Christian Delhon of Berck-sur-Mer, France, combines traditional ornamental turnings (*bottom*) with a unique contemporary structure. Its height is 30 in. (750 mm), its diameter is 24 in. (600 mm).

    Bottom, this combined star-in-sphere and Chinese ball was shown in 1816 in plate XXI, Vol. II of the second edition of *Manuel du Tourneur* by Louis-Eloy Bergeron, revised by Pierre Hamelin-Bergeron. A similar sphere is also shown in *L'Art de Tourner* (1701) by Charles Plumier.

Figure 4.43   A *Kyoto* lamp. It is 32 in. (820 mm) high, and based on the traditional Japanese candlestick which has a thicker and upwards-tapering stem and a base carved with gadrooning (see page 136), not with rings.

4.2.5 TRUTH TO MATERIAL

The finished state of a material depends on its innate qualities and on the ways it has been worked. Truth to material, the concept that materials should be used truthfully and naturally, and should not be used to imitate other materials, therefore sensibly includes truth to process.

Truth to material is a powerful concept—I was once almost prevented from exhibiting turnings because they were painted not clear finished. Another example is the commercial advertizing of furniture as being constructed from "*natural* wood"—is there any other?

An early writer on the issue was Vincenzo Scamozzi who wrote in volume VII of his L'*idea della architettura universale* (1615),

> it is not very laudable for an architect to attempt, as it were, to do violence to the material, in the sense that he always seeks to subordinate Nature's creations to his own will, in order to give them the forms that he desires.[35]

This view was not unchallenged. Daniele Barbaro (1513–1570), a translator of Vitruvius, did not believe that material should dictate form; nor was he concerned by the use of stuccoed brickwork to imitate stone walls and columns.[36]

Truth to material did not become an important issue until the nineteenth century when the development of new materials and processes and the rapid growth of a less-discerning middle class gathered pace. This made rejection of the concept, whether knowingly or otherwise, easier and profitable. Therefore most of the writings on the concept are nineteenth century, and the concept is often wrongly attributed to Gottfried Semper who in 1834 wrote:

> Let materials speak for themselves and appear, undisguised, in whatever form and whatever conditions have been shown by experience and knowledge to be best suited to them. Let brick appear as brick, wood as wood, iron as iron, each according to the structural laws which apply to it.[37]

The concept was also supported by John Ruskin and others, including Adolf Loos (1870–1933) who wrote in 1898:

> Every material has its own formal language, and no material can assume for itself the forms of another material. These forms have emerged from the way in which each material has been produced and employed: they have come into being *with* the material and *through* the material. No material permits interference with its own set of forms.[38]

Wood was then still a hugely important constructional material. Also the way in which it has been worked is graphically recorded by its fibrous surface. It was therefore used in an example in 1895 by P. Rioux de Maillou of the consequences of ignoring truth to material:

When stamped, compressed, or tortured, wood is wood no longer. Whatever you do, it will never look like anything but papier-mâché. Its special character, its aesthetic beauty, resides in the affirmation of its fibrous identity, and in the felicitous working of the tool that works the fibrous substance. Crush those fibers, and you kill your material. Wood that is stamped or compressed is nothing but the corpse of wood. It has not been worked but murdered.[39]

The reaction revealed in the above quote is not strongly moral (the "truth" in truth to material is a moral term); it is mainly aesthetic, and would be popular with many. However, this popularity does not validate the concept, and would evaporate if its inherent restrictions were realized. These restrictions are listed below in italics, my comments in Roman type :

1. *The material should show its natural surface.* What is the natural surface of wood (figures 4.44 and 4.45)?
2. *The material should not be covered by paint, a veneer, plating, or similar.* Paint has been used as decoration, and protection, and to communicate for thousands of years. Its ability to deceive is limited, as has been its use in deception. Are translucent staining and clear-finishing also taboo?
3. *The material should not be worked so as to imitate a different material.* This denies the economy and aesthetic

Figure 4.44 Naturally exposed wood. Wood in nature is usually hidden beneath bark. Only when a tree has been damaged, here by borers, is wood naturally exposed. Mechanical damage, for example when a major branch splits off, also exposes the wood.

Wood can be worked to expose or retain a natural surface (next figure), but can wood be worked to imitate a natural surface? It can, but I suggest that the imitation would rarely be accurate; nor would it always be popular or appropriate on functional turnings.

Tooled, unsanded surfaces such as that in figures 4.5 and 4.40 do not resemble a naturally exposed surface (tooled surfaces are discussed in the next section).

Figure 4.45 A retained natural surface on the outside of an inverted bowl. Sometimes the surface of the sapwood is exposed naturally by the bark coming away. Here the sapwood's surface was exposed without damaging it using high-pressure water blasting (see *Woodturning Techniques*, p. 115).

Figure 4.46 An imitation of a basket made by turning a conglutination of woods of different colors. Made by Lincoln Seitzman of Longboat Key, Florida. A basket can also be imitated by carving a turning (figure 8.27). Baskets have often been imitated in clay.

pleasures which can be associated with imitation (figures 4.46 to 4.48). This distinction was noted by Ruskin in his acceptance that in architecture gilded surfaces would not be mistaken for the surfaces of huge masses of solid gold.

4. *The material should be processed using traditional techniques.* What is inherently objectionable about new techniques such as power wire-brushing, waterblasting, sandblasting, knurling, laser cutting, and chainsawing (figure 4.8)? The reason these techniques are not traditional is that they were not technically possible until recently, not because they are inherently wrong. While the surfaces left after applying these new techniques may not resemble that left after cutting with a sharp, properly presented edge, they have valid aesthetic properties and uses. Whether a technique is traditional is surely far less important than whether it has been applied in a workmanlike manner.

5. *The material should be used in its traditional roles and not in fresh roles.* In times without sophisticated structural calculation there was perhaps an implicit safety consideration in this restriction—I can see no other valid reason for it.

Apart from the quasi-moral strictures against deceit and imitation in 2 and 3 and the implication of structural conservatism in 5, the restrictions of truth to material are arbitrary and conservative. They can force a higher quality of result, although at greater cost. For example, more care has to be taken when selecting multiple component pieces of wood if the resulting clear-finished object is to have a consistent appearance. Also, faulty workmanship cannot be hidden beneath paint or veneer.

Figure 4.47 Poking fun at the concept of truth to material, a lidded "brick" bowl by John Ambrose of Ely, Cambridgeshire, England.

Figure 4.48 **The lidded bowl from the preceding figure closed.**

4.3 CONCEPTS CONCERNED WITH THE PRODUCTION OF TURNINGS

Truth to material includes truth to process. In this section I discuss the related concepts of workmanship and deskilling.

4.3.1 WORKMANSHIP

A lathe machine is essential to woodturning and dictates that every turned cross section perpendicular to a turning-axis shall be circular or annular. Perhaps this truth overshadows the fact that the profile and the surface of a hand woodturning are produced directly by the hand-manipulation of tools. Workmanship is therefore an appropriate term to apply to hand woodturning, the inclusion of "man" excluding the application of the term to the production of fully automated machines.

David Pye wrote "The designer proposes, workmanship disposes".[40] Whether or not you are to be the worker (the person who makes, as distinct from the person who designs), in our case the turner, an essential part of designing is to specify to the worker the workmanship required. In turning this means:

1. How far the turned dimensions can depart from the designed.
2. The desired qualities of the finished surfaces. This will require the specification of any sanding grits and polishing materials and procedures.
3. The freedom the worker has to modify and express.

To specify these parameters you, the designer, need to be aware of what is possible and at what approximate cost. You also need to be able to grade the possibilities with reference to your design intentions.

You cannot of course specify everything, especially as situations may arise during the making which the designer has not foreseen—one advantage of combining both the designing and making functions in the one person is that such situations can be addressed immediately.

ROUGHNESS AND OVERT TOOLING
To discuss roughness and overt tooling in detail I need to define some associated terms. My source for these definitions (given in figure 4.49) and my main reference for this section has been David Pye's *The Nature and Art of Workmanship* (1968).

Although the cantankerousness of wood as a material for mass manufacturing shielded it somewhat, the Industrial Revolution greatly accelerated the trend to machine-based production, the division of labor, and the lessening of hand skills. What was formerly produced by hand could be imitated en masse at lower cost and less roughly by machine.

Before the Industrial Revolution the usual aim of workmanship was perfection. Workmanship was, however, often imperfect because of lack of time, lack of skill, etc., or the knowledge that rough was appropriate in that particular situation (figure 4.50). Ruskin undermined that simple belief. He wrote in the *The Seven Lamps of Architecture* (1849) that "Ornament. . .has two entirely distinct sources of agreeableness, one, that of the abstract beauty of forms, which, for the present, we will suppose to be the same whether they come from the hand or from the machine; the other the sense of human labor and care spent upon it".[41] Ruskin was not the first to conclude that the precision, which until the Industrial Revolution characterized the best hand workmanship, could henceforth be excelled by machine. But after Ruskin, precision could no longer be the sole criterion on which to judge hand workmanship. Two more criteria were added: the imperfections and rhythms of the happy hand craftsman, and expression. These additions were consistent with Ruskin's belief that the only true beauty was found in nature, and that it derived from God. Man thus could not create beauty which rivalled that produced by God, but when man was happy and thereby communing with God, he was best able to create beauty which approached God's. Machines, however, could only produce counterfeits of beauty.

During Ruskin's lifetime the Japanese aesthetic was introduced to the West (page 33). In Japan, roughness and inaccuracy have been regarded in three ways:[42]

1. As an honest and accidental occurrence during the process of seeking perfection. In this description Kakuzo Okakura in his *The Book of Tea* was specifically referring to the unintended departures from the intended which happened inside a pottery kiln during firing. Not every unintended occurrence within a kiln resulted in beauty. Thus the "art of imperfection", a term coined by Okakura, is perhaps one of selection.
2. Buddhist aesthetician Shin'ichi Hisamatsu rejected Okakura's belief, and countered that imperfect was

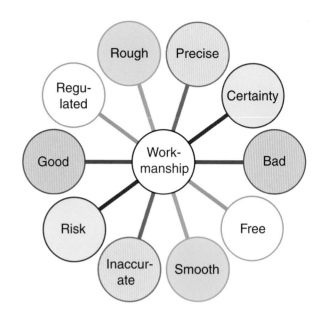

Figure 4.49 The five pairs of terms used to describe workmanship by David Pye in *The Nature and Art of Workmanship*:

1. Good workmanship complements the designer's intentions. Bad workmanship conflicts with the designer's intentions.
2. The more freedom the designer allows the worker, the less regulated the worker is. Regulation refers to the tightness of the design specification.

    Classical music scores regulate. They define notes and timing. They also often specify the emotions, using terms such as *animato* meaning spirited, which the composer wishes the players (workers) to communicate through their playing. Specifying such terms requires players to consciously express, to employ artifice, but does not prohibit, and implicitly encourages, artistic expression by players as long as it is in harmony with the composer's intentions. In jazz, players are less regulated, are free within the restraints of the melody to express and to play notes of their own choice. It is similarly appropriate in woodturning to specify where and to what extent the worker is free to change and to express.
3. Rough and smooth refer to surface finish. If a rough surface is specified, it is thus regulated. If a rough surface is produced, as long as it is either specified or was not specified but still complements the design intentions, it is good.
4. Approximate and precise refer to how closely the turned dimensions and profile conform to the specified dimensions and profile.
5. Risk and certainty refer to the likelihood of the workmanship being as specified.

The ten terms defined above are not absolute, but are ones of degree.

Figure 4.50 Workmanships in a turning-tool handle. The fitting of the ferrule has to be precise and the spigot diameter is therefore regulated by the inside diameter of the ferrule. The profile of the rest of the handle was not drawn beforehand, but "eyed" during turning, and was not therefore highly regulated. It would be impossible for anyone not privy to the mental construct which I used to eye the profile to judge the precision of the profile. The rough, unsanded surface was intended and is therefore good. Except for the ferrule area, I use rough workmanship on tool handles because the resulting surface gives a better grip.

Figure 4.51 Windsor chair underframes, hand turned in huge numbers. Although the turner or turners of the legs and stretchers would have been working "on automatic" (as a machine), there would not have been emotional takeover. Absolute precision in the turning of the ornament was unimportant, but was adequate and resulted both from the turners skill and his familiarity with the form. An example of less-regulated, free workmanship rather than of expression.

purely a negative concept, and could not therefore constitute beauty. Imperfect could only be beautiful if it was a positive rejection of the perfect involving a search for and deliberate refining of the imperfect, a form of artifice. Followers of Hisamatsu therefore deliberately throw their pottery off center and deform it. They also fire it in such a way that something normally regarded as an unfortunate accident is likely to happen.

3. Soetsu Yanagi (1889–1961) had reservations about both of the above beliefs. For Yanagi beauty was neither a stage on the way to perfection nor a rejection of it in favor of artifice, but resulted from a worker who was focussed on making something serviceable. The design was not rigidly regulated, and thus enough roughness and inaccuracy was allowed that competent workers could "just make what they make without any pretension". It is alas a small step from this situation to that where workers are forced to work like machines.

While Yanagi's idea was similar to Ruskin's, Yanagi realized the importance of self-discipline (self-regulation) in work, and that unregulated freedom led to bizarreness.

These Japanese ideas were not developed in response to the economic and aesthetic pressures of modern manufacturing, or in a society in which wealth and taste were often strangers, but all three remain influential. In Western societies they have become integrated with the theories of Ruskin, Morris, and others. The consequence is that overt tooling (rough workmanship) has become more desirable in woodturnings since the 1970s. The following beliefs have been at play:

1. Ruskin's idea that the imperfect workmanship of the supposedly happy, carefree workman is preferable to the dead precision of the machine remains powerful. But in modern times buying handmade by a Western worker means paying more than for the machine-made equivalent. Overt tooling proves that an object is handmade or handturned; it suggests artistic expression; it may be abused as a communicative marketing tool to justify a higher price. The overt demonstration to the experiencer that something is handmade is, of course, dependent on the assumption in truth to process that machines cannot and would not be used to imitate hand work.
2. Overt tooling can be a prop to the less competent hand worker—if you can't make it well, make it rough and nullify, even glorify, remnant catches, poor profiling, and poor design. It might fool someone.
3. Overt tooling results in detail, texture, and variability. These can be aesthetically pleasing in themselves—a positive side of roughness.
4. If the perception of hand workmanship adds to an experiencer's pleasure and desire to buy, should maker's intentionally use the artifice of rough workmanship? It

also depends on experiencers having the conceptual knowledge to appreciate the handmade. Will such artifice become irrelevant because the next generation's knowledge of manual skills will be restricted to manipulating a computer mouse?

5. Rough workmanship can result from a desire for faster and therefore less-costly production in areas where precision is not necessary. It can also reflect the adequate, acceptable, and economic standard of workmanship which a market is used to and which therefore there may be no point in exceeding. Both reasons would be approved by Yanagi.

6. Overt tooling can be a factor in depressing prices; even if it does not imply incompetence, it demonstrates that the worker is free and happy. The wealthy who believe that making money without using their hands deprives them of true work satisfaction feel free to force prices down with a clear conscience.

7. Perfection does not permit expression. According to Collingwood, art is associated with unconscious expression, craft is not. While this is a valid distinction according to Collingwood's narrow definitions of art and craft, it fails when applied to the usual understandings of the two concepts. Overt tooling also ensures uniqueness (an important characteristic of art) even when turnings are similar in form.

8. Overt tooling demonstrates that the artist did not care about the quality of his workmanship. For some this was and is an expression of artistry. "Technique is cheap" was a popular art mantra in the1960s and 1970s; concept was everything, and the manner of its manifestation was an unimportant distraction. This attitude is not restricted to the fine arts. I recall several art woodturners who excused themselves with "I'm not really a woodturner" when their poor technical abilities were exposed during demonstrations.

9. Overt tooling reinforces the separation of the fine arts (which should imitate natural appearances which are rarely smooth and polished) from less exalted practices which stress the importance of surfaces free of tool marks.

10. Overt tooling can be a feature of a personal style.

A knowledgable experiencer can distinguish between an unsanded spindle which was pole-lathe turned, and one hand turned on a lathe powered to give continuous (not continually alternating) rotation, although the differences are small. It is improbable that even a knowledgable experiencer could distinguish between turnings done on an electrically-powered hand lathe, a lathe person-driven via a Great Wheel, or a lathe turner-driven via a treadle and flywheel. Despite the differences between tooled surfaces produced on different types of hand lathe being insignificant or nonexistent, the type of lathe used and the particular tooled surface produced by a turner can be magnified into great significance by

promotion. This promotion typically includes that of the turner. Thus experiencers get a sense of knowing the turner through the promotion. This promotion may also focus on the materials and workshop location, and be leavened with nostalgia; it is a powerful marketing force.

Such promotion exploits the idea that an experiencer's perception that something is handmade can create a bridge of empathy between the maker and an experiencer, and was introduced on pages 53 and 54. This empathy is assumed to be absent for a machine-made object even though it results from human intention, because the object is not the *direct* result of a human act. Whether we consider machine-made as alien, as from a source that we may identify as not in ourselves, is unclear. It may also be that such identification is weakening as handworking lessens in importance.

Pye stated in 1968 that overt tooling as a marketing tool would eventually discourage purchase of the handmade because a genuine aesthetic could not be based on a mere artifice used to differentiate the hand turned from that turned on an automatic lathe.[43] Overt tooling seems less common in the twenty-first century than it was in the late twentieth, but I doubt whether Pye's writing has been directly responsible. For Pye the real benefit of handworking was that it enabled diversity. The increase in art turning is one manifestation of this, one-offness being a characteristic but not universal property of art. But what about multiples and diversity?

Traditionally in turning the workmanship for multiples was desired to be regulated and precise. If you caliper a flight of handturned balusters you will be surprised at how large the variations in dimensions are, but because once installed they are viewed en masse as a screen and not subjected to minute examination, extreme precision is not needed. However, similar dimensional inaccuracy in a pair of finely finished candlesticks displayed close together would be noticeable, and would therefore not be appropriate.

The baluster example above suggests that there is no necessity for high regulation in many turnings produced in multiples. Pye's belief that workmanship should be used to produce diversity, not roughness, suggests that where being handmade is important for marketing, you should produce only one small batch of any particular design, with succeeding batches of the theme object each incorporating minor design changes. An alternative artifice would be to intentionally produce or allow minor differences between objects in the same batch. Fortunately for some turners these minor variations do not require conscious effort.

4.3.2 DESKILLING

A worker's appreciation of workmanship can be combined with the desire to compete to become an urge to show workmanship by being able to handle extra complication, accuracy, or risk. Such workmanship may be appreciable by experiencers. Similarly experiencers may also be able to perceive when workmanship is too rough or inadequate for the job.

Pye's concepts of the workmanships of risk and certainty were described near the bottom of the legend of figure 4.49. There is a commonly-held moral view that by intentionally lessening risk a worker cheats and decreases the worth of the resulting object. There are several implicit issues:

Honest workers don't lessen risk. Hand workers improve their workmanship through consciously and unconsciously acquiring and applying knowledge, and through repeatedly applying that knowledge (practice). The knowledge acquired can be preexisting or be generated by the worker through experimentation, invention, and development. It is to the advantage of both the worker and society that a worker improves his or her workmanship because this produces a better product, more quickly, and with less waste: it is not being dishonest.

Part of a worker's knowledge concerns tools. By designing, shaping, sharpening, and using most turning tools optimally they become self-jigging and risk is lessened.

In hand woodturning risk cannot be much diminished by approaching the desired result more slowly. In bead rolling an error is just as likely with a first thick rolling cut as with a final thin skim. Some turners design out the more risky cuts, but this restricts the range of profiles which they can attempt; for example, those who turn beads with gouge, not a skew, cannot turn adjacent beads which are near semicircular in profile. Therefore the desirability of texts such as *The Fundamentals of Woodturning* which are essentially to

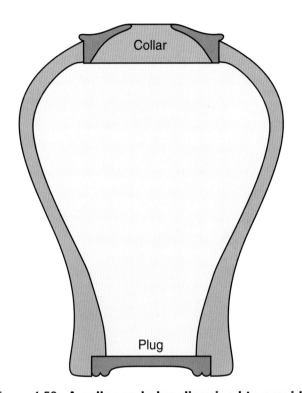

Figure 4.53 A collar and plug disguised to provide far greater tool access. Some hollow turnings have either a bottom plug or a collar which are intentionally joined invisibly to the body after the hollowing is completed. An essence of hollow turnings is that their excavation is difficult, exacting, and expensive because it is done through a small access hole at the top. Is the careful fitting of such plugs and collars an attempt to deceive an experiencer about the exact means of production, and therefore morally fraudulent? The turner who uses plugs and collars might argue that there is no legal fraud because the vessel is not advertised as "turned in one piece". Even the advertisement "turned from one piece" would not be legal fraud because the plugs and collars are usually cut from the same piece of wood as the body of the vessel. The turner could also argue that he is just selling an object, that that does not imply any particular method of manufacture, and that any implication the buyer makes about the making process is entirely the buyer's own.

Fortunately for turners who have moral concerns, there is new equipment which makes hollowing quicker and more certain (figures 4.54 to 4.58).

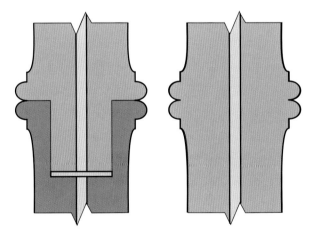

Figure 4.52 A fraudulent joint. *Left,* the shafts of many commercial standard lamps are constructed from two sections with the joint between them rendered invisible by being hidden in a groove. This is done to simplify manufacture and reduce the cost. But is it also a fraud, an implication that the shaft is turned in one piece and has the strength of a one-piece turning (*right*)? If it is a fraud, it is not a serious one because the two-piece shaft is still strong enough not to break in normal use.

widen scope and lessen risk, to increase the probability that a reader will achieve his or her desired result.

Lessening risk means lessening the workmanship input. Deskilling involves lessening risk by redistributing some of the need for workmanship backwards along the chain of production. For example, if you tune and sharpen your turning tools so that they are self-jigging, your tools become easier to control and you lessen the risk of a catch. If you use a machine such as a planer (jointer) to flatten wood, your need to be able to hand plane precisely is eliminated by the efforts of those involved in designing, making, and setting the planer.

Lessening the need for handworkmanship increases the overall workmanship input. It would be uneconomic to design and manufacture a planer to plane one piece of wood. Whether to deskill is usually an economic decision, not a moral one.

It is moral to lessen risk by using better tools, but not by using machines? Is there a moral difference between using a tool and a machine (here differentiated by having moving parts)?

Consider drilling. Is there any moral difference between using a medieval brace which had no moving parts and a hand-operated egg-beater drill? If "no", what moral difference does applying electric power to the hand drill and thereby increasing productivity make? Converting an electric hand-drill to a drilling machine decreases the need for workmanship, but what is the moral or other benefit in not decreasing the likelihood of wrongly directed holes?

Is it immoral to replace physical workmanship with mental? The two are inseparable. Mental ingenuity and the application of acquired conceptual knowledge (experience) are both essential to superior workmanship.

Should you lessen risk through design? If the lessening of risk through improvements in the workmanship and equipment used by those who make an object is acceptable, there cannot be any objection to lessening the risk through modifying the design of the object, particularly as there are likely to be associated reductions in cost and waste. There is however a qualification: when design modifications to

Figure 4.54   Frank Sudol using his medium boring bar. Such devices greatly reduce the risk of losing control by spreading the need for workmanship backwards along the production process, here to the design, making, and setting-up of the boring bar. Such devices also reduce the need for personal strength.

reduce risk would compromise the aesthetic, functional and other intended qualities of the object, the pros and cons need to be considered. Two examples are discussed in figures 4.52 and 4.53.

There are no moral issues concerning deskilling providing that there is no misdescription of the method of making (deskilling difficult or impossible to police). There is no logical place to stop deskilling if the completed object is not adversely effected because of the benefits such as lower cost, less fatigue, and freeing the worker to concentrate on activities which still necessitate hand skills. The only objections to the improvement of workmanship and the concomitant lessening of risk are that the gains should not come at the expense of the environment or of workers' emotional and financial rewards and physical conditions.

Deskilling is not just not a negative concept, it is a positive duty. It has been among the main catalysts for material advancement. A deskilling advance in developed for woodturning might require new advances in forestry,

mining, and engineering. These advances in turn allow and catalyse advances in other activities.

Workmanship is valued by buyers and experiencers not only because of empathy, but because it is a rare commodity which should enhance the value of an object it is applied to. The object will also be rare and valuable because there will not be enough expert workmanship available to make many similar objects. The machine destroys this paradigm. A photograph of a scene is usually less costly than a painting of the same scene and can be reproduced as many times as desired. However if it became known that the painting was done by projecting a slide of the scene onto the canvas and then matching the paint to the projected image, that painting might fetch less than one painted directly from the scene. However those painters, the hyporealists who emphasized that this was their method, now fetch large prices. We should not be attempting to downplay the lathe machine's involvement to turning, but promote how we exploit it.

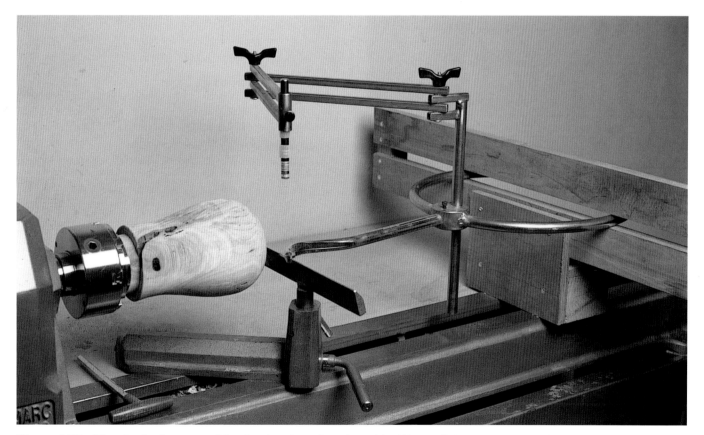

Figure 4.55 The Articulaser and its boring bar. Developed by Wayne Shipman of Walnut Creek, California, and Robert Whitworth of Martinez, California, the Articulaser enables a turner to know exactly where the tool tip is during hollowing. It does this by allowing the turner to position a laser pen's beam in any fixed position relative to the boring tool's tip (next figure). Then by observing how the laser beam shines onto the outside of the vessel, the turner can accurately judge the vessel's wall thickness at that location (figures 4.57 and 4.58). The Articulaser thus further lessens the risk and improves the efficiency of hollow turning. The pen and its positioning mechanism can be supplied separately for use on any boring bar.

Figure 4.56 The positioning of the Articulaser's laser beam relative to the tool tip can be varied. The next figure below shows the laser beam positioned so that when the desired wall thickness is being cut, the laser just ceases to show on the outside of the wall.

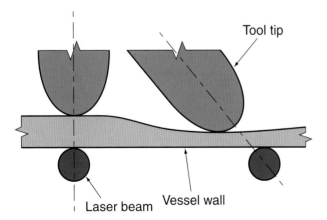

Figure 4.57 Using the Articulaser correctly. *Left*, the correct alignment between tool tip, wall direction, and laser beam. *Right*, poor alignment leads to the overestimation of wall thickness.

Figure 4.58 Using the Articulaser. The beam is here adjusted to point as shown on the left in the preceding diagram. When the laser beam just leaves the wood the required wall thickness has been reached.

4.4 MORAL CONCEPTS

This section discusses the moral issues of forgery, conservation and restoration, plagiarism, borrowing, and reproduction.

4.4.1 FORGERY

An excellent discussion of forgery and its associated mental gymnastics in the fine arts is given in *The Forger's Art* where Denis Sutton defines a forgery as "represented as genuine with the intention to deceive".[44] In woodturning I suggest that accidental or unintentional misrepresentation is more common. Through carelessness, ignorance, or wishful thinking, objects tend to be misrepresented as being older, or rarer, or by a more noted turner, or in a more costly wood than they are (figure 4.59). Thus many forgeries were not originally made to deceive; only subsequently was a signature added or a knowingly wrong or optimistic claim made as to origin or material.

Why are forgeries despised? It isn't because of inferior technical or aesthetic qualities because in these respects some forgeries surpass the originals. Nor is it because forgeries are copies because many aren't—they are unique designs but in a particular style.

Consider for a moment what happens to a supposedly genuine object when is discovered to be a forgery; its monetary value and reputation are slashed, yet the object has not changed. What have changed are the criteria by

Figure 4.59 A forgery? Muffineers' domed tops were usually threaded in the eighteenth century. This muffineer's top is a push fit onto the lower part. Was this unthreaded muffineer made innocently for use? and when? or was it made recently as a forgery by a turner without the resources to cut threads in wood?

Muffineers were used, particularly in the eighteenth century, to sprinkle spices, usually cinnamon, on muffins or on hot buttered toast.[45]

which we judge it. Its essence has vaporized; it has lost the romance and associations that we attach to a particular maker or a particular period. The discovery that this intangible quality, which may have constituted the major component of the object's monetary value, is but a mirage causes the object not merely to be downgraded, but to be assessed as if it were now a different category of object.

The rarity component of an object's monetary value is vulnerable to forgery. The discovery of one forgery opens the possibility that there may be many. And where the forgery is so good that it can only be suspected of being a forgery, or proved to be one with great difficulty, the value of genuine examples will be lowered.

It can be argued that forgeries are not necessarily harmful. Many unrevealed forgeries give great pleasure to their proud owners in addition to having given financial succor to those along the supply chain. The only harms unrevealed forgeries promote are distortions to the history of objects and the reputations of makers, and a lowering of the monetary values of originals because the number of originals is believed to be greater than it truly is. Only when a forgery is exposed does its buyer become aware of his monetary loss, and does the possibility of public confidence being undermined arise.

Forgeries aren't always made from scratch; many are the result of what are euphemistically called "improvements" or "marriages". In the nineteenth century and earlier, people were less concerned with an object's integrity, and the incorporation of pieces of earlier carving or turning was a popular and accepted practice.[46] Other "furniture-restoration" techniques exposed in *Is It Genuine?* include: reducing the sizes of antique pieces of furniture to suit today's smaller rooms; carving surfaces which were originally plain; changing moldings, feet and handles to those of an earlier period; and converting an object made to serve a now obsolete function to serve a currently desired one—for example, converting pole screens to tripod tables.[47]

4.4.2 CONSERVATION AND RESTORATION

Improvements were and are sometimes carried out during restoration. The debate between the conservation approach promoted by Ruskin and Morris and the improvement-to-permit-current-usage approach of Viollet-le-Duc continues. The current practice is towards conservation rather than extensive restoration, but for less-expensive objects sensitivity and care is still rejected to exploit the unaware consumer, and the stripping and spraying of antique woodwork continues apace.

The conservation/restoration debate is fundamentally about ownership. No longer is a piece regarded solely as its owner's private property for the owner to do with as he or she decides. Ruskin's belief that we are minders for posterity, curators of links in the chain of human history (page 33), prevails at the informed, more expensive end of the market. Obviously the poorer the condition of a piece, the greater the tendency to restore rather than conserve. Indeed the restoration may be so great that it could be argued that the restorer has created a reproduction; or if the restoration work has been especially well disguised, a potential forgery.

4.4.3 PLAGIARISM

If you found that your work had been plagiarized you might be flattered, at least initially. Plagiarism, the passing-off of another's ideas as one's own, is far more common in woodturning than forgery.

The concept of plagiarism is dependent on the belief that design ideas are the intellectual property of their originators. Governments have judged the ownership of original ideas inappropriate for legislative protection, electing instead to restrict protection to the manifestations of original ideas. Patent protection was developed for the manifestations of new principles; design registration for new shapes and arrangements of parts. The legislation also recognizes that after a period the protection should lapse.

The rationale is to encourage invention and development by permitting a period of unfettered exploitation by the inventor without allowing permanent progress-preventing monopolies.

Patenting is expensive, and it and design registration both depend for their effectiveness on a willingness to privately litigate against infringers—the patenting or registrating authority does not legislate at its cost on your behalf. There is design protection under copyright, but this is appropriate only to one-offs and very small batches, and is again dependent on a willingness to litigate. Patenting is rarely appropriate for woodwork designs and copyright, and design registration become increasingly ineffective the further the offending plagiarism is from being an exact copy.

Although few of today's best-known woodturners are likely to have their works forged, some will have had them plagiarized. There are several categories of plagiarism:

1. *Active*, in which the plagiarizer states that he or she originated the idea. This can be:
   i. Knowingly false.
   ii. Unknowingly false because the plagiarizer does not know that he or she was not the first to design that particular aspect or object.

Figure 4.60 Copies in an unusual medium, a teapot, cup and saucer made from the mulberry tree which William Shakespeare (1564–1616) planted at New Place, Stratford-on-Avon. The tree was felled by Rev. Francis Gastrell in 1756.[49] Illustration supplied by Birmingham Museum and Art Gallery, England.

2. *Passive*, which is more common than active. The passive plagiarizer presents his work without any reference to the source of the work's concept or style. This can be further divided into:

    i.   Deliberate, the plagiarizer hopes that an ignorant experiencer will assume that the plagiarized idea or style is the invention of the plagiarizer.

    ii. *Unthinking*, being unaware of the concept of plagiarism.

    iii. *Resulting from the plagiarizer's ignorance of who is the inventor.* This may be due to a refusal to do the research necessary to identify the inventor, or because the research has not identified the originator.

    iv. *Unbelieving*, believing that there is no moral need to acknowledge the originator. As will be explained, there can be several complicating factors.

Passive plagiarism should not be excused, but often is. There is also a mistaken belief or a tacit understanding that plagiarizing is permissible if there is no intention to sell.

Many accusations of plagiarism are well founded, but not all. The design process is not a series of isolated original inspirations. It is rather a process in which new designs inevitably repeat or are developed from earlier ones (figures 4.60 to 4.63), or are fresh or unorthodox arrangements or associations of preexisting design elements (figures 4.62 and 4.63). Even when catalyzed by new materials or techniques;

originality is impossible without some degree of copying. For both legal and moral accusations of passive plagiarism to be valid the copying must be very close, if not creation would be severely stiffled. Every new creation needs a trigger, and that trigger will often have a visual connection with an earlier work. Brent Brolin has highlighted impossibility of creating without borrowing: "The notion of borrowing from the past to aid in creating new ornamental designs is probably as old as the second artisan".[48]

There is a wide grey area between plagiarism and borrowing. The following points indicate the problems which

Figure 4.62 *Tea Set* **(1997) by Merryll Saylan,** box elder, painted, 6 in. high x 6 in. dia. (150 mm x 150 mm). This is not a plagiarism of earlier wooden teacups and saucers because:

1. Merryll did not promote *Tea Set* as the first, so there was no active plagiarism. That the teacup has been replicated in wood for centuries (figures 4.40, 4.61, and 4.63) is widely known and therefore *Tea Set* is not an example of passive plagiarism.

2. The forms of this teacup and saucer are different to those of other wooden teacups and saucers, and are copied from crockery owned by Merryll.

3. *Tea Set* is more than a replica. Its large scale and distortion of the form of the saucer make it a unique parody. It is also the teacup has been a vehicle for parody in the crafts for decades.

Figure 4.61 A pearwood replica teacup and saucer, English, circa 1825. Illustration supplied by Birmingham Museum and Art Gallery, England. This, and the teapot, cup and saucer in figure 4.60 are part of the Pinto Collection. This collection was assembled by Edward H. Pinto, and is now housed in the Birmingham Museum and Art Gallery.

can arise when attempting to classify a turning as one or the other:

1. There is inverted plagiarism—a design evolution which seeks to parody its ancestry (figure 4.64).
2. New ideas are frequently exaggerations, refinements or reappraisals (figures 4.65 to 4.67). A notable example is the warping of green-turned bowls which was, I suspect, considered until recently an inescapable evil. Its exploitation as a decorative technique probably did not start until the 1970s.
3. Similar ideas can occur independently to different designers, and so plagiarism does not apply (figure 4.68).
4. A turner may get a new idea by unconscious recollection or association, and thus not be aware of the idea's source.
5. Many techniques and design features are difficult if not impossible to attribute to an originator, particularly when of some age.
6. New designs are often fresh associations of a number of plagiarized design elements. Such compound plagiarism is rarely considered plagiarism at all.

Figure 4.64   A parody of plagiarism, *Eat your heart out David Ellsworth*. To appreciate the parody the experiencer must be aware that David Ellsworth was the first to promote and develop the technique of hollow turning for art turnings. The work's title implies, "Why attempt to copy Ellsworth's exacting technique like all the other turners? There's an easier way". In the collection of Bonnie Klein.

Figure 4.63   Tea chest teapot, cup, saucer, and teaspoon. Made in about 1985 from tea tree (*Melaleuca quinquinervia*), and the plywood and steel trim of a tea chest. Points 1 and 2 from the legend in the preceding figure apply to this cup and saucer which are copied from porcelain examples made by the Spanish company Bidosa. While I stole Bidosa's design, did I do damage to the company? The teapot combines two preexisting objects to create a new parody.

Figure 4.65 **The inception for the carving board in the next two figures.** Here the larger the diameter of the channel, the deeper it is turned. This meat carving board in teak is 12.5 in. (310 mm) square, and was designed by Jens H. Quistgaard. It was made by Dansk Designs, Denmark. Illustrated in Rathbone Holme and Kathleen Frost, eds., *Decorative Art 1958–1959*, volume 48 (London: The Studio Ltd., 1958), p. 71.

7. After a period of time knowledge becomes public (figure 4.69). This doesn't imply that we shouldn't acknowledge the originator, but perhaps allows that the acknowledgment is less critical because the public should already be familiar with the idea and its source, or because ample time has elapsed for the originator to adequately exploit the idea.

8. Design ideas may be plucked from other media such as ceramics and silversmithing (figure 4.69). Inter-medium plagiarism is less likely to be discovered, it may also be more difficult to prosecute under design registration, I don't know. Another example, the dimpled bowl bottoms which I have long used (*The Fundamentals of Woodturning*, page 181) are common in blown glass. I found they are not new in woodturning either—one is shown in *Das Drechslerwerk* published in 1940.[50]

9. Many woodturners teach and demonstrate their individual styles and methods. While the resulting

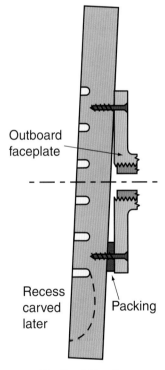

Outboard faceplate

Recess carved later   **Packing**

Vertical Section Along Lathe Axis, Board Shown in Diagonal Section

Figure 4.66 **A carving board (1980).** I used the concept in the preceding figure, but developed it by packing the board before turning the channels so that the channels are deepest along the radius leading to the meat juices reservoir (next figure).

Figure 4.67 **Mounting the carving board shown in the preceding figure for turning.**

income is welcome, it surely encourages plagiarism and makes any protestations against plagiarism less than convincing, particularly against students who paid to attend classes or buy teaching materials (figure 4.70).

10. Major success in the art end of the woodturning market is not solely dependent on originality. Marketing success may be heightened if you can found a "school" who copy you. The difficulty is to encourage copying but with source acknowledgment to ensure that the limelight remains on oneself.

Figure 4.68 Similar but independently conceived designs based on the hyperboloid.

Above, candlesticks (c. 1952.) by Rude Osolnik (1915–2001), of Berea, Kentucky. Tallest candlestick 9.5 in. (240 mm) high. Photograph supplied by The Wood Turning Center, Philadelphia.

Right, candlestick in silver or polished brass, on a teak base. Designed by Sven Aage of Holm Sørensen. Made by Holm Sørensen & Co., Denmark. Illustrated in Rathbone Holme and Kathleen Frost, eds., *Decorative Art 1958–1959*, volume 48 (London: The Studio Ltd., 1958), p. 57.

Figure 4.69 Inter-medium borrowing. Egg-shaped peppers in silver (c. 1800) and wood (2000). Instead of directly threading the wood, plastic threaded parts from a milk carton (*right*) were glued into the top and onto the base spigot of the wooden pepper. The illustration of the silver pepper is taken from Peter Waldron, *The Price Guide to Antique Silver* (Woodbridge, Suffolk: Antique Collectors' Club, 1982), p. 93, and reproduced courtesy of the Antique Collectors' Club.

Perhaps the best defence against plagiarism is a greater public awareness of it. There has been successful litigation against plagiarism, but it is rarely well publicized, particularly when there is an out-of-court settlement with the terms being kept confidential. The woodturning media sometimes even encourages plagiarism by showing work which to the knowledgeable (and media editors should be knowledgable about their subject areas not merely competent journalists) is plagiarized. Therefore if you see your work plagiarized in the media, demand a correction, although some may then judge you as big-headed or mean-spirited?

How should we react to plagiarism? Whether active or passive, deliberate or unthinking, it is the theft of someone's intellectual property. I suggest that we make our personal judgements on a three-tier basis in which we have to:

Figure 4.70 Promoted plagiarism, turned boxes made by your author following the designs and instructions in the three instructional videos by Ray Key of Bretforton, Worcestershire, England. Three issues arise:

1. If I sign the boxes with my name, am I stating merely that I turned them, or am I also implying that I originated the designs?
2. By selling the videos has Ray Key lost any legal rights to the box designs that he might have had?
3. By selling the videos has Ray Key lost any moral rights to the designs?

The sale of these videos has not lead to enormous numbers of boxes of the three Ray Key designs being offered for sale. This suggests that turners have used them to improve their own designs and techniques, rather than to produce multiple copies to sell. Perhaps the videos, and books and articles by Ray Key featuring the boxes have so publicized his box designs that potential plagiarists have not dared risk exposure.

1. Decide whether plagiarism has occurred, and if so and if possible whether it was deliberate or not.
2. Judge the extent of the plagiarism, and any mitigating factors.
3. Assess the benefits to the plagiarizer and the damage to the originator. It is only here that one might look less harshly on the amateur than the professional. A beginner's early pieces are almost inevitably attempted copies, but plagiarism by competent amateurs does adversely affect originators. Some amateurs sell work, if the plagiarism not sold but kept or given away the originator is possibly deprived of sales; in either case the originator's reputation as the originator is likely to be adversely affected.

The pressures to plagiarize are strengthening. The erosion of isolation has smothered regional styles, the once gentler pace of stylistic evolution and the forces of artistic conformance have been blown away. Whereas originality was once the means to achieve greater beauty or efficiency, the tendency now is for means and ends to be transposed, for originality (and personal reputation) to be the prime aim, and for bizarreness and shallowness to be the result. A further result of universal media penetration, of the instant omniscience of the World Wide Web, is that those rare individuals who do evolve individual styles of true integrity must exploit them quickly before they are rendered passé by the terrible twins of plagiarism and overexposure.

It is not just practitioners of woodturning who have their ideas plagiarized. Woodturning writing is another fertile field for those short on ideas and talent. Regrettably woodturning writers, editors, and publishers usually seek to expunge any hint of academe by omitting footnotes and references, and this is a major factor lessening the tendency to acknowledge sources.

But all is not negative. The awareness of copying and plagiarism is growing. Exhibitors are sometimes asked to list their influences in artists statements. Acknowledgment of sources benefits originators and heightens the reputations of those who combine and develop others' ideas.

4.4.3 REPRODUCTION

Reproduction tends to be applied to the use of the features of a style. *Replica* and *copy* are more accurately applied to a copy of an object, with replica having overtones of higher quality or greater accuracy. None of these three terms has any moral associations.

The term reproduction has a benign overtone: its use implies that a knowledgeable experiencer will readily be able to tell that the reproduction is not "original". This may be because the woods, the finishing, or the workmanship used are different, the fittings are modern, the reproduction is labelled as such (permanently we hope), or that the function is modern—the Queen Anne television cabinet. Reproductions are also sometimes advertized as such. Although the term is usually associated with antique styles and designs where the originators are long dead, modern classics and primitive and tribal objects are now commonly reproduced. The potential of reproductions to become forgeries has already been mentioned.

Many choose to make reproductions because those styles are in demand—for the professional turner they are an economically safe option, for the amateur they tend to ensure acceptance and admiration. Some reproduce because the design problems are essentially micro, concerned with detail rather than concept. The wish to concentrate on mastering and practicing traditional skills is also a factor in the continuing popularity of making reproductions.

However the acceptance of reproductions is not universal. British designer Richard La Trobe-Bateman argues that reproduction is a sham, and that it is untruthful not to strive to design something fresh and of its time. I agree, but ironically, if such a design becomes widely admired, it is likely become a "classic", and likely to be reproduced in the future.

Reproduction is perhaps an admission of inadequacy, but we live at a time when solid wood is a tried, known, and almost obsolete material; all the techniques for working it are known; there are no new species to be discovered—in fact the number of available species and range of available sizes is declining; and the major categories and functions of woodwork are old. Perhaps the potential for major stylistic progress is contracting. Reproduction and plagiarism are a sham; bizarreness is only momentarily satisfying, if at all. I expect that we will see more, not less, of all three.

Figure 4.71 A reproduction, a stool in the style of the late seventeenth century. This stool is not a copy, nor is its design strongly based upon any original.

4.5 ENDNOTES

1. Roger Scruton, *The Aesthetics of Architecture*, 2nd ed. (New Jersey: Princeton University Press, 1980).

2. Sebastian Gardner, "Aesthetics," A.C. Grayling, editor, *Philosophy; A Guide Through The Subject* (Oxford University Press, 1995), p. 599.

3. Michael Kelly, editor in chief, *Encyclopedia of Aesthetics*, vol 1 (Oxford University Press, 1998), p. 243.

4. Scruton, pp. 179–187.

5. A. C. Pugin, *Gothic Ornaments Selected from Various Buildings in England and France* (1828–1831; reprinted as *Pugin's Gothic Ornament*, New York: Dover Publications, 1987), p. 81.

6. Gardner, p. 617, summarizes content from R. G. Collingwood, *The Principles of Art* (Oxford University Press, 1938).

7. Scruton, p. 7.

8. Peter Dormer, *The Meanings of Modern Design* (London: Thames and Hudson, 1990), p. 152.

9. Hanno-Walter Kruft, *A History of Architectural Theory from Vitruvius to the Present* (New York: Princeton Architectural Press, 1994), p. 211.

10. Albert B. LeCoff, ed., *Challenge V: International Lathe-Turned Objects* (Philadelphia: Wood Turning Center, 1993), p. 43.

11. Scruton, p. 38.

12. Gyorgy Doczi, *The Power of Limits* (Boston: Shambhala Publications, 1981).

13. Doczi, p. 144.

14. Robin Hopper, *Functional Pottery*, 2nd ed. (Iola, Wisconsin: Krause Publications, 2000), p. 94.

15. Kruft, p. 147.

16. John Ruskin, *The Seven Lamps of Architecture* (1849; reprint, New York: Dover Publications, 1989), p. 129.

17. Richard Eales, *Chess The History of a Game* (London: B.T. Batsford, 1985), pp. 66–67.

18. Edmund Burke, *A Philosophical Enquiry into the Origin of our Ideas of the Sublime and Beautiful* (1757; reprint, Oxford University Press, 1990), p. 85.

19. Scruton, pp. 210–211.

20. Scruton, p. 235.

21. Scruton, p. 211.

22. Scruton, p. 220.

23. Kruft, p. 322.

24. Leon Battista Alberti, *The Ten Books of Architecture* (1755 Leoni ed.; reprint, New York: Dover Publications, 1986), p.113.

25. Alberti, p. 203.

26. Ernst H. Gombrich, *The Sense of Order*, 2nd ed. (Oxford: Phaidon Press, 1984), p. 42.

27. Peter Dormer, "The ideal world of Vermeer's little lacemaker," *Design After Modernism*, John Thackara, ed., (London: Thames and Hudson, 1988), p. 142–143.

28. The illustrations are scanned from: Frederick Lichfield, *Illustrated History of Furniture* (London: Truslove & Hanson, 1893), p. 80; Thomas Chippendale, *The Gentleman & Cabinet-Maker's Director* (1762, reprint; New York: Dover Publications, 1966), plates XXXIV and XXXV; Thomas Sheraton, *The Cabinet-Maker and Upholsterer's Drawing-Book* (1793–1802, reprint; New York: Dover Publications, 1972), opposite p. 225; and, *The Victorian Cabinet-Makers Assistant* (1853, reprint; New York, Dover Publications, 1970), plate LXXXV.

29. David Springett, *Turning lace Bobbins* (Rugby, Warwickshire England: C & D Springett, 1995); and, Christine and David Springett, *Success to the Lace Pillow* (Rugby, Warwickshire, England: C & D Springett, 1997).

30. Michael Kenny, vol. 2, p. 412–415.

31. Anthony Kenny, ed., *The Oxford Illustrated History of Western Philosophy* (Oxford University Press, 1994), p. 210.

33. Geoffrey Killen, "Wood Turning in Ancient Egypt," *Turning Points* (Summer 1998), pp. 18–21.

34. Robin Wood, "In Praise of Rough Work," *Turning Points* (Winter 2001), pp. 26–29.

32. Barry Bergdoll, *European Architecture 1750–1890* (Oxford University Press, 2000), p. 173.

33. Kruft, pp. 98–101.

34. Kruft, pp. 85–86.

35. Kruft, p. 311.

36. Kruft, p. 364.

37. *The Theory of Decorative Art*, ed. Isabelle Frank (New Haven: Yale University Press, 2000), p. 188.

40. David Pye, *The Nature and Art of Workmanship* (Cambridge University Press, 1968) David Pye was Professor of Furniture Design, Royal College of Art, London, 1963 to 1974. His contribution to woodwork is described in *David Pye. Wood Carver and Turner* (London. Crafts Council, 1986).

41. Ruskin, p. 53.

42. Soetsu Yanagi, *The Unknown Craftsman* (Tokyo: Kodansha International, 1989), pp. 120–123.

43. Pye, p. 82.

44. Denis Sutton, *The Forger's Art* (University of California Press, 1983).

45. Excellent color illustrations of muffineers are shown in Jonathan Levi, *Treen for the Table* (Woodbridge, Suffolk: Antique Collectors' Club, 1998), pp. 84–90.

46. Victor Chinnery, *Oak Furniture The British Tradition* (Woodbridge, Suffolk: Antique Collectors' Club, 1979), pp. 561–569.

47. W. Crawley, *Is It Genuine?* (London: Eyre & Spottiswoode, 1971).

48. Borrowing is dicussed in Brent C. Brolin, *Flight of Fancy* (New York: St. Martin's Press, 1985), pp. 292–310; the quotation is on page 293. The use of borrowing rather than copying suggests that the borrowing designer does not intent to promote the borrowed idea as originating from him or her.

49. Edward H. Pinto, *Treen and Other Wooden Bygones* (London: G. Bell & Sons, 1969), pp. 296–297..

50. Fritz Spannagel, *Das Drechslerwerk* (1940; reprint, Hannover: Verlag Th. Schäfer, 1981), pp. 153, 161, 166.

ANSWERS ON THE PROPORTIONS OF CYLINDERS AND BOXES

Figure 4.17. *Left to right*, the heights of the cylinders in multiples of the diameter are: 1.0, 0.95, 1.05, and 1.1.

Figure 4.18. *Left to right*, the heights of the cylinders in multiples of the diameter are: 0.95, 1.1, 1.0, and 1.15.

Figure 4.19. *Left to right*, the heights of the boxes in multiples of the diameter are:1.5, 1.55, 1.62 (the Golden ratio), 1.75, and 1.85.

Chapter Five

STAGE 1 DESIGN

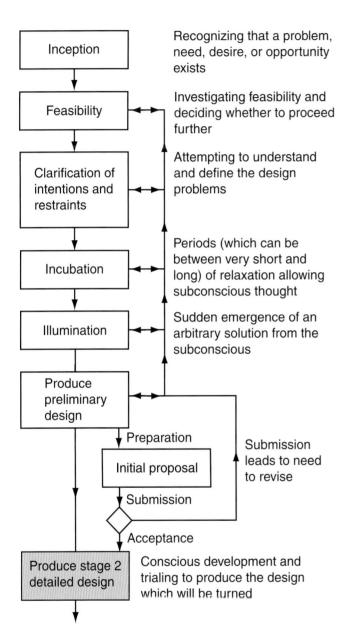

Inception — Recognizing that a problem, need, desire, or opportunity exists

Feasibility — Investigating feasibility and deciding whether to proceed further

Clarification of intentions and restraints — Attempting to understand and define the design problems

Incubation — Periods (which can be between very short and long) of relaxation allowing subconscious thought

Illumination — Sudden emergence of an arbitrary solution from the subconscious

Produce preliminary design

Preparation

Initial proposal — Submission leads to need to revise

Submission

Acceptance

Produce stage 2 detailed design — Conscious development and trialing to produce the design which will be turned

Figure 5.1 Stage 1 of the design process described by Brian Lawson, but amended to be compatible with figure 1.5.[1] The design process for a particular turning will not always include all seven steps, and may include much churning.

Illumination, with or without discernable incubation, can occur not just where shown above, but at any time during the design process. Illumination is also an essential part of the design process because it is the emergence of the arbitrary design solutions which you then trial and attempt to rationalize.

Stage 1 of the design process usually results in the creation of a preliminary design, and sometimes in the preparation of an initial design proposal. Stage 1 typically includes the seven steps in the yellow rectangles in figure 5.1. In this chapter I discuss those steps.

5.1 INCEPTION

The inception, the trigger which starts the process which may ultimately result in a turning, may be:

1. An approach from a client.
2. A suggestion from someone.
3. A turning or other object which the turner sees and decides to copy, improve, or develop.
4. The recognition of a functional need or a way to improve functionality.
5. Seeing an economic opportunity such as a way to lessen the production cost, or exploit or create a new market.
6. A desire to design a more beautiful example of a turning, or to design a turning which will cause a particular aesthetic reaction.
7. An idea which arises in the turner's mind for a fresh combination of preexisting ideas (figure 5.2) which can be communicated through the medium of a turning.
8. The realization that particular design restraints can be ignored.
9. Suggested by a particular species or piece of wood, other materials, a process, or an item of equipment.
10. A need, a desire, or an idea which has a personal rather than any public relevance.

5.1.1 SOURCES OF INSPIRATION

Microbiologist Louis Pasteur (1822–1895) said "Chance favors only the prepared mind". Such "An unexpected discovery, a chance observation, or simply a sudden crazy idea"[2] can be the inception or the illumination in figure 5.1. You can improve the probability and quality of such a chance happening not merely by being prepared, but by being proactive. Discussion and questioning may lead to ideas which you can reuse unaltered, or which you can develop, combine, or parody. You can also use techniques such as lateral thinking and brainstorming (pages 9 and 10), and search likely sources such as:

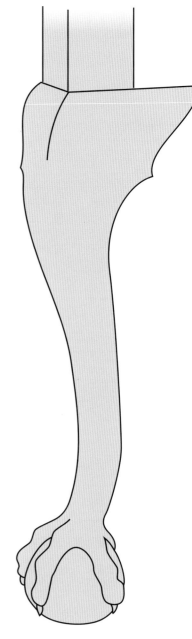

A cabriole leg with claw-and-ball foot.[3]

Figure 5.2 A fresh combination of ideas. Made in 1999 by Stephen Hogbin of Lake Charles, Ontario, Canada, thid table combines preexisting ideas in a new and conceptually ambiguous way.

The legs seemed to combine the eighteenth-century claw-and-ball foot (*above, right*) with Stephen's earlier salad servers (*next page, top, left*), although the two-way split of the salad servers has become a four-way split. For turning the legs, four separate pieces of wood were clamped together, not glued together with paper joints. The hollowing of each leg to house a ball could have been done as shown *next page, middle, left*.

The table-leg balls are in a darker wood to emphasise their separateness. Closer inspection showed that they were not housed in recesses in the bottom of the legs, but were glued *onto* the legs as shown in the diagram, *next page, bottom, left*. The sectors cut out of the balls are fitted to the stretchers.

The forms projecting upwards from the table top are fixed. They express the clutter usually left on tables. If a table top becomes and stays cluttered in normal use, Stephen asks, "Why should a table top be empty when you buy it?"

Salad servers by Stephen Hogbin which resemble the leg and the claw parts of a claw-and-ball feet.

Figure 5.3 **Sources of inspiration.** Egyptian ceramic vessels, 3850–3100 B.C., at the Virginia Museum of Fine Arts, Richmond. Vessel forms don't seem to have changed much over 5000 years. Photograph supplied by Virginia Museum of Fine Arts.

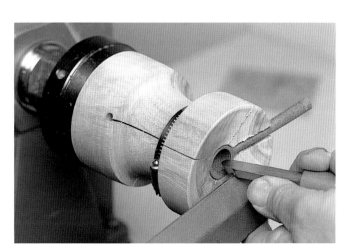

Hollowing the bowl of a spoon, a method which could be used to hollow the bottom of a leg to house a ball. This illustration appeared previously on page 143 of *Woodturning Methods*.

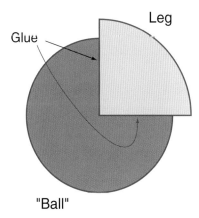

A horizontal section through a foot of Stephen Hogbin's table showing the construction used.

Figure 5.4 **An imitation of a spacecraft, *Voyager*.**

Figure 5.5 The Colosseum in Rome, and, in the next figure, a turning which it inspired.
Illustration from A. Rosengarten, *A Handbook of Architectural Styles*, trans. W. Collett-Sandars (London: Chatto and Windus, 1878), p. 138. The engraving was originally by Piranesi (page 230, figure 12.31).

1. Galleries, collections, exhibitions, and museums (figure 5.3).
2. Man-made forms and objects—pottery, silverware, machinery, plumbing components, and buildings are among the favorites (figures 5.4 to 5.6).
3. Natural forms including natural objects photographed at unusual magnifications; and shapes derived from animals, geological formations, and plants (figures 5.7 to 5.10).
4. Books, magazines, and websites which include content on:
   Antiques and treen (objects made from wood excluding furniture and building components).
   Archeology.
   Architecture (figures 5.5 and 5.6).
   Arts and crafts, including those which do not use wood and those from foreign cultures.
   Design.
   Fashion.
   Furniture and woodwork..
   Interior design.
   Marketing and publicity.
   Woodturning.
5. The media generally—especially if you intend your turning to communicate a political, environmental, or other message.

Figure 5.6 Inspired by the Colosseum, *Colosseo* by Dewey Garrett of Livermore, California; oak, 8 in. high x 14 in. diameter (200 mm x 350 mm).

The name "Colosseo" confirms the intention that the piece should echo the architecture of ancient Rome and in particular the Colosseum. The Colosseum had five storeys not two, was elliptical not circular in plan, and had its peripheral columns and entablatures vertically above one another; the column orders were also different on each storey (page 232, figure 12.34). Both tiers of *Colosseo*'s columns are similar to Roman Tuscan, but lack the astragals, fillets, congees, and abacuses proper to the Tuscan order. Do these departures matter? In my view "no" as *Colosseo* does not attempt to be a scale model, but an imitation "in the spirit of".

Figure 5.7 A natural form, a pine cone. Three turnings inspired by a pine cone's shape and texture are shown in the next three figures.

Figure 5.9 A box with a threaded lid, an ornamental-turning by Geoff O'Loughlin of Beaumaris, Victoria, Australia.

Figure 5.8 *Pine Cone* by Henri Groll of Sassenage, France. Turned in 1997 from black walnut, 6.5 in. high x 6 in. dia. (150 mm x 170 mm).

Figure 5.10 A cone box with vertical fins, also by Geoff O'Loughlin.

5.2 FEASIBILITY

After the inception, you have to decide whether to proceed further with the stage 1 design. Base your decision on your assessment of the likelihood of the design and turning process being successful. Your decision may be influenced by factors such as:

1. What is the client's budget? Is it elastic? Is it likely to be sufficient? Should you suggest differently priced options? The greater the client's confidence in you, the higher the budget is likely to be. You can raise the client's confidence by showing the client drawings, photographs, and examples of previous work. Showing sketches which lead to final designs for previous projects encourages a client to believe in your creativity and your ability to satisfy the special needs of individual clients.
2. Do you have the interest, the time, and the resources?
3. Can the inception be manifested? If "yes", by an acceptable commitment?
4. After reflection, is the inception as good as you first thought?
5. Is turning the appropriate technique to use? Is wood the appropriate material? Is wood of suitable size, species, and moisture content available and affordable?
6. Do you want or need to sell the turning? What is the likelihood of a sale at your required price if there is no commissioning client?

For this initial feasibility study you may need to do some rudimentary design, costing, and other research. If you keep and compare records of estimates and actual costs of earlier jobs, you will be able to estimate more accurately (figure 5.11). If you then decide to proceed, you might still churn back later in the design process to check and refine earlier information, assumptions, judgements, and decisions. At any stage before the completion of the turning it is possibe that a review will lead to a halt or to cancellation.

Job description:						
Job no.			Client:			
Day	Date	Worker	Start	Stop	Duration	Remarks
Total duration spent on job						

Materials used	Quantity	Rate	Total
Total cost of materials used			

Estimated materials	Quantity	Rate	Total
		Total	

Cost center	Estim'd	Actual	Difference
Labor Materials Design Subcontractors Supervision + overheads Cartage, postage, packing			
Cost totals			
Sale price			
Cost			
Gross profit			

Figure 5.11 A job card for recording estimated and actual costs. *Left*, the front of the card is for the turner to record the actual labor and materials used. *Right*, the rear of the card is used to summarize actual costs and calculate profits, and the differences between estimates and actual costs.

You can estimate the cost for a turning job by summing your cost estimates from the six cost centers listed in the center of the back of the card. The hourly rate you charge could be based on what you need to earn, or what similar local businesses or tradespeople charge. If you cannot make sales if you charge based on the rates of other tradespeople, you might then reduce this rate using a *desperation divider*. Turners who are very successful might still be able to sell after multiplying the other-tradespeople-based rate by a *fame factor* greater than one.

Your estimate of the sale price may include contingencies in the gross profit. If selling direct to the public or a client, you should add a retail mark-up so that your sale price doesn't undercut that charged by retailers who sell your work. You may also need to include government taxes.

5.3 INTENTIONS

A major reason for formalizing the design process is to force the designer to clearly define his or her intentions, what he or she should be trying to achieve with and through a design. These intentions can be classified as:[2]

1. *Reproductive.*
2. *Functional.*
3. *Economic.*
4. *Aesthetic,* intended to cause an experiencer to have a particular aesthetic reaction.
5. *Communicative.*
6. *Focused on the materials, techniques, or equipment used.*
7. *Personal and not necessarily intended to be apparent to others.*

Classifying intentions is not an exact science, so do not be too concerned by any untidiness when you attempt to list your intentions for a turning. You will also have to rank your choice of intentions when they conflict in order to choose between them. And you may need to change the rankings and add or ignore intentions during the design and production processes. The final intentions manifested in the finished turning may thus be much different to your initial intentions.

If you intend your design to be experienced by others, you should attempt to forecast how your intentions and their manifestation the turning will be received by intended or likely experiencers. The greater your ability to do this and make any appropriate design changes, the greater the likelihood that the turning will be appreciated as you intended.

5.3.1 REPRODUCTIVE INTENTIONS

The reproductive intention is primary when you wish to design replacements or copies. It should be, and usually is, mated with an intention to improve on the original when the original does not have to be copied exactly.

The intention to work in a particular style is also reproductive (figures 5.5 and 5.6). It is also often associated with aesthetic and communicative intentions.

5.3.2 FUNCTIONAL INTENTIONS

A sewing needle is one of the few purely functional man-made objects. If you design useful objects which are only slightly more complicated, you have to clarify intentions and make choices in other areas besides function (figure 5.12).

"Intended to be useful" as demonstrated in figures 5.12 and 5.13 is not the only meaning of "functional". Jean-Nicolas-Louis Durand had supported *economic* functionalism early in the nineteenth century (page 30). More recently, David Pye stressed that functional is often abused as a catch-all adjective meaning cheap, streamlined, light in weight, having the lowest price, or convenient.[4] For example, the most structurally efficient form for a leg or other structural spindle would vary somewhat in diameter along its length. If you elect to use a dowel, this is usually an economic decision and has little to do with function.

The intentions that turnings shall be "used" as ornaments or shall "function" as works of art are generally aesthetic and communicative. The intentions to ridicule function displayed in figures 5.14 to 5.17 could be classified as functional, but are more accurately regarded as communicative.

Figure 5.12 The designs of rolling pins, which are supposedly purely functional, result from both arbitrary and rational decisions.

Arbitrary decisions may include the detailed shape, wood, and color of the handles.

The size and shape of the roller is largely an economic/functional choice. Whether the handles and roller are integral, the handles are glued into the roller, or there is a mechanism so that the roller can rotate freely with respect to the handles is largely an economic choice.

Figure 5.13 A functional turning, a Chinese wooden vibrator for muscle relief. Turning the handle rotates the slightly-out-of-balance weights shown in the bottom photograph at high speed. This causes the head of the machine to vibrate. Photographed courtesy of The Village Pump Antiques, Exeter, New South Wales.

Figure 5.14 Ridiculing function, *The Bush Potty.*
The trigger was an invitation to enter an exhibition called The Po Show in 1981. Brainstorming suggested possible desirable features which were developed as suitable branches and other natural materials were found.

This has every convenience for those "caught short" in the Australian bush: there is a scraper, a brush made from the flower head of a banksia tree, and soft paperbark from the tree *Melaleuca quinquinervia* held in place by counterweight-operated lever. The functional intent is clearly little more than a peg on which to hang humorous and risqué communicative intents.

I also did the painting and frame. The corner blocks of the frame are turned to imitate squash.

Figure 5.17 **The plug removed.**

Figure 5.15 **The wondrous facilities of *The Bush Potty* in close-up.**

Figure 5.16 **A functional *plug bowl*.** The plug enables the bowl to be emptied without inversion and thus more easily.

5.3.3 ECONOMIC INTENTIONS

An economic intention can be chosen by the designer, or can be imposed by a real client or one imagined by the turner. A common economic intention is to restrict the cost and/or the employment of resources to the minimum or to below a specified level. This specified level may be based on the client's budget, a selling price, a production time, a cost of wood, etc. An economic intention may cause the turner to modify a design to use a particular piece of wood to avoid having to buy another, or to use wood which would otherwise be waste (figure 5.18).

Economic intentions can lead to an increase in cost and an increased employment of resources. You may decide to use more costly woods because they turn better and produce a net cost saving. For turnings in some woods, because of promotion or because of their appearance, you can charge a premium which makes the woods' extra costs worthwhile. And there are unique and notable individual tree specimens which have associations which are deemed worth remembering and exploiting; for example, the mulberry from Shakespeare's garden (figure 4.60, page 80). The intentions described in this paragraph are related to or could also be classified as material intentions (pages 103 to 108).

One way to reduce unit costs is to produce more of a turning. You may then need a new marketing strategy to shift the greater production (figure 5.19). You may also find the repetitive turning less enjoyable.

Plagiarism, forging, undercharging, and overcharging are usually economic intentions. Faking to deceive or for revenge would be a personal intention.

Economy is both the friend and enemy of turning. Being a relatively speedy shaping process, turning is favoured where funds are insufficient for carving. If funds are too limited, a spindle turning can be just turned to a dowel or, worse, be left unturned except for any connecting pins.

Figure 5.18 The satisfaction of multiple intentions. The functional intention is that of play. The economic intention is that they should be inexpensive and therefore likely to sell in large numbers.

These tops can often be made from scrap wood, an economic benefit. Their appeal is enhanced by each being named with its wood species—a communicative intention. Having them for sale in a variety of species (a material intention) increases the likelihood of a buyer buying several, and assists experiencers in wood species identification—another communicative intention.

The uniqueness of the wood of each tree species is a valuable marketing aid. Until man started shifting species from their native habitats, every species grew in specific and restricted regions. Even now when many species are grown far outside the regions to which they are native, particular species are still associated with particular areas or countries; for example, maples are still associated with Canada, and the kauri with New Zealand.

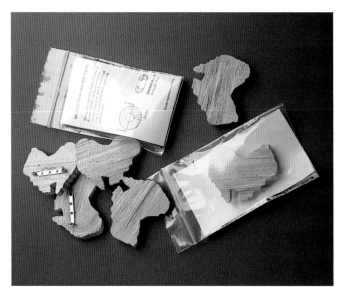

Figure 5.19 A brooch imitating Australia. The economic/communicative intention was to produce a turned Australian wooden souvenir of low cost. The trigger was the thought that I could exploit the technique of riving rings (*Woodturning Techniques*, pages 93 to 97).

5.3.4 AESTHETIC INTENTIONS

People respond to objects aesthetically. You should therefore design each turning to cause a particular aesthetic response in those who will experience it (figure 5.20).

Designers often intend their designs to be beautiful. Other equally-valid aesthetic intentions include that a turning should be striking, angular, flowing, or ugly. An intention to conform to a known style is aesthetic if the reason for the conformity is aesthetic, or communicative if you intend that experiencers should recognize the style; both intentions often apply.

Aesthetic intentions need not be primarily emotional; they can include intellectual exercises associated with form, such as novel arrangements of cylinders, spheres, and cones (figure 5.21).

A common aesthetic intention is that a turning should harmonize, share stylistic features, with its intended surroundings (figures 5.22 and 5.23).

Figure 5.20 **An aesthetic intention strengthened by downplaying woodiness, *Volume* by Maria van Kesteren** of the Netherlands. The legend to this illustration on page 128 of *Enter the World of Lathe-Turned Objects* included: "She designs and executes pure forms . . . Van Kesteren explores the radial symmetry of circular forms and employs color to downplay the grain in the wood".[5] Photograph supplied by The Wood Turning Center, Philadelphia.

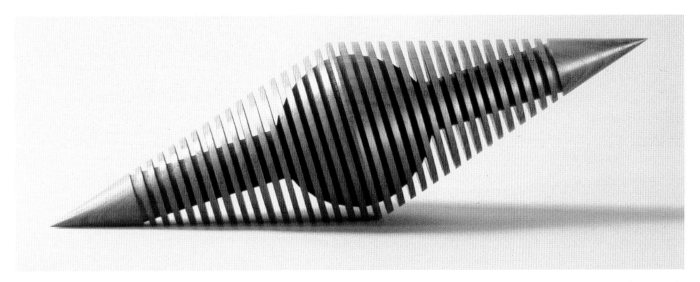

Figure 5.21 ***Double Cone/Sphere* (1995) by Timothy Stokes of Great Britain;** black walnut, 14.5 in. (370 mm) long. Geometric playfulness is an intention which is common in postmodern design. Here there is also the communicative intention to symbolize (represent) inner and outer existences to experiencers. Finned forms were popular in the 1990s (figures 5.8 to 5.10.) The finned turnings shown in figures 5.38 to 5.40 are turned in unseasoned wood in order to exploit the subsequent distortion which accompanies seasoning. Photograph supplied by The Wood Turning Center.

Figure 5.23 **The interior of the banking chamber of the Bank of Victoria in Melbourne.** The chair in figure 5.22 is one of the set pictured which was made in about 1860. The chairs were probably designed by architect J. Ross Anderson who also designed the interior of the Bank's head office. This photograph suggests that the chair backs were intended to echo the circularity of the table and of the banking chamber. Comfort was unimportant as the chairs were designed to seat the bank's customers, and only for a short duration. Photograph and information courtesy J. B. Hawkins Antiques, Moss Vale, New South Wales.

Figure 5.22 **A chair which is exceedingly uncomfortable because of its turned back.** I wondered why this obvious and major design fault had been allowed in such a finely-made chair. When I later saw the photograph above, it was clear that design harmony had been the dominant intention.

5.3.5 COMMUNICATIVE INTENTIONS

As the market for art woodturnings grows, the communicative intention becomes more important. Successful communication depends on the the designer and the experiencer having sufficient conceptual knowledge in common for the imitation and/or representation to be perceived by the experiencer. Communicative intentions can be manifested in the form of:

1. A *sign* such as that in figure 5.24.
2. An *imitation or a representation*. An imitation requires an experiencer to have just sufficient knowledge to *recognize* the subject (figures 5.25 to 5.27), a representation requires an experiencer to have sufficient knowledge to *understand* the subject represented (figures 5.28 and 5.29).
3. A *pun, parody, or similar* (figures 5.28 and 5.29).
4. A *boast*. Technique is a common area in which to boast— I can turn bigger, or thinner, or am more skilled (figure 5.30).
5. *Conformance to a style*. Use of a particular, recognizable style may increase saleability or status.
6. A *rejection*, commonly of function (figure 5.31). Is the absence or rejection of function a necessary property of a work of art?

Designers and turners can also seek to convey expression. For this to be successful, the designer and experiencer must have an appropriate emotional empathy, the experiencer may also need the conceptual knowledge to be able to distinguish expression from, say, rough workmanship.

Figure 5.25 **Imitative *Deepings Dolls*** turned by Adrian Hunt and painted by Marie Boots. "The Deepings" is the name of the Hunts' property in Tasmania. The intentions are to generate income through selling craftsmanship, draftsmanship, and nostalgia. Such pieces appeal to doll collectors and are often bought as souvenirs.

Some doll designs are associated with particular countries rather than with particular turners; for example, the nutcracker dolls of Germany, and the Matroshka dolls of Russia (figure 10.11).

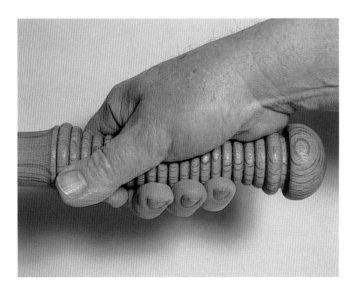

Figure 5.24 **The reeding is a sign that the truncheon should be gripped there.**

Figure 5.26 **A manifestation of imitative, functional, economic, and communicative intentions.** A buffet tray, toothpick holder, and souvenir in the shape of a Mexican sombrero. (Hayman Island is in Australia, not Mexico). The 11.5 in. (290 mm) dia. tray was turned by Frank O'Brien of Rocklea, Queensland.

Figure 5.27 An imitative turned souvenir which communicates by reminding the buyer of a building or of a building style common in the area visited.

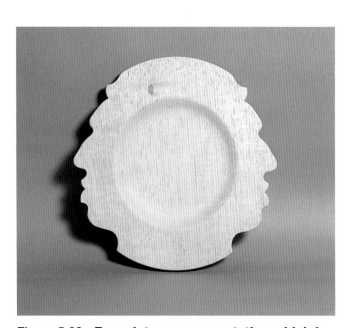

Figure 5.28 *Faceplate*, a representation which is a pun or equivoque. The titles of works should assist experiencers to understand the works—too often titles mystify or suggest that the work is an artifice. Only an experiencer who is familiar with lathe accessories will "get" this pun.

The inception for *Faceplate* was seeing a similar plate by Stephen Hogbin with facial outlines which he had carved into the turned rim. Here the faces are turned into the rim with the workpiece mounted on second turning-axis passing through a diameter (here vertical) of the plate.

Figure 5.29 A representational turning, *The Russian Caravan Teapot*. Those experiencers whose conceptual knowledge does not include the Russian caravan blend of tea might "get" the imitation, but cannot "get" the representational pun.

This teapot does pour and is therefore nominally functional. However, as it implicitly ridicules its functionality, must it be art? There were also economic intentions: to be an entry for a teapot exhibition and sale, and to thus gain publicity and commissions, and be able to charge more for future works.

Figure 5.30 **A boast,** a translucent bowl 0.5 mm thick over its whole surface. The thinness eliminates any pretense at functionality. It is a demonstration of skill.

Figure 5.31 **A drip scoop.** Does its rejection of function mean that it is art? If so, is it an example of significant art?

5.3.6 MATERIAL INTENTIONS

Turning designers exploit their working materials, primarily wood, to manifest their intentions, but the properties of working materials can also trigger intentions. As your knowledge of materials' properties grows, more intentions will be triggered, and you will be better able to select and exploit materials to realize design intentions. The properties of woods which you can exploit include:

1. *Colors which are particular to a species* (figure 5.32). These colors can be used singly, or be exploited by decorative conglutination (pages 180 to 184, and *Woodturning Techniques*, pages 25 to 28).
2. *Color variations and patterns within single pieces of wood.* These include those due to prominent medullary rays,

sapwood/heartwood contrasts (figure 5.33), layers of differently colored cells and areas of contorted grain (figures 5.34 to 5.36). Insect or bacterial attacks (rot) can also create color effects (figures 5.34 and 5.44).

3. *Bent and contorted grain.* Wood with straight and axial grain is usually preferred for use in structures. Pieces of wood with bent grain are preferred for the knees of boat frames. The contorted grain of burls ensures that vessels turned from them are dimensionally stable.

Figure 5.32 **Exploiting the different colors of woods,** *Double-Wall Ball Box* **by Hans Joachim Weissflog** of Hildesheim, Germany; African blackwood and boxwood, 3.2 in. (80 mm) diameter.

Figure 5.33 **Sapwood/heartwood contrast in a lignum vitae barrel,** 5.5 in. high x 7 in. dia. (140 mm x 180 mm). This turning is imitative because of its barrel shape and the bands, functionally redundant but imitating the iron hoops used to hold barrel staves together. Photographed courtesy of Connor Galleries, Moss Vale, New South Wales.

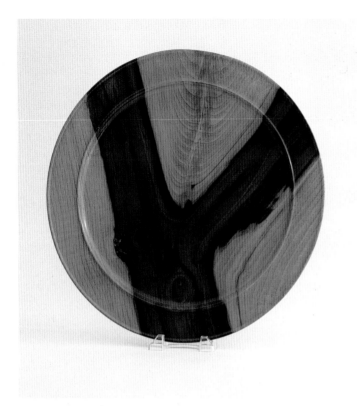

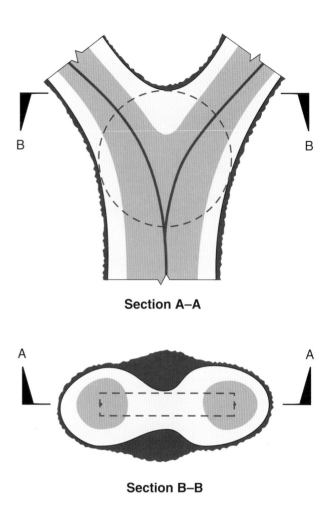

Section A–A

Section B–B

Figure 5.34 **Crotch figure and bacterial staining contrast** in a *Magnolia grandiflora* platter turned by Wayne Shipman of Walnut Creek, California. The blank has to be carefully cut and the form designed so that the crotch figure is retained in the tuning (figure 5.36). This platter is 18 in. (450 mm) in diameter.

Figure 5.36 **The extent of crotch figure.** It is restricted to a narrow layer shown dashed, and lies mainly in the triangle between the piths.

Figure 5.35 **A raised platter is another form which enables the crotch figure to be retained and displayed in the finished turning.** The stem is hollowed (page 210, figure 11.2).

4. *Hardness, softness, heaviness, and lightness.*
5. *Toughness.* Tough (both hard and springy) woods such as ash, hickory, and spotted gum are used for axe, hammer, and other tool handles, chair frames, etc.
6. A *reluctance to split.* Elm is used for wheel hubs and for English Windsor chair seats because when seasoned it is reluctant to split. Woods which split easily are preferred for shingles.
7. *The ability to turn and machine well.*
8. *Silica inclusions.* Teak, Queensland walnut, and brush box are among the species which contain free silica, and rapidly blunt cutting edges. They are however hard wearing and therefore excellent for flooring.
9. *Wax or oil content which imparts water resistance and an ability to lubricate.* Lignum vitae was used for the outer bearings of boats' propeller shafts.
10. *Low shrinkage during seasoning.* The differences between woods' three shrinkage coefficients requires special joints to allow for wood movement in some types of wood construction. Woods which have low shrinkage coefficients are therefore preferred, other properties being equal, for components. Woods with lower shrinkage coefficients also suffer less degrade during seasoning. In some forms of wood construction, such as Windsor chairs, the parts have different moisture contents when they are assembled so that the damper parts will shrink onto the fully-seasoned parts and hold them tightly.
11. *High shrinkage during seasoning* is desirable in only a small number of situations (figures 5.37 to 5.42).
12. *Thermoplasticity.* When the temperature of wood is raised above 80°C, the lignin which binds the cellulose together softens. The wood can then be bent. When the wood is allowed to cool the lignin hardens, and the new shape is retained.
13. *Calorific value.* In some parts of the world, wood is still much used for heating and cooking. Charring is used in art turning to produce blackness and texture.
14. *Resonance.* Some woods are preferred for musical instruments because of their superior acoustic properties.
15. *Smell or its absence.* The true cedars and camphor laurel are often used in furniture for clothing storage because their smell repels moths. Woods used to store food should not smell.
16. *Susceptibility or resistance to rot and insect attack.* Woods which spalt reliably and attractively are kept by some woodturners in conditions which promote spalting (figure 5.44). Timbers rich in extractives, such as western red cedar, are resistant to attack.
17. *Translucency.* Wood becomes translucent when turned thinly, especially if pale in color (figures 5.45 and 5.46). This property can be used to monitor wall thickness during the turning of thin-walled vessels.

Figure 5.38 Vessel by Paul Clare of Great Britain; 6 in. high x 6.8 in. dia. (150 mm x 170 mm). The deep parting cuts into the wet burl oak enabled the fins to distort independently as they seasoned. In contrast to the turnings in figures 5.21 and 5.39, the shape of the core left after the parting cuts is both hidden and unimportant.
Photograph supplied by The Wood Turning Center.

Figure 5.37 A poppadum bowl turned in 1980 illustrates how wood with high shrinkage coefficients can distort as it seasons. The extreme distortion is also due to the use of crotch wood. The wood is peppermint gum

18. *The regional specificities of tree species, and the associations which particular specimens or particular pieces of wood have.* Some trees are individually well known, and objects made from their wood can be more desirable because of the tree's associations.

19. *Large sizes* are becoming relatively rarer and more prized.

20. *Cost and rarity.* These are related to what's left rather than what was.

21. *Holes, cracks, and other naturally-occurring features which would usually cause the wood to be scrapped* (figure 5.43).

22. *The turnability of nuts, cones, and seed cases.*

23. *Mixed media*, the combination of wood with other materials (figure 5.47).

Figure 5.40 *Big Fish, Little Fish II* **by Marlowe McGraw** of Louisiana. Wood's limited plasticity and the distortion and shrinkage which occur as wood seasons enable the two forms to grip each other long-term. Bleached madrone; 6 in. (150 mm) high. Photograph supplied by The Wood Turning Center, Philadelphia.

Figure 5.39 *Shifting Currents* **by Melvyn Firmager** of Wedmore, Somerset; 11 in. high x 6.5 in. dia. (280 mm x 165 mm).

The species used, *Eucalyptus gunnii*, Alpine cider gum, has circular juvenile leaves which have no perceptible stalk. The turned form therefore echoes the juvenile leaves. The two forms at the top of the turning also echo eucalyptus seed cases (gum nuts), although they are squatter than the gum nuts of *E. gunnii*.

Figure 5.41 **A madrone hat worn by its maker Johannes Michelsen** of Manchester Center, Vermont. By turning the form to a 1/16 in. (1.5 mm) wall thickness, the form is free to go oval and curl under the action of its differential shrinkage coefficients as it seasons. To increase curling, the hat is seasoned in a bending rack (next figure).

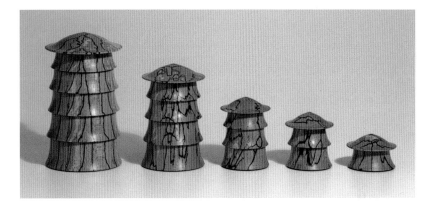

Figure 5.42 Johannes Michelsen's bending rack. The rubber bands force the brim to curl more as it seasons. So that this curling will be towards the crown of the hat, the brim lies within a layer parallel to a diameter through the log with the top of the crown close to the bark.

Figure 5.44 Spalted-beech, tiered, pagoda boxes by Ray Key of Bretforton, Worcestershire. Spalting is an intermediate stage in rot. These forms combine a Chinese pagoda with the traditional, cylindrical, European spice tower.[6]

Figure 5.43 A spalted yellow birch bowl (1981) by Mark Lindquist of Quincy, Florida; 28 in. (710 mm) diameter. Instead of scrapping the blank because of its seasoning cracks, Mark transformed them into an asset.

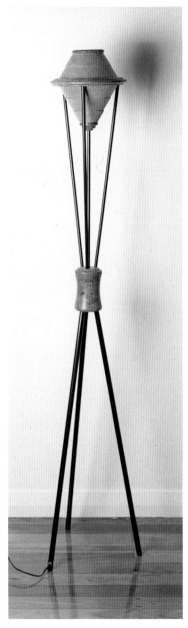

Figure 5.46 A translucent bowl by Ron Kent of Kailua, Hawaii; 9 in. high x 15 in. dia. (230 mm x 380 mm).

After turning and fine sanding, the pine bowl is immersed in Danish oil for a minimum of 12 hours, wiped dry, and allowed to stand for at least 24 hours. This cycle is repeated at least a dozen times. A second and different cycle is then repeated several-dozen times. For this second cycle the Danish oil is rubbed into the surface with wet-and-dry abrasive paper for about 15 minutes, then allowed to dry for 24 hours or more. The oil polymerizes and gradually builds up within the wood expressing any air to leave the wood with an amber-like translucence.

Figure 5.45 A standard lamp by Michael Cassidy of Exeter, New South Wales. The shade has not been sealed or polished, and is not therefore as translucent as, for example, Ron Kent's bowl shown in the next figure.

Figure 5.47 Mixed media, *The Green Submarine*. The title was inspired by the Beatles' yellow one, but the form was inspired by the silver-mounted, emu-egg inkwells made by nineteenth-century Australian silversmiths.

5.3.7 TECHNIQUE AND EQUIPMENT

The exploration or exploitation of a particular technique or item of equipment is a common intention in woodturning. There are economic gains such as enabling the operation to be done better, faster, and with less risk. Operations which were previously impossible may become possible, but there is not always an aesthetic gain. When there is, fame and fortune, generally alas of the modest variety, may follow. Examples include: David Ellsworth and his development of hollow turning; and Stephen Hogbin's explorations in which he saws turnings into parts, and reassembles the parts from each turning into a new form (pages 111 and 112).

Intentions in this category need not be associated with exploring through *forward* development; they can involve self-imposed restrictions. Figure 5.48 shows one example, and as detailed on page 66, Robin Wood has been successful through rejecting not just electric power, but the Great Wheel, and the treadle.

5.3.8 PERSONAL

Turners produce turnings for reasons which may not be apparent to later experiencers. Turnings such as practice pieces and trials of new tools or techniques, for example, may have been intended for the scrap bin, not for public display.

Figure 5.48 A *Lopez* chess set. The inception was the desire to design a chess set which did not need any carving (a personal intention, and one also associated with technique, or rather the exclusion of one). This sparked the arbitrary illumination to use cones for the bodies. The use of woods of different colors, the grading of the heights, and the differentiation of the heads result from the traditional and functional restraint that the Lopez men should echo the standard Staunton pattern and thus be instantly recognizable to any Western chess player.

5.4   RESTRAINTS

Restraints are obstacles. They may block your intended design path and force you to give up, may cause you to detour, or may force you to branch onto a different path. You may have direct knowledge of some restraints; others may be your assessments. Many restraints are unconsciously accepted; others flow from the intentions which you have chosen because every decision to pursue an intention imposes a restraint.

Restraints may result from:

1. *Convention or tradition* (figure 5.49).
2. *The dictate of function.* The more efficiently a turning design fulfils its intended function, the more its form and size are prescribed. This truism perhaps explains the antagonism between art and function.
3. *The subject turning being a component, or one of a series.* Factors which may be prescribed in a series include: the proportions, the dimensions of each member of the series, the wood species and grain directions, the design style, and any decoration and finishing.
4. *The choice of a style* restrains design freedom by limiting the types of detail which are appropriate.
5. *The limitations of the available materials.* For example, the species you want to use may not be available seasoned in large sizes.
6. *The limitations of the available resources.* Is the readily available equipment suitable? Are their enough people with suitable skills available?
7. *Shortcomings in turning and other skills.* Some turners compromise their designs by excluding design elements which they would find risky to produce.
8. *Insufficient time.*
9. *Client instructions.*
10. *Your assessments of what design features are acceptable and, where relevant, affordable.*
11. *The intentions to use other techniques.* For example, the specks of color in the boxes in figure 5.50 are produced by exposing dowels glued into drilled holes. The preferred forms for the box bodies are therefore cylindrical or conical. Robin Wood's use of a pole lathe is another example (page 66),
12. *The tyrannies of turned roundness and symmetry* which restrain us from exploring other design avenues (figures 5.51 to 5.53, and 5.55).
13. *The assumption that wood surfaces must be fine-sanded.*
14. *The sacredness of wood* which results in a powerful reluctance to hide it beneath paint or similar.
15. *The convention that hollowed turnings should have even wall thicknesses.* This is a pottery-firing imperative which is largely irrelevant to wooden workpieces which are already seasoned. It imposes the restraint that the turning's outside and the inside surfaces shall closely follow one another.
16. *The unthinking acceptance that an earlier design is a summit of design excellence*, and can be reused with, at most, minor modifications.
17. *Good practice.* The sound ways of working and turning wood impose restraints which may unnecessarily limit design freedom; they are discussed on pages 162 and 163.

Restraints can also be internal. Summoning the will to start is among the most powerful..

Figure 5.49 **Restrained by the unchanging ritual of the Japanese tea ceremony.** Innovation in the design of the form of Japanese tea boxes (*natsumes*) is actively discouraged. Their special lid design is detailed in figure 10.17C.

Figure 5.50 *Boxes with Lines and Dots* **by Hans Joachim Weissflog** of Hildesheim, Germany; 2 in. (48 mm) dia. The decoration is revealed by the ornament.

Figure 5.51 A *Walking Bowl* **by Stephen Hogbin** of Lake Charles, Ontario. Made in 1999, it ignores the turning convention (restraint) "roundness is inviolate". It was produced by gluing together the two halves of a *cup-on-a-board* turning in a fresh way. The separation of the two halves is described in the next figure.

The form is as though a walking bowl was suddenly frozen in mid-stride.

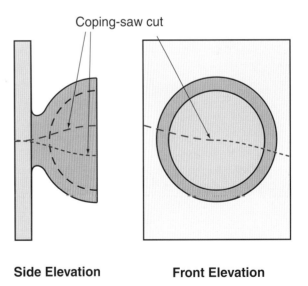

Coping-saw cut

Side Elevation   **Front Elevation**

Figure 5.52 Sawing apart a cup-on-a-board turning to create the components for a walking bowl.

The type of movement implied can be varied by altering the relative rotation between the two "halves", and by changing the form of the turning.

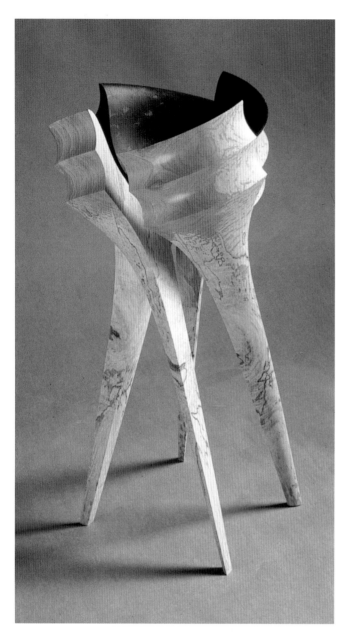

Figure 5.53 Further restraints rejected. *Progress of Walking, Happenstance* by Stephen Hogbin (2000). The walking bowl in the preceding figure conformed to the restraint "when parts are reassembled, the form should flow continuously across the joint". Rejecting that restraint lead to the rejection of two others: "the original form shall be cut into two pieces", and "there shall be no open joints".

This static piece implies movement by resembling a snapshot of a moving object (*frozen motion*). You can also imply movement in a static object by designing the object to be unstable (figure 4.9), or to resemble something which we associate with movement (figure 6.28).

5.4.1 EXPLOITING RESTRAINTS

We usually properly take into account the restraints we are conscious of when designing. It is the restraints we accept unconsciously which unnecessarily limit our designs. Many of the triggers for new designs are conscious realizations that an unconsciously accepted restraint need not restrain. Thus figures 5.51 to 5.53 show how movement can be expressed through turning by rejecting the sacred restraint of roundness.

We are not conscious of many restraints because they have merit, and our minds wisely save us from consciously questioning them again and again. Simply choosing to reject these meritorious restraints may lead to poor functionality or bizarreness. The better approach is to:

1. Define and list all the restraints, investigate them, and then decide which to retain and which to scrap. Scrapping a restraint unlocks an infinitely-vast hall crammed with infinite number of new design choices. It also shuts the access door to the hall of the restraint which was previously accepted.
2. Trial the replacement of existing restraints with new ones.

Figure 5.54 *Floorwalker* by C. R. "Skip" Johnson of Stoughton, Wisconsin. Frozen motion is suggested by its articulated 20 in. (510 mm) high structure.

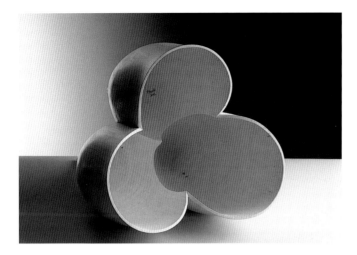

Good designers naturally do these two steps more and better than poor designers, and may be able to process more variables simultaneously. The value of exploring restraints is demonstrated in the designing of watch stands in figures 5.56 to 5.59. The examples also illustrate how challenging one restraint often sets of a chain reaction which results in the challenging of other restraints.

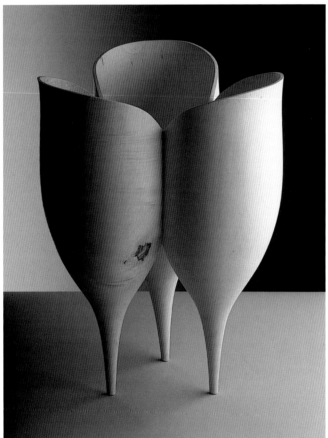

Figure 5.55 *Not Walking but Standing*, **a vessel conglutinated from three identical turnings by Peter Hromek** of Sinntal, Germany. This vessel is static, in contrast to Stephen Hogbin's walking vessel in figure 5.53.

The surfaces don't flow through the joints, but meet symmetrically at them. The technique of combining turnings is described on page 18 of *Woodturning Techniques*.

Bowls of similar but less elongated form have been carved from single pieces of wood in Scandinavia from medieval times.[7]

Figure 5.56   An eighteenth-century watch stand. This is a practical, economic, and aesthetically attractive design which has been in continuous production for well over two centuries in various forms (*Woodturning Techniques*, page 92, figure 5.19).

Watch stands enabled a pocket watch to function as a bedside clock when the watch's owner was not wearing his or her day clothes. Watch stands now tend to be used to permanently display pocket watches. Photographed courtesy of J. B. Hawkins Antiques, Moss Vale, New South Wales.

Figure 5.57 A Holtzapffel watch-stand design published in 1881 which essentially reproduces the eighteenth-century design shown in the preceding figure.[8]

The continuation of the basic form suggests that there were no strong market pressures to change its design during the nineteenth century. Equally, there may not have been any market pressures not to change its design. Where there have been no relevant technological advances, external pressures for design change come from feedback from the market, and new and successful designs from other designers.

This design conforms to many restraints, most of which were unconsciously accepted as valid by Holtzapffel. These restraints include:

1. The arch shall be semicircular.
2. The arch's radial cross section shall be constant and symmetrical.
3. The columns shall be vertical.
4. The columns shall project perpendicularly from the top surface of the base.
5. The columns shall be fully turned.
6. The columns shall be turned on one central turning-axis.
7. The columns shall be identical.

8. There shall be two columns.
9. The base shall essentially be of even thickness.
10. The base shall be fully turned.
11. The style of ornament shall be eighteenth or nineteenth century.
12. The stand shall be symmetrical about a vertical centerline.
13. The watch shall hang from a central, small, brass hook.
14. One species of wood shall be used.
15. The wood shall be unstained and clear finished.

Scrap one of the first thirteen restraints and any others which intimately associated, and a new infinitely large family of forms becomes possible. Scrap more restraints, and the scope for new families of forms widens further. However, introduce too much design freedom and the mind cannot cope.

Figure 5.58 Another Holtzapffel watch-stand design published in 1881 which ignores restraints 1, 3, and 9 listed in the legend of figure 5.57. Ignoring the restraint to keep the columns vertical while retaining restraint 4 required that restraint 9 be ignored.[9]

This stand is more costly in wood and labor, and less functional because there is not a recess between the pillars for the watch chain. I suggest that it is also less aesthetically attractive.

Figure 5.59 **A watch stand design which ignores figure 5.57 restraints 1 to 4, 6, 7, 11, 12, and 14.** Its design was triggered by a demonstration by Rémi Verchot (figure 10.2, page 197), and also owes much to the work of Mark Sfirri (*Woodturning Methods*, pages 123 to 124).

Figure 5.60 **The building blocks for any design.** The basic blocks are shown in the two columns on the left and the column on the right. Any elevation of, or section through, a form can be produced by distorting, rotating, and cutting away parts of blocks, and by combining blocks by stacking, overlaying, and subtraction.

5.5 INCUBATION AND ILLUMINATION

During the process of designing a turning you should try to allow time for subconscious processing to yield illuminations. There is no minimum length of time which is necessary or advisable for a successful incubation, nor any guarantee that one or more illuminations will result, nor that their quality will be high.

At some time during stage 1 you will need to commit something to paper or its equivalent. How far you develop this first design to produce the preliminary design will vary from situation to situation.

5.6 THE PRELIMINARY DESIGN

The culmination of stage 1 is the preliminary design with, when appropriate, the initial design proposal. You produce the preliminary design after any combination of:

1. Subconsciously selecting, combining, and developing forms and ideas held or taken into your conceptual knowledge. After an incubation, your subconscious outputs an illumination. There may, of course, be a succession of incubations and illuminations mixed with analysis, research, and decision-making.
2. Selecting existing designs to copy, adapt, or combine.
3. Attempting to synthesize a form by combining form building blocks as described in figure 5.60.

Although many woodturners designers design alone, involving others through brainstorming or asking them their opinions can bring great benefits.

5.7 THE INITIAL DESIGN PROPOSAL

The scope and formality that is appropriate for an initial design proposal will depend on the circumstances, especially whether you or someone else is the client, your relationship with the client, and the cost involved.

A formal initial design proposal might include the following:

1. The preliminary design, plus if appropriate, design alternatives.
2. A schedule for any further design, and for the production.
3. A specification of the materials and processes.
4. A specification of the quality of the workmanship, including the accuracy of the dimensions of the finished object to the design, and qualities of the finished surfaces, including the fineness of any sanding.
5. Contract terms; including the costs, the timings and amounts of client payments, and a dispute resolution procedure.

Where there is an external client, the presentation of the initial design proposal, not just its content, is likely to influence its acceptance. The drawings may be sketchy and/or formal and highly finished. The proposal may include photographs, etc. of earlier projects, an offer to arrange for an inspection of earlier projects, samples, and models.

5.8 ENDNOTES

1. Robin Roy and David Wield, eds., *Product Design and Technological Innovation* (Milton Keynes: Open University Press, 1986), p. 61.
2. Roy and Wield, p. 60.
3. Also known as a talon-and-ball foot, it was introduced into England late in the sixteenth century. It is particularly associated with English furniture in the period 1720 to 1760. John Gloag, A *Short Dictionary of Furniture* (London: George Allen and Unwin, 1969), pp. 229–230.
4. David Pye, *The Nature and Aesthetics of Design* (New York: Van Nostrand Reinhold, 1968), p. 13.
5. Judson Randall, ed., *Enter the World of Lathe-Turned Objects* (York, Pennsylvania: York Graphic Services, 1997), p. 128.
6. Spice towers are stacks of identically shaped and sized small boxes in which the base of a box locates with the lid of the box below. They are pictured in: Jonathan Levi, *Treen for the Table* (Woodbridge, Suffolk: Antique Collectors' Club, 1998), p. 108; and Edward H. Pinto, *Treen and Other Wooden Bygones* (London: G. Bell & Sons, 1968), p. 65, and plate 141.
7. An eighteenth-century example is pictured in Levi, p. 71.
8. John Jacob Holtzapffel, *Hand or Simple Turning* (1881; reprint, New York, Dover Publications, 1976), p. 502, illustration 679.
9. Holtzapffel, p. 502, illustration 681.

Chapter Six

ORNAMENT AND MOLDINGS

In this chapter I discuss ornament, and how it differs from decoration. The ornaments usually produced by turning are termed *moldings*. I detail their naming and usage in the second and largest part of this chapter.

The vase in figure 6.1 features ornament and decoration. These two related categories differ:

1. An ornament does not have a physical or structural function. It is a relatively-small physical addition to, or subtraction from, the three-dimensional unornamented form of an object.

2. A decoration is two-dimensional and applied to, or laid onto, a surface without affecting the shape of that surface. Shallow texture and carving could be classified as ornament or as decoration; I have treated them as decoration because I have chosen to discuss pattern in chapter 8 on decoration.

Figure 6.1 Ornament and decoration, *The Jerusalem Vase* by Eli Abuhatzira, the Wood Craft Center, Jerusalem, Israel. 12 in. high x 9.5 in. dia. (300 mm x 240 mm).

The castellations are repetitive, imitative ornament. The representational conglutination is decoration not ornament, and is organic because the woods' natural colors are utilized. Although the conglutination in ebony and maple is successful aesthetically, its primary intention is communicative and is to represent the Jerusalem city walls and the gates through them.

Figure 6.2 Applied ornament on a caster. The groups of flush beads are "applied" in the sense that they were turned after the unornamented paperbark body had been finish-turned. The bead at the bottom of the black-apple lid could not have been applied in the same sense because it had to be finish-turned before the rest of the lid.

The concepts of *application* and *unornamented form* are also pursued in the next two figures.

6.1 ORNAMENT

Ornament is the elaboration of otherwise complete objects. It is applied to a completed structure or an unornamented form, and is therefore conceptionally optional (figure 6.2). The application can consist of fastening the ornament onto an otherwise completed object. It can also consist of carving or molding the ornament into an otherwise completed object without lessening the integrity of that object. This second concept of application is, however, not widely applicable to woodturning because many turned ornaments are *process* ornaments, and have to be produced as the form is produced. Only concave moldings such as coves and the flush beads in figure 6.2 can be turned into an otherwise completed turning.

The concept of applied turned ornament is further complicated by the problem of defining the unornamented form. In many turnings the form and the ornament are one because their forms were primarily designed to be ornamental. Their unornamented forms would then be their starting blanks or those blanks after rough turning (figure 6.3).

Applied ornament is sometimes contrasted with *organic* (inherent in the object's function or materials), although "organic" is more often used to refer to the natural colors and patterns in woods.

The concept of application thus has little relevance to the turning of ornament. It is however relevant to the design-by-drawing of turnings because you can readily add ornament to or subtract it from the drawn unornamented form, and may want the unornamented form to be apparent to those who experience the completed turning (figure 6.4).

Figure 6.3 Which is the unornamented form?
Left, a hollowed blank, an unornamented form, makes a fully functional eggcup.

Center, a more refined unornamented form from which the eggcup on the right could be turned.

Right, a more ornamented version of the center eggcup, and an ornamented version of that on the left.

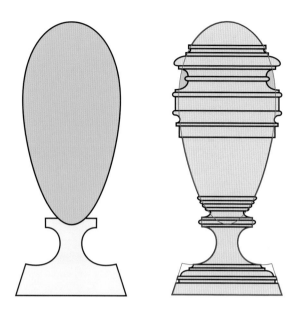

Figure 6.4 Applying moldings to an unornamented form in design-by-drawing.
Left, the unornamented form. *Right,* the ornamented caster elevation was produced by drawing moldings both onto and into the unornamented form.

The caster is based on one pictured in A. Graef and M. Graef, *Moderner Drechslerarbeiten* (1889; reprint, Hannover, Germany: Th. Schäfer, 1982), plate 4, fig. 5.

6.1.1 THE HISTORY OF ORNAMENT

Man is attracted by ornament (in this section the term "ornament" also includes decoration), and has an inborn desire to create it. This is demonstrated by its presence on the earliest extant things that man used. The attraction of and the desire to create ornament remain strong in modern man, and is demonstrated at a mundane level by the doodling in my sons' school exercise books. Ornament is also important in communication—Coca-Cola commercially exploits its ornate bottle and decorative logo in the same way that some art turners use particular ornament and decoration to establish a personal "brand". Even where there is no commercial motive, designing ornament provides pleasurable challenges which are distinct from, but related to, the inborn desire to employ skill.

The development of ornament is related to the development of the crafts and technology. During the Upper Paleolithic period (38,000 to 8,000 B.C.), some ornament was geometric, but most was imitative. During the Neolithic (8,000 to 3,500 B.C.), man-made walls and pottery provided surfaces which could be ornamented. Weaving was also invented during the Neolithic, and stimulated invention in geometric decoration and in imitative, stylized, geometric decoration. This was because in weaving the decoration is produced as the cloth is produced using threads of different

Figure 6.5 Ornamental-turnings in which the ornament is usually applied to an unornamented form. In ornamental turning the wood, ivory, metal, or other material is usually first plain turned to the unornamented form which is then ornamentally machined.

In the related specialty of rose-engine turning (*Woodturning Methods,* page 152) the two stages are usually combined, and the concept of unornamented form has little application.

Center, the watch stand is a more ornamented version of those in figures 5.56 and 5.57.

Photograph supplied by J. B. Hawkins Antiques, Moss Vale, New South Wales.

colors to produce differently colored squares and rectangles (*process decoration*).

Woodturning was invented later than weaving, probably about 1000 B.C. Among its important features is the ease with which it can be used to ornament. The specialty of ornamental-turning was initially developed during the sixteenth century (figure 6.5).

6.1.2 RECENT ATTITUDES TO ORNAMENT

The modernist fashion for cosmophobia—the fear or mistrust of ornament— was powerful through much of the twentieth century. It originated in the nineteenth century when ornament became mass producible, and ceased to depend on costly materials and caring craftsmanship (William Morris's doomed efforts to improve the quality of manufactured goods through a return to handworking were introduced on pages 35 and 36). The standard of design, which largely reflected the dictates of manufacturers, also declined.

The rise of democracy during the nineteenth century helped to undermine ornament. Costly ornament had long been used to confirm status and to heighten ceremony, but from the realization that divisions in society were man-made not God-dictated, came the conclusion that personal wealth does not always reflect personal worth. Excessive ornamentation bought by the unworthy becomes at best undue ostentation, even when of the highest quality and cost. And each time that ornament was discovered to be imitation (figure 6.6), the belief that buying and owning ornament raised your status took a further knock.

Ornament is debased by being twice associated with exploitation. Those who accumulate suffcient wealth to be able to afford expensive ornament must be exploiters; and because of the labor-intensive nature of ornament, it is usually commissioned from the lowest labor cost sources.

Ornament is linked to waste. At the end of the nineteenth century democracy was associated with socialism, and socialism with economic functionalism. In 1910 Austrian architect Adolf Loos (1870–1933) published an influential essay "Ornament and Crime". In it he called for the rejection of all ornament, not for reasons associated with aesthetics, falseness or exploitation, but for economy. Ornament was a waste of labor, money, and materials. Like many crusaders, he did not entirely practice what he preached. His most famous building was erected in Vienna between 1909 and 1911, and is now known as the *Looshaus*. It has a lower facade clad in costly cipollino marble which displays strong, natural swirlings in green and white. These swirlings are decoration, and are the two-dimensional equivalent of ornament! What the Looshaus really illustrates is that man is reluctant to live without ornament even if he

believes it is wrong, and that the modernist sleight of hand whereby naturally-occuring-man-selected-and-revealed two-dimensional organic decoration is substituted for man-made ornament and decoration is intellectually corrupt. Organic decoration also demands the careful selection and working of the materials—cheap it is not. Nor is it modern—it has been practiced in stone and wood for centuries.

Ornament was associated with deception, exploitation and waste; it was also base. If mankind enjoyed ornament and decoration, the uncivilized, uneducated, and uncultured enjoyed them also. Those who regarded themselves as superior shouldn't wallow and share in such enjoyment, but what to replace it with? If discernment was needed to distinguish the genuine from the sham, then extreme discernment and its sometime partner patronising amusement, signified great separation from the savage and

Figure 6.6 Not deceptive decoration. Although gilt, this vessel by Glenn Krueg of Newark, California, would not be mistaken for a gold one. Even purist John Ruskin conceded that gilding "in architecture [and surely in woodturning] is no deceit, because it is therein not understood for gold". 12.5 in. x 6.5 in. dia. (310 mm x 160 mm). Collection of Carol Shipman.

their contemporary equivalent, the hoi polloi. The confirmation of extreme discernment as a mark of superiority was providentially aided by the introduction of a similar Japanese aesthetic called *shibui*. It had two strands:

1. An astringent taste based on rightness and on a minute appreciation of subtlety. Indeed so subtle are some works of art that we could be forgiven for thinking that they resemble the royal garments in the Hans Christian Andersen fairy story "The Emperor's New Clothes". A less extreme example is classic simplicity, a belief that rightness of proportion determines beauty. This belief remains powerful even though it took a knock from the revelation by Jacques Ignace Hittorff in 1830 that ancient classical temples were originally gaudily painted, and were not left pristine so that their proportions could be appreciated without distraction.[1]

2. An appreciation untainted by base instincts and false refinements. This appreciation includes a love of the unspoiled, the natural, and the innocently man-made without the taint of the sophisticated rustic or other artifices.

In the eighteenth century art separated from craft. In the mid-twentieth century the separation became antagonism. Art was no longer different to craft, or even just superior; art was concept, and shouldn't be soiled by craft which was merely concerned with workmanship. Even the manifestation of concept through craft skills and craft knowledge into a durable form was rejected by some. The attitude was contagious. Weak-willed craftspeople rejected their heritage, the need to master skills and the need to formally design.

During the second half of the twentieth century workmanship and craft knowledge became more appreciated. Ornament is no longer taboo, but is it appreciated as it once was? The belief that contemporary man has been losing his ability and even his need or desire to appreciate ornament is longstanding as evidenced by Otto Wagner's statement quoted on page 54. Whether this belief can be proved, I doubt. Perhaps sensual bombardment and the myriad of modern distractions allow less contemplative time. However, the fact that you are reading this book

Figure 6.7 The classical ornament of a sculpture niche. An engraving from Andrea Palladio, *The Four Books of Architecture* (1570, Isaac Ware edition, 1738, Fourth book, plate LVIII. Reproduced courtesy of Dover Publications.

Figure 6.8 Classical ornament in the late twentieth century. Classically inspired postmodern window surrounds and the entablature below on a building in San Francisco. This building is richly ornamented compared to most of its contemporaries, but compare its amount of detailed ornament with that in the preceding figure.

suggests that the pessimism is overdone, and that at least some are keen to:

1. Devote the time needed to fully appreciate more complex ornament.
2. Understand the relationships of ornament to form.
3. Understand the heirarchy of ornament.
4. Identify ornamental styles.
5. Recognize motifs and patterns.

In woodturning these five endeavours require a knowledge of moldings, the subject of the rest of this chapter.

6.2 MOLDINGS

This section describes the forms and uses of turned parts called moldings (spelt mouldings in British English). I prefer to use "molding" when the subject part is relatively small compared to the size of the object of which it is a part. I prefer "profile" when referring to the outline of a major part of a turning.

The importance of moldings in woodturning design is illustrated in two sentences from Plumier's L'Art de Tourner which were quoted earlier on page 1: "In order to become a skillful turner, it is insufficient only to thoroughly know the machines and the expert handling of the lathe tools. In addition one must understand the profile in order to give the best style to the workpiece". Regrettably in the twenty-first century the desirability of understanding profiles continues to be rejected or ignored by some woodturning designers.

The source for much of the information in this chapter's first four sections is C. Howard Walker, *Theory of Mouldings* (Cleveland, Oregon: J. H. Jansen, 1926). He shows that in woodturning, moldings are:

1. Produced by the prolongation of a cross section around a turning. The flutes or reeds which commonly run along shafts can also be considered as moldings.
2. Not essential to the structure, but are often used to define and emphasize the structure. The moldings on small objects are often relatively larger than the moldings on buildings. Many turnings can be considered to be mainly or entirely composed of moldings.
3. Used to add interest, definition, and emphasis, especially by producing parallel bands of shadow, highlight, and graduated shading.
4. Used at boundaries, at junctions, and at discontinuities. At such locations where there are often changes of color, surface, material, and/or direction.

Molding cross sections are of two main types:

1. *Subtractive*, made by carving into a surface. Medieval and Gothic architectural moldings are generally subtractive, being derived from stone construction. Subtractive moldings are little used in woodturning design.

2. *Additive*, produced by combining elements, and often derived from wood or brick construction. Ancient Egyptian, classical, and oriental moldings are generally additive.

6.2.1 DERIVATIONS

Many of the profiles which can be used on turnings and which are usually classified as moldings resulted from:

1. The need to restrain natural materials and their distortions under load. If you can imagine a world without metal, you can appreciate the difficulty of crosscutting wood with stone tools. Bundles of reeds were therefore favored as a domestic constructional element by those who lived along the banks of the Nile even though wood was plentiful. The distortions and bindings of bundles of reeds (figure 6.1) and the structural demands of other natural materials suggested forms for ornamenting in ancient construction, and determined essential molding types.
2. The need to cover and seal the joints of structures against the weather. Moldings were also introduced and designed to shed water, and to provide deep undercuts and overhangs to prevent water running down walls.
3. The desire to cover joints and remove the need to produce close fits in difficult circumstances—the bolection molding is an example (page 135).
4. The desire to allow more light to enter by chamfering the sides of window openings and window mullions.
5. The removal of sharpness from corners to lessen the possibility of damage to both person and object. The chamfer is an obvious example of this.
6. The removal of unnecessary weight from structural members such as vault ribs.
7. The desire to ornament, differentiate, and define. Although tending to flow from the physical and functional imperatives, the ornamental potential of moldings has been exploited from the earliest times. Moldings provide a means to use light to decorate and define: shadows give dark stripes, highlights give pale stripes. The tones are uniform with the straight moldings, and graduated with the curved moldings.
8. The desire to texture and pattern surfaces (figure 6.9).
9. The desire to imitate natural forms, for example: the acorn (page 132), the thistle (page 145), and the classical column capitals.
10. The desire to express movement, structure, and force; and to funnel and spread forces.
11. Their location. Building moldings are usually angled and shaped to look best to pedestrians at ground level (figure 6.17). The resulting conventions are also used for moldings on furniture and on smaller objects.

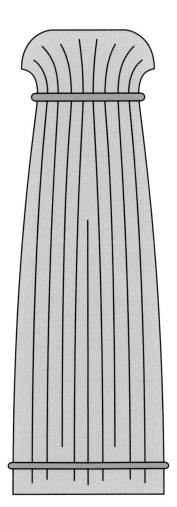

Figure 6.9 Reeds and the moldings based on them.

Above, an impression of a bundle of reeds, used singly for columns and in rows for walls in Ancient Egypt and elsewhere.

Above center, the rippled surface texture of a bundle of reeds is usually run axially.

Above right, the rippled reed texture can run around a turning.

Right, the spread of the tops of bundles above the top binding may have been a source of the column capital, and the gorge molding. The bindings are probably the precursors of the moldings found around the tops, bottoms, and along the shafts of wood and stone columns.

A French-made, reeded, dining-table leg. This leg profile is particularly associated with Jacques-Emile Ruhlmann (1879–1933), the leading decorator and furniture designer in Paris in the 1920s.

Reedlike moldings which do not run axially, but are wrapped around a turning are called rings. These rings on the handle of a truncheon give texture which aids gripping.

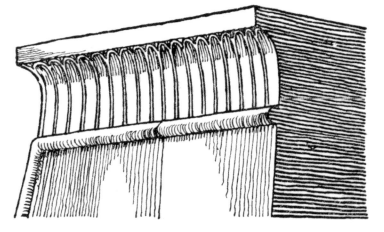

A gorge molding is a combination of three moldings, a fillet, a cavetto below, and a bead (or roll) below the cavetto which recalls the top binding of a bundle of reeds.[2] In Egyptian architecture a gorge crowned walls and pylons, and formed the cornices over doorways.

6.2.2 THE BASIC MOLDINGS

There are approximately sixteen basic moldings of which seven are straight. In the drawings on this and the following two pages the exact extent of each molding is shown by the thickened line.

The basic moldings can be modified within the constraints of their definitions, and combined to suit your design intentions. There is generally no restriction to how a molding is angled relative to a turning's turning-axis, although in the drawings in this section the turning-axes are vertical.

THE STRAIGHT MOLDINGS

Bevel   A straight flank typically neither parallel nor at right angles to the turning's turning-axis. *Splay* is a related term particularly describing the bevelling alongside windows to allow more light to enter.

Chamfer A bevelled corner, typically leaving straight profiles both parallel to and at right angles to the turning-axis. *Cant* is a synonymous term.

Channel   A groove of rectangular cross section, sometimes called a *sunk fillet*. Channels grouped close together and separated by *lands* of the general diameter of the turning in the area are termed *channeling*.

Fillet   A relatively small, often projecting molding, usually of flat or rectangular section. The term is also applied to the narrow flat bounding a projecting molding, and to the land between the flutes on column shafts.

The alternative term *listel* has become obsolete. A fillet around the top or bottom of a column shaft may be termed a *cincture*. Fillets are usually best parallel or at right angles to the turning-axis. Fillets which are slightly concave are more brilliant. Concave or convex fillets are used when the tangents (colored magenta) to the curves which join the fillet are not parallel.

Quirk   A V-cut used alongside a bead or similar to add definition. A quirk's flanks need not be straight in cross section. Whether a bounding V-shaped groove is a quirk or part of the main molding is often debatable.

V-cut A vee-shaped groove used to create a shadow line without greatly disturbing the profile.

V-bead, *V-ring*   Terms invented by your author. "V-ring" is preferred for relatively-small sizes. The apex may be left sharp or be rounded. These moldings seem to be common on Indian turnings, but whether that is the intended profile or they are merely poorly shaped beads or rings I don't know.

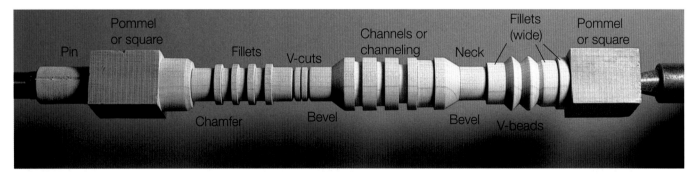

Figure 6.10 A spindle with straight moldings. The four fillets at the left-hand end project from the general level of the spindle. Because the bottoms of the grooves between the fillets are not below the general level of the spindle in the proximity, the grooves are not channels. The term *neck* can be used whether its profile is straight or concave.

THE CURVED PROFILES

There are six basic curved moldings. Their definitions vary between reference books, an unsatisfactory situation which I have corrected by redefining some of the profiles. A major factor in the naming of a curved molding is how much you would axially rotate if you were able to walk along its outline. I have expressed this rotation in degrees rather than in the customary fraction of a circle.

Convex moldings are sturdy and robust, and accent with highlights. Concave moldings weaken, and accent with shadows. Mating the two types creates contrast.

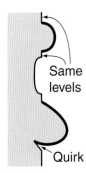

Bead   A convex, projecting molding often of semicircular cross section, typically with a rotation of between 90° and 180°. The ends of the bead spring from surfaces at the same level. I suggest that an asymmetrical bead be called a *canted bead*.

In woodturning "bead" is now used for both large and medium examples. In the past a large bead might have been called a torus, but I have narrowed the definition of torus to that defined below. Where a bead is relatively small it is termed a *ring*.

Cavetto   A concave molding with a rotation of 90° or less, quieter than a scotia. Sometimes also confusingly called a cove (see below), or a hollow (a term better reserved for the inside of a bowl or vessel). Where the end of a cavetto runs without a break into a surface parallel to the turning-axis it is called an *apophyge*.

Cove   The reverse of a bead; a concave, often semicircular section, with a typical rotation between 90° and 180°. The ends of a cove descend from surfaces at the same level. An asymmetrical cove can be called a *canted cove*.

Ovolo   From the Greek meaning egg-shaped; a shallow asymmetrical convex molding with a rotation of about 90°. The term is also applied to shallow symmetrical convex moldings.

Torus   From the Latin for rope. A convex molding, with a rotation of between 90° and 180°, the opposite of a scotia. The ends of a torus spring from different levels.

Scotia   A concave molding of between 90° and 180° rotation, the opposite of a torus. Its ends spring from surfaces at different levels. A scotia produces a band of heavy shadow, and is aptly named after the Greek goddess of darkness and the underworld. Scotia was also the Roman name for Ireland.

THE S-SHAPED PROFILES

The S-shaped moldings are collectively known as ogees, two other names are also used for particular forms. William Hogarth called one particular version of this curve *the line of beauty* (page 24 and figure 6.11). Ogees are often bounded by channels, fillets, or quirks; and are often "broken" by fillets.

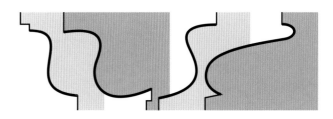

Ogee   The general term for an S-shaped profile. The rotations of the convex and concave parts can each exceed 90°. An earlier term for an ogee molding was *ressaunt*.

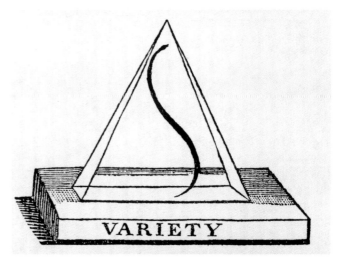

Figure 6.11   William Hogarth's serpentine line of beauty is appropriately pictured in the form of a serpent on the title page of his book *The Analysis of Beauty*.[3]

Figure 6.12 An ogee profile on a bottle coaster.

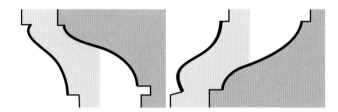

Cyma Reversa A less accentuated ogee in which the rotations of the concave and convex sections do not exceed 90°, and in which the object diameter at the convex part of the cyma is larger than that at the concave part.

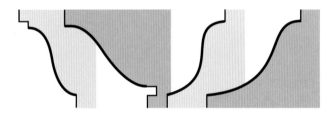

Cyma A less accentuated and less "gutsy" ogee in which the rotations of the concave and convex sections do not exceed 90°. If, as above, the object diameter is larger at the concave part of the cyma than at the convex part of the cyma, the molding is called a *cyma recta*.

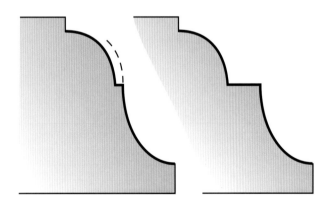

Figure 6.13 Cyma rectas broken by fillets. *Left,* the small fillet at the point of inflection on the ogee does not destroy the visual continuity of the ogee which is indicated by the dashed line. *Right,* if the fillet is large, the continuity of the ogee is destroyed, and the ogee is divided into separate ovolo and cavetto moldings.[4] The length (width) of a fillet should therefore be appropriate to the size of the curve on which it lies. Another criterion is that it is desirable that all the fillets on a turning have the same length. The two criteria often conflict; part of detailed design is to achieve the most appropriate compromise.

THE FILLET

Although some contemporary designers ignore the fillet, this small molding has a usefulness and power which belies its size. The fillet provides a longitudinal reference and calipering point to aid accurate and repetitive turning, it bounds curves, and it divides into parts. If used wisely, it can add definition and crispness to a design without greatly disrupting flow and continuity (figures 6.14 to 6.16).

Figure 6.14 The roles of fillets. *Left,* a vase without fillets; *center,* a similar vase but with well-positioned fillets; *right,* a similar vase but with poorly-postioned fillets.

Fillets should be positioned so that they articulate (explain) the design by dividing the form into logical parts. Therefore position fillets on ogees at points of inflection where the curvature on an ogee changes from convex to concave (compare the three vases). At such fillets the concave and convex parts of the ogee should usually meet the fillet at 90°. A fillet should be narrow when its role is restricted to articulation and the addition of crispness.

One of the advantages of woodturning is the ease with which crisp fillets can be produced.

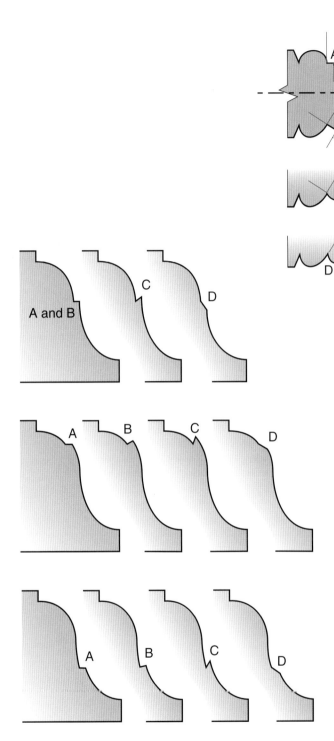

Figure 6.15 **The placement and inclination of fillets.**

Top row, the fillets are placed at the points of inflection of the ogees, and look better than the fillets with the same letters in the rows below.

All rows, I suggest that the horizontal fillets *A* look better than the fillets *B* which are at 90° to the adjacent surfaces. Fillets *C* are aggressive, yet have fragile edges. Fillets *D* have lost much of their definition.

Figure 6.16 **Fillets on spindles.** For maximum brightness and contrast fillets should meet adjacent profiles at 90°.

At *A,* the fillet alignment is axial. Both the bead and the ogee meet the fillet at 90°. The ogee's curvature has to increase rapidly as it nears *A* for it to meet the fillet at 90°

At *B,* the fillet is canted or kicked-up to be at 90° to the canted bead. This facilitates increasing the diameter at *E.* The edge of the fillet is delicate because of the short grain although the included angle between the fillet and the ogee is 90°.

At *C,* because the fillet is curved, both the bead and the end of the ogee (which is at 90° to the turning-axis) meet the fillet at 90°. Curving the fillet (especially if it is wide) adds life, and durability. A less defined solution would be to replace the curved fillet with a small bead as at *D.*

Between *B* and *I,* the profile of the ogee has to be adequately defined if it is to be turned to the designed shape. The magnitudes of the maximum and minimum diameters on the ogee and their longitudinal positions along the turning-axis must therefore be defined. Even this is inadequate as the dashed lines between *E* and *F* demonstrate. You must also define further points on the ogee and/or clearly define the ogee's required profile on a drawing (figure 7.12, page 153).

At *G,* the rolling cut from *F* to *G* is too deep, and the resulting V-cut destroys the visual flow from the ogee through the fillet into the cove.

At *G* and *H,* the fillets are aligned axially and not at 90° to the adjacent curves, thus lessening brightness.

At *I* and *J,* kicking the fillets up gains brightness and offers the opportunity to increase the spindle diameter at the bottom of the cove without deadening the spindle's form. Although not as durable as axial fillets, having the edges of the fillets with a 90° included angle imparts some strength to the short grain.

The visual transition from the spindle into the plate at *K* is abrupt. By introducing a fillet *L,* or a torus *M* and a fillet *N,* you make a gentler transition. Adding an apophyge at *O* further smooths the transition.

6.2.3 DESIGNING AND USING COMPOUND MOLDINGS

Figures 6.17 to 6.24 describe guidelines which you will find valuable when you are designing moldings, whether basic or compound, to enhance the beauty and delight of a turning.

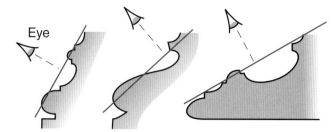

Bases low down

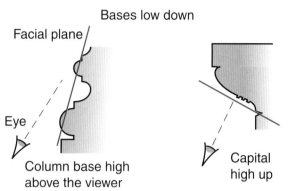

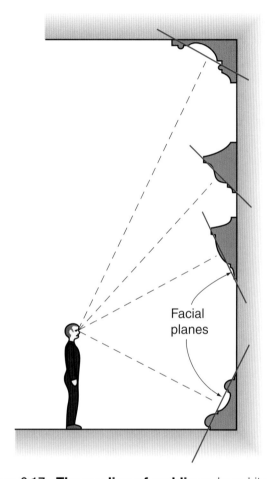

Figure 6.17 **The angling of moldings.** In architecture, the height of buildings is typically large compared with the height of people, and the eye height of viewers and a typical horizontal distance away can often be assumed with reasonable accuracy. Therefore moldings on buildings are designed and placed so as to lie along facial planes (drawn magenta) at about 90° to the assumed sight lines. However, a viewer looking along a molded surface or a colonnade sees moldings in the distance in profile with near-horizontal sightlines.

Furniture moldings are usually angled in the same way that architectural moldings are. The same conventions are applied to moldings on small, movable turnings, although viewing positions are far less predictable because our conceptual knowledge associates certain facial-plane inclinations with particular parts such as bases and capitals.

Figure 6.18 **Molding facial planes adapted to the anticipated line of sight.** *Bottom left,* the facial plane of this column base cannot be distorted to be at 90° to the expected line of sight. Nor has it been stretched vertically so that the base's height as projected onto a viewer's retina would be similar in size to that projected when the viewer's line of sight was at 90° to the facial plane. Such stretching, which is recommended on page 51 of Walker's *Theory of Mouldings*, is unnecessary because a viewer's brain will automatically process the sensed foreshortened image so that the viewer perceives the true profile.

When assessing the shadow and highlights on moldings, particularly outside, the light is generally assumed to be descending at 45°. In particular conditions it may be appropriate to use different angles.

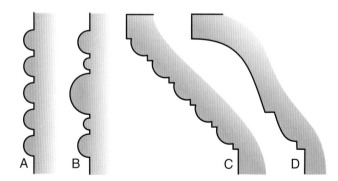

Figure 6.19 **Avoiding monotony in moldings.** Groupings of the same moldings side-by-side as in *A* and *C* are considered to be monotonous. Grouping moldings with variety as in *B* and *D* is preferred. Grouping small identical flutes, reeds, and/or other moldings side-by-side gives tactile and visual texture.

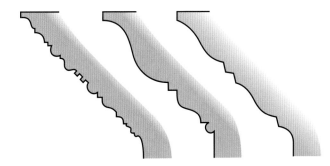

Figure 6.20 Confusion and contrast in moldings.
Left, an excess of compound moldings confuses.
Center, use simple moldings for main accents, compound moldings for secondary, intimate developments. The sizes and shapes of component moldings should vary considerably, and should spring at 90° for maximum impact and contrast.
Right, a weaker effect resulting from using two main component mouldings similar in shape and size, with junctions at angles greater than 90°.

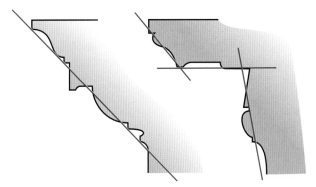

Figure 6.21 The role of facial planes in compound moldings. *Left,* harmony results if there is one facial plane. *Right,* the use of three component facial planes produces an uncouthness.

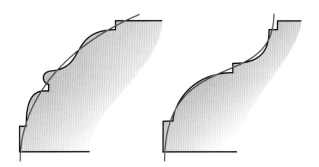

Figure 6.22 Harmony in a compound molding can also be achieved by having its facial plane lie along a discernible curve.

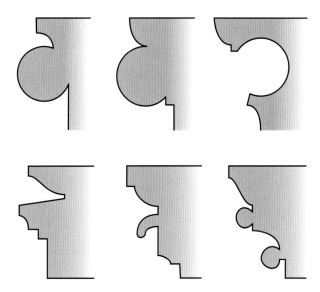

Figure 6.23 Uncouth moldings. The causes of uncouthness are difficult to define, but include abruptness, the grossly inappropriate size of a part, structural illogicality, and the use of an appropriately sized but inappropriately shaped part. Are uncouth moldings ugly because they are unconventional?

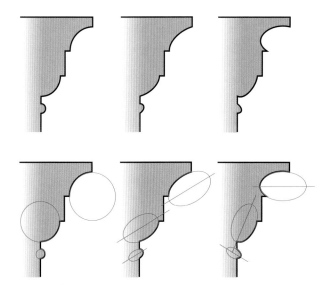

Figure 6.24 Arcs and conics in compound moldings.
Left top and bottom, circular cross-sections, particularly when quarter round, are sometimes described as stale.[5] A more accurate description might be "unable to express directional force, stress, or even movement". When you wish to express such qualities you should therefore prefer molding profiles with continuously-varying curvatures.
Middle top and bottom, unity is greater when the axes of conics are parallel to each other.
Right top and bottom, When the curve axes are not parallel the resulting compound molding lacks harmony.

6.2.4 EXPRESSING WITH MOLDINGS

The placement, sizing, and shaping of profiles and moldings can be used expressively to imply weakness, massiveness, force, support, and even motion. It seems that there is an unconscious appreciation of these factors which draws from our conceptual knowledge and influences our perceptions. Another illustration of this is our reaction to the thickness of structural members in different materials. For example, were the cast iron columns in figure 12.44, page 237, of wood, you would doubt their strength; were they stone you wouldn't go near them!

The structurally-efficient shaping of some members can be calculated, or an approximation can be readily visualized (figures 6.25 and 6.26). Figure 6.27 shows how the expressiveness of a common detail can be varied.

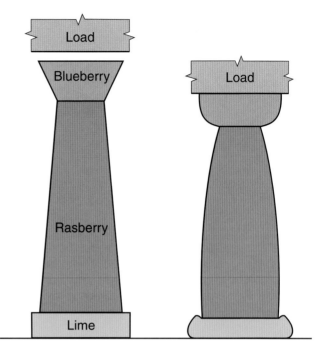

Figure 6.26 The jelly analogy. *Left,* the unloaded column is a stack of three lumps of stiff jelly which are unable to expand at their horizontal interfaces. *Right,* when the load is applied the jelly will distort. This distortion expresses loadbearing, and is a useful aid to visualizing the expressive shape of loaded components: it reflects the statement by Karl Philipp Moritz in 1793 that the column capital represents a "visible sign of pressure".[6]

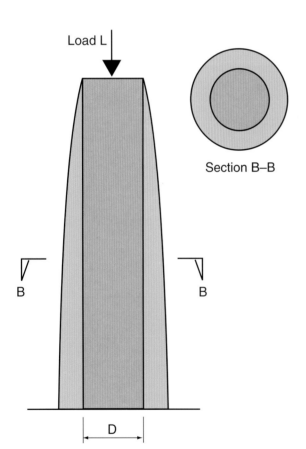

Figure 6.25 A structural derivation for the diminution of column shafts.

The diameter of the column at the top, D, is just strong enough to support the applied vertical load L without crushing. The shaft must grow in diameter downwards from the top so that at any level the total self weight of the column above is just supported by the annular area colored green.

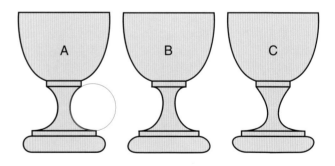

Figure 6.27 Three eggcups showing molding directionality. *Eggcup A,* the cove is a circular arc and the bead below is semicircular. *Eggcup B,* the raising of the smallest diameter of the cove and the distortion of the bottom bead into a torus give an impression of upward thrust. *Eggcup C,* lowering the minimum diameter of the cove and inverting the torus produces a confusing form.

The preferred impression given by the distortion of the moldings in *eggcup B* is also aided by the shifting of mass downwards and by increasing the diameter of contact with the table top.

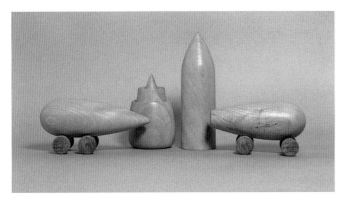

Figure 6.28 **Motion in moldings.** The impression of
motion can be created with moldings. These four
streamlined forms resemble real objects which are
associated with motion. The impression of motion is
affected by the orientation and placement of a form. The
rocket could be about to take off, but the unfamiliar
placement and orientation of the aircraft-engine-like form
lessens any impression of motion. The left of the two
wheeled airship-like forms could move to the left or to the
right, but the cannon-like form on the right could only
move to the right.

Reproduced
courtesy of
Dover
Publications.

6.2.5   GLOSSARY OF MOLDINGS

Many applications and combinations of moldings have
particular names. This section gives an alphabetical list.
Some of the terms are architectural, but are applicable to
woodturning.[7] In the drawings made specially for this
chapter, the named molding is distinguished by being
shaded darker or having a thicker outline.

Some profile terms are directional. For example, when
a baluster form is upright but its bulb is at the top of the
form, the qualification "inverted" should be added.

I have taken the liberty of suggesting clearer alternatives
to traditional terms which are vague or confusing. I also
propose and use the following conventions when building
names for compound repeating moldings:

1.   The term for the main repeating profile should start the
     name, followed by *and* and the term for the subsidiary
     or separating profiles.
2.   When the subsidiary or separating profiles are small and
     recessed, such as V-cuts or small coves, their names
     need not be included in the overall molding name in
     the interest of brevity.
3.   Where a separating profile projects, its term should be
     included in the overall molding name.

Abacus   The uppermost division of a capital, usually in the
form of a square plate (figure 6.31). Sometimes the four
sides are concave in plan.[8] Abacuses which are octagonal[9]
or circular in plan[10] are associated with Gothic styles.

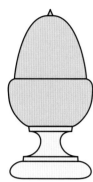

Acorn A form copied from the fruits of oak trees and used for knobs, finials, and drop finials (finials which hang down). There are about 450 species of oaks in the genus *Quercus*.

Annulated An adjective applied to shafts and spindles which are plain except for bands of moldings at intervals along them (figure 6.29).

Annulet The term is used almost exclusively to refer to the projections low on the echinuses of Greek and Roman Doric column capitals (figure 6.31).

Apophyge The cavetto flowing tangentially from the top and bottom of a column shaft, terminating at a fillet or other molding (figure 6.31). Also called a *congee, congé,* or *scape.*

Arcade A line of arches supported on columns. When applied as a decoration to an unpierced wall the arcade is blind (figure 6.30).

Arcature A miniature arcade.

Archivolt An architrave consisting of a simple or compound molding running around the vertical face of an arch (figure 6.30).

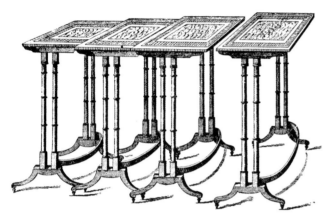

Figure 6.29 Columns with annulated shafts on quartetto (a nest of four) tables from Thomas Sheraton's *The Cabinet Dictionary* (1803), plate 75.

Figure 6.30 A blind arcade from Stoneleigh, Warwickshire *circa* 1190.[11] The archivolts are carved with rows of chevrons.

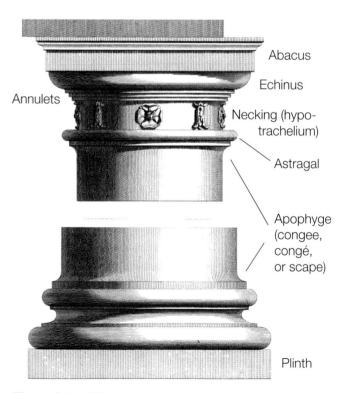

Abacus
Echinus
Annulets
Necking (hypo-trachelium)
Astragal
Apophyge (congee, congé, or scape)
Plinth

Figure 6.31 The moldings of a Roman Doric column.[12] The moldings particular to the different column types are discussed in chapter 12. Reproduced courtesy of Benjamin Blom.

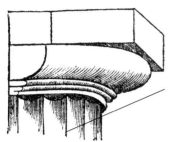

Arris An edge, particularly that between adjacent column flutes on Greek Doric columns.[13] A sharp edge which has been slightly rounded is often referred to as *arrised*. Reproduced courtesy of Dover Publications.

Astragal Derived from the Greek for knuckle bone. A small bead, usually half round. The term is particularly applied to the small bead and fillet combination below the capitals of Roman columns (figure 6.31).

Bag A useful term for a shape similar to a tall cup tapering convexly towards its rim. *Right*, when the form is upside-down and vertical it is called an inverted bag or a canopus.[14]

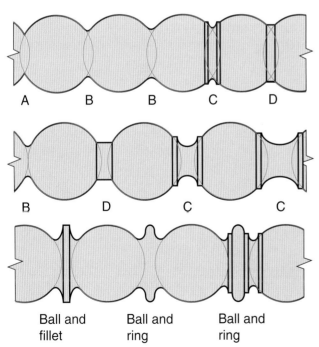

Ball turnings Spindle forms based on spheres which overlap, touch, or are separated. The spherical surfaces may: A, join at cusps; B, be connected by coves; C, be connected by coves and fillets; or D, be connected by fillets alone. Other moldings can also be used to connect the spheres.

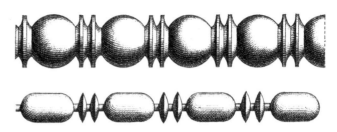

Ball and reel turnings *Top*, the reels in this ball and reel turning are short. As shown later under *bead and reel*, reels can be relatively longer. *Bottom*, a sausage and reel turning.[15]

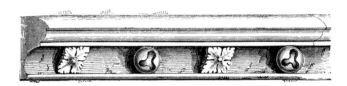

Ballflower A spherical ornamental feature generally arranged in rows with its outer layer partially carved away in the form of three joined petals to reveal a ball within.[16]

Figure 6.32 Ball-turned spindles on an easy or lounging chair, *circa* 1850, pictured in Kevin Fahy and Andrew Simpson, *Australian Furniture: Pictorial History and Dictionary, 1788–1938* (Sydney: Casuarina Press, 2000), p. 233. Reproduced courtesy of the Casuarina Press.

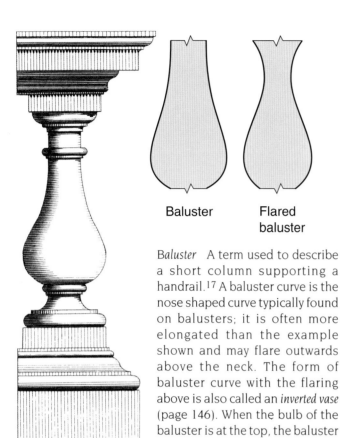

Baluster　　　Flared
baluster

Baluster　A term used to describe a short column supporting a handrail.[17] A baluster curve is the nose shaped curve typically found on balusters; it is often more elongated than the example shown and may flare outwards above the neck. The form of baluster curve with the flaring above is also called an *inverted vase* (page 146). When the bulb of the baluster is at the top, the baluster is *inverted*. Reproduced courtesy of Benjamin Blom.

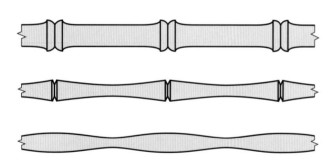

Bamboo turning　*Top*, a spindle turned to resemble bamboo. The turning of split bamboo moldings is described in *Woodturning Techniques*, pages 16 to 17.

Less-accurate imitations are also termed bamboo. *Center*, the spindle retains vestigial nodes. *Bottom*, the design is so degraded that it could barely be described as bamboo.

Band　The moldings or suites of moldings which encircle slender column shafts at intervals (figure 6.29). Such a column is called an *annulated column*.

Bandelet or bandlet　A small flat molding, an annulet.

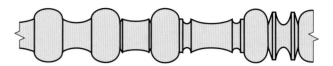

Bead and reel turning　The four variations show different relative lengths of reel.

Bell of a column　The transition from the shaft to the abacus which lies beneath the decorations of acanthus leaves on Corinthian capitals. A *bell capital* is plain and usually has the form of an inverted bell (see figure 12.5, page 217).[18] Reproduced courtesy of Dover Publications

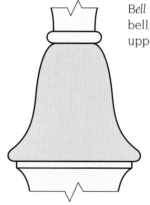

Bell　A turned shape resembling a bell. When the mouth of the bell is uppermost, the bell is *inverted*.

Bezant (*besant* or *byzant*)　A shallow disk usually arranged in rows and standing proud from the bottom of a shallow recess or channel (figure 6.33). When the surface from which the disks project is not recessed, the term *pellet* is preferred (page 141).

Figure 6.33 **A patera with a central domed pellet and a circle of bezants.**

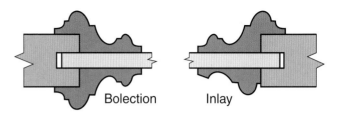

Bolection (various similar spellings) A molding which projects beyond the outermost surfaces which it ornaments. It is often used to conceal a joint between components at different levels, and may also be used to locate one component relative to another. The turning of bolection moldings is detailed on pages 104 to 110 of *Woodturning Techniques*.

Billet A cylinder, half-cylinder, or a prism having a cross section with three straight sides at right angles and the fourth convex. Billets are staggered when used in multiple and adjacent rows to ornament moldings (figure 6.42 and page 144).

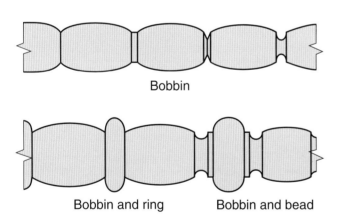

Bobbin A profile resembling a barrel.

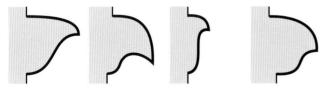

Bird's beak A projecting molding with its top an ovolo, and its lower element a cyma recta.

Figure 6.34 **Bobbin and ring turned spindles** on a bedroom chair pictured in Thomas King, *Modern Style of Cabinet Work Exemplified* (1829; reprint, New York: Dover Publications, 1995), plate 20. Reproduced courtesy of Dover Publications.

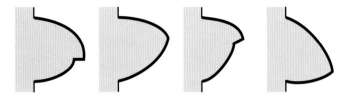

Bowtell (plural *bowtelles*) *boultine, boutell* A projecting moulding of two opposed ovolos meeting at a point or with a fillet inserted between them.

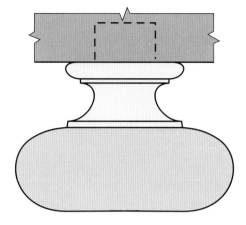

Bun A form resembling the flat round bread roll containing spices and dried fruits. Often used in the form of bun feet (see also figure 6.35).

Gadrooning

Bulb A swelling on a spindle, larger in diameter than the thickness of any pommels. Sometimes called a melon bulb, the profile can resemble an inverted plant bulb or a squat sausage. Where, as here, there is a pronounced division into two parts, the form is known as a *cup and cover*.[19] The carved, lobed ornament on the cover is gadrooning.

Figure 6.35 Bulbs on the legs of a seventeenth-century draw-table. The table is supported on bun feet.[20]

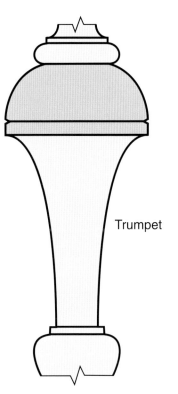

Trumpet

Cup   A form resembling a dipper cup, often mated with a cover (see bulb), or used inverted with a trumpet as here. The term "cup" may be retained if its rim is slightly flared or the cup is elongated.[21]

Cup and cover   See bulb.

Cabling   A convex molding worked in the flutes of columns and pilasters (figure 12.75, page 256). The cables rarely extend higher than a third of the way up the shaft.

Channeling   A series of close-together grooves, running around a form or, as in column flutes, running along or even spiralling around. The term is also applied to column flutes.

Chaplet   An astragal or bead molding.

Chevron   A zigzag (or dancette) molding (figure 6.30). In heraldry a chevron is a V-shaped stripe pointing up or down.

Cincture or *girdle*   The molding around the top or bottom of a column shaft.

Corbel   A bracket, sometimes semicircular in plan, often supporting the end of an arch.

Cornice   A projecting molding which crowns the part to which it is affixed. The gorge molding pictured in figure 6.9 is a cornice.

Cushion or *cubiform* capital   A plain capital having the form of a round-ended pommel.

Figure 6.36 Inverted trumpet legs and onion feet on a dining chair. *Photographed courtesy The Village Pump Antiques, Exeter, New South Wales.*

Dado or die The middle portion of a column pedestal between the base (or plinth) and the surbase (figure 6.37).

Dodai-ishi   The opposite of a cushion capital. The junction of a square-cross-section wood post with a dome-shaped foundation stone used in Japanese architecture.

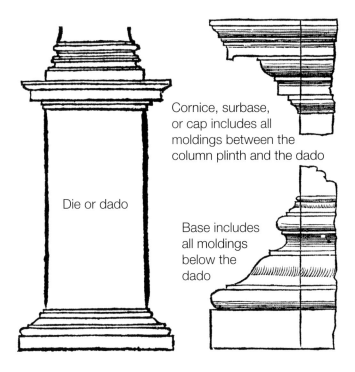

Die or dado

Cornice, surbase, or cap includes all moldings between the column plinth and the dado

Base includes all moldings below the dado

Figure 6.37 A column pedestal of the Composite order (the proportions and moldings of the pedestals for the different orders differ).[22] Reproduced courtesy of Dover Publications.

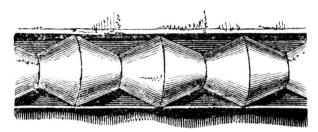

Double-cone molding   A Norman molding enriched with longitudinally split cone frustums joined alternately base to base and top to top.[23]

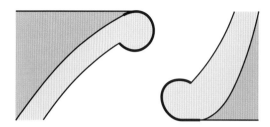

Edge roll Left, an edge roll attached to a rim. *Right,* footrims and bases also often incorporate edge rolls.

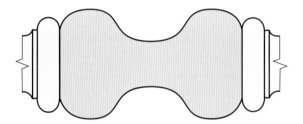

Dumbbell   A form based on an apparatus used for exercise and for the silent practice of bell ringing.

Flushbead A bead which is recessed below the general, usually cylindrical, surface of the turning. Flushbeads may be single or grouped. The term includes the bounding quirks.

Bobbin and reel astragal   Echinus

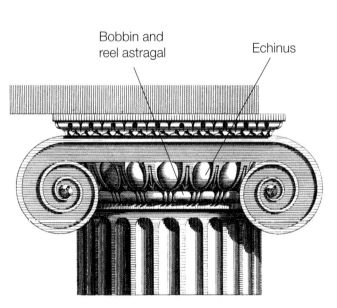

Echinus A carved egg and dart molding of ovolo profile under the abacus of Ionic and Composite columns.[24]

The name is also confusingly used for any uncarved ovolo molding, but is properly used only for the plain ovolo molding beneath the abacuses of Greek and Roman Doric and Tuscan columns. The term is derived from the Greek word which meant both a sea urchin and a wide-mouthed jar.[25] Reproduced courtesy of Benjamin Blom.

Flutes (or *flutings*)   The concave grooves cut into the shafts of columns, spindles, legs, bedposts, bowls (figure 6.38), etc. The edges of adjacent flutes may join at an edge called an arris, or be separated by fillets. Although flutes usually run straight and axially along a shaft, they can be helical as in this column from the crypt of Canterbury Cathedral, England.[26]

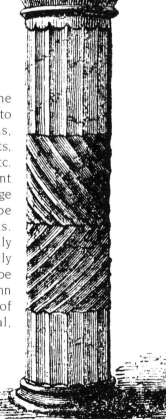

Figure 6.38 A bowl with a fluted outside by Al Stirt of Enosburg Falls, Vermont.

Gorge   The form of cornice associated with the tops of Egyptian buildings (figure 6.9).

Hypotrachelium, gorgerin   The neck between the astragal or sinkage and the lowest annulet or its equivalent in Doric and Tuscan columns (figures 6.31 and 6.44).

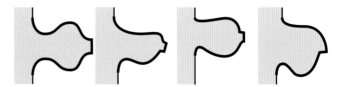

Lamb's Tongue   A Gothic molding of considerable projection composed of two opposed ogees separated by a fillet.

Melon bulb   See bulb.

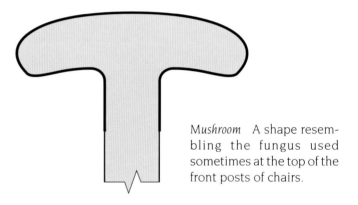

Mushroom   A shape resembling the fungus used sometimes at the top of the front posts of chairs.

Kokoshniki

Kokoshniki   The tiers of corbeled arches around the drum supporting a cupola in early Russian architecture.[27]

Nail head   A V-bead molding carved using a straight chisel to resemble a row of forged, square, nail heads.

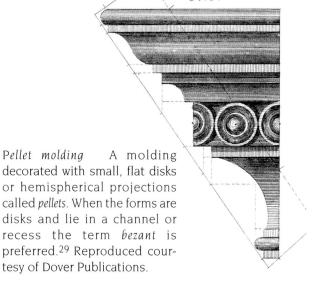

Pellet molding   A molding decorated with small, flat disks or hemispherical projections called *pellets*. When the forms are disks and lie in a channel or recess the term *bezant* is preferred.[29] Reproduced courtesy of Dover Publications.

Pommel   A length of square-cross-section spindle blank left unturned; also called a *square* (figure 6.10). A square length narrower in thickness than the general diameter of the spindle should be called a square rather than a pommel.

Onion   A shape based on the bulb of the *Allium cepa*, often used in turning, especially in finials, box knobs, and feet (figure 6.36). These onion domes are on the Cathedral of the Assumption in the Kremlin in Moscow. The term is interchangeable with *turnip*.[28]

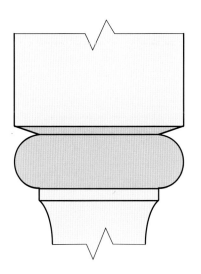

Quirked bead   A bead at an abrupt narrowing bounded on the side of greater diameter by a quirk.

Figure 6.39 Helically reeded front legs on a "Nelson" chair designed by Thomas Sheraton in 1806.[30]

Reed One of a group of adjacent, usually parallel, relatively small beads running axially or nearly axially, usually carved into the turned surface (figures 6.39 and 6.40). The smaller the reeds in relative size, the more the effect is to create texture rather than a group of similar profiles.

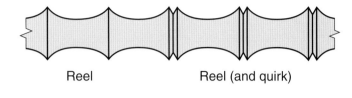

Reel   Reel (and quirk)

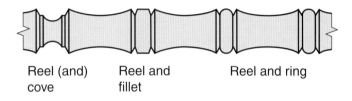

Reel (and)   Reel and   Reel and ring
cove   fillet

Reel A spindle profile resulting from turning coves. The length of reels can vary considerably (see bead and reel turnings, page 134).

Ring A small bead used in isolation to separate larger profiles and grouped to create texture (figures 6.9 and 6.41).

Figure 6.40 **A reeded vessel, *Narcissa Garden* by Bill Hunter** of Rancho Palos Verdes, California.

Roll and fillet molding Of almost circular cross section with one or more proud fillets.

A bead retains its individuality even when grouped

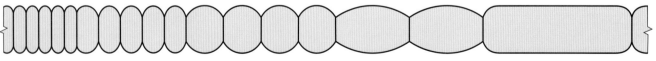

A ring is a relatively small bead which when grouped creates texture

A ball has the same full diameter as the spindle irrespective of the balls' overlap or separation

A bobbin is a wide, shallow bead with an arclike profile

A sausage is wider and flatter than a bobbin

Figure 6.41 **The shapes and relative sizes of the symmetrical convex moldings.**

Figure 6.42 **A stand decorated with roll billet moldings** (essentially cylindrical billets partially recessed into semicircular grooves). Both flat and domed pellets are glued around the hexagonal plinth.

Roll billet molding   A molding consisting of cylindrical billets let into grooves of semicircular cross-section. When there are multiple grooves, the fillets are usually staggered (figure 6.42).

Rosette (*rosace*)   A disk turned and carved to resemble a conventionalized floral motif.[32] Reproduced courtesy of Dover Publications.

Figure 6.43 **Roundels carved on the doors of a sixteenth-century oak chest.**[31]

Roundel A flush bead cut into a corner angle or square edge. The quirks are included in the term. In woodturning it is sometimes used at the edges of rims and bases. If the roundel stands proud, it is called an edge roll (page 139).

The term "roundel" is also used to describe a carving surrounded by a turned frame (figure 6.43).

The term also refers to thin wooden disks resembling table mats used in England in the sixteenth and seventeenth centuries, plain on one side and having poesies written on the other. The diners sang or recited these poesies after their meals.[33]

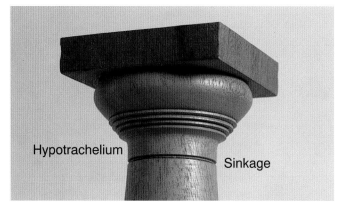

Figure 6.44 A Greek Doric capital. The *sinkage* is the narrow groove denoting the top of a Greek Doric column shaft. The *hypotrachelium* or *gorgerin* is the neck between the sinkage and the annulets at the base of the echinus.

Sausage turning Profiles resembling this delectable food item with the questionable contents, similar to but slenderer than melon bulbs (figure 6.41).

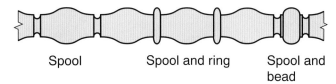

Spool   Spool and ring   Spool and bead

Spool A profile resembling a wound spool. If spools are separated by small channels, coves or V-cuts, the separating moldings are not usually mentioned in the compound molding's name: projecting separating features such as rings or fillets are usually mentioned.

Segmental billet A molding formed by billets with cross sections which are segments, usually semicircular, of a circle in cross section, glued onto a flat surface or the bottom of a channel.

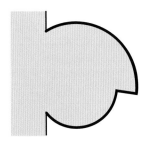

Scroll molding A molding which resembles a scroll with the outer free end hanging down in cross section.

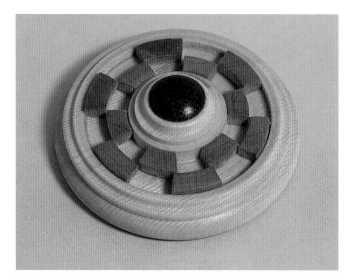

Square billet molding Composed of separated projecting cubes or billets of square or rectangular cross section. The cubes or billets are staggered where there is more than one row of them.

S-*curve* An ogee.

Sinkage The groove below the necking of a Greek Doric column (figure 6.44).

Sunk fillet   A channel.

Surbase   The top moldings or cornice of a column pedestal above the die or dado (figure 6.37).

Sikhara (sikra)   A convex tapering tower characteristic of Indian temples. The decorated, somewhat mushroom-shaped top is called an *amalaka* (*amalasari* or *amalasila*).

Thistle   The form of the flower of the Scottish thistle *Onopordum acanthium*, used particularly to communicate a connection with Scotland.

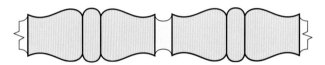

Toad-back   A moulding of two cymas connected by a small bead. It is so named because it resembles the profile across a toad's back. The longitudinal section through a toad's back lacks the serpentine curves, and is therefore ugly according to William Hogarth (page 23).

Tee   A finial in the form of a vertical stack of stylized umbrellas. Originally used on pagodas, tees are sometimes incorporated into the designs of chessmen.

Treacle molding   The derivation of the name is obvious.

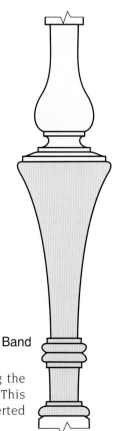

Band

Trumpet   A spindle form resembling the natural horn musical instrument. This trumpet is *banded*.[34] Legs with inverted trumpets are shown in figure 6.36.

Urn   Lidded vessels of many shapes have been used for funerary purposes and thus qualify as urns. If however the term "urn" is to be useful to describe form, the range of forms to which the term is applicable needs to be restricted. I propose that urn shapes should resemble that of the knife box in figure 6.45. The two darker component forms in the spindles in figure 6.46 might also qualify.

Figure 6.46   **Two urn forms in spindles.**[36]

Figure 6.45   **A knife box urn** on the pedestal of a sideboard. The pedestal door is ornamented with a rosette.[35]

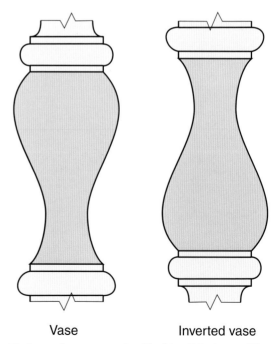

Vase   Inverted vase

Vase   Various shapes are signified by this term. These are my recommendations. An *inverted vase* is similar to a flared baluster .

6.2.6 USING MOLDINGS

When designing ornament you can use moldings:

1. Singly.
2. Adjacent to one another in part-groups (figure 6.47).
3. To create a pattern—this is often done by repeating a single molding or group of moldings (figure 6.48).
4. To create texture—the individual moldings do not have to be identical for this.

The designing of the size, shape, placement and integration of moldings is at the heart of detailed design, and is discussed in the next chapter.

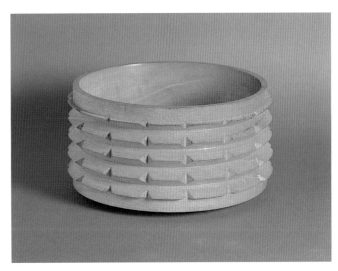

Figure 6.48 **A repeating pattern of ornament formed by circumferential V-rings and vertical V-cuts.** The turner is unknown.

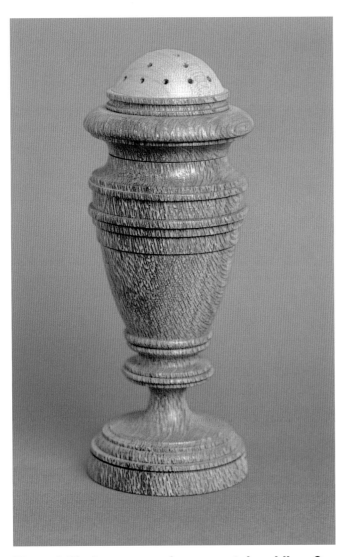

Figure 6.47 **An excess of ornamental moldings?** This caster is similar to that pictured in figure 6.4. Does the complexity of the moldings prevent an experiencer from perceiving the underlying ovoid? In my view "Yes", and this is a design fault.

6.3 ENDNOTES

1. Barry Bergdoll, *European Architecture 1750–1890* (Oxford University Press, 2000), p. 176.

2. F. M. Simpson, *A History of Architectural Development*, vol. I (London: Longmans Green, 1921), p. 30.

3. Ronald Paulson in p. xxi of his notes to William Hogarth, *The Analysis of Beauty* (New Haven: Yale University Press, 1997) explains that the transparent pyramid enclosing the serpent symbolizes the Holy Trinity. In the pyramid the serpent replaces the Tetragrammaton, the four Hebrew letters that form the name of God. The use of the serpent is also an allusion to the following verse from Milton's poem "Satan Tempting Eve" which is printed higher on Hogarth's title page:

    > So vary'd be, and of his tortuous train
    > Curl'd many a wanton wreath, in fight of Eve,
    > To lure here eye.

    John Milton (1608–1674) was an English poet, remembered particularly for "Paradise Lost" (1667) and "Paradise Regained" (1677).

4. This property was detailed in Owen Jones, *The Grammar of Ornament* (London: Day & Son, 1856; reprint, London: Studio Editions, 1986), p. 67.

5. C. Howard Walker, *Theory of Mouldings* (Cleveland, Oregon: J. H. Jansen, 1926), p. 11.

6. Hanno-Walter Kruft, *A History of Architectural Theory from Vitruvius to the Present* (New York: Princeton Architectural Press, 1994), p. 190.

7. The recent reference books that I found most useful on naming of moldings are:

    John Gloag, *A Short Dictionary of Furniture* (London: George Allen and Unwin, 1969).

    Cyril M. Harris, ed., *Illustrated Dictionary of Historic Architecture* (1977; reprint, New York: Dover Publications, 1983).

    J. Henry Parker, *Classic Dictionary of Architecture* (1875; reprint, Poole, Dorset: New Orchard Editions, 1986).

    Dora Ware and Maureen Stafford, *An Illustrated Dictionary of Ornament* (London: George Allen & Unwin, 1974).

8. Sebastiano Serlio, *Tutte l'opere d'architettura et prospettiva* (*The Five Books of Architecture*) (Venice, 1584; reprint New York: Dover Publications, 1982), third book, fourth chapter, folio 62v.

9. Capital from Warmington church, Northhamptonshire, c. 1280, pictured in John Henry Parker, *A Glossary of terms Used in Grecian, Roman, Italian, and Gothic Architecture*, part II, 4th ed. (London: David Bogue, 1845), plate 30.

10. Capital from Bloxham, Oxfordshire, c.1220, pictured in John Henry Parker, plate 30.

11. John Henry Parker, plate 5.

12. William Chambers, *A Treatise on the Decorative Part of Civil Architecture* (1791; reprint, New York: Benjamin Blom, 1968), opposite p. 46.

13. Serlio, fourth book, sixth chapter, folio 17v.

14. The name "bag" is taken from Franz Sales Meyer, *Handbook of Ornament* (1888; reprint, New York: Dover Publications, 1957), p. 304, plate 181. Canopus was a city in ancient Egypt, and the name recalls the shape of burial jars for the viscera removed during mummification. The naming of the canopy of a parachute has the same source.

15. A. Graef and M. Graef, *Moderner Drechslerarbeiten* (1889; reprint, Hannover: Th. Schafer Druckerei, 1982), plate xxiii.

16. John Henry Parker, plate 38.

17. Chambers, plate opposite p. 103.

18. Andrea Palladio, *The Four Books of Architecture* (1738; reprint, New York: Dover Publications, 1965), opposite p. 107.

19. Gloag, pp. 160 and 279. The illustration is based on the drawing in Ware and Stafford, p.69.

20. Frederick Litchfield, *Illustrated History of Furniture*, 3rd ed. (London: Truslove & Hanson, 1893), p. 106.

21. Illustration based on Wallace Nutting, *Furniture Treasury* (New York: Macmillan Publishing, 1928), figure 4772.

22. Serlio, fourth book, ninth chapter, folio 59r.

23. John Henry Parker, plate 81.

24. Chambers, plate opposite p. 52.

25. George Hersey, *The Lost Meaning of Classical Architecture* (Cambridge, Massachusetts: The MIT Press, 1988), p. 6.

26. J. Henry Parker, p. 116.

27. A. Rosengarten, *Architectural Styles* (London: Chatto And Windus, 1878), p. 194.

28. Rosengarten, p. 193.

29. Thomas Sheraton, *The Cabinet-Maker and Upholsterer's Drawing-Book* (1791–1794; reprint, New York: Dover Publications, 1972), plate 59.

30. Lichfield, opposite p. 206.

31. Lichfield, p. 72.

32. Paul N. Hasluck, ed., *Manual of Traditional Wood Carving* (1911; reprint, New York: Dover Publications), p. 303.

33. Owen Evan-Thomas, *Domestic Utensils of Wood* (1932; reprint, Wakefield, Yorkshire: EP Publishing, 1973), p. 63.

34. Illustration based on Wallace Nutting, figure 4774.

35. Litchfield, opposite p. 200.

36. Illustrations based on Meyer, candelabrum 2 on p. 223; and leg 2 on p. 323.

Chapter Seven

THE DETAILED DESIGN OF FORM

In this chapter I discuss detailed design, the process by which you refine the preliminary design and all the assumptions and decisions on which it was based. Detailed design will usually give a superior version of the preliminary design. It may also lead to you rejecting the preliminary design, and either returning to stage 1 to produce a new preliminary design, or delaying or abandoning the project.

One approach to detailed design is to follow rules or laws. Franklin H. Gottshall in *Design for the Craftsman* provides fifty-eight "universal laws of design" on form, plus another thirty-six on ornament and decoration.[1] Gottshall's laws are unwieldy in number, and attempt the impossible task of defining appropriateness. In contrast, in *Woodturning Design* I concentrate on attempting to give you an appreciation of appropriateness, and question design laws rather than advocate them. I also stress the roles of parts, introduced in the description of Hogarth's *The Analysis of Beauty* on pages 23 to 27.

The concept that a form is built-up from parts is not new, although its usefulness in the producing a design and in analysing a finished design has been underrated. This utilization of the concept of parts I call *design-by-parts*. It complements design-by-drawing. Like most techniques it uses tools, the subject of this chapter's first section.

Chapters 4 and 5 discussed concepts and intentions and their practical applications. The second section of this chapter discusses other factors which are important in detailed design. It also leads into the major section, 7.3, on designing by parts, and the last major section which illustrates the combined application of design-by-parts and design-by-drawing to two preliminary designs.

7.1 DESIGN TOOLS

Many woodturning profiles contain sections which approximately, even if unknowingly, follow mathematically-defined curves. However, I suggest that there is usually little gain from accurately calculating and plotting such curves when designing turnings—French curves and similar are quicker, or you can draw the curves freehand. The turner, who may be you, will usually be "drawing" these curves freehand on the wood when it is spinning in the lathe, so why not practice drawing them freehand when designing? Whether formally plotted, traced, or freehand, you will still need to define on the design drawing, the turning gauges, and the rotating wood, the longitudinal position of, and the

diameter at reference locations such as maximum and minimum diameters and sharp changes in direction.

The second design tool described in this section is the regulating line.

7.1.1 CURVES

The profiles of parts can have straight or curved edges. The curves can be arcs (curves cut from circles), or can vary in curvature along their lengths.

Design texts sometimes state that arcs are more boring and less beautiful than varying-curvature curves, a view which I broadly support. There are often sound aesthetic and other reasons for using arcs in profile, but varying-curvature curves are more expressive. Consider the analogy of driving round and round the helical ramp of a multistory car park. Once the front wheels are at the correct angle you can become bored because you do not have to adjust the steering wheel as you pass between floors. Similarly, as you drive around a tightening bend, you concentrate more, and your expectation that something new will happen rises.

Curves of varying curvature can, as shown on pages 130 and 131, express force and even motion. Our perceptions of these in turn contribute to our feelings that some varying-curvature curves can be particularly beautiful.

Form profiles which give an impression that they incorporate curves of continuously-varying curvature can be constructed solely from arcs (figures 7.1 and 7.2).

A curve which tangentially connects two arcs (a straight line can be considered as an arc with an infinitely-long radius of curvature) and has an orderly change in curvature along its length is often called a *transition curve*.

Among the infinite number of mathematically defined curves with varying curvatures are the catenary, and the conic-sections or conics: the ellipse, the parabola, and the hyperbola. These are described in figures 7.3 to 7.7. Logarithmic spirals are described in figures 7.8 to 7.10. I have not detailed other families of curves such as roulettes, glissettes, and involutes.

It is important to define sufficient reference points on a designed curve so that the turner can replicate the design accurately on the wood (figure 7.11). This is especially so with serpentine curves because relatively small variations in the positions of the sections of maximum and minimum diameter and points of inflection greatly affect curve expressiveness (figure 7.12).

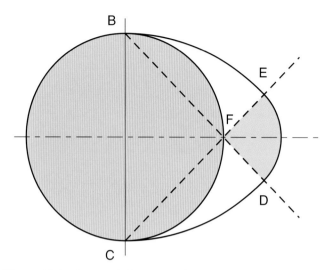

Figure 7.1 An oval drawn only from arcs of three curvatures. Although there are abrupt changes in perimeter curvature at *B*, *C*, *D*, and *E*, they are not obvious when one arc joins another tangentially.

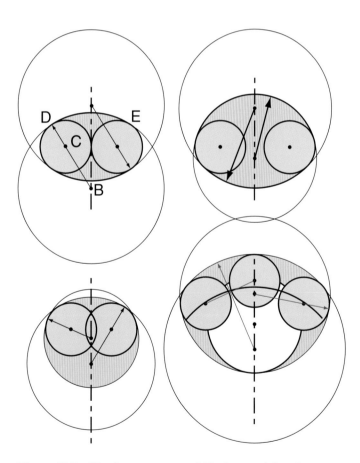

Figure 7.2 Circles, arcs, and their combinations.
Arcs can be combined to produce outlines with apparently continuously-varying curvatures. Although the abrupt changes in curvature are disguised because the arcs join one another tangentially, arcs are better joined by transition curves.

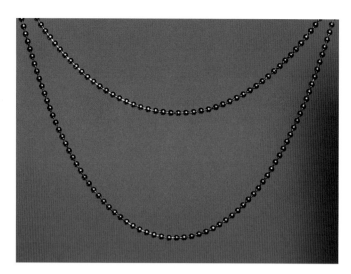

Figure 7.3 The catenary is the curve in which a perfectly flexible chain or cable hangs between two points. Its general equation was discovered by Leibniz and Huygens in 1691.[2]

Any part of the length of a catenary can be used in a design, and the axes of the curve from which the segment is cut do not have to be horizontal and vertical (this applies to all curves).

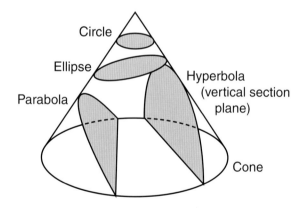

Figure 7.4 How to slice through a cone to reveal the four conic sections.
The conic sections were first studied in detail in the fourth century B.C. by Menaechmus, a pupil of Plato. Other early Greek contributions to the understanding of conics were by Euclid, Archimedes, and Apollonius of Perga. The general equations for the four conics are:

Circle	$r^2 = (x - a)^2 + (y - b)^2$
Ellipse	$1 = x^2/a^2 + y^2/b^2$
Parabola	$y = ax^2 + bx + c$
Hyperbola	$y = x/a$

where a, b, and c are constants which can have any value. The ellipse, parabola, and hyperbola are described in the next three figures.

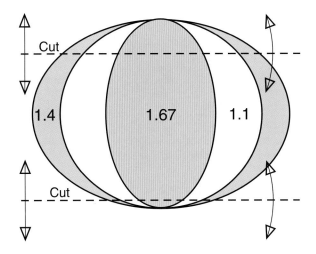

Figure 7.5 **Ellipses are symmetrical closed curves with continuously varying curvatures.** The ratios of the length of the major axis (longest "diameter") to the minor axis (shortest "diameter") can be varied, and three are pictured. Ellipses can be cut through at different heights and at different angles to produce an infinite number of different curves. The geometry of the ellipse is detailed in *Woodturning Methods*, p. 149.

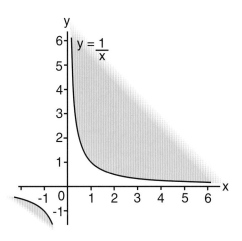

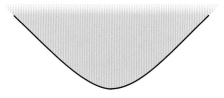

Figure 7.7 **The hyperbola y = 1/x.** In the lower diagram the same hyperbola has been redrawn after being rotated until it is symmetrical about a vertical axis.

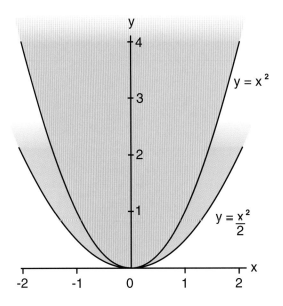

Figure 7.6 **The parabolas y = x², and y = x²/2.** The parabolas are perhaps the most elegant of the conics. Ignoring air resistance but not gravity, the path of a thrown object viewed in side elevation is a parabola.

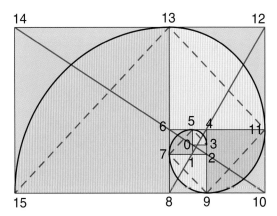

Figure 7.8 **The logarithmic spiral based on the Golden rectangle** is typical of shell growth. Each consecutive extension to the spiral is what Jay Hambridge calls a "whirling square."[3] Thus starting from the Golden rectangle *0123* a square of side length *03* is added to form the new, next larger Golden rectangle *1245*. The process can be continued ad infinitum, both outwards and inwards.

Some shells tend to grow in this spiral, although their spirals have a continuously changing curvatures, and are not built from tangentially joining quarter circles as shown here.

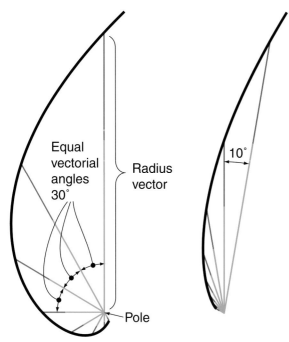

Figure 7.9 Logarithmic spirals based on the equal vectorial angles of 30° (*left*) and 10° (*right*), and radius vectors whose lengths increase according to the Golden ratio (see next figure below).

An infinite number of different spirals can be drawn by varying the vectorial angle between the radius vectors and by using different formulae to calculate or draw the lengths of the radius vectors. The center from which the radius vectors radiate is called the *pole*.

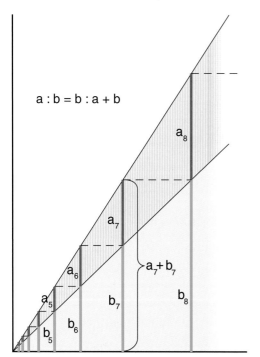

Figure 7.10 The construction of the lengths of the radius vectors used in the preceding figure. The lengths are based on the Golden ratio.

7.1.2 DEFINING CURVES

Figures 7.11 and 7.12 discuss what should be specified on the final design drawing and on the turner's gauge for the turner to be fully informed on the profiles to be turned. A lack of care in preparing pencil and other gauges, and a reluctance by the turner to study the design and become clear on both the design's intentions and the details, rather than poor turning technique, is often the cause of imprecise replication of the designer's intentions. When you, the designer, are also the turner, the tendency is that you rush the design, and expect to clarify what you neglected to clarify in the design stage while you're turning.

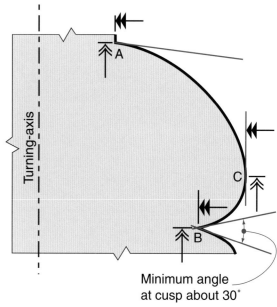

Figure 7.11 Defining curves which are convex or concave. The straight magenta lines are tangents. The following information needs to be clearly drawn on the detailed design drawing and be clear in the turner's mind:

1. The diameters and distances along the turning-axis of each end of the curve (at *A* and *B*, although the turner will not be able to accurately calliper the diameter at *B*).
2. The slope of the tangent to the curve at each end of the curve (at *A* and *B*).
3. The diameter and distance along the turning axis of the minimum or maximum diameter (here at *C*). At this diameter a tangent to the curve will be parallel to the turning-axis. Obviously the circle the turner pencils on the rotating workpiece at a minimum diameter will soon be turned off, but knowing where it was and having a picture of the curve, both mental and on the gauge, will help the turner replicate the designed curve profile accurately.

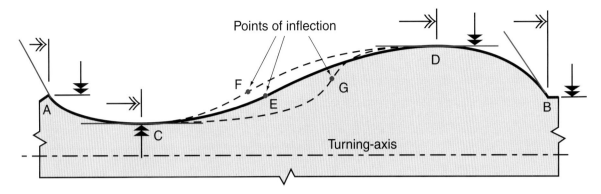

Figure 7.12 Defining serpentine curves. Specifying the details at the ends and at the maximum and minimum diameters of a serpentine curve is not enough. The long profile between the maximum and minimum diameters C and D is particularly liable to be misshapen by the turner. The information which the turner needs to turn a serpentine curve precisely is:

1. The diameters and distances along the turning-axis of each end of the curve.
2. The slope of the tangent to the curve at each end.
3. The diameter and distance along the turning axis of each maximum or minimum diameter. At these diameters a tangent to the curve will be parallel to the turning-axis.
4. A clear picture of the curve between maximum and minimum diameters. Just three of the infinite number of possible curves between C and D are shown. You could define the diameter and distance along the turning-axis of one or more points along the correct curve between C and D. More commonly, the turner will eye the curve from that drawn on the design drawing or gauge.

7.1.3 REGULATING LINES

Regulating lines are straight lines or arcs used to align and position parts of a design so that those parts will be in definite spacial relationships to one another. Figure 7.13 shows the use of regulating lines in the design of a church. Figure 7.14 shows three vases designed using regulating lines.

Proponents of regulating lines believe that they give a perceptible logic to the design, and that the definite spacial relationships add harmony to the design.[4] Whether the eye always perceives the nice relationships is doubtful, especially when the experiencer cannot view the object in the same way as the draftsman who drew the regulating lines.

Is a regulated arrangement of parts more beautiful? If you can perceive the relationships established by using regulating lines, does this make the object more beautiful? A design produced using regulating lines is more likely to express harmony and symmetry. It is also likely that if a design does not perceptibly quite conform to a regulated arrangement of parts, the imprecision will distract and prevent unfettered enjoyment of the beauty.

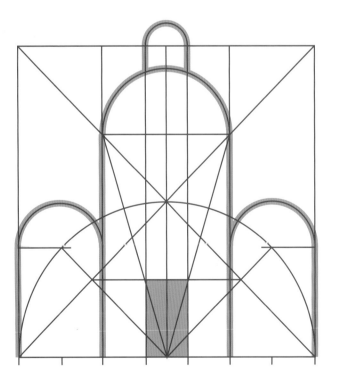

Figure 7.13 Regulating lines used to design a section through the nave and aisles of a church, copied from drawings by Francesco di Giorgio and Philibert de l'Orme.[6]

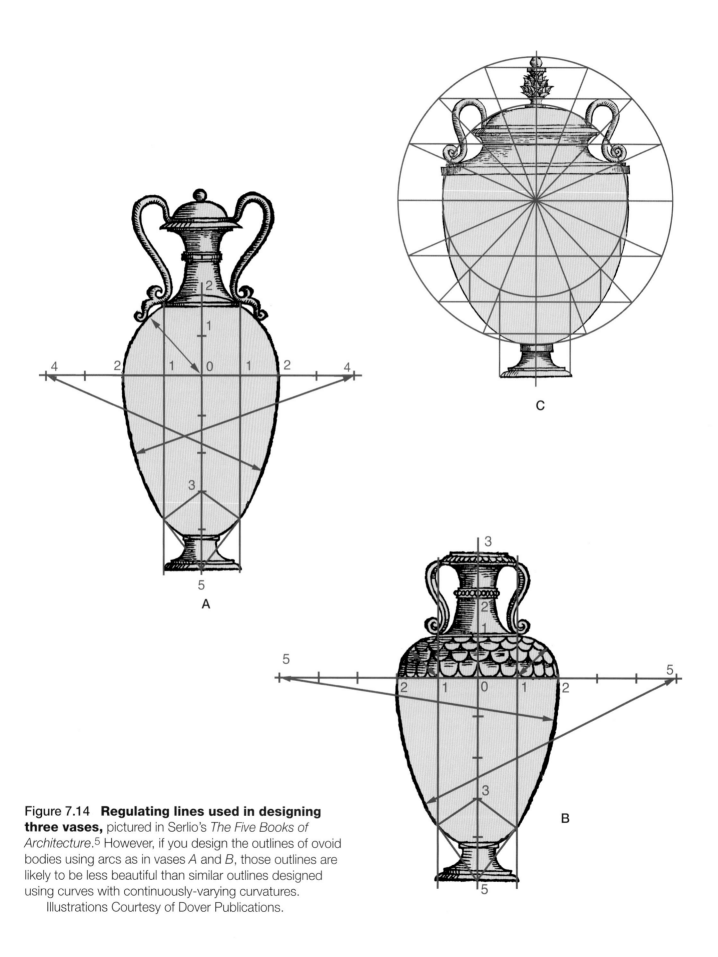

Figure 7.14 **Regulating lines used in designing
three vases,** pictured in Serlio's *The Five Books of
Architecture*.[5] However, if you design the outlines of ovoid
bodies using arcs as in vases *A* and *B*, those outlines are
likely to be less beautiful than similar outlines designed
using curves with continuously-varying curvatures.
　　Illustrations Courtesy of Dover Publications.

7.2 WHOLISTIC DETAILED DESIGN

Figure 7.15 outlines the process of detailed design. This section discusses eight factors which govern or influence the design of the overall form, and through it the designs of the part-groups and parts. These factors, together with the intentions, the design style, the restraints, etc. form the context, albeit one which can still be varied, within which you design the part-groups and the parts in detail.

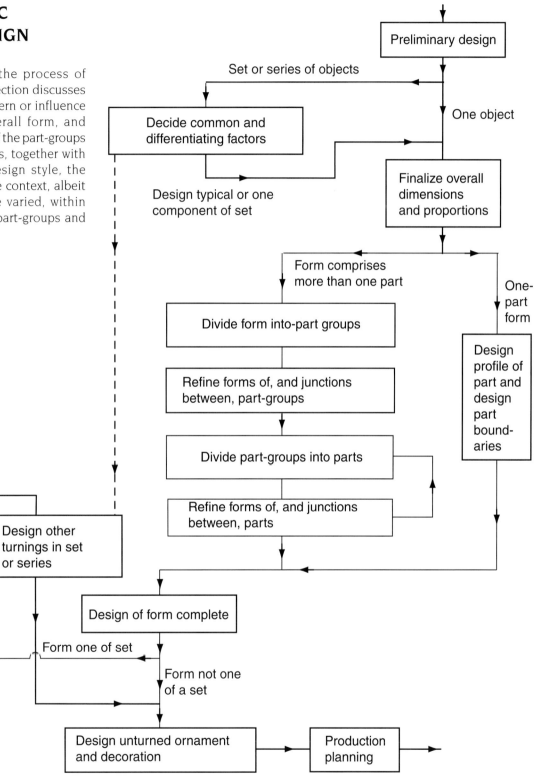

Figure 7.15 An idealized and orderly description of the process of detailed design. The actual process is likely to be less orderly and include much more churning back to reassess and possibly change earlier design decisions. These then have to be followed forwards which may reveal unforeseen consequences which may necessitate further changes.

7.2.1 ABSOLUTE SIZE

If not specified in the preliminary design, the first step in the detailed design is often to fix one or more the object's basic dimensions, especially the overall height and/or the maximum diameter. Basic dimensions may be imposed (figures 7.16 and 7.17), be variable within limits, or be able to be chosen arbitrarily. The following factors are material:

1. Whether the turning is functional. Utility is an intention which usually determines that the size of the turning must lie within a restricted range. If the turning is nominally utilitarian, distorting its customary size or proportions may be an artifice because of the implied rejection of utility (figure 7.18). Such departures may not be more or less beautiful than the customary, but are more likely to jolt our senses. Some items can properly be found in widely differing sizes.
2. The available sizes of working materials (figure 7.16). Where freedom from cracking is important, the advisability of excluding the pith and the sapwood, may further limit the dimensions of the pieces of wood which are suitable.
3. Whether the turning is a component and has to fit with or within other components and objects.
5. Your resources, budget, and equipment (for example, lathe capacity), may influence the choice of size.

6. The desire to exploit size expressively. For immense objects there is a respect that the makers were able to source, afford, and shape the huge mass of material. For tiny objects there is a wonderment at the skill needed to work tiny pieces of material. Designs which are many times greater or smaller than customary are artifices, and may provoke experiencer reactions in addition to those of respect and wonder.

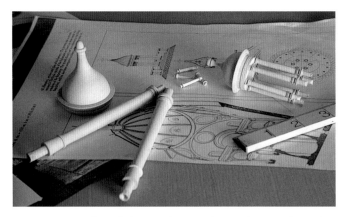

Figure 7.17 Small in both absolute size and scale, a lantern for an architectural model of a dome. The sizes were determined by the sizes of the full size original and the scale of the model. A piece of doll's house furniture is also both full-sized and a reduced-scale copy.

Figure 7.16 A large spindle, the central column for a pole house, 19 ft. (5.8 m) long. The length was specified, the form was designed by the client within the material restraint of the power poles which were available.

Figure 7.18 Unusual proportions. The tall box and eggcup jolt because of their unusual overall proportions. The needle case which has a similar ratio of length to diameter does not jolt because its proportions are customary.

7.2.2   PROPORTIONS OF THE FORM

I showed on pages 47 to 53 that the beauty of an object has little connection with its overall proportions. I also showed that we are sensitive to slight departures from the common geometric norms such as straight, square, cubic, circular, conic, spherical, etc. A related, almost contradictory belief is that we find simple overall proportions boring, and should therefore avoid them in our designs. In view of the difficulty of defining overall proportion discussed in chapter 4, a sounder guideline might be: if the overall proportions of a design are recognizable, unless there is an overriding reason otherwise, they should be modified to be not readily recognizable. The point is not that recognizable proportions are less beautiful or more boring, but that they are a distraction from an object's other more important properties.

7.2.3   STABILITY

Most turnings are designed to rest in a particular orientation which is signalled by the presence of a base, footrim, feet, or similar. High stability reinforces the impression of mass and strength. Instability can heighten the impression of delicacy (figure 7.19). Some wrongly believe that narrow bases on vessels require high turning skill

There is no quantitative measure for stability. Neither is it related solely to form. You assess stability according to what you sense and according to what you reasonably assume. Subjects for assumption include densities and wall thicknesses. For example, in assessing the stability of the lamp in figure 9.5 on page 191, you would not assume that

Figure 7.19 Intentional top-heaviness in a vessel by Michael Hosaluk of Saskatoon, Saskatchewan. The success of this design does not lead to the general conclusion that top-heaviness or instability or the presence of three legs is necessary for a vessel to be regarded as a work of art.

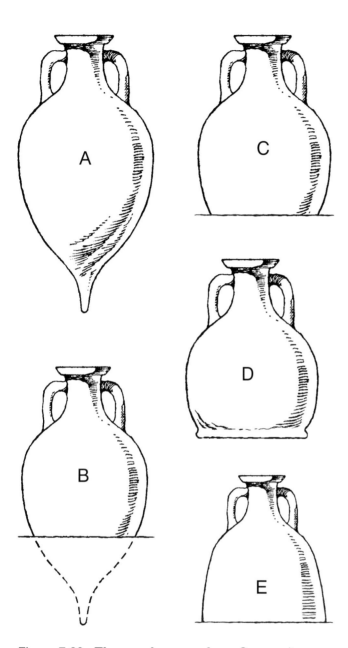

the lampshade is a solid mass of heavy material.

Some writers believe, incorrectly in my view, that we assess stability using what I shall call the amphora analogy (figure 7.20).

Stability is not only concerned with an object in static isolation. What could reasonably be expected to happen to the object is also relevant. A table with feet which project out past the rim of its top may be more stable than one with feet which do not project, but there is an additional risk of knocking the first table over when you trip on the projecting feet. A container's stability will also vary according to how full it is, and with what.

7.2.4 AVAILABILITY OF COMPONENTS

The availability and affordability of materials and other resources has been discussed under various headings, notably that of feasibility (page 94). A related issue is the availability of manufactured components. Check what is available early in the design process to avoid having to later redesign or abandon the project (figure 7.21).

Figure 7.20 The amphora analogy. Some writers maintain that we assess the stability of a form by imagining that the form continues below the hard surface on which it rests like a pointed-bottomed amphora, *A*, which is standing in sand, *B*. They claim that our assessment of the stability of an object such as vessel *C* standing on a hard surface is related to the size and form of the imaginary buried volume shown dotted in *B*.

This analogy ignores our conceptual knowledge that none of the volume of an object standing on a hard surface is buried below that surface. Further, for vessels *D* and *E*, what volume does one imagine lies buried below the surface? and if you cannot reasonably assume a volume, do you then assess the vessel as stable or unstable?

The image of the amphora is reproduced courtesy of Dover Publications.[7]

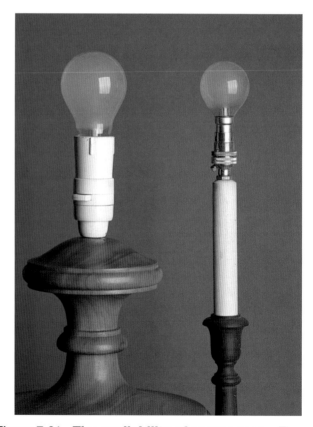

Figure 7.21 The availability of components. The plastic bulbholder is widely available, the small brass one is not. The appearance of many small lamps is spoiled by their having the large plastic bulbholder.

7.2.5 GRADING AND SETS

When designing turnings which will form a set or series you have to design the features which they have in common, and any features which distinguish different turnings in the set. These features may include: size, form, ornament, color or decoration, wood species, grain orientation, and communicated meanings. Figures 7.22 and 7.23 show series in which the individual turnings only vary in size. The relationships between the members of the chess sets in figures 4.21 and 5.48, and the pagoda boxes in figure 5.44 are more complicated.

If you intend the members of a set to fit together to form an additional entity, you should design the turnings so that both the separated individual members and the assemblage satisfy your design intentions.

Figure 7.22 **A nest of five bowls from the same blank by Mike Mahoney** of Orem, Utah. Mike parts the largest bowl free first, then the second largest, then the third largest, etc. The five bowls are obviously a nesting set because of the similarities in the wood. Mike has also ensured that the forms of the individual bowls are related.

Figure 7.23 **An ambiguous series of vessels by Christian Burchard** of Ashland, Oregon. At first sight some might assume that this is a nest of bowls turned from one circular madrone blank. Thought would then show that each bowl had to have been turned from its own separate blank.

7.2.6 EDGES, HOLES, AND PROFILES

Most turnings have edges, sometimes in the form of rims, footrims, or shoulders; some turnings have holes. Holes and edges may be natural or man-made. Holes can be completely or partially filled.

The discontinuities associated with edges and holes alert our senses and therefore need design attention. They also provide design opportunities. Edges, holes and profiles are often used to manifest intentions, especially to imitate (figures 7.24, 7.27, and 7.28), to express (figures 7.25, and 7.26), to ornament (figure 7.29), and to represent (figures 7.27, 7.28, and 7.30).

Figure 7.25 **Expression with edges, holes, and the texture of redwood burl;** *Fractured Millstone I* **by Robyn Horn of Little Rock, Arkansas;** 17 in. (430 mm) high.

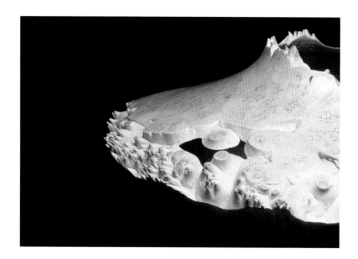

Figure 7.24 *White Stone Desert (top)* and *Two Canyons Mesa (bottom).* **Natural edges and bleaching are exploited by Michael Peterson of Lopez Island, Washington, to express weathered rock formations.** Care has been taken to keep crisp boundaries between the natural and sanded surfaces. Photographed by Jerry Davis.

Figure 7.26 **Natural, turned, and sawn edges,** *Fractured Millstone II* **by Robyn Horn;** 23 in. (580 mm) wide. The open texture of the jarrah burl is also critical to the success of the piece.

Figure 7.27 Pictorial profiles in *Wake* by potter Greg Payce of Calgary, Alberta. Its not the form of the objects which defines the idea, it's the spaces between them. *Wake* is therefore related to the face/goblet illusion (page 6). The jars are each 7 in. (180 mm) high.

Greg's inspiration was apothecary's jars which had concave profiles so that fingers could fit in between them to remove a jar when they were tightly packed on shelves.

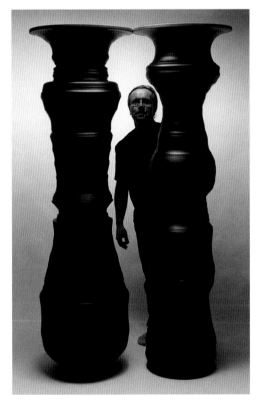

Figure 7.28 *Al Barelli* by Greg Payce, an enlarged version of the figure in *Wake* which allows people to interact with a virtual figure of their own size.

Figure 7.29 *The Edge* by Hans Joachim Weissflog of Hildesheim, Germany. The precise, square holes were turned; Amazonas rosewood burl, 6.5 in. (160 mm) diameter.

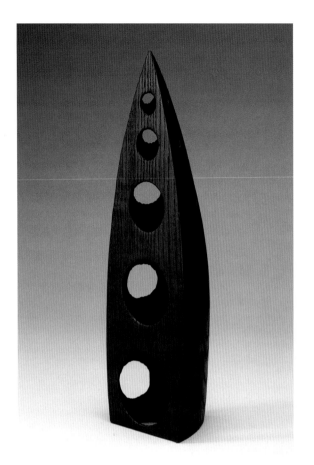

Figure 7.30 *Missing Home* by Graeme Priddle of Northland, New Zealand; in scorched and burnished ash. The inspirations were a weathered shipwreck and the work of American furniture maker George Nakashima. The five turned holes represent particular people and also the holds in a ship.

Graeme is one of the few turners whose work has been pictured on a postage stamp.

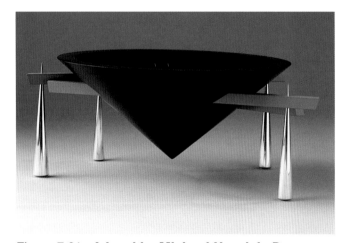

Figure 7.31 A bowl by Michael Hosaluk. Beams pass through holes in the bowl. The beams and conical legs are appendages, and have been designed to be appropriate in style, size, and decoration to the bowl.

7.2.7 APPENDAGES

An appendage is a subordinate attached part such as a knob, a handle, or a foot. The design of any appendage should be appropriate to the design of the rest of the object (figures 7.31 and 10.16). When harmony is an aesthetic intention, an appendage should be in the same style as the rest of the object, and should echo or repeat features from the rest of the object. The appendage should also be joined to the rest of the object appropriately.

7.2.8 GOOD PRACTICE

Designing in accordance with good practice restrains design freedom to a limited extent, but rewards by saving time and cost. If the design is to be produced in quantity, the savings can be considerable. Other possible gains include improved dimensional stability and less vulnerabilty to damage. You have to decide whether the potential gains are worth any required design compromises.

Good practices include:

1. Minimizing wood wasteage by designing to suit the sizes and condition of the wood likely to be used. Design within maximum diameters and maximum thicknesses which allow for any roughness, lack of straightness, cupping, and similar which are likely to be present in the wood.

2. Specifying any particular properties which are desirable in the wood. For example, for wide platters, bases, and similar turned from disks cut from planks, specify quartersawn planks to minimize future cupping.

3. "Softening" the ends of the squares, often by making them slightly convex, makes them less vulnerable and less aggressive (figure 7.32, and *Woodturning Methods*, page 44, figure 2.13).

4. Designing to minimize calipering during the turning. Will the appearance of the turning be significantly affected if diameters which differ slightly are made equal?

5. Designing to minimize the number of tool changes during turning, and the number of different drill diameters used.

6. Designing to avoid awkward-to-turn details such as beads next to pommels, deep narrow coves, and rings at the bottom of coves (figure 7.32). This is not the same as omitting details because you have not mastered how to turn them.

7. Designing to simplify chucking and the later turning-off of features which have to be temporarily incorporated just for chucking.

8. Designing slender spindles to avoid having to use, or, if this is not possible, to suit, steadies (*Woodturning Methods*, pages 62 to 70).

Figure 7.32 Good and bad practices.
Left, the long fillet between the pommel and the bead has allowed the right-hand half of the left-hand bead to be turned with a wide skew, thereby saving an unnecessary tool change. The end of the left-hand pommel has also been rounded which is easier to turn and less liable to be damaged.

Center, the design of the cove, both because of its outer ends and because of the ring at its bottom, has made it more demanding to turn.

Right, the square-ended pommel and the adjacent bead are both more difficult to turn than the similar details to the left.

7.3 DESIGN-BY-PARTS

A finished object may be considered as being composed of one or more whole components. Each component may be considered as being composed of one or more part-groups, each of which is composed of one or more parts. Figures 7.33, 7.35 and 7.36 illustrate this hierarchical subdivision. Figure 7.34 shows that dividing a form into part-groups and parts is not always as straightforward as figure 7.33 implies. Fortunately it doesn't matter if you have to make arbitrary choices when dividing.

The concepts of part-groups and parts were foreshadowed by Hogarth (figures 3.15, 3.16, and 3.18). What I call design-by-parts itself has two parts: the hierarchical subdivision of forms; and the designing of forms or the analysis of existing forms using the hierarchical subdivision as your framework. Design-by-parts complements design-by-drawing, and is like it a development and formalization of something you already often do. Essentially, design-by-parts allows you to organize your designing or analysing of a design so that at any stage you are focusing on a manageable number of variables. The process is described diagrammatically in figure 7.37.

7.3.1 DIVISION OF AN OBJECT

Some definitions:
1. A *component* is a entity produced separately, and added to other completed or partially-completed components or assemblages of components to build the completed object. In many cases the turned object is a single turning, and can be considered as the sole component.
2. A *part-group* is one part, or a group of connected parts, which form a distinct form and an often nameable entity within the component's form such as a lid, a base, or a column.
3. A *part* is the smallest single entity of volume. In a turning it is typically a disk-like volume with a single revolved molding such as a fillet, bead, cove, or ogee, as its periphery. Some solid forms may consist of one part. A part may be:
    i. Major, or minor, or somewhere between.
    ii. Fulfilling a special function such as connecting, accenting, breaking the flow, separating, or terminating.
    iii. Dual-role, an ornament on a part, such as an astragal on a Roman Doric or Tuscan column shaft, and a part in its own right.
    iv. Negative or subtractive. The outside of a bowl can be a part which approximates to a solid hemisphere. The inside surface of the bowl is produced by subtracting or turning out an inside part, a smaller solid hemisphere.

7.3.2 DESIGNING AND ANALYSING

Design-by-parts is especially important during detailed design, but is also used during stage 1 in the production of the preliminary design. If, for example, you were designing an urn similar to that in figure 7.33, you would follow the process in figure 7.37 and:

1. Design an overall wholistic outline that is compatible with your intentions and the restraints which you are conscious of, indicating the components, in this case two, the lid and the base.
2. Divide each component into part-groups, and design each part-group to be successful in itself, and in its relationships with the other part-groups.
3. Divide the part-groups into parts. Then design each part so that it is successful in itself, and in its relationships with the other, particularly adjacent, parts.

While designing part-groups and then parts, you should also check back that earlier design decisions are not being compromised. Analysing the design of a finished object would proceed along a similar path. Examples of design analyses are shown on pages 191 to 196, and 207 to 208.

Figure 7.33 Dividing a form. *Left*, the whole urn divided into lid and base components. *Center*, the urn divided into three part-groups. *Right*, each of the three part-groups divided into parts, seventeen in total.

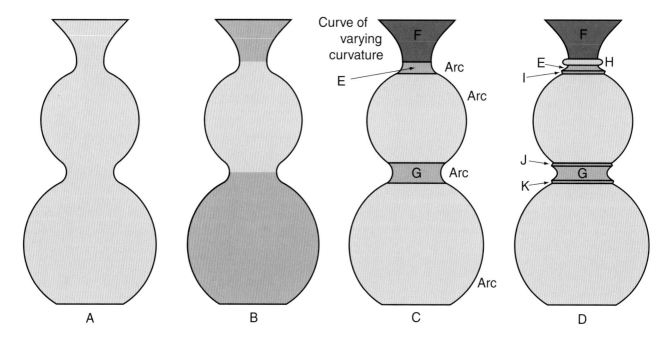

Figure 7.34 The problems of division. This double-gourd form could be considered as: *A*, one compound single part; or *B*, a three-part part-group; or *C*, as a four or five parts depending whether *E* is separate from or included with *F*. In *C* the divisions between parts are at the abrupt changes in curvature. The introduction of the fillets and ring in *D* creates more definite breaks, but *E*, *F*, *H*, and *I* are still best considered as one part-group. Similarly *J*, *G*, and *K* are usually considered as a part-group following the convention that fillets are associated in a part-group with the adjacent concave profile rather than with the adjacent convex profiles.

Figure 7.35 **Three Totemic Sculptures, a graphic illustration of design-by-parts by Mark Lindquist** of Quincy, Florida; heights 5 to 8 ft (1.5 to 2.4 m). *Left*, a stack of three part-groups. *Front*, a single part. *Right*, two single-part part-groups on a two-part part-group.

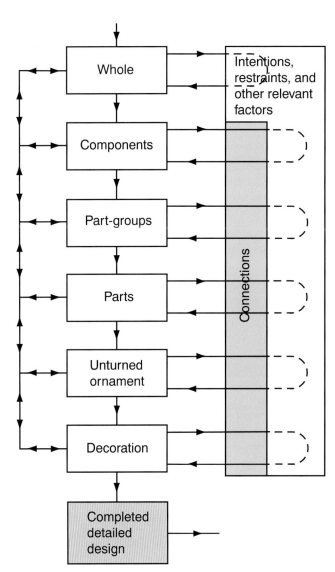

Figure 7.37 **Design-by-parts.** The orderly process represented by the primary downwards path does not exclude the need to churn backwards. The loops to the right represent the need to constantly consider the physical and visual connections between components, part-groups, parts, etc. The loops also refer to the need to constantly refer to, and where necessary refine and revise, your intentions, the restraints, and any other relevant factors.

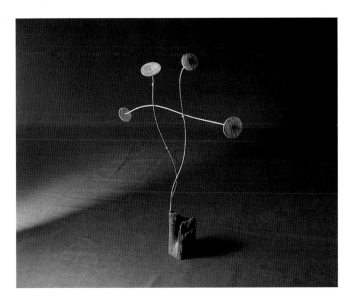

Figure 7.36 **Carpenter's Dilemma, a cross comprising two part-groups, one horizontal, one vertical by Ernie Newman** of Blaxland, New South Wales. Although joined, the horizontal and vertical part-groups retain their separateness because there is no significant structural or visual continuity across the joints between the two.

This work represents, among many things, the dilemma of the carpenter from Galilee, whether "to be a carpenter or a prophet?".

7.3.3   DESIGNING A SIMPLE PART

The simplest turning designs have one part. It can be a cylinder, a cone, or be produced by rotating a convex, concave, or serpentine curve about a turning-axis (figure 7.38). There may not be definite ends (figure 7.39), but if there are, they need not be perpendicular to the turning-axis or flat (figure 7.40). If one-part forms are hollowed they become forms with two or more parts (figures 7.38 and 7.40).

Figure 7.38 explores the design of a simple part with ends which are flat and perpendicular to the turning-axis. When beauty is sought and the form is not prescribed:

1. A curved outline is preferred to a straight one.
2. A convex outline may be preferred to a concave outline.

Figure 7.39   Parts without ends. Which is more beautiful, the sphere or the bun? Perhaps the bun, but sometimes you want the sphericity.

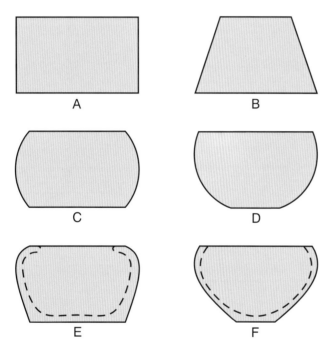

Figure 7.38   The beauty of a simple single part. *C* and *E* are constructed with arcs, *D* and *F* with curves of varying curvature.

Part *B* may be more notable than *A*, but is it more beautiful? Part *D* is more beautiful than *C* or *E*.

F is more beautiful than *E* or *D*. Are *A* and *B* less beautiful than *C*, *D*, *E*, and *F*? or does the comparison of straight with curved forms have little meaning?

These drawings suggest that a single simple part is more beautiful when its ends have unequal diameters and its side profiles are curved, but not with arcs.

Single part forms are often hollowed as indicated by the dotted lines in *E* and *F*, and thus become two-part forms. You should obviously design the inside and outside parts of each hollowed object in concert.

Figure 7.40   A three-part form by Peter Hromek of Sinntal, Germany. The turned inside and outside are each one part, and don't have a flat, top end perpendicular to the turning axis. The surface of the sapwood, which is a type of rim, can be considered as a third part.

3. An outline of varying curvature is preferred to one which is an arc.
4. The maximum or minimum diameter should not be halfway up or along the part.
5. The end diameters should not be equal.

Assuming that these guidelines have validity (which I do), it does not follow that to maximize the beauty of a multi-part object, all the parts should conform to these five recommendations. Too much harmony is boring; delight is better but depends on contrast in which the aesthetic properties of individual parts are accentuated by the presence of other parts with complementary forms.

7.3.4 INTERFACES BETWEEN PARTS

When parts flow continuously into one another, they must be distinguished by a change in material, and/or a change in texture, or decoration. More often there is a discontinuity

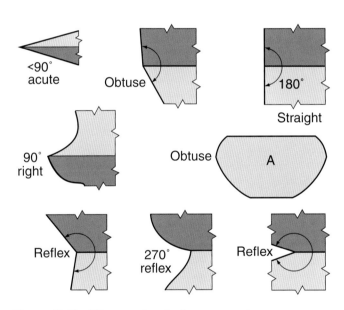

Figure 7.41 The angles between parts.
Angles of less than 180° do not always signify a junction between parts; they can signify what could be regarded as a discontinuity within a part, for example in a V-bead, or as shown in the elevation of form *A* where the effect of the obtuse angle is similar to that of a curve.

Obtuse and reflex angles close to 180° are visually indecisive.

Reflex angles of about 270° are preferred at junctions between parts (particularly where curves meet fillets), but can be as large as 330°.

The meetings of parts can be softened or ornamented by the presence of a small molding, often a fillet, bead, flushbead, or cove.

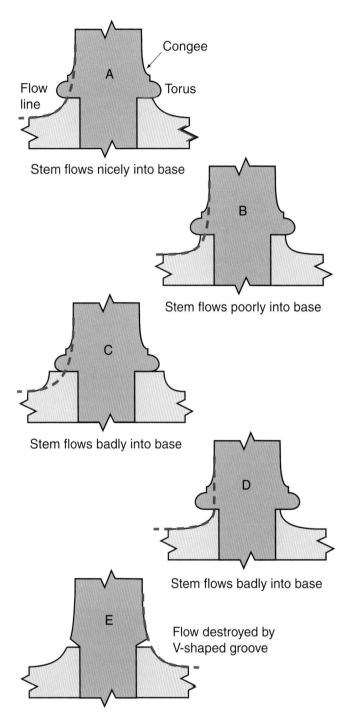

Figure 7.42 Flow-through from a stem into a base. The congee at the bottom of the stem is a signal that the dashed flow line (which represents the flow of shape and/or force) is about to change direction. For visual continuity, the congee and the surface of the base should follow the flow line. In *D* the change in direction of the flow line is too abrupt and the flow line does not attempt to follow the congee. Where there is strong visual continuity through a junction as in *A*, any feature at the junction is perceived to be outside the flow line. If the flow line is severed as in *E*, the feeling of continuity is lost.

in the profile where parts meet (figure 7.41).

When designing part-groups and parts, and thus the junctions between them, you should take care that the junction expresses the correct meaning:

1. Should the junction communicate that the parts are separate or separable? This can be implied even if the parts are not physically separable. Large reflex angles are effective at this.
2. Should there be a sense of structural continuity flowing through from one part-group or part into the next (figure 7.42).

The form of a design often has meaning. The response a designer usually seeks from an experiencer is "Yes!" not "Why?" or "What's happening?". A questioning reaction results from a lack of structural clarity, an ambiguity between form and meaning, or a clash between an experiencer's expectation or knowledge (usually of what is customary), and what the experiencer perceives.

7.3.5   THE FREE ENDS OF PARTS

Some parts have one or more free ends, free in the sense that their design is not governed by having to interface with adjacent parts. Free ends are typically the ends of spindles, the tops and bottoms of boxes, and the rims, footrims, and similar of vessels. Although free ends are usually flat and perpendicular to the objects main turning-axis, they do not have to be either (figure 7.43). They are also areas which require design attention because they are exposed.

Figure 7.43   A turning with two free carved ends by Peter Hromek.

7.3.6   GUIDELINES FOR DESIGNING PARTS

William Hogarth's huge contribution to the understanding of part-groups and parts (pages 23 to 27) was developed and formalized into rules of proportion by William H. Varnum in his *Industrial Arts Design* (1916).[8] I adapted Varnum's rules to woodturning design in my first book *The Practice of Woodturning*. However, I called Varnum's "laws" "guidelines" because they need to be applied with much more flexibility than "laws" implies. Although the guidelines are presented below as if they are only applicable to parts, they are just as applicable to part-groups.

The guidelines are broad-brush, and are few and short. They are a restricted attempt to flesh and "quantify" Scruton's sense of detail and appropriateness. They tend to reflect what is conventionally beautiful and harmonious, and has therefore become customary. Only if conventional beauty and harmony are among your major design intentions for an object should you consider following them closely.

GUIDELINE 1
When a form is divided by a horizontal into two parts and there is no overriding reason to make their heights equal, make their heights unequal.

Vertical symmetry (about a horizontal axis) is absent in nature except for reflections on still water. Perceptibly equal parts are therefore unusual, and jolt; their equality is a distraction rather than causing a lessening in beauty. To avoid the distraction the unequalness should be sufficient so that an experiencer does not question whether equalness was intended (figure 7.46).

Is there a preferred ratio of unequalness such as the Golden ratio? This question is explored in figures 7.44 and 7.45. I conclude that there is not a preferred ratio for the heights of two parts, that the transition from beautiful to not beautiful is gradual, and that as parts become less appropriate to one another in harmony, contrast becomes an increasingly desirable option (figure 7.47). There is also the additional problem for any who still support laws of proportion of defining the proportions of uncooperative forms, explored in figure 4.16, page 49.

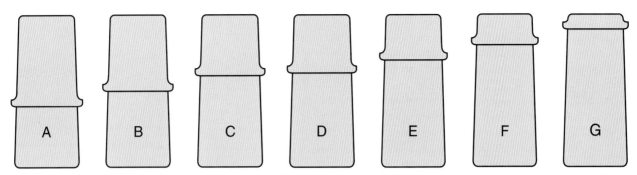

Figure 7.44 A series of boxes with different ratios of exposed lid height to exposed base height. The ratio of box *D* is the Golden ratio. I doubt that one could say that any one of the boxes *A* to *G* is significantly uglier than the rest, but *A*, *F*, and *G* are outside the customary range of proportions. The next figure shows alternative lid designs having the same lid height to base height ratios as *G*.

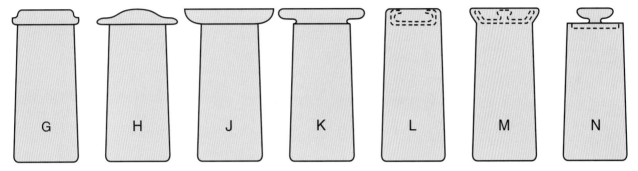

Figure 7.45 Alternative lid designs to that in *G*. Boxes *H* to *N* show just six of the infinite number of possible lid designs which could be more appropriate than that of box *G*. It seems that extreme ratios of height are more appropriate where the lid and base parts are dissimilar in form.

Figure 7.46 A silky oak *bound bowl* "pulled" into two parts by tensioning a stainless steel wire.

Figure 7.47 Box by David Pye, aesthetically successful despite the relatively small height of its lid because of the contrast in form between the lid and base parts; 5 in. (125 mm) high.

GUIDELINE 2.

When a form is divided by horizontals into three parts, all part heights should be unequal with the largest height placed between the other two. Alternatively, the parts may be placed in order of part height with the shortest or tallest at the bottom.

While sound, this guideline gives no guidance to the preferred ratios of the heights of the three parts. I advise that the respective heights should neither be almost identical nor vary by huge amounts (figure 7.48).

GUIDELINE 3.

When a form can be divided by horizontals into more than three parts, the parts should first be combined into two or three parts and/or part-groups. After these have been designed using guidelines 1 and 2, the parts within the part-groups should be designed also using guidelines 1 and 2.

The converse also applies when you are analysing a design: *any part-groups should be subdivisible using guidelines 1 and 2.* For example, the lowboy leg in figure 7.49 divides readily into part-groups, and is therefore more beautiful than the table leg in figure 7.50 which does not divide as readily.

Figure 7.48 Guideline 2 applied, a *Woznot* (derived by combining "whatnot" (a tiered display stand) and "Oz" (a slang term for Australia).

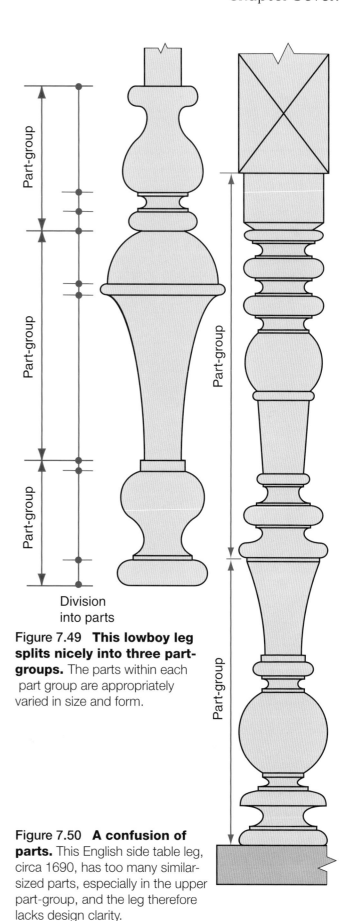

Division into parts

Figure 7.49 This lowboy leg splits nicely into three part-groups. The parts within each part group are appropriately varied in size and form.

Figure 7.50 A confusion of parts. This English side table leg, circa 1690, has too many similar-sized parts, especially in the upper part-group, and the leg therefore lacks design clarity.

GUIDELINE 4.

To avoid a top-heavy or unstable look, a form should usually decrease in width and depth (or diameter) towards the top. Top heaviness is also related to such ratios as overall height to base size, and the height of the perceived center of gravity to the base size. Figure 7.51 shows a top-heavy table.

Figure 7.51 Top-heaviness due to the deep rail and the lack of mass low in the legs.

GUIDELINE 5.

When a form is to be divided by a vertical into two parts or part-groups, if the parts are similar in form and transposed, it is preferable they be alike in size.

Compare the tables in figures 7.52 and 7.53.

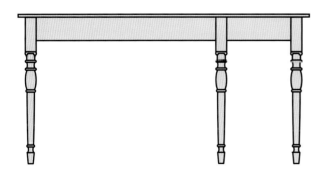

Figure 7.52 Uncustomary asymmetry. This asymmetrical table jolts because its design is not customary. Had one of the two bays been a stack of drawers, the reason for the different bay widths would have been apparent, and you would perceive its design as customary.

GUIDELINE 6.

When a form is divided by verticals into three parts, it is preferable if the central part is the widest, and the two outside parts are of equal width if they are similar in design.

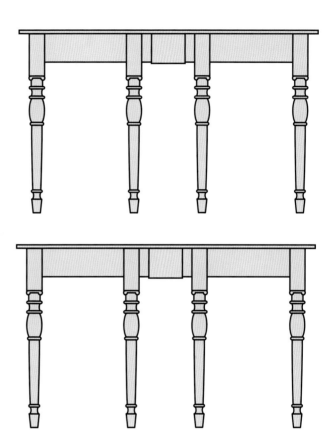

Figure 7.53 Three-part tables.
The upper table looks more beautiful, but there is no rational reason why it should. The validity of guideline 6 was recognized by classical architects who stipulated that the central space in a portico colonnade should be wider than the spaces between the other columns (page 245).

GUIDELINE 7.

When a form can be divided by verticals into more than three parts, the parts should first be combined into two or three parts and/or part-groups. After these have been designed using guidelines 5 and 6, the parts within the part-groups should be designed also using guidelines 5 and 6.

The converse also applies: *any part-groups should be subdivisible by verticals using guidelines 5 and 6.*

7.4 DESIGNING FOR APPROPRIATENESS

This section consists essentially of figures 7.54 and 7.55. They show the detailed design of a baluster and a caster, and demonstrate that by combining work with design-by-drawing and design-by-parts you can achieve appropriateness.

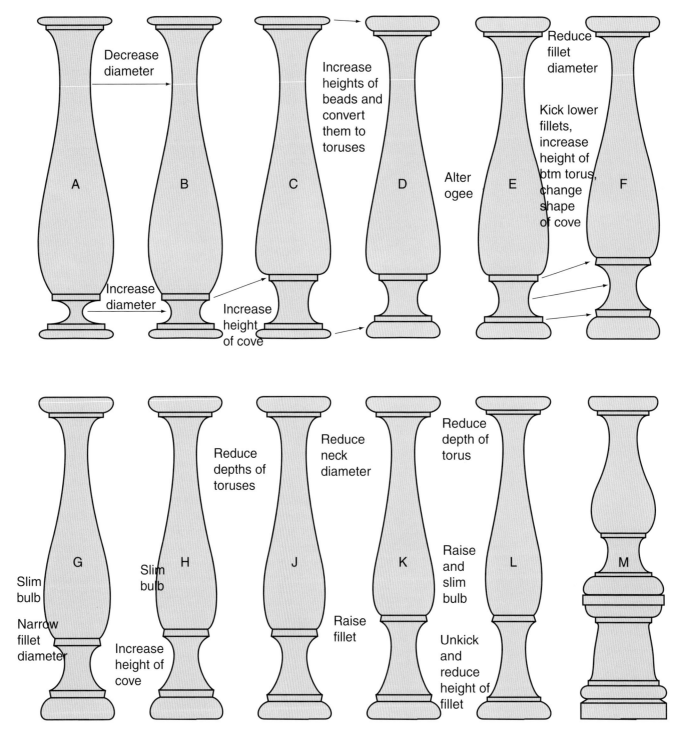

Figure 7.54 The detailed design of a baluster. The preliminary design *A* is unusually poor, but by *G* has been greatly improved. The modifications trialed in *G* to *L* illustrate that there are an infinite number of appropriate forms which will satisfy any but the simplest design problem. The column on the pedestal *M*, offers another infinite number of appropriate solutions to the same design problem.

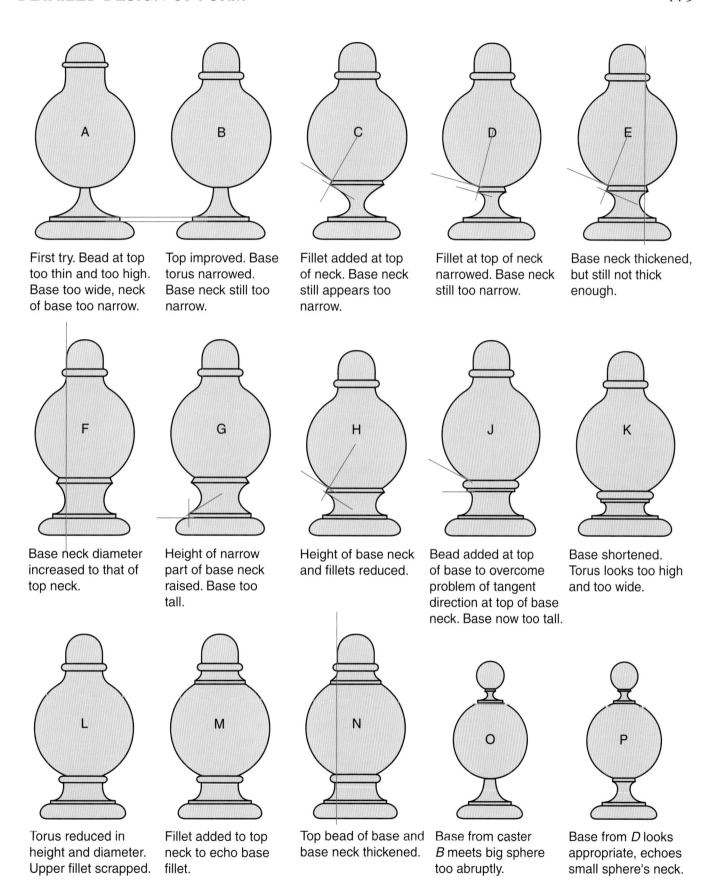

First try. Bead at top too thin and too high. Base too wide, neck of base too narrow.

Top improved. Base torus narrowed. Base neck still too narrow.

Fillet added at top of neck. Base neck still appears too narrow.

Fillet at top of neck narrowed. Base neck still too narrow.

Base neck thickened, but still not thick enough.

Base neck diameter increased to that of top neck.

Height of narrow part of base neck raised. Base too tall.

Height of base neck and fillets reduced.

Bead added at top of base to overcome problem of tangent direction at top of base neck. Base now too tall.

Base shortened. Torus looks too high and too wide.

Torus reduced in height and diameter. Upper fillet scrapped.

Fillet added to top neck to echo base fillet.

Top bead of base and base neck thickened.

Base from caster *B* meets big sphere too abruptly.

Base from *D* looks appropriate, echoes small sphere's neck.

Figure 7.55 The detailed design of a caster. There seems to be a need for the minimum diameter of the base neck to be at least as large as the diameter of the top in both caster *N* and the top neck in finial *P*.

The examples show that as detailed design proceeds, each new modification you trial tends to be less arbitrary and more based upon the knowledge gained in the preceding trials. Design conceptual knowledge thus builds, and as a designer gains experience he or she is able to reach an appropriate solution more quickly. As experience increases, so unfortunately does the likelihood that a designer's new solutions will resemble his or her earlier solutions. This is the process of building a personal style; accompanying it is the danger of calcification of that style.

In both examples the appropriateness sought was that of customary beauty. Neither "appropriateness" nor "beauty" can be defined except when you experience them, and can then point and say "That is beautiful" or "That is appropriate".

7.5 ENDNOTES

1. Franklin H. Gottshall, *Design for the Craftsman* (New York: Bonanza Books, 1940), pp. 131–133.

2. The formula for the catenary is $y = a\cosh(x/a)$ where a is a constant, cosh is the hyperbolic cosine, and $\cosh x = 0.5(e^x + e^{-x})$.

3. Gyorgy Doczi, *The Power of Limits* (Boston, Massachusetts: Shambhala Publications, 1981), p. 53.

4. Jonathan Hale, *The Old Way of Seeing* (New York: Houghton Mifflin, 1994), pp. 45–108.

5. Sebastiano Serlio, *The Five Books of Architecture* (1611 English edition; reprint, New York: Dover Publications, 1982), pp. 31, 32.

6. Joseph Rykwert, *The Dancing Column* (Cambridge, Massachusetts: The MIT Press, 1996), pp. 64, 65.

7. Franz Sales Meyer, *Handbook of Ornament* (1892; reprint, New York: Dover Publications: 1957), p. 305.

8. William H. Varnum, *Industrial Arts Design* (Peoria, Illinois: The Manual Arts Press, 1916 and 1933).

Chapter Eight

DECORATION

Decoration is essentially two-dimensional. It is applied to a surface, or laid onto a surface, without affecting that surface's shape, to produce differences in color, and/or gloss levels. Painting, staining, polishing, and veneering are three ways in which you can decorate wood. Another decorative technique is to produce motifs or patterns by conglutinating pieces of woods of different species (several examples were shown in *Woodturning Methods*, pages 23 to 28). Utilizing the visual properties of materials, such as the natural colorings of woods and stones, is called *organic* decoration.

I shall also treat as decoration the surfaces left when wood is coarsely sanded, shallowly chiseled or machined, wire brushed, sandblasted, impressed, or similar. Although this arbitrary decision blurs the distinction between decoration and ornament, I have taken it because I decided to discuss pattern in this chapter rather than in chapter 6 on ornament.

8.1   COLOR

There are many books on color.[1] This section therefore gives only a brief introduction to the science of color before discussing aspects of the decoration of woodturnings.

8.1.1   THE PROPERTIES OF COLORS

Sir Isaac Newton discovered that sunlight would split into the colors of the rainbow if passed through a glass prism (figure 8.1). He also discovered that these colors would recombine to produce white light if passed through a second prism. This additive recombination of colors to produce white differs from the subtractive addition of pigments and dyes (figure 8.2).

What light is was not discovered until two centuries later. James Clerk Maxwell, a Scottish physicist, defined light in the 1870s as a vibrating electromagnetic field. Red light has a lower frequency and a longer wavelength than violet light. Albert Einstein then refined the concept by explaining that light was also composed of particles or quanta of light energy called photons. (Alas, Maxwell's and Einstein's explanations do little to help me visualize what light is and how it behaves).

Color has its own precise terms:

1. H*ue* is the colour defined in terms of the five principal hues of pure colours red, orange, yellow, green, blue

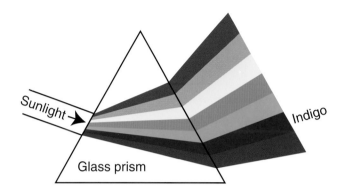

Figure 8.1   **The colors of white light.** In 1666 Sir Isaac Newton discovered that when a shaft of sunlight is passed through a glass prism it emerges as a spectrum of colors. This process is called refraction. Because there are seven notes in the musical scale, Newton decided that the spectrum should contain seven colors. Red, orange, yellow, green, blue, and violet were valid and obvious choices. The inclusion of indigo is barely justified.

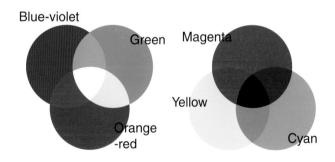

Figure 8.2   **Primary colors:** *left,* of light; and *right,* used for printing inks.

Left. When green, orange-red, and blue-violet lights shine onto a white surface they mix as shown to reflect white and the secondary colors yellow, magenta (a bluish-red), and cyan (a greenish-blue). This surprising result is because the three primary colors are "added" together; it was discovered by Thomas Young at St George's Hospital, London in 1801. Young also suggested that we see color using what are now called cones in the retina which are sensitive to red, green, or blue light. The sum of the responses R + G + B defines the brightness; the ratio R : G : B defines the color.[2]

Right. If yellow, magenta, and cyan pigments are mixed, the results are predictable to us because the process is subtractive. The pigments absorb all the colors of white light except those that they reflect.

and violet. Thus pink is not a hue because it is a combination of the hue red and white which is not a hue (neither is black).

2. *Value or tone* is varied by mixing the hue with black and/ or white.

3. *Chroma or saturation* is the intensity of the colour. The more you dilute a watercolour paint before you brush it on, the more you reduce its chroma. The same effect would not be produced by adding more white and/or black.

4. *Pure* or *saturated* colours have no black or white and are at their maximum chroma.

There are an infinite number of colors, and man has sought a means to organise them. A simple arrangement for saturated colors is the color wheel (figure 8.3). For tonal colors containing black and white, and unsaturated colors, three-dimensional arrangements such as color spheres, or fans with each blade having say a range of tones and/or saturations, are used.

We may see colors when white light strikes a surface through two means:

1. *Scattering* which includes refraction (what happens in Newton's prism). Irridescence is also caused by scattering.

2. *Absorption* in which a material absorbs the energy of the colored light which has a frequency corresponding to its own. The colors whose frequencies do not correspond pass through the material if it is transparent or translucent, or are reflected.

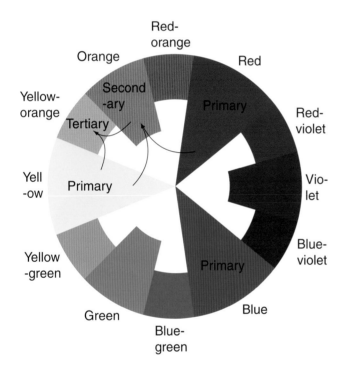

Figure 8.3 A color wheel, one of many variations.[3] The circle contains the three primary hues used by painters, red, blue, and yellow. The three secondary hues are orange, green, and violet. The six tertiary hues are produced by mixing a primary with its neighboring secondary.

Complementary hues such as red and blue-green are diametrically opposite one another on the hue wheel and produce a neutral or grey when mixed in the right proportion.

Contrasting hues are complementary or almost opposite one another on the hue wheel.

Harmonious hues are adjacent or close to one another on the hue wheel.

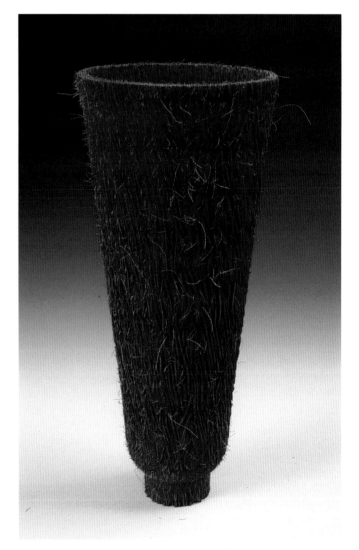

Figure 8.4 *Red Palm* by Dewey Garrett of Livermore, California; 10 in. high x 5.5 in. dia. (250 mm x 140 mm).

8.1.2   COLOR ASSOCIATIONS

The reactions to different colors vary between societies, and between individuals in a society. The distinctions between reactions which are innate and those which are learned are far from clear. Through a knowledge of an experiencer's likely reactions to colors, you can use color to reinforce your design intentions. The main colors and the likely reactions to them are listed below:[4]

1. *Red* symbolizes primitive, emotional, sexual (red-light district, scarlet women): it is an aggressive, exciting, advancing color (figure 8.4). Imagine looking at a painting with blue, yellow, purple, and red areas. Red rays are refracted less by the eye's lens than yellow and purple, and thus focus behind the retina. To focus the red the lens has to bulge more as if the red were nearer. Similarly blue is a retiring, receding colour. Its rays are refracted more than those of yellow and purple, and to focus blue the lens has to flatten as if the blue were further away. When looking at a design in blue and red, the lens will tend to pulsate in an attempt to focus on both colors simultaneously.
2. Yellow is warm, sunny, and optimistic; its lacks the aggression and forwardness of red. The bright clear yellows are regarded as gay and lively; the darker, greenish yellows are associated with disease and treachery.
3. *Purple* is a mixture of red and blue; it is rich, stately, royal. It was originally obtained from a rare shellfish, and was costly, and hence the preserve of the rich. Duller and bluer purples can be solemn, resigned and negative. (The 1890s in Britain was dominated by the aged Queen Victoria and known as the "mauve decade").
4. *Blue* is cool, passive, and tranquil ("feeling blue", "singing the blues"): it is also sincere and aloof ("blue-blooded", "true blue"). Blue as a color is rare in living things and naturally-occuring solids.
5. *Green* has similar characteristics to blue, and is passive and restful (figure 8.5). It has religious meanings of faith, immortality and contemplation, resurrection and baptism.
6. *White* is positive, stimulating, airy, light, and delicate.
7. *Black* is solemn, profound, and depressing (a "black mood", the "black spot" of *Treasure Island*). A black background with white or gold gives smartness and formality.
8. *Grey* lies between white and black, is neutral and mellow. A middle grey is an ideal background for colours. A pure color looks best on a grey tinted with the color's complement.

Point 8 suggests that our perceptions of colors vary according to the surrounding colors. Chemist Michel Eugene Chevreul, the Director of Dyeing at the Gobelin tapestry works, was the first to research this phenomenum. He published his findings in 1839 in the book *On the Harmony and Contrast of Colors*. Five of the effects are that:

1. Contrasts intensify one another. For example, blue emphasizes the warmth of orange, black makes grey and white seem brighter. Such contrasts can create vibration. Thus intense vermilion on a strong blue-green background glows and pulsates.
2. Adjacent hues induce their complement in each other. Thus if yellow and red are adjacent, the yellow will appear slightly green and the red a little more purple.
3. A hue of strong chroma will induce its opposite in a neutral grey. Thus a grey spot will appear greenish on a red background, and would need to be warmed if it were to harmonize with the red. The induced hue is strongest when the neutral has the same colour as the color.
4. A light hue of moderate chroma will appear weak on a black background because the contrast of value overpowers the hue and chroma. A light hue of moderate chroma will appear much stronger in chroma when placed on a white background
5. A strong tonal contrast overpowers and neutralizes hue and chroma.

These effects can be utilized in color schemes.

Figure 8.5 *Sea Palm* by Dewey Garrett. 6 in. high x 4 in. dia. (150 mm x 100 mm).

8.1.3 COLOR SCHEMES

The science of color may be fascinating, but can it contribute to a more successful use of color in design? It is popularly assumed that there is a secret to the successful choice and arrangement of colors, much in the same way that there is thought to be to the design of beautiful forms. Philip Ball denies that there are laws for successfully using color:

> Color does speak to our emotions—but not, it seems, in a way that everyone agrees on, independent of cultural conditioning . . . It is futile to be dogmatic about color. There can be no consensus about what colors "mean" or how to use them "truthfully". Color theories can assist the construction of good art, but they do not define it. In the end, the modern artist's struggle to find form for color is an individual quest.[5]

Designing color is thus similar to designing form, it requires knowledge, intuition, and trialing; in short, work. As with form, guidelines, often in the form of color schemes, can help. For example, Edith Anderson Feisner distinguishes seven basic color schemes:[6]

1. *Monochromatic*, one hue varied in tone and/or chroma.
2. *Analogous*, based on three or more hues next to each on the color wheel.
3. *Complementary*, based on two hues opposite each other on the color wheel.
4. *Double complementary*, based on any two hues and their opposites on the color wheel.
5. *Quadrad*, based on four hues equally spaced around the color wheel.
6. *Split complementary*, one hue and the two hues at each side of the complement.
7. *Triad*, three equally spaced hues.

To start designing the colors for a turning you can select an established color scheme, and then develop a final scheme through trialing. However our ground (wood) is not white.

8.1.4 WOODS' ORGANIC COLORS

The emphasis of woodturning design is on form. We need to more consciously use and exploit color, both applied color, and the organic colors and patterns of colors of wood. To do this you need a knowledge of the colors and color patterns which are characteristic to particular species (which is outside the scope of this book). A knowledge of the general nature of woods' organic colors is also useful, and is given below:

1. Wood occurs in almost every hue except blue and hues which include blue.
2. Sapwood is always pale. It can be white, buff, beige, cream, or yellow.

3. Heartwood can be darker than the sapwood in value and chroma, and different and darker in hue.
4. Medullary rays differ in chroma to the surrounding wood. Other multicolor effects are due to annual rings, large pores, particular grain patterns, etc.
5. Some woods display vivid colors on just-cut surfaces, but these colors become less vivid over time.
6. All wood surfaces weather eventually to a silver grey. Exposure to light and air, but not rain, can cause wood colors to change in hue and chroma.
7. The colors of woods are altered by bluestaining, by more advanced forms of rot, and sometimes by insect attack. Sapwood is richer in nutrients than heartwood and contains fewer toxic compounds, and is therefore more vulnerable to attack.
8. Clear finishing and even wetting enrich the colors of wood. They do this by reducing the scattering of the light reflected from the surface.

   Light travels at different speeds through different mediums. It travels slower through water than through air. This change in speed is denoted by the magnitude of what is called the refractive index. Light from unpolished wood has experienced a greater change in refractive index and is scattered more than light from polished or wet wood.[7] Therefore polished or wet wood looks richer than unpolished or dry wood.

8.1.5 COLORING WOODTURNINGS

We have a wide and marvellous pallet of wood colors. You often accept and exploit the colors in the wood you have. Alternatively, you might search for wood which has the colors you desire. There is another option. We readily accept applied colors on ceramics and metals, we should be less reluctant to accept them on turned wood.

Wood can be colored using opaque pigments, usually in the form of paints, or translucent stains and dyes (a dye is a stain specially formulated to color cloth). More "violent" techniques for coloring wood include fuming (usually with ammonia), charring, and bleaching.

The lathe is not just a shaping machine, you can use it to apply color both in broad areas and in patterns such as colored rings (figure 8.6) and radial runs (figure 8.7). You can also use the lathe in decorating by selectively removing colored material (figure 8.8).

In charring the harder parts of the wood structure burn less. Brushing off the ash leaves a surface which displays the wood's structure (page 67, figure 4.41).

The color of stained wood depends on both the organic color of the wood and the color of the stain. For the color of stained wood to resemble the color of the stain, the wood must be near white, either naturally or through bleaching, or be close to the color of the stain. Stains may be applied to the raw wood, usually before applying a clear finish. Stains can also be applied by being mixed into the clear finish which is applied to the unstained, raw wood. This eliminates a step and the problem of sanding through the stained outer cells of the wood, but the resulting appearance is inferior because the wood is partly obscured by a finish which is less translucent.

Over time all applied translucent finishes yellow or become browner, stains fade, and the wood itself changes color. The color changes may not be in the one direction; for example, the wood may first darken, then fade. These color changes slow with time. They create a fundamental problem when staining and finishing a new wood surface to match an old surface. The color of the new surface will change rapidly in the short and medium term, whereas the color of the old surface will be much more stable. You have to choose whether you want to achieve an immediate color match but a poor color match over the long-term, or vice versa.

Figure 8.7   Radial runs produced by applying paint to a rotating surface. I first used this technique in 1993.

The usual method of using a lathe to apply paint to a rotating workpiece in a decorative pattern involves holding the brush against the revolving surface. This produces encircling rings of color.

8.2   PATTERN

Patterns commonly occur in nature, but their regularity is often disturbed by interference from other natural patterns or by natural events or human actions. It is also in man's nature to create patterns, sometimes solely for their aesthetic effects, but also to satisfy other intentions. For example, the ears of wheat carved around bread boards signal use and support symbolism and ritual.

That we recognise patterns and look for them demonstrates the existence of Gombrich's sense of order. James Trilling in *The Language of Ornament* explains that both ornament and decoration consist of motifs arranged in patterns. The motifs in a pattern may be identical, similar or related, or different. They may be further classified as one or a combination of:[8]

1. *Freeform*, non-geometric (figure 8.8).
2. *Geometric*, such as straight or regularly-wavy lines, circular dots, or triangles (figures 8.9 to 8.20).
3. *Imitative or representational*. Such motifs can imitate flowers, animals (figures 8.8 and 8.9), human beings, buildings. Imitations and representations can vary enormously in their degree of stylization. Some motifs are so stylized as to be ambiguous.

Figure 8.6   Decoration with charring.

The top two pale rings were produced by turning off upstanding fillets which had been charred with the rest of the box. Had the fillets been a little thicker, the rings would have been more prominent.

The two bottom pale rings were produced by turning channels into the outside surface of the box base.

Although not every pattern conforms nicely, James Trilling defines four types:

1. *Unitary*, consisting of one main motif used once. Most people would regard a unitary pattern as a design rather than a pattern, a reservation which also applies to the next type.
2. *Additive*, consisting of a number of different motifs in an unordered arrangement.
3. *Repeating*, using the same motif or motifs or similar motifs in an ordered arrangement.
   i. The order can be because the arrangement is geometric (figures 8.9 to 8.19). The witty geometric patternings of geometric motifs of Op(tical) Art, at its height in the 1960s, have influenced many of the woodturners who specialize in creating geometric pattern by conglutination (figures 8.10, and 8.14 to 8.19) and by other means.
   ii. The order can be due to a perceptible concept other than one which is purely geometric. One which is used in some of the turnings illustrated is *uniform randomness* in which the motifs are sized and arranged so that there aren't any areas which jolt (figures 8.20 to 8.23, and 8.25). *Restrained randomness* is a better term where the motifs which are arranged randomly or "naturally" are relatively large and therefore perceived individually (8.24).

4. *Hypotactic*, using a number of different motifs in an ordered arrangement (figure 8.26).

These patterns can be created on woodturnings by the following methods, either separately or in combination:

1. Selecting and revealing the wood's organic color, grain, and ray patterns.
2. Applying, manipulating, and removing finishes such as paint or charring selectively.
3. Applying decorative motifs.
4. Shallow turning, machining, and carving. These processes can remove, alter, or produce texture.
5. Conglutination, usually followed by turning or other operations.

Figure 8.9 **A repeating pattern using a decoratively-turned, imitative, geometric motif;** a bottle coaster by John Rea of Llandilo, New South Wales.

Figure 8.8 **A repeating pattern of three freeform, imitative snake motifs;** *Yokut Snake Basket Illusion* by Lincoln Seitzman of Longboat Key, Florida; oak, paint, and ink, 10 in. high x 12 in. dia. (250 mm x 300 mm).

Figure 8.10 **An imitative, geometric, repeating pattern** in wenge, cherry, and chechen; *Petrified Sewing Basket* by Lincoln Seitzman; 7 in. x 13 in. dia. (180 mm x 330 mm).

Figure 8.11 A geometrically patterned mural by Vic Wood of Burwood, Victoria, made for the conference room of the Housing Industry Association, Melbourne. The mural consists of 16 panels, each composed of 26 boards of Victorian ash. The boards for each panel were clamped together and mounted on a very large faceplate for turning. Each panel was turned separately.

Figure 8.12 Decoration by conglutination, boxes by Jean-Luc Merigot of Saint Alban, France.

Centre, box 5 in. (130 mm) diameter turned from a blank conglutinated from strips of different species. The apparently random conglutinations must, if the glue joints are to be tight, result from careful design and workmanship, not from the carelessness which tends to be associated with randomness.

Left and right, boxes with inlaid lids.

This photograph and those in figures 8.13, 8.15, and 8.17 were generously supplied by Gérard Bidou, and were earlier published in Gérard Bidou and Daniel Guilloux, *Woodturning in France* (Dourdan, France: Éditions H. Vial, 1998).

Figure 8.13 **A repeating geometric pattern** produced by turning a lamination of walnut and sycamore planks which were not even in thickness. By Luc Caquineau of Tramayes, France; 4.5 in. high x 12 in. dia. (110 mm x 300 mm).

Figure 8.15 **A mosaic tray with geometric pattern** by Luc Caquineau, 2.75 in. high x 15 in. dia. (70 mm x 370 mm).

Cherry and mahogany strips were first glued alternately and side by side to form a wide plank-like blank. This was mounted with the turning-axis passing through a joint between two strips, and turned into chamfered rings. Every second ring was then rotated 180° from its orientation in the first blank. All the rings were then nested and conglutinated into a circular blank for the final turning.

The angle of the parting-cuts is calculated as described in the next figure. Parting-cut techniques are described on pages 19 to 22 of *Woodturning Techniques*.

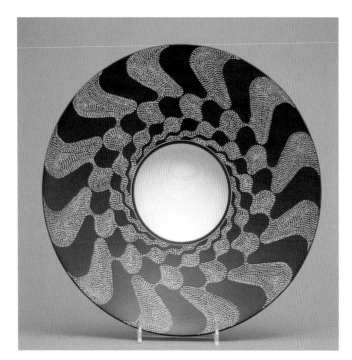

Figure 8.14 **A repeating geometric pattern** produced by drilling shallow holes through a black-painted surface into the pale sugar maple below. The "Transforming Wave" pattern is thus both visual and textural. Created by Al Stirt of Enosburg Falls, Vermont, this bowl is 16 in. (400 mm) dia.

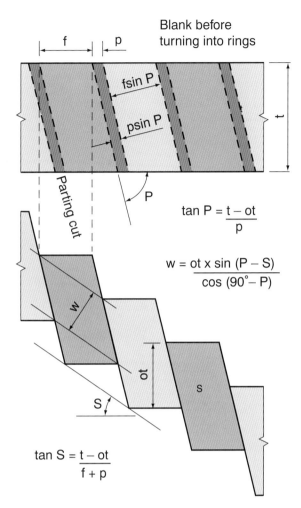

Figure 8.16 **The geometry of nesting rings.**
This diagram shows how to determine the angle at which you should part off rings when you want the rings to nest. (Figures 1.40 and 1.41 of *Woodturning Techniques* show the parting-cut angles when you want the rings to stack).

As an example, consider cutting a blank of thickness t = 40 mm which you want to cut into rings f = 20 mm wide, using a p = 4 mm wide cut. If you want the rings to overlap 60% so that ot = 24 mm, then:

$$\tan S = \frac{40 - 24}{20 + 4} = \frac{16}{24} = 0.667 \quad \text{Then } S = 34°$$

$$\tan P = \frac{40 - 24}{4} = \frac{16}{4} = 4.0 \quad \text{Then } P = 76°$$

$$w = \frac{24 \sin(76° - 34°)}{\cos(90° - 76°)} = \frac{24 \times 0.656}{0.9703} = 16.2 \text{ mm}$$

If you wanted to conglutinate a flat tray with S = 0°, you would need two cut two identical, conglutinated, disk-like blanks into suitably sized rings. You would then conglutinate the tray blank from rings obtained alternatively from one blank then the other.

Within the diagram (Figure 8.16):

Blank before turning into rings

fsin P

psin P

Parting cut

P

$$\tan P = \frac{t - ot}{p}$$

$$w = \frac{ot \times \sin(P - S)}{\cos(90° - P)}$$

$$\tan S = \frac{t - ot}{f + p}$$

Figure 8.17 **Geometric patterning in a bowl by Jean-Luc Merigot,** 20 in. (500 mm) dia.[7]
Elm and cherry strips were first glued alternately and side by side to form a wide blank. This was mounted in the lathe with the turning-axis passing through the centre of an elm strip, and parted into chamfered rings using a method and geometry similar to that used described in figure 8.16. The rings were assembled into a nest with every ring rotated slightly clockwise with reference to the ring immediately inside it. The rings were then conglutinated into a circular blank for turning.

Figure 8.18 **Geometric patterning on the inside of a bowl by Gary Johnson** of Bridgeton, Missouri; 6 in. high x 7.75 dia. (150 mm x 200 mm). Gary's method is described on page 28 of *Woodturning Techniques*.

Figure 8.19 **A elevation of the bowl shown in the preceding figure.**

Figure 8.20 **A geometric motif, a vee, in an ordered "Crowded Square" pattern** which is reinforced by the jagged rim. The uniform randomness needs to be designed with great care to avoid areas which would disrupt the evenness of the effect. Al Stirt produced the design by carving through the black-painted surface into the sugar maple below to create both pattern and texture. The bowl is 15 in. (380 mm) dia.

Figure 8.21 **A pyrographed squiggle motif in a uniformly random pattern on a sugarberry vessel,** 10 in. high x 7 in. dia. (250 mm x 180 mm).

This figure and the following four figures show a series of ordered, random patterns by Simon Levy of Nashville, Tennessee.

Figure 8.22 **A uniformly random V-shaped freeform motif engraved into the surface of a cherry vessel, and filled with white acrylic paint.** The vessel is 8.25 in. high x 5.75 in. dia. (210 mm x 145 mm).

Figure 8.23 **Different but related motifs in a uniformly random arrangement engraved into the surface of a boxelder vessel and filled with grey acrylic paint.** The vessel is 9.5 in. high x 5.5 in. dia. (240 mm x 140 mm).

Figure 8.25 **Related freeform motifs drawn in a uniformy random pattern in black ink over part of a bleached boxelder vessel.** The vessel is 8.5 in. high x 5.75 in. dia. (215 mm x 145 mm).
Photographs for figures 8.21 to 8.25 by John S. Cummings.

Figure 8.24 **Related wavy-line motifs carved into the surface of a maple vessel, and filled with grey paint. The pattern is one of restrained randomness.** The vessel is 7.5 in. high x 6 in. dia. (190 mm x 150 mm). Collection of Dave and Ruth Waterbury.

Figure 8.26 Applied decoration, folk art painting by
B. Willmott, 12 in. (300 mm) dia.
    Center, a hypotactic pattern of repeating, imitative,
floral motifs.
    Rim, the gold lines emphasize the ornamental bead
and the edge roll, and enclose a repeating pattern of
imitative leaf motifs.

8.3 TEXTURE

You do not have to fine-sand every wood surface. You might
decide to retain an existing natural surface or specify a man-
made surface or texture, either sanded or unsanded. The
textures you design should reinforce or at least be
compatible with your design intentions, and can, say, be:

1. *Functional.* Sanded smooth and polished surfaces are
   easy to clean and don't snag. Off-the-tool surfaces aid
   gripping and satisfy the economic intention of being
   cheap to produce.
2. *Aesthetic.* You can specify textures and surfaces for their
   aesthetic effects. You might contrast rough against
   smooth.
3. *Communicative.* Off-the-tool surfaces indicate rusticity and
   handmade. Wood can be textured to imitate man-made
   surfaces associated with other materials (figure 8.27),
   and natural surfaces such as snake skin, a bed of leaves,
   or feathers (figure 8.28).
4. *Economic.* Unsanded, unpolished surfaces are cheaper
   to produce and serviceable. Unfortunately, buyers have
   been conditioned to expect that wood shall be sanded
   and polished.

Texture can be produced:

1. *During a tree's growth.*
   i. The pores of hardwoods form cavities which texture
      the wood's surface.
   ii. The sapwood surface immediately beneath the
       cambium layer can be retained undamaged by
       carefully removing the bark. High-pressure water
       blasting can be used to remove stubborn bark
       (*Woodturning Techniques,* page 115).
   iii. The bark can be left in place, for example on bowl
        rims.
2. *By "natural" damage before a tree is harvested.*
   i. Splitting or fracturing leave striated or jagged
      surfaces.
   ii. Insect attack and rot can leave usable textured
       surfaces if not too far advanced.
3. *After a tree has fallen or been harvested, but before turning.*
   i. Off-the-tool surfaces left after dimensioning by
      chopping, riving, or sawing.
   ii. Seasoning and collapse can produce undulating
       surfaces, and cracking both coarse and fine. Because
       of its contorted grain, burl warps little as it seasons,
       and develops many fine, short cracks running in
       different directions .

Figure 8.27 Carved basket weave texture. *Carob #
436* by J. Paul Fennell of Scottsdale, Arizona; 10 in. x 8
in. dia. (250 mm x 200 mm). Collection of Marilyn
Friedman.

iii. Usable surfaces are produced by weathering, by charring, and by prolonged abrasion in moving water.
4. By *intentional texturing*.
   i. Turned or carved, small, abutting, repeated details such as rings, coves, flutes, and reeds coalesce to produce texture.
   ii. Process decoration by overt tooling. Traversing a turning tool along rotating workpiece produces a helical groove

Figure 8.29 Textures produced by ornamental-turning on an African blackwood box by Jon Sauer of Pacifica, California; 3 in. high x 3 in. dia. (75 mm x 75 mm).

Figure 8.28 Imitative motifs in a restrained-random arrangement; *Magpie Bowl* by Frank Sudol of Paddockwood, Saskatchewan, 9.5 in. high x 5 in. dia. (240 mm x 125 mm).

Figure 8.30 Deep, crisp texture and subtle patterning produced with an ornamental-turning, elliptical cutting frame by John F. Edwards of Tonbridge, Kent, England.

on the workpiece surface. By slowing the lathe, speeding the traverse of the gouge along the toolrest, and using a gouge with a deep, narrow flute, the helix becomes more apparent (page 73, figure 4.50).

iii. Other techniques including coarse sanding, wire brushing, knurling, and chatterwork (*Woodturning Techniques*, pages 81 to 83) which can be applied to a rotating workpiece. Applying rotating tools such as chainsaws and Arbortechs to rotating wood is possible but dangerous unless done using proper precautions. Rose engines can also be used to texture wood.

iv. By hand-carving and machine-carving processes on a stationary workpiece. Chainsaws, Arbortechs or similar, rotating sanding disks, rotating circular wire brushes, and pyrographs are among the tools which can be used.

v. By ornamental-turning (figures 8.29 and 8.30).

vi. By impact.

vii. By driving components into, or sticking materials or components onto, the wood surface. Eggshell texturing is one such finish.[10]

Turned surfaces usually do not blend convincingly into natural surfaces or those produced by other means. The best solution is therefore to create a definite boundary between different types (*Woodturning Techniques*, page 115, figure 6.3).

8.4   GLOSS LEVEL

Your specification of gloss level and how it is to be achieved will depend on your aesthetic preference, fashion, and client expectation. Durability, ease of application, and ease of repair are other likely factors in the choice. Gloss level also affects the display of texture and colour—a matt surface dulls both, a high gloss can confuse with bright refections.

A 70% "satin" gloss with minimum surface build is commonly specified on the dubious ground that it is "natural". A thick, high gloss finish gives an aura of artificiality, is even the antithesis of naturalness. It is also associated with costliness and luxury.

The gloss level need not be the same over the whole surface of a turning, and can be varied to reinforce intentions, as a decorative device, and to lessen the polishing cost. You can of course abolish the polishing cost by specifying "no finish", an option which is too often ignored.

Factors which affect the gloss level of a wood surface include:

1. *The characteristics of the raw wood*. The hardness, the size and distribution of pores, and the presence of resins

and other compounds in the wood affect its ability to take a surface gloss.

2. *Burnishing*. Gloss is increased by incidentally crushing the surface cells by bevel pressure during turning, and by intentional methods such as pressing shavings against the revolving surface. Light burnishing of applied finishes can also increase their glossiness.

3. *Abrasion*. The more complete the series of abrasive grits used, and the finer the last one, the glossier the resulting surface.

4. *Wetting, oiling, or waxing* will increase the glossiness of a surface, even if only temporarily.

5. *Filling the pores and scratches* in the surface of the raw wood by applying a film to it. Compounds which set hard and can be worked to give the desired gloss level for the long-term are often preferred.

6. *Time*. High-gloss surfaces will tend to become worn and damaged; they are likely to break down if exposed to sunlight and weather. Low-gloss surfaces which are often handled and/or waxed will become glossier as a patina builds. Regularly maintaining surfaces, say by reoiling or rewaxing, can restore or increase gloss levels.

8.5   ENDNOTES

1. Four of the many approachable books on color are: Philip Ball, *Bright Earth: the Invention of Colour* (London: Viking, 2001); Helen Varley, ed., *Colour* (London: Mitchell Beazley, 1980); Edith Anderson Feisner, *Colour* (London: Laurence King, 2000); and Maitland Graves, *The Art of Color and Design* (New York: McGraw-Hill, 1951.

2. Geoffrey Underwood, ed., *The Oxford Guide to the Mind* (Oxford University Press, 2001), p. 4.

3. The first color wheel was pictured in Sir Isaac Newton's *Opticks* of 1706. Newton used a wheel because he thought that the spectrum was circular, whereas we now know that the colors of visible light are but a short part of a long linear spectrum of electromagnetic radiation.

4. Richard Box, *Colour and Design for Embroidery* (London: B. T. Batsford, 2000). pp. 25–44.

5. Ball, pp. 22 and 24.

6. Feisner, pp. 75–76.

7. Ball, p. 37.

8. James Trilling, *The Language of Ornament* (London: Thames & Hudson, 2001), pp. 36–53.

9. A similar Op Art pattern is shown printed on a 1960s wallhanging in Philippe Garner, *Sixties Design* (Koln, Germany: Taschen, 2001), p. 78.

10. Dan Braniff, "Eggshell Texturing," *American Woodturner* (Spring 2001): pp. 31–33.

Chapter Nine

DESIGNING SPINDLES

The preceding chapters have concentrated on the process of design. This and the following three chapters concentrate on design of specific categories of turnings, namely: spindles, boxes, vessels, and columns. The design approach is similar for each, in part because a short spindle, a box, a vessel, and a short column can be similar in elevation. The first two chapters also include show-and-tell sections which mimic the critical appraisal sessions which are part of the meetings of many woodturners' groups.

In these chapters I shall not discuss inception, feasibility, restraints, or the initial proposal, nor shall I differentiate between the stage I and detailed design.

9.1   INTENTIONS

The seven types of intention first listed on page 95 are entirely relevant to boxes, and are:

1. *Reproductive.* The wish to reproduce, or develop, perhaps by combining new features, is perhaps the most common inception and intention in spindle turning (figure 9.1).

2. *Functional.* This includes structural sufficiency which relates to slenderness, and to the positions and magnitudes of minimum diameters. Obviously these are made on the basis of our experiences of similar spindles which have been satisfactory. The minimum diameters (often at the bottoms of coves) should not decrease downwards as a general guideline.

3. *Economic.* Where low cost is the imperative, spindles can often be left as unturned square-cross-section blanks without any reduction in utility. Dowelling produced using a doweller would only be slightly dearer. In designing spindles you will therefore usually be more concerned with satisfying the nonfunctional intentions.

4. *Aesthetic,* intended to cause an experiencer to have a particular aesthetic reaction. The choice of style is often related to a reproductive intention (figure 9.2). The chosen style does not have to be a named style; it can be defined by adjectives such as rounded, sharp, or aggressive.

5. *Communicative* (figures 9.3 and 9.4).

6. *Focused on the materials, techniques, or equipment used.*

7. *Personal and not necessarily intended to be apparent to others.*

Figure 9.1   Unusual ornament on a row of otherwise conventional pillarettes beneath a balcony in York, Pennsylvania. The ornaments are at graduated heights, and were perhaps intended to imitate a swag. The effect is heightened by decorative painting.

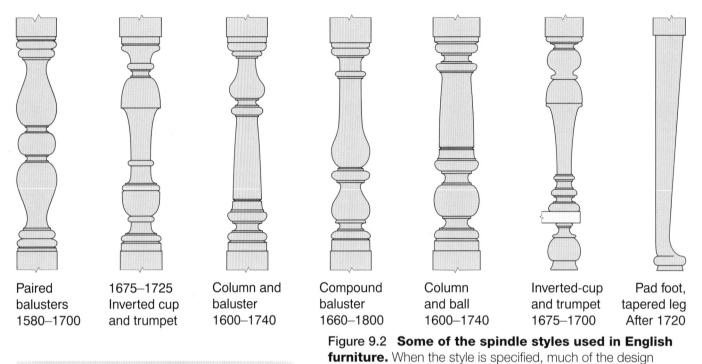

| Paired balusters 1580–1700 | 1675–1725 Inverted cup and trumpet | Column and baluster 1600–1740 | Compound baluster 1660–1800 | Column and ball 1600–1740 | Inverted-cup and trumpet 1675–1700 | Pad foot, tapered leg After 1720 |

Figure 9.2 **Some of the spindle styles used in English furniture.** When the style is specified, much of the design becomes prescribed. These drawings are based on just seven of the thiry-two legs illustrated in Victor Chinnery, *Oak Furniture* (Woodbridge, Suffolk: The Antique Collectors' Club, 1979), p. 191.

Figure 9.3 **An imitative assemblage of eight component spindle turnings** in a cricket trophy for Tudor House School, Moss Vale, New South Wales. The silversmith was Nicholas Deeprose of Bowral, New South Wales.

Figure 9.4 **Imitative spindles.** The turned legs of *The Elephant Table* are carved with the correct number of toe nails.

9.2 SHOW-AND-TELL

So far this book has been explanatory and advisory; it has not been critical. Many woodturners' clubs include a show-and-tell session in their regular meetings during which members describe and answer questions and criticisms on turnings which they have brought along. The value to all attending, and especially to those who designed the subject turnings, is greatly reduced if frank, critical discussion is discouraged.

In the show-and-tell sections in this and the next chapter I will detail my personal design thoughts on selected turnings. Some of the subject turnings are by others, some are synthesized by me to illustrate design shortcomings. I assume that each subject turning exactly replicates its design.

I shall organize my criticisms using the framework provided by design-by-parts, introduced in pages 163 to 171. I shall also show how I would redesign the subject turnings. I have done this by refining the original design rather than by making major changes.

I do not provide these criticisms and redesigns to demonstrate my superiority as a designer. I have explained how arbitrary many design choices are, and how they are influenced by the designer's unique conceptual knowledge. Thus you may validly view my opinions as inferior, or too traditional, or . . . No matter, the purpose of these show-and-tell sections is to encourage *you* to become more searching and more informed in your criticisms; and to stimulate *you* to develop your own views, not acquire a taste which is identical to mine. Only by becoming more critical, and especially of your own designs, will you increase your ability to design. This is confirmed by the subject turnings which suffer from a lack of design work and knowledge, rather than a lack of flair or inspiration.

9.2.1 TABLE LAMP

The lamp in figures 9.5 to 9.7 was designed and turned by Fred Robjent of Moss Vale, New South Wales. He has generously agreed to it becoming a show-and-tell subject.

WHOLISTIC
Many woodturners would be pleased to have designed and turned this lamp. It has some excellent features:

1. The overall proportions are attractive. The base is substantial, and therefore the lamp is stable. Fred designed the lamp, the shade, and the bulbholder wholistically. Many poorly designed lamps result from designing the wooden lamp alone, then being unable to source a bulbholder and/or a shade which are appropriate (figure 7.21, page 158).

2. The lamp is tall (26 in. (660 mm) to the top of the stem), a quality too often neglected in lamps which might be used for reading.
3. The stem has crisp detail and fillets, the base does not. Both should conform to the same style.
4. The overall feeling is a little stolid. There could be bigger differences between maximum and minimum diameters, and the curved profiles could have been more lively and less jerky.

Figure 9.5 Fred Robjent's lamp. The wood is camphor laurel.

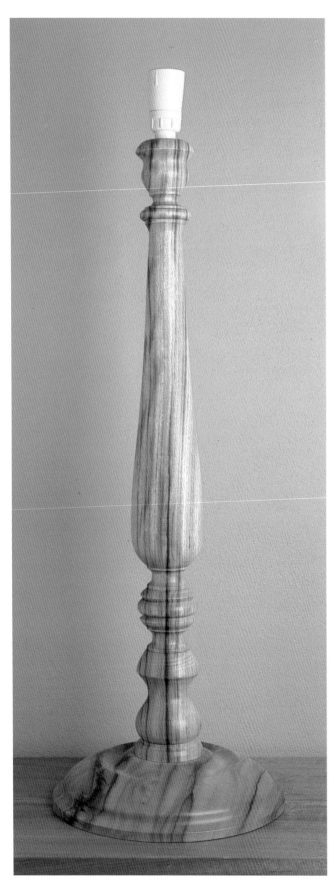

Figure 9.6 Fred's lamp without the shade.

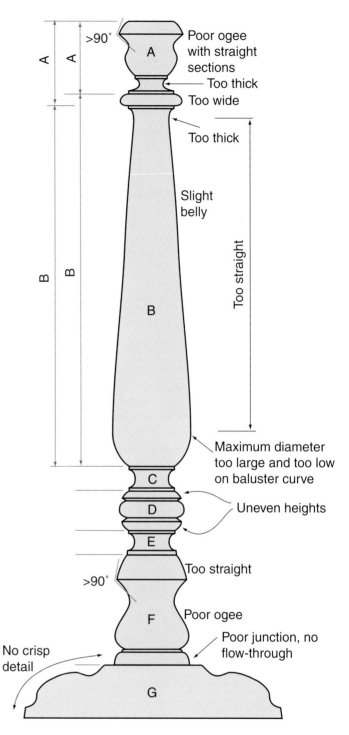

Figure 9.7 My comments on Fred's lamp. The stem is in elevation, the base in diagonal section.

The subdivision into parts is somewhat arbitrary:

1. Should part *A* include the torus?
2. Should fillets between coves and other curves be grouped with the coves as in part-groups *C* and *E*?
3. Should *C* be a part-group? should it be grouped into *B*? or should it be grouped with *D* and *E*? Similarly, should *E* be a part-group? should it be grouped with *F*? or should it be grouped with *C* and *D*?

Figure 9.8 My redesign of Fred's lamp. It has greater variations in diameter, more-flowing curves, and its visual weight is lower.

Right, the lamp design should be done taking into account the visual mass of the shade. The exposed part of the stem has about the right visual weight, whereas if the shade is ignored, the lower half of the stem (*above*) looks a little heavy.

PART-GROUPS

You often have to decide the boundaries between part-groups somewhat arbitrarily. The range of possibilities outlined in the legend of figure 9.7 is common. Fortunately your choice has negligible effect upon the final design.

Regarding the part-groups selected in figure 9.7, their relative sizes could be varied to advantage: sconce *A* is too small; and the tall baluster part-group *B* is too large and dominant. To lessen the dominance of *B*, in the redesign in figure 9.8 the height of *F* has been increased, and so has the size of *D*.

PARTS

My detailed criticisms of parts are shown on figure 9.7. In general:

1. Curves have too little curvature and the changes in curvature are too jerky.
2. The tapering upper length of the baluster curve in *B* is too straight, and even bellies out where its should be concave.

The coves *E* and *C* are joining parts which connect *B* to *D*, and *D* to *F*. The top cove is part of the sconce (part-group A). Fred has correctly designed the minimum diameters of all three coves so that they decrease towards the top of the lamp. This structurally sound practice is too often ignored.

Closely compare figures 9.7 to 9.8 and you will see that there are many additional refinements. They may be small, but together they give a much greater coherence.

9.2.2 STANDARD LAMP/TABLE

John Harris of Welby, New South Wales, has been turning for about two years. His combined standard lamp and table, shown in figures 9.9, 9.10, 9.12 and 9.13, is impressive, useful, and stylistically influenced by traditional design detailing. I thank him for allowing it to be a subject. My redesigns are shown in figures 9.11 and 9.14.

WHOLISTICALLY
John had not designed or obtained a shade. Although the wooden components cannot be properly designed without also designing the shade and its placement, I have chosen to assume that this lamp/table is complete as shown in figure 9.9.

The general arrangement and styling of the wooden components are good, except that:

1.   The spindles have lots of sharp detail, the table has none. It shares this undesirable duality of styles with Fred's lamp discussed previously. Perhaps amateur turners are less confident about turning crisp detail on faceplate work than on spindles.
2.   The combination of areas with considerable detail and areas without detail gives variety and delight.
3.   In the stem above the table the part-groups have the feeling of being stacked one on another. There is little feeling of continuity of structure through this stem. The main reason is that convex curves are generally separated from concave curves by V-cuts, not by fillets.
4.   The column below the table is visually a little light.
5.   The four legs have large bulbous ends, but still do not provide enough weight or spread for stability. A disk-like base, or perhaps three legs spreading to a greater radius could have overcome this.

PART-GROUPS IN THE UPPER STEM
I have split the lamp/table into the part-groups shown. As usual some of the splitting is arbitrary. For example, the cove and fillets at the bottom of *A* could have been assembled into a separate part-group, or been included in the part-group *B* below. Also:

1.   Part-groups *B*, *C*, and *D* are too similar in shape, size, and orientation.
2.   Part-group *E* lacks clarity of form.

PARTS IN THE UPPER STEM
Detailed comments are shown on figure 9.10.

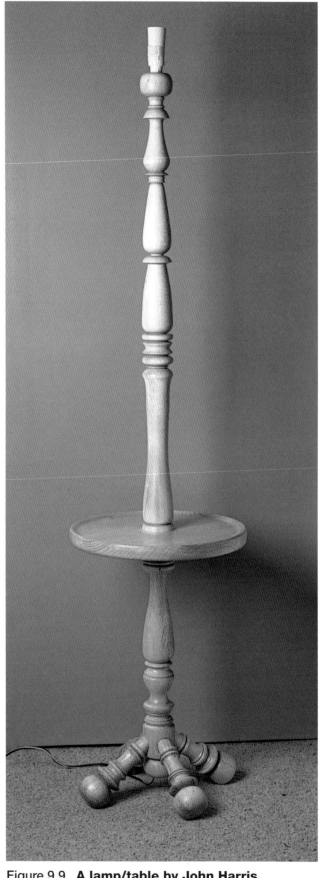

Figure 9.9 **A lamp/table by John Harris.**

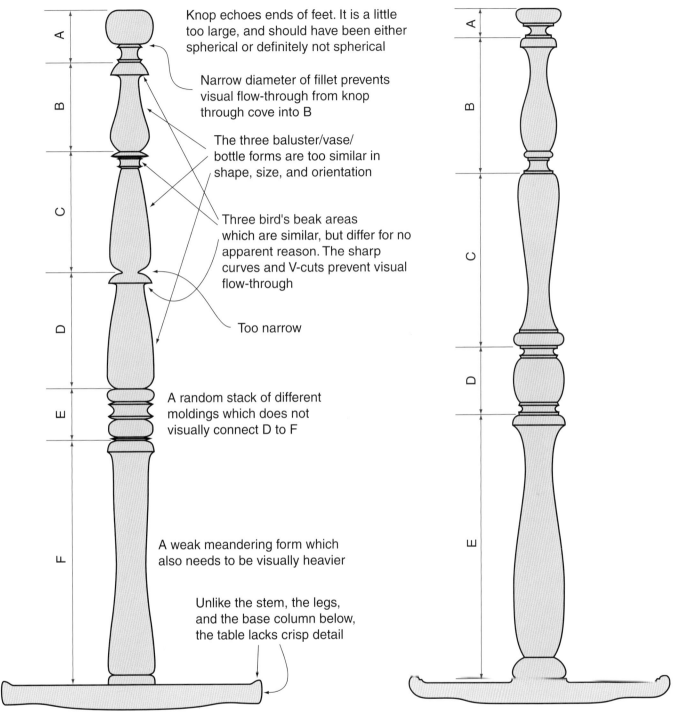

Knop echoes ends of feet. It is a little too large, and should have been either spherical or definitely not spherical

Narrow diameter of fillet prevents visual flow-through from knop through cove into B

The three baluster/vase/bottle forms are too similar in shape, size, and orientation

Three bird's beak areas which are similar, but differ for no apparent reason. The sharp curves and V-cuts prevent visual flow-through

Too narrow

A random stack of different moldings which does not visually connect D to F

A weak meandering form which also needs to be visually heavier

Unlike the stem, the legs, and the base column below, the table lacks crisp detail

Figure 9.10 The upper stem of John Harris's lamp/table with my comments.

Figure 9.11 The upper stem redesigned. I decided to radically redesign the part-groups and scrap one, in part to overcome the similarities of *B*, *C*, and *D*.

Here the styles of all the parts are consistent, the ogees are better shaped, the stem flows with some continuity into the table, the minimum diameters decrease upwards, and the more detailed areas have clarity.

PART-GROUPS IN THE BASE COLUMN
The lower part of part-group *G* and the upper part of part-group *H* are too dominant, largely because *H* and *J* are too light, *H* is the wrong way up, and *J* is too short.

PARTS IN THE BASE COLUMN
My comments on the designs of parts are shown on figure 9.13. The redesigned base column is shown in figure 9.14.

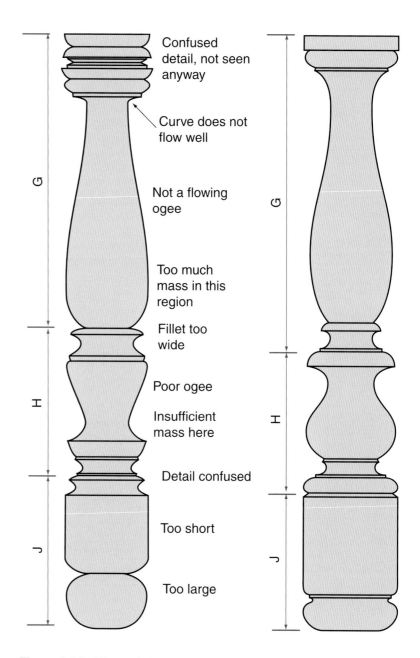

Confused detail, not seen anyway

Curve does not flow well

Not a flowing ogee

Too much mass in this region

Fillet too wide

Poor ogee

Insufficient mass here

Detail confused

Too short

Too large

Figure 9.13 The original base column with my comments.

Figure 9.14 The base column redesigned.

Figure 9.12 The base column and legs of John Harris's lamp/table.

Chapter Ten

BOX DESIGN

A box is a hollow container with some form of lid. The lid is usually able to be removed and replaced many times, but might be glued in permanently.

Most turned wooden boxes are small and simple in form (figure 10.1). Therefore the design process is usually compressed, and there is not a clear demarcation between a box's stage 1 design and its detailed design. Nor will there be in this chapter which concentrates on five box design topics:

1. Intentions.
2. Influences on form, especially how function influences the way a box stands, hangs, etc.
3. Guidelines for hollowed forms. These concern wall thicknesses, and the styles of forms' insides and outsides.
4. Fitting lids.
5. Lid:base height proportions.

This chapter ends with a show-and-tell section.

Figure 10.1 A functional box made to hold a seal. Photographed courtesy of Connor Galleries, Moss Vale, New South Wales.

10.1 INTENTIONS

The seven types of intention first listed on page 95 are entirely relevant to boxes, and are:

1. *Reproductive.*
2. *Functional.* Most contemporary turned wood boxes are not designed for a specific use; they are intended to be objets d'art. They have become an affordable vehicle for the exploration of form, ornament, and decoration, unrestrained by the need to fulfil a useful function. Boxes, however, can be designed to fulfil, even if only nominally, a host of functions: storage, safekeeping (figure 10.1), display, dispensing, and transport. Examples include casters (figure 6.47), pomanders, salts and pepper shakers (figure 10.2), flasks (figure 10.3), and boxes for drills (figure 10.4).

   An important aspect of box functionality is lid design. This is discussed on pages 203 to 207.
3. *Economic.* The volume of wood in a box is small in proportion to the labor input. You can therefore usually afford to turn boxes in more costly and usually more decorative woods. If so, use chucking methods which do not require long waste spigots.
4. *Aesthetic.* Boxes offer unlimited scope for variations in form, ornament, and decoration. Organic decoration, which exploits woods' natural colors and grain patterns is commonly used (figures 10.5 and 10.6).

Figure 10.2 Functional boxes, salt and pepper shakers, each turned on two turning-axes by Rémi Verchot of Queanbeyan, New South Wales.

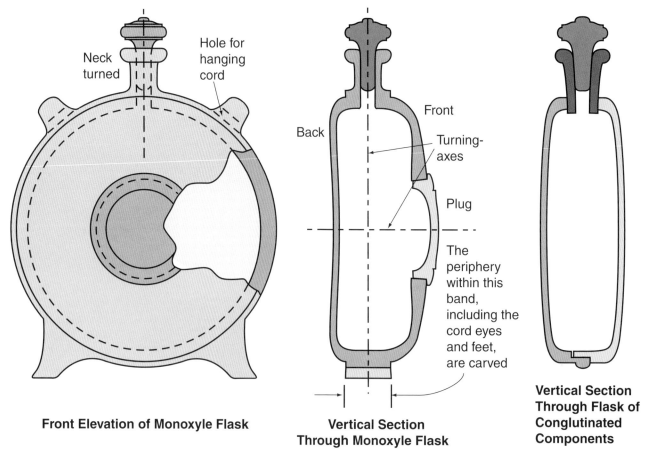

Figure 10.3 **Monoxyle flasks** (also called pilgrim flasks) turned on two turning-axes.

Left and center. A true monoxyle (or monoxylous, "made from one piece of wood") flask. As most turnings are made from one piece of wood, the implication of "monoxyle" is that the type of object of which the subject is an example is normally made or can be made from several pieces of wood, and that a high degree of skill and ingenuity is required to make the subject from one piece. Pierre Mille in his excellent article details the history and making of monoxyle flasks, the insides of which were waterproofed with beeswax.[1]

Right, a flask assembled from three (excluding the stopper) component turnings, and not deserving of the status of monoxyle.

Figure 10.4 **A box for drills.** It is labelled, as is the size of the drills which should be stored in each of the cylindrical compartments. The rotating lid allows any compartment to be accessed without the drills stored in the other compartments falling out. The box can stand vertically. It can also rest horizontally, but will not roll because the bead on the base has been facetted.

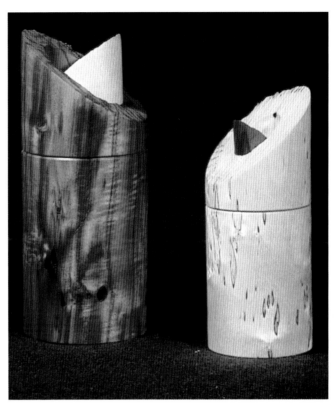

Figure 10.6 ***The Opposite,* boxes turned by Bernd Pfister in 2001.** A complementary pair of cylindrical boxes in almond and birch with inset ornaments contrasting in color and direction. The starkness of the cylinders contrasts well with the ornaments and textures on the lids. The exposed heights of the lids are appropriate to those of the bases.

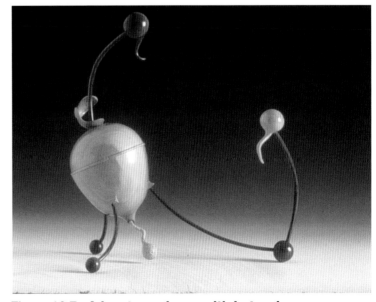

Figure 10.5 **Organic decoration in a Bahia rosewood box turned by Bernd Pfister** of Eschelbronn, Germany, in 2002. The box is 5 in. (130 mm) high

Contrast the concave top of its lid with the convex top in figure 10.18.

The mating surfaces of the box's outside-fitting lid and base spigot are cylindrical, the most common arrangement.

Figure 10.7 **A box turned on multiple turning-axes,** *Putting into orbit,* by Jean-François Escoulen of Puy Saint Martin, France. The woods are Pernambuco and green ebony; the height is 12 in. (300 mm).

Figure 10.8 Imitative *Lips* boxes turned on two turning-axes by Rémi Verchot of Queanbeyan, New South Wales.

5. *Focused on the materials, techniques, or equipment used.* You can use seed cases and nuts to make small boxes; you are not restricted to solid wood. Turning boxes is enjoyable because of the variety of techniques and intricate skills which can be applied (figure 10.7). Little special equipment is needed, threading being the most likely to demand extra expenditure.
6. *Communicative.* Boxes can be turned to imitate natural or man-made forms (figure 10.8). A neglected communicative facility is the labelling of contents (figure 10.4).
7. *Personal and not necessarily intended to be apparent to others.*

10.2 INFLUENCES ON FORM

The intentions you choose for a box will influence its form. For example, the intended function will influence whether a box should be designed to:

1. Stand on a horizontal surface.
2. Be carried (figures 10.3 and 10.9).
3. Hang in essentially one orientation (figure 10.10).
4. Rock about an equilibrium position.
5. Roll in a line or a circle, or not roll (figure 10.4).
6. Rest on one or more supports or locators which are an integral part of the box.
7. Be supported on a separate stand; locate in a hole or recess; or locate on a pin or similar.

    Other variables which may influence form include:

1. Whether a box will be one of a series or set (figures 10.11 and 10.12).

Figure 10.9 A box designed to hang from a belt. Based on the Japanese *inro*, this box does not need a flat base. Some inros have a locking (*ojime*) bead which slides along the cords. To secure the inro into the belt a *netsuke* is used. Netsukes are often beautifully carved.

Figure 10.10 A string box, made to hold a ball of string. Although similar to the box in the preceding figure, this box hangs statically and its lid does not have to be secured to cope with non-vertical orientations and movements. The top is outside-fitting, and a tight push fit. The hanging cord could have also been routed through the base in a way similar to that in the preceding figure so that the base could not fall off unexpectedly.

This box is also a communicative souvenir, and an example of the transfer-printed Mauchline ware made in the Scottish town of Mauchline between 1850 and 1933.[2]

2. Whether the box will have more than one compartment (figures 10.13 and 10.14).
3. Should stackable boxes be able to stack in a fixed or variable order (figure 10.15)?
4. Should the boxes be able to nest (figure 10.11)?
5. Whether the box will be turned on one or more turning-axes (figures 10.2, 10.3, 10.5, 10.7, 10.8, and 10.18).
6. The need for knobs, gripping features, or projecting handles (figure 10.16). These can be turned with the turned form, be carved into or from the turned form, or be appendages. You may need to design local thickening where a handle attaches.

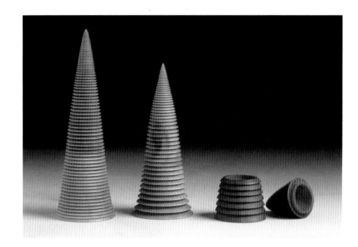

Figure 10.12 Three boxes by Henri Groll (1996) of Sassenage, France. They are staggered in height, and continue the sharp-ring (or V-cut) ornament used on the *Pine Cone* box shown in figure 5.8, page 93.

Figure 10.11 Nesting boxes called Russian or Matroshka dolls.[3] Collection of Mr and Mrs John Carroll.

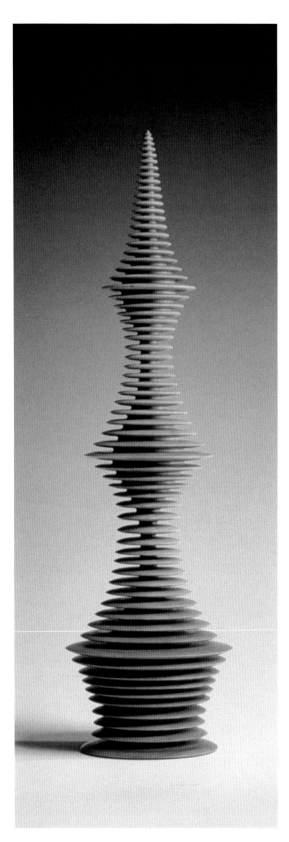

Figure 10.13 **A stacking double box**
***Asiatic Temple* (1999) by Henri Groll;**
persimmon, 17 in. high x 5 in. dia. (430 mm x
130 mm).

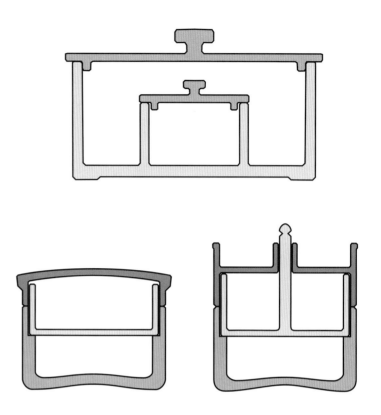

Figure 10.14 **Boxes with multiple compartments,** shown in
diagonal section; just three of the infinite number of
arrangements.[4]

Figure 10.15 **Stacking boxes** (shown in diagonal section) can
be designed as complete boxes which stack (*left*), or as box
bases which stack with one lid (*right*). Both types of stacking
boxes can be designed to stack in any order (*left*), or in a set order
(*right*). In eighteenth- and nineteenth-century spice towers the
separate boxes often screwed together.

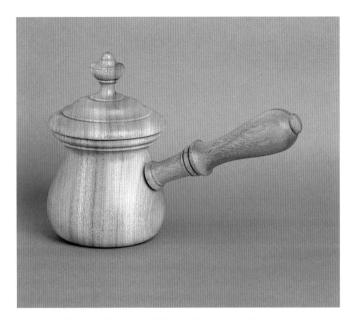

Figure 10.16 A box with a side handle.

7. Whether a box is designed to store specific contents (figure 10.4). Some contents such as matches or toothpicks may need to project well above the base when the lid is removed. A label or symbol may also be needed.
8. Your choice for the style of the box.

10.3   GUIDELINES

I detailed seven design guidelines on pages 168 to 171. I propose two more for all hollowed turnings, including boxes and vessels:

1. *The walls and similar of hollowed turnings should be of even thickness unless you decide otherwise*. This guideline does not demand even thickness, but requires that there be some feeling or logic to your designs' departures from the guideline.

    Even wall thicknesses are essential to prevent pottery cracking in the kiln. A similar situation applies to turnings which are roughed prior to seasoning or finish-turned with thin walls from unseasoned wood. For them the guideline has aesthetic, material, and functional bases. Boxes, however, must be turned from seasoned wood if their lids are to fit long-term. Even wall thicknesses are not therefore critical for boxes, and for them the guideline is essentially an aesthetic requirement (figures 10.26 and 10.29).

2. *The inside and the outside of a hollowed turning should be stylistically coherent in form, ornament and decoration*.

Restating these guidelines in terms of parts: *inside and outside parts which combine to create a hollowed turning should correspond in both form and style*.

10.4   LIDS

It is the presence of a lid which distinguishes a box. Different types of plain-turned lid are described in figures 10.17 to 10.23. Slot-located, and hinged lids are not pictured. Threaded lids are discussed in *Woodturning Techniques*, pages 129 to 186.

Care needs to be taken if a lid is to conform to your intentions. There are four main issues:

1. *Achieving a long-term fit*. Short- term problems due to the relaxation of internal stresses can be eliminated by rough-turning the box and then delaying the finish-turning for a few days even if the blank was seasoned. Unseasoned wood should be left for a longer period after roughing to allow seasoning. Because the diurnal changes in relative humidity will affect the fit of lids, prefer species with low shrinkage coefficients. The plastic compressibility of wood is best countered by using harder species.

    Another factor is grain direction. Pages 4 to 7 of *Woodturning Techniques* stated that wood movement with changes in moisture content is negligible parallel to the grain, and that the tangential movement is approximately double the radial. The difference between the radial and tangential shrinkage coefficients also causes seasoning wood to cup away from the pith (figure 10.24). These factors determine that:

    i.   Axially grained boxes have the best long-term fit.
    ii. The larger the diameter, the more the fit changes with changes in moisture content.
    iii. When the grain is perpendicular to the turning axis, ensure that the lid and base will cup in sympathy with moisture content changes, or better, use quartersawn blanks.
    iv. It is preferable that the grain directions in the lid and base be the same.

2. *The appropriate design and tightness of the lid*. This depends on how you intend the box to be used, and whether the lid will be removed (if at all) with one or with two hands.

3. *Gripping the lid*. The functional intention of a knob and the ornamental intention of a finial are often combined. The size and strength of attachment of a knob should reflect the designed tightness of the lid.

4. *The lengths of mating spigots* are typically 1/4 in. (6 mm). If you want the top of the base to be high in a box, but the rim of the lid to appear much lower, you would need to design an unusually-long base spigot.

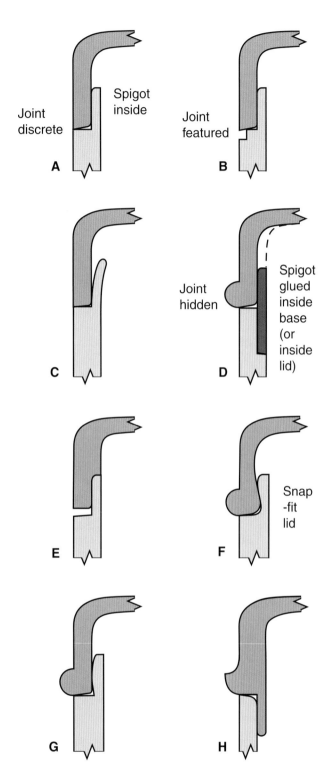

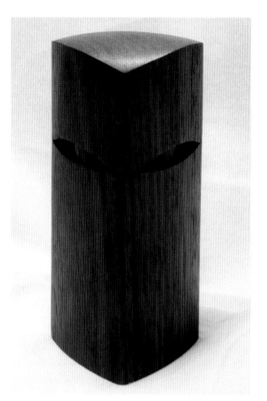

Figure 10.18 Padauk box turned by Bernd Pfister in 2002; 4.8 in. (120 mm) high. The technique of turning thermed boxes is described in *Woodturning Methods*, pages 116 to 118. When using the technique, care has to be taken to achieve a straight joint between lid and base. Here, instead, the joint is featured. The top of the lid is convex to echo the lid's bottom edge.

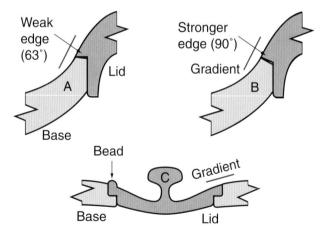

Figure 10.17 Fitting lids. *C* is used in *natsumes* (Japanese boxes used to hold powdered tea) so that as soon as the lid is lifted, air can enter and the tea will not billow. *D* is used when the grain running through the lid and base is contorted, and you want to minimize grain mismatch across the joint. *F* snaps shut.[5] *G* is supposed to be less exacting and give a better long-term fit than *A*, *B*, and *E*.[6] All the lids are outside fitting, except *H* (or *D*) which are inside fitting.

Figure 10.19 Inside-fitting lids in sloping surfaces. With an inside-fitting lid with mating surfaces which are vertical or horizontal, the greater the gradient of the outside surface, the weaker are the exposed edges of the lid or base. Thus *B* is preferred to *A*. The addition of the bead in *C* makes the edge of the lid more durable, but has destroyed the uninterrupted flow of the surface across the joint between lid and base.

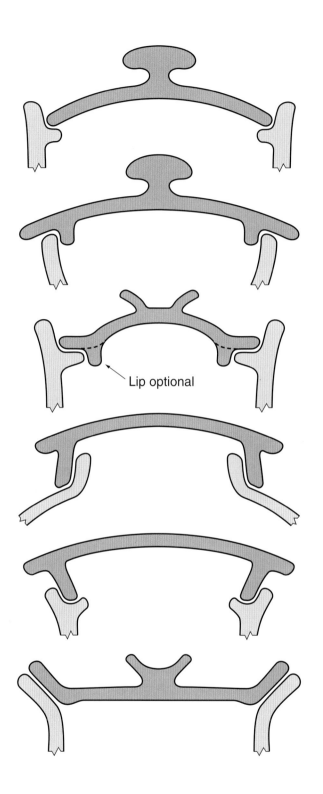

Figure 10.20 Pottery lid designs are equally suitable for turned wooden boxes.[7] The tight, precision fit which has become standard in woodturning is sometimes neither essential nor appropriate. The fitting of lids in the above and similar designs can be as exact or as sloppy as you decide. Although the edges and corners are shown rounded in these diagonal sections, they can, of course, be designed squarer or otherwise.

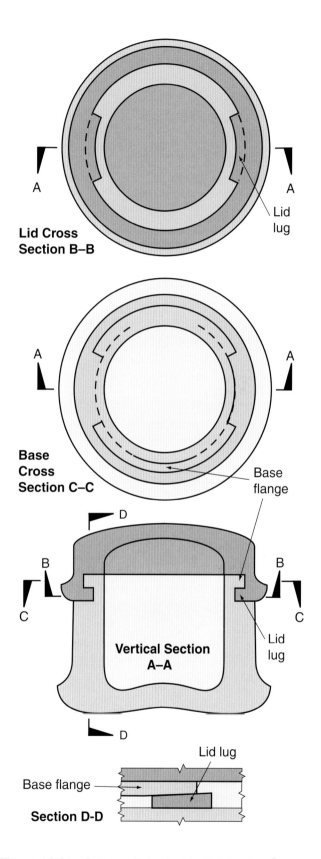

Figure 10.21 A turned, lockable lid design.[8]
Section D–D, carving slight slopes on the mating surfaces stops the lid being freely rotated. However, overzealous tightening can break the lugs and flanges away.

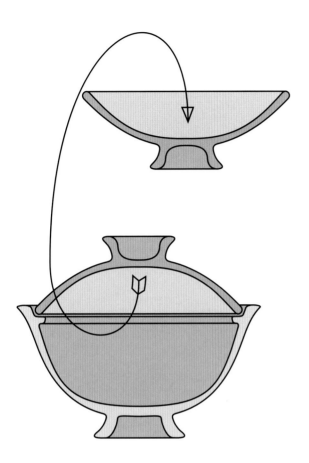

Figure 10.22 Bowl (or box) with reversible lid. The lid can be used as a bowl by removing and inverting it. This design is based upon the rice bowl of the Far East.

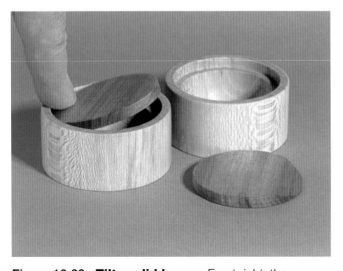

Figure 10.23 Tilt-up lid boxes. *Front right*, the underside of the lid is bevelled at about 20°. The edge of the lid should taper downwards so that the lid does not jam as you press down.

Figure 10.24 A bowl lid which no longer fits. To minimize cupping when the grain runs across the turning, the lid and base should be quartersawn.

Figure 10.25 A glued-in lid. An imitative paperweight. Lead shot was glued inside the body; the lid was then glued in place.

10.5 LID/BASE PROPORTIONS

Overall external proportions have little influence on beauty. A proportion which has been the subject of recommendations by turning teachers is lid height to base height. What is certain is:

1. No single ratio can apply to all boxes or even to one form of box.

2. The ranges of the proportion which are most appropriate will be different for different forms.

3. Other intentions, usually functional, may require that the lid height to base height proportion be outside the aesthetically preferred range. To overcome this objection, change the form of the box to one which satisfies both aesthetic and other intentions.

10.6   SHOW-AND-TELL

Two boxes are discussed, the first is turned in London plane (figure 10.26), the second in a bluestained softwood. As in the preceding chapter, my views will be gathered under the three headings wholistic, part-groups, and parts.

10.6.1   A LONDON PLANE BOX

WHOLISTIC
The overall proportions are attractive. The knob is visually separate, and thus I have excluded it when calculating the ratio of the exposed height of the lid to that of the base which is 0.72:1.00, a ratio which lies well with the usual range. The overall height to maximimum diameter are also within the normal range and the diameter at the bottom of the base is ample for stability.

PART-GROUPS
The profile of the lid part-group is built from straight lines, the sides of the base part-group consist of two curves. Here, and in general, straight lines, which tend to be aggressive

and static, do not harmonize well with curves, particularly with curves of varying curvature. Figure 10.27 shows a box in which lid and base share the same style.

PARTS
A major design fault is the difference in styles between the base and lid outside parts. Other design flaws, including the lack of correspondence between the inside and the outside parts, are described in figure 10.26.

Figure 10.27   **A box with its lid and base in the same style,** and similar in design to that on the right in the figure below. Turned in cocobolo (*Dalbergia retusa*) by Richard Raffan of Tharwa, Australian Capital Territory; 2 in. (54 mm) high x 2.75 in. (70 mm) diameter.

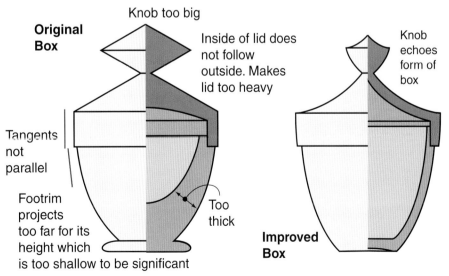

Figure 10.26   **A London plane box,** 4.25 in. high x 3 in. dia. (109 mm x 73 mm). *Left and center,* the original box. *Right,* the improved design. A positive detail of the oriiginal box is that the slopes of the knob relate to that of the top of the lid.

10.6.2 FINIAL BOX

WHOLISTICALLY
The finial box in figures 10.28 and 10.29 is
nicely turned, but wholistically stolid. As it
is a freestanding box, you can assume that
it will be treated with care and that its thinner
sections do not therefore have to be
especially strong.

PART-GROUPS
The finial is best split into two or three part-
groups. They are similar in style, although
the lowest is more substantial than it need
be.

PARTS
The parts arc timidly designed, and there is
poor flow-through from the outside of the
cup into the stem, and the from the stem
into the plinth (figure 10.29). A contributing
cause is that the tangents to curves where
the curves are broken by small details, such
as fillets, are not parallel or at 90°—this is
demonstrated by the pairs of magenta lines.

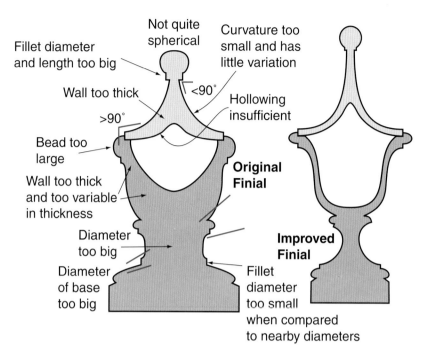

Figure 10.29 **The finial box from the preceding figure.** *Left*,
comments on the original. *Right*, an improved design with two alternative
transitions from the cup into the waisted stem, and much greater
correspondence between the inside and outside parts.

10.7 ENDNOTES

1. Pierre Mille, "Studies of Medieval Monoxyle Flasks," *Papers from the* 1997
   World Turning Conference (Philadelphia: Wood Turning Center, 2000), pp.
   26–36. Other references for monoxyl flasks include: Rolf Steinert,
   Drechseln in Holtz (Leipzig: Fachbuchverlag Leipzig, 1993), p.248; Chris
   Stott, *Turned Boxes 50 Designs* (Lewes, East Sussex: GMC Publications,
   2002), pp. 150–151; Jonathon Levi, *Treen for the Table* (Woodbridge, Suffolk:
   Antique Collectors' Club, 1998), p. 182; and Fritz Spannagel, *Das
   Drechslerwerk* (1940, reprint 1981; Hannover: Th. Schafer, 1981), p. 206.

2. John Baker, *Mauchline Ware and Associated Scottish Souvenir Ware* (Princes
   Risborough, Buckinghamshire: Shire Publications, 1985).

3. Gary Roberts, "Matroshka Dolls," *American Woodturner* (Spring 2001): pp.
   41–43.

4. A range of containers with multiple compartments are pictured in Klaus
   Pracht, *Woodturning* (London: Dryad Press, 1986), pp. 110, 111, 119.

5. William L. Stephenson, "Boxes with Snap-On Lids: The Production
   Techniques of Judy Ditmer," *American Woodturner* (December 1994): pp.
   28–30.

6. Richard Raffan, *Turning Boxes* (Newtown, Connecticut: The Taunton Press,
   2002), pp. 84–89.

7. Two books which show a range of lid designs for pottery are Robin
   Hopper, *Functional Pottery* (Iola, Wisconsin: Krause Publications, 2000);
   and Neal French, *The Potter's Directory of Shape and Form* (Iola, Wisconsin:
   Krause Publications, 2000), pp. 36–37, 52–53.

8. Drawing based on Spannagel, p.110; and Pracht, pp. 110, 117.

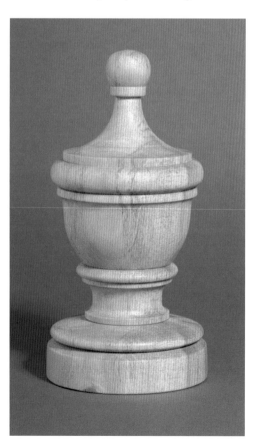

Figure 10.28 **A finial box,** 4.75 in. high
x 2.3 in. dia. (120 mm x 58 mm).

Chapter Eleven

VESSEL DESIGN

A vessel is a utensil for holding something. No particular shape is implied, and the contents are usually but not exclusively liquid. In recent years this meaning has widened to include bowls, platters, and hollow turnings which are intended to be works of art and which may be useless as containers (figure 11.1).

11.1   STAGE 1 DESIGN

For vessels, the inception and the first design are often triggered by the availability of a particular piece of wood. For other triggers, the test of feasibility is often whether you can source wood which is suitable for the intended design. Because the majority of vessels are turned from one-piece blanks, many turners cut their blanks directly from freshly-felled trees. If you do this, you should study the physical characteristics of each tree, decide on the approximate designs of the vessels, etc. that you will use its wood for

(figure 11.2), and only then start to cut the blanks. As you proceed with the cutting, more of the tree's structure, colors, flaws, etc. will be revealed, and you may revise your earlier decisions about how to blank the remaining part of the tree.

Once you have confirmed that a design is feasible, the next step is to establish the restraints and your intentions in whichever of the seven areas listed in page 95 are appropriate. These areas are reproductive, functional, economic, aesthetic, communicative, materials etc., and personal.

11.2   DETAILED DESIGN

You can regard a vessel as an assemblage of one or more outer parts from which is deducted an assemblage of one or more inner parts. These inner parts are the wood you turn away to create the hollow or cavity. You can equally regard a vessel as an assemblage of, say, a rim, a body, and

Figure 11.1 **Communicative, imitative, lidded bowls by Michael Brolly** of Mertztown, Pennsylvania. *Left, Frog Bowl II* (1992); mahogany, maple, bubinga, and ebony; 5 in. (125 mm) high; collection of Irving Lipton. *Right, Frog Bowl* (1988); maple and mahogany; 4 in. (100 mm) high; collection of the Wood Turning Center.

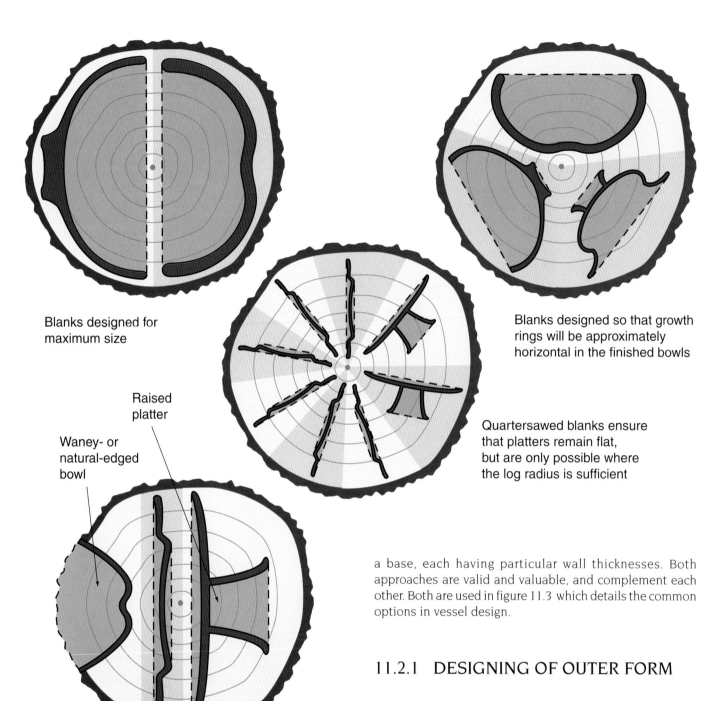

Blanks designed for
maximum size

Raised
platter

Waney- or
natural-edged
bowl

Blanks designed so that growth
rings will be approximately
horizontal in the finished bowls

Quartersawed blanks ensure
that platters remain flat,
but are only possible where
the log radius is sufficient

The two platter blanks ensure maximum
diameters, long-term flatness, and
quartersawed figure (or strong crotch figure
if cut from a crotch)

**Figure 11.2 Converting tree cross-sections into
vessel blanks.** The pith (and sometimes the sapwood)
should not be included in blanks to reduce the possibility
of cracking during seasoning. True quartersawing is
wasteful as the central cross section shows.

a base, each having particular wall thicknesses. Both
approaches are valid and valuable, and complement each
other. Both are used in figure 11.3 which details the common
options in vessel design.

11.2.1 DESIGNING OF OUTER FORM

Some vessel outsides consist of only one part. In elevation
this part can be cylindrical, conical, or based on a rotated
convex, concave, or serpentine curve (figure 11.4). There will
be at least one end because a vessel must have an opening.
Ends need not be flat or perpendicular to the turning-axis.
Even with these simple one-part forms the choices of
elevation are infinite, and vary in the aesthetic reactions
which they engender. Thus for arcs, the greater the rotation,
the greater the impact. Similarly for curves with varying-
curvatures, the greater the total rotation(s) and the greater
the acceleration(s) of curvature, the greater the impact.

The outer forms of many vessels are composed of more
than one part arranged in one or more part-groups (figures
11.5 and 11.6). You can shorten the design process by using

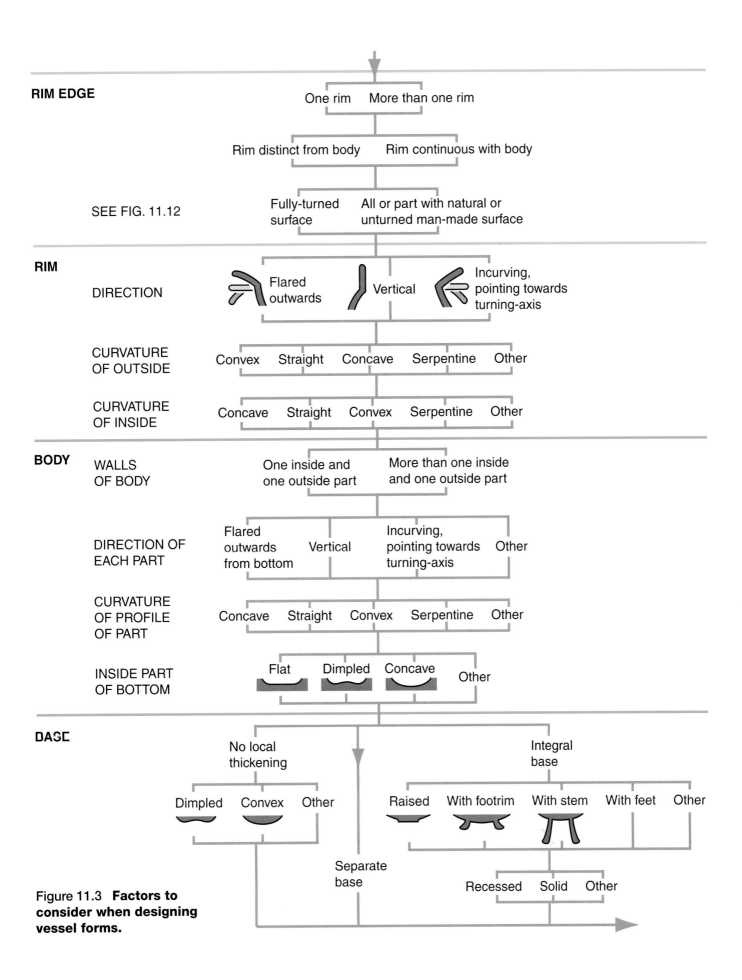

Figure 11.3 **Factors to consider when designing vessel forms.**

guidelines, by choosing a particular style, even by some degree of copying, but you can only ultimately determine what is appropriate by design work, by trialing different solutions.

11.2.2   DESIGNING THE INSIDE

When designing the inside of a vessel, rather than designing the part volumes which have to be turned out, you can design the wall thicknesses with reference to the outside form. (Alternatively you can first design the inside, and add the wall thicknesses to design the outside form). The guidelines concerning equal wall thicknesses and sameness of style between the inside and outside stated on page 203 apply.

Wall thickness here includes the thicknesses at any place on a vessel, not just in the main body, and can be:

1. Thick, medium or thin depending on your intentions and the restraints (figure 11.7).
2. Constant or variable in thickness. Any changes in

thickness can be gradual or abrupt (figure 11.8). Edges, rims, and footrims are often thickened to aid durability; and bottoms and bases are often thickened to aid stability (figure 11.9). Thin walls are used to imply exceptional workmanship, create translucency, lessen weight, and enable rapid seasoning without cracking but with distortion.

Figure 11.6   A vessel with two major outside parts, both rotated serpentine curves, *Eat Your Heart Out David Ellsworth* previously pictured in figure 4.64. The brightness and starkness of the fastenings stresses their representational role.

Figure 11.4   A one-outside-part oak bowl, its silhouette a revolved cyma recta.

Figure 11.5   A silky oak krater, similar in form to the preceding bowl, but composed of two part-groups: the upper one, a fillet surmounted by a cavetto; the lower one, an ovolo above or overlaid by a region of textural/ornamental rings.

Figure 11.7   A bowl with a thick wall and a flat horizontal rim by Holger Graf of Hilzingen, Germany. The single outside part (the rim and the inside are the other two parts) has ringed ornament.

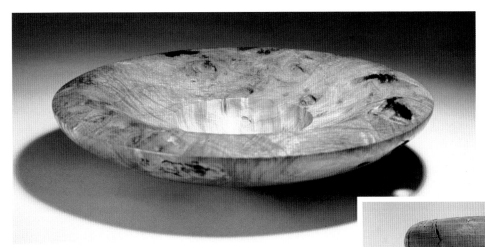

Figure 11.8 **Breaking the wall thickness guideline, a shallow bowl by Holger Graf.** The sudden hollowing rejects the wall thickness guideline, and creates an ambiguous inside rim—is it a rim? or is it part of the body?

11.2.3   ORNAMENT & DECORATION

Vessels commonly provide large surfaces which are ideal for organic or other decoration, and for communication (figure 11.10). These surfaces can also be ornamented by retaining earlier man-made or natural features (figure 11.11), by turning, or by other means.

Rims are obvious areas for ornamentation—some turned options are shown in figure 11.12, carved examples are shown in figures 11.13 and 11.14. The insides of vessels are less often ornamented, in part because of restricted tool access: even turned concentric ripples in the bottoms of vessel insides are rare.

Figure 11.10 **Communicative decoration, *Graffiti Bowl* (1988).** The whole rim is an edge roll.

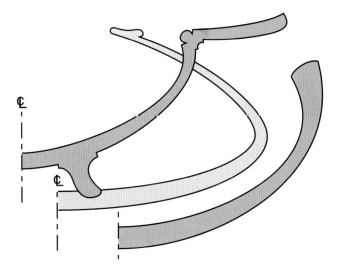

Figure 11.9 **Bowl halves with thickened rims and bottoms shown in vertical diagonal section.**

Figure 11.11 **The surface of the sapwood of jarrah burl retained as ornament.**

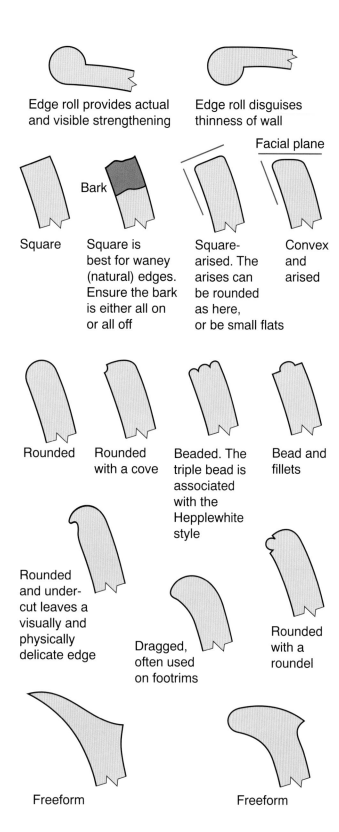

Edge roll provides actual and visible strengthening

Edge roll disguises thinness of wall

Facial plane

Bark

Square

Square is best for waney (natural) edges. Ensure the bark is either all on or all off

Square-arised. The arises can be rounded as here, or be small flats

Convex and arised

Rounded

Rounded with a cove

Beaded. The triple bead is associated with the Hepplewhite style

Bead and fillets

Rounded and under-cut leaves a visually and physically delicate edge

Dragged, often used on footrims

Rounded with a roundel

Freeform

Freeform

Figure 11.12 Rims, just a few of the infinite number of possibilities. Should the facial plane, where there is one, be at 90° to the angle of the wall? Some of the rim designs can also be used on footrims and at the bottoms of stems.

Figure 11.13 A vessel with a waney-edged and ornamented rim by Peter Hromek of Sinntal, Germany.

Figure 11.14 The wide, ornamented, and functional rim of a negus strainer. Antique examples are pictured in Jonathan Levi, *Treen for the Table* (Woodbridge, Suffolk: Antique Collectors' Club,1998), page 179; and Owen Evan-Thomas, *Domestic Utensils of Wood* (Wakefield, Yorkshire: EP Publishing, 1973), plate 61.

Law's Grocers' Manual, edited and revised by C. L. T. Beeching, 3rd edition (London: William Clowes & Sons, 1930) states that negus was invented in the reign of Queen Anne (1707–1714) by colonel Francis Negus, and is a drink of port, sherry, or other wine, hot water, sugar, grated nutmeg, lemon juice, and grated lemon rind.

Chapter Twelve

COLUMNS

One of my specialties has been turned wooden columns. I will therefore discuss turned columns in detail, tracing the history of the circular-cross-section column, and particularly that of the classical column, before detailing column designing and making. Aptly, the term "classical" is derived from the Latin *classicus* meaning "of the highest of the five classes into which the Roman citizenry were divided".[1]

Since man started to construct shelters he has made columns from wood and from stone. Few wooden columns have survived from antiquity, therefore many of the illustrations in this chapter show stone columns. By about 2500 B.C. stone columns had become an architectural focus for the Egyptian civilization, and their shafts and capitals often imitated on plants. Thereafter the column's form and usage continued to develop, particularly around the eastern end of the Mediterranean Sea. In the Egyptian and Greek architectures the column was a critical structural element, but in Roman and later architectures columns were less important and were also used just as ornaments.

The only text which included column design to survive from ancient times was Vitruvius (page 13). During and following the Renaissance, numerous architects and scholars formalized the five Roman orders (the Tuscan and Composite plus Vitruvius's Doric, Ionic, and Corinthian). In the eighteenth century Greek architecture was rediscovered and revived, and this ushered back into the architectural lexicon my favorite column, the Greek Doric.

Ancient Egypt, Greece, and Rome are not our only sources for column designs. Ancient civilizations in other parts of Europe, the Near East, and Asia developed unique column designs, and within Europe the classical column was subsumed and adapted by Romanesque and Gothic architects during the millennium following the fall of the Western Roman Empire. Since the eighteenth century column design has continued to both develop and degrade due to the demands of commercial fashion-lead eclecticism, the availability of new materials and processes, and the relative increase in the cost of skilled labor.

Architectural styles concern the forms of structures and buildings. These architectural styles have have also influenced the designs of joinery, garden structures, furniture, and treen. While all these man-made structures and objects may incorporate columns, the designs of those columns need not follow the dictates of a particular version of a style. Neither does the design of a column have to conform to the dominant style of its surroundings. Thus columns, including those of classical design, remain both a relevant and a creative resource in the twenty-first century.

12.1   COLUMNS IN ANCIENT EGYPT

The civilization of ancient Egypt depended on the Nile. Along its banks were sited the major settlements (figure 12.1). Many of the associated stone-built temples and tombs have survived to the present (figures 12.2–12.15). Their columns display vegetable references in their capitals and shafts through both their form and decoration, with the edges and cusps in the carving used to define color boundaries. The shafts which were basically circular in cross-section were:

1. Plain round, often with low-relief carving.
2. Reeded, echoing the bound bundles of reeds used singly as columns and in rows as walls in domestic buildings.
3. Fluted.

These three shaft types still dominate today.

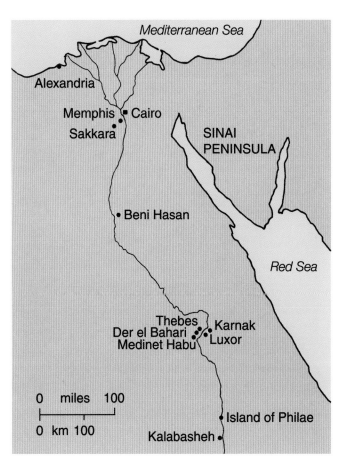

Figure 12.1 Ancient Egypt. The square denotes that Cairo is a modern city.

Figure 12.2 Polychromed columns with papyrus capitals, in the portico of the temple of Isis built between 283 and 247 B.C. on the island of Philae in the Nile. Isis was an important goddess with powers concerning protection, illness, and the dead. She was the wife of Osiris and the mother of Horus.

Illustration sourced from Samuel Manning, *The Land of the Pharaohs* (1880).

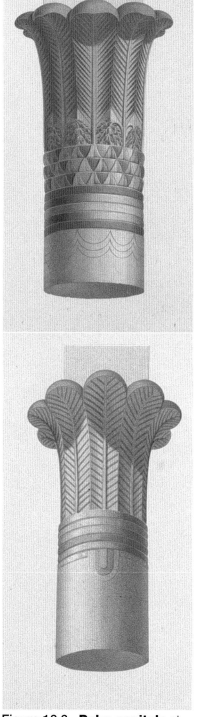

Figure 12.3 Palm capitals at Philae, pictured in G. Perrot and C. Chipiez, *Histoire de l'Art Egyptien.*

The other plants usually featured in Egyptian capitals are the lotus, both the flower and the bud, and the papyrus.

Figure 12.4 The processional hall at Karnak showing remnants of the original painted decoration. The stone surfaces were thinly stuccoed; the stucco surfaces were then burnished before being painted.

Polychromy was widespread in the ancient world, but had almost completely eroded from the Greek and Roman buildings which were the only ones accessible to Europeans until the eighteenth century. There was consternation in the early nineteenth century when the pale stone structures of the ancient Greek and Roman empires were shown to have been brightly painted.[2]

Polychromy was a major feature of twentieth-century postmodernism, although, as the next figure shows, modern efforts pale in comparison.

Photograph by Russell Brooks, Sydney.

Figure 12.5 An impression of the original low-relief carving and polychrome on a column with a bell capital at the mortuary temple of Rameses III at Medinet-Habu (1198 B.C.).[3] The column is 29 ft 10 in. (9.1 m) high.

Figure 12.6 **Columns with bell columns at Karnak.** Photograph by Russell Brooks, Sydney.

Figure 12.7 A bell capital at the Ramesseum, Thebes (1301 B.C.).[4]

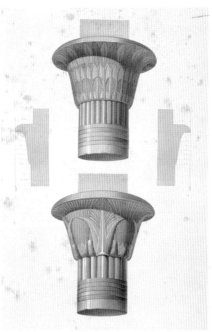

Figure 12.8 **Papyrus capitals.**[5]

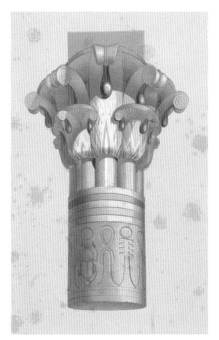

Figure 12.9 **A volute capital at Philae.**[6]

Figure 12.10 **Columns with bud capitals at Karnak.** Photograph by Russell Brooks, Sydney.

12.1.1   FLUTED AND REEDED SHAFTS

The earliest known fluted shafts were carved circa 2778 B.C. in the tomb of Third Dynasty king Zoser (or Djoser). This tomb incorporated the first pyramid, one with six steps, and is the earliest known large stone monument. Reeded columns are also used in the tomb—the reeding echoes the surfaces of the bundles of reeds used in earlier and domestic Egyptian buildings.

Fluted shafts were used elsewhere in Egypt—examples are shown in figures 12.11 to 12.13. The trigger for the introduction of fluting is unknown, but could have been:

1. A desire to invent a variation on a preexisting design. Fluting is the reverse of reeding, which was earlier in origin.
2. A desire to add interest to column shafts which lead to the arbitrary illumination of fluting.
3. The illumination that there was no need to fully round a shaft. Stone shafts may have first been carved square, then by repeatedly trimming first to eight facets, then to sixteen, etc., brought round. It was seen that if this process was halted before completion, the resulting pattern of facets (or flutes if a tool with a convex edge was used) was highly ornamental.
4. The illumination that the method used to straighten a tree trunk could be adapted to also ornament it. An adze or chisel with a blade of convex cross section would probably have been used to remove lumps and to trim tree trunks straight. If the cuts were regularly spaced around the trunk's periphery, a fluted surface would result.
5. The sight of the fluted (cannulated) stems of certain plants, or an attempt to imitate bark.

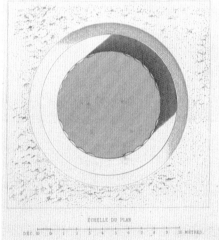

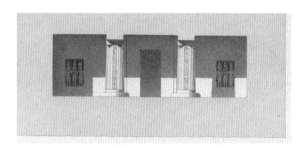

Figure 12.11   Fluted columns at Kalabsheh, XIX dynasty, Ramases II, circa 1300 B.C.[7] These columns have 24 flutes; plus four flat vertical strips or chutes, carved with cartouches, which divide each column shaft into quarters.

Figure 12.12 **The portico at Beni-Hasan** where thirty-nine tombs were constructed between 2130 and 1785 B.C. The proto-Doric columns at Beni-Hasan have sixteen flutes, a slight taper from top to bottom, and incipient capitals and bases. The capitals were in the form of square plates, and were the precursors of the abacus. Defined earlier on page 131, an abacus is the plate immediately below the entablature which first conveys the load down to the ornamented lower part of the capital, and thence to the shaft.[8]

Figure 12.13 **Rock-hewn, proto-Doric columns in the Temple of Hatshepsut at Deir-El-Baharee,** Thebes, 1520 B.C. Fluted columns were also built in the southern temple at Karnac.[9]

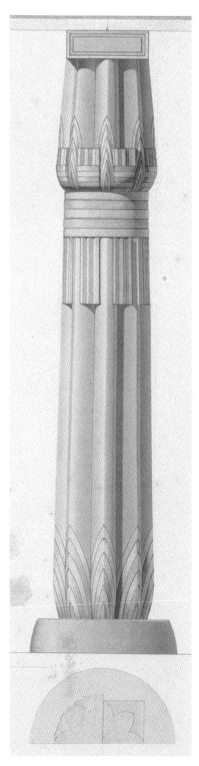

Figure 12.14 **Reeded columns with lotus bud capitals at Karnac, commissioned by Thothmes III.**

    Stone column shafts are more often fluted than reeded because flutes are easier to carve in stone. For wooden columns the shafts are first turned, and the flutes or reeds are then often run using a scratch gauge or similar, or a fast-rotating cutter. Using this process, reeding is easier than fluting, and therefore wooden shafts are more often reeded than fluted.

Figure 12.15 **An impression of the polychrome on the columns shown left,** pictured in G. Perrot and C. Chipiez, *Histoire de l'Art Egyptien.*

12.2 COLUMNS IN THE ANCIENT NEAR EAST

Empires were surprisingly large in the Bronze and Iron Ages, and people travelled long distances to colonize, to trade, and to war. For example, Egypt did not merely control both banks of the Nile between the Third Cataract and the sea. At its height during the early part of the New Kingdom under Thothmes III (1501–1447 B.C.), the Egyptian empire encompassed Nubia, Abyssinia, the Sudan, Arabia, Syria, Palestine, Mesopotamia, Crete, Cyprus, Kurdistan, and Armenia. However, Egyptian architecture was not widely adopted outside Egypt because the Egyptians did not attempt to impose their culture on the societies which they conquered. Design and technological influences did spread widely, but were modified as they spread, and adapted to local conditions including climate, wealth, religious practices, and population densities. Local architectures were particularly affected by the local materials. Where suitable timber and stone were rare, as in the alluvial plains of the Tigris and Euphrates rivers, sun-dried bricks were used in engaged and isolated columns supporting arches, vaults and domes. In Persia where readily worked limestone and timber were plentiful, the architecture was columnar. A plentiful supply of timber permitted the widespread use of fired bricks and fired tiles. When used on roofs, fired tiles superseded thatch and shingles.

Crete is in the center of the eastern Mediterranean. In ancient times it was fertile and well wooded. About 2000 B.C. large palaces were built there. The peoples were known as the Minoans after King Minos, who legend has it was the son of Zeus and was given Crete to rule. About 1625 B.C. the early palaces were destroyed by an earthquake; they were then rebuilt more grandly. The second palace at Knossos was at least two stories high, and covered 4 acres (1.6 hectares). Its columns were downward-tapering and had cypress shafts (figure 12.16).

About 1425 B.C. Crete was invaded by the Mycenaeans. The people of the Mycenae area in the Peloponnese (figure 12.19) had begun to farm more efficiently, thus creating surpluses for trade. The population also increased, which encouraged the Mycenaeans to colonize. When they did, they took their column designs with them (figure 12.17).

The primary remains of the Persian columnar architecture are at the Palace of Persepolis, begun in 518 B.C. by Darius, continued by Xerxes I, and completed by Artaxerxes in about 460 B.C. The major columns were stone (figure 12.18), but those in the lesser apartments had wooden shafts which were plastered and polychromed.

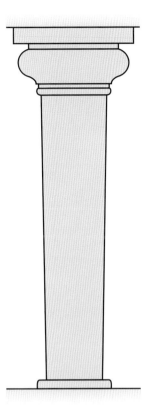

Figure 12.16 The outline of the downward-tapering cypress Minoan columns used in the palace at Knossos. Their heights varied from 5.6 to 9.9 ft (1.7 to 2.9 m).

Shafts were ornamented (*right*). Fluted shafts are shown on a fresco at Knossos, and on the half-columns flanking the entrance of the Tomb of Clytemnestra at Mycenae.[10]

Figure 12.17 One of the two half-columns of hard green limestone patterned with chevrons and running spirals which stood on each side of the entrance to the Treasury of Atreus at Mycenae in southern Greece. The columns were carved between 1350 and 1250 B.C., and are 18.7 ft (5.7 m) tall. This column is housed in, and this photograph was supplied by, The British Museum.

12.3 ANCIENT GREEK COLUMNS

The European Dark Ages (A.D. 476–1000) followed the overthrow of Roman civilization in Europe. Greece also had a Dark Age which started in about 1100 B.C. when the Mycenaean civilization fragmented. By about 700 B.C. a revival was well advanced (the first Olympic games was in 776 B.C.). Cities developed, and each competed with the others to provide its protecting gods with the grandest temples. A pan-Hellenic movement grew, and with it a Greek culture and architecture, the confidence to trade overseas, and the surplus population to colonize. Coastal settlements were founded in Sicily in about 733 B.C., and later southern Italy, Turkey, and around the Black Sea. Isolated settlements were also founded on the coast of north Africa, and on the southern coasts of France and Spain. Settlements tended to be established where natural resources were abundant, and so became wealthy and able to afford grand architecture.

The development of the two major of the three Greek orders occurred during the later part of what is termed the Archaic period (before c. 550 B.C.). The Greek (to distinguish it from the different Roman) Doric order is named after the Dorians who had invaded the Peloponnese from northwest and north central Greece. The Ionic order originated in Ionia (western Turkey), and in the Aegean islands. The Hellenic (or Classical) Age (550–323 B.C.) which followed was a period of increasing trade and prosperity for the Grecian city-states, but one adversely affected by struggles with Persia (lead first by Darius and later by Xerxes), Sparta, and Macedon. The power of Greece declined after the death of Alexander in 323 B.C., and Greece was absorbed into the Roman Empire from 27 B.C.

Greek temple building was at its height during the Hellenic Age. The Greek Doric (figures 12.20–12.22) and Ionic orders (figures 12.23 and 12.24) were first used in temples during this period. The Corinthian order (figures 12.25–12.29) appeared in the fifth century B.C., as a decorative variant of the Ionic. Although Egyptian and Greek architectures are both columnar, the colonnades (peristyles) which run round the hallowed cella (the main internal structure) of Greek temples are a Greek innovation. In early temples these peristyles were tree trunks, and were thus strong reminders of

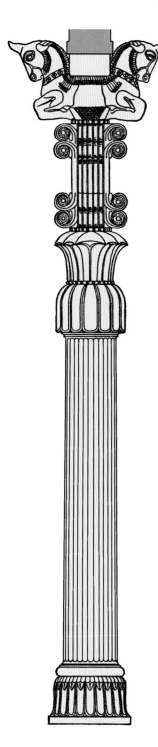

Figure 12.18 A column with a double bull capital from the Apadana (grand audience hall), Persepolis. These columns are 37 ft (11.3 m) high, and were commissioned by Xerxes I (486–465 B.C.). Other similar columns at Persepolis are up to 76 ft (23.15 m) high.[11]

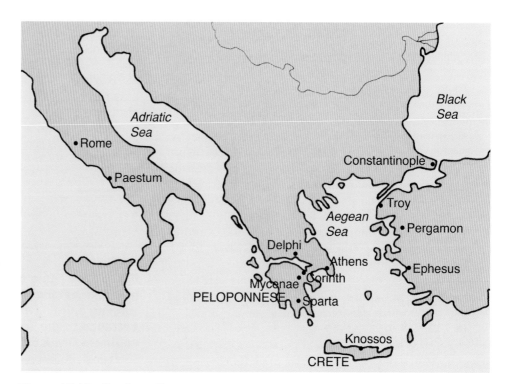

Figure 12.19 Ancient Greece.

the sacred forests in which the gods lived. Thus Greek architecture was in many ways original, although undoubtedly influenced by Egyptian which had become accessible when the Egyptian king Psamtek I (664–610 B.C.) encouraged overseas contacts.

12.3.1 GREEK DORIC COLUMNS

The Greek Doric column and entablature was a sculptural representation in stone of earlier wooden articulated structures. The Greek Doric column:

1. Stands without a base.
2. Looks marvelously gutsy, and varies in height from about 4 to over 7 times the shaft diameter at the base.
3. Has, like all classical columns, a shaft with a slightly convex profile. This looks better than, and counteracts the apparent waisting which results from, a straight shaft taper.
4. Has a shaft with a greater taper than that of other column types. The diameter of at the top of the shaft is typically between 65% and 75% of the base diameter.
5. Has a shaft which is usually fluted (but not always as in the Temple of Apollo at Delos). There are usually 20 shallow flutes separated by sharp arrises; but there can be 12, 16, 18, or 24 flutes.
6. Has a capital consisting of an echinus supporting a plain square abacus. The echinus became smaller later.
7. Does not have a base to the shaft or an astragal on the shaft a little way below the capital. In these respects it differs from the later Roman Doric column.

Since the first Greek revival columns were built in 1805,[13] the Greek Doric has been considered as having the most gravitas. It has therefore been used extensively in law courts, memorials, prisons, and mausoleums.

Figure 12.20 A side view of the temple of Neptune, circa 460 B.C. One of twenty-two views of the three Greek temples at Paestum published in 1778 by architect, etcher and archeologist Giovanni Battista Piranesi (1720–1778). The columns are about 29 ft (8.8 m) high. This height is 4.3 times their lower shaft diameter of 6ft 9in. (2.0 m).

Although close to Naples, the Greek remains at Paestum (Posidonia) remained ignored and therefore preserved until the eighteenth century because the area at the mouth of the river Silarus had become a malodorous marsh.[12]

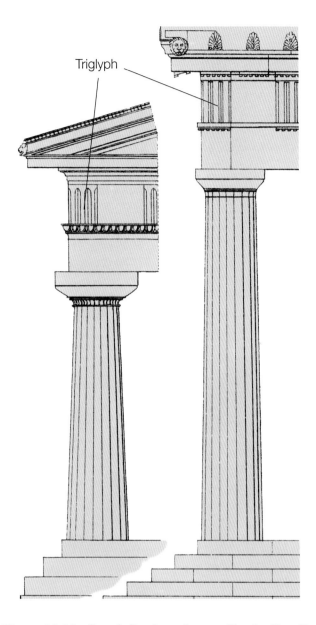

Triglyph

Figure 12.21 **Greek Doric columns illustrating the range of proportions.**[14]

Left, from the Temple of Ceres, Paestum, built c. 510 B.C. The column height is 19.5 ft (5.9 m), which equals 4.08 times the maximum shaft diameter.

Right, from the Propylaea of Elreusis, built 436–431 B.C. on the Acropolis at Athens. The height is 27 ft (8.2 m), which equals 5.72 times the maximum shaft diameter.

The stepped structure on which the columns sit is called a *crepidoma*. Its top step is a *stylobate*.

Here the triglyphs are at the corners of the friezes. In Roman and later Doric entablatures, the end triglyphs are centered over the columns below, and the innermost face of the corner of an entablature aligns vertically with the outside of the column neck (figures 12.60 and 12.61).

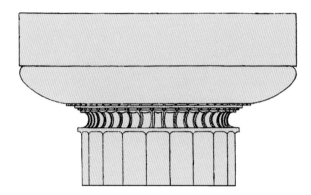

Temple of Hera (Neptune) at Paestum, circa 460 B.C.

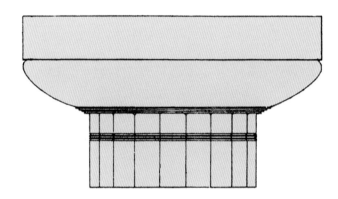

Athenian temple to Apollo, Delos, 426 B.C.

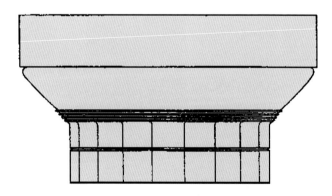

Temple of Theseus, Athens, circa 421 B.C.

Figure 12.22 **Greek Doric capitals.**[15] The earlier the column, the squatter it is and the broader its capital.

12.3.2 THE GREEK IONIC ORDER

The Greek and the later Roman Ionic columns were similar. They were also slenderer than their respective Dorics. Greek Ionic columns (figure 12.23):

1. Have a height between 9 and 10 times their maximum shaft diameter.
2. Usually have 24 flutes which are separated by fillets. Early examples may have 40, 44 or 48 flutes; those of the Peloponnese usually have 20 flutes.
3. Use canted angle volutes in the capitals of corner columns (figure 12.24).
4. Have two principal types of base, that used in the eastern Greek area, and that developed in Athens which subsequently became the dominant type.

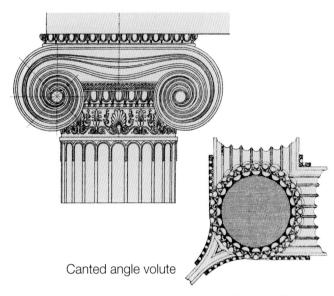

Canted angle volute

Figure 12.24 An Ionic corner capital viewed in elevation, and looking upwards.[17]

12.3.3 THE GREEK CORINTHIAN ORDER

The Corinthian (named after the city of Corinth) order was developed in the fifth century B.C. as a decorative variant of the Ionic—the coiled form at the top corners recalls the Ionic volute (figure 12.25). The Corinthian was first used only in internal colonnades and fanciful monuments (figure 12.29). The Ionic and Corinthian shafts and entablatures are similar, but the Corinthian has a deeper and more decorated capital which has several variants (figure 12.26).

The Corinthian capital may have been derived from the bell capitals of Egypt. Whether its fabled origin has any truth we shall never know (figures 12.27 and 12.28).

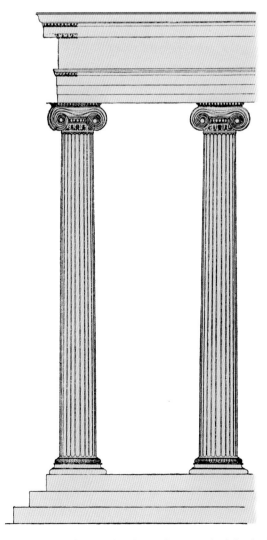

Figure 12.23 Greek Ionic columns, height 25 ft (7.6 m), in the north portico of the Erechtheum, Athens, built 421–406 B.C.[16]

Figure 12.25 A Corinthian capital from the Temple of Jupiter in Athens.[18]

Figure 12.26 **Greek Corinthian columns.** *Left*, an early form from the Tower of the Winds, Athens; *center*, from the Choragic Monument of Lysicrates, Athens (figure 12.29); *right*, from the portico of the Pantheon (447–436 B.C.), the Acropolis, Athens.[19]

Figure 12.28 **A leaf of *Acanthus mollis*,** similar to the leaf of *Acanthus spinosus* which was probably the species which was the model for Corinthian capitals.[22] Perhaps the use of the acanthus was derived from the Egyptian use of plant motifs in capitals. The acanthus was probably selected because it was symmetrical, sculptural, and native to Greece.

The acanthus leaf continued to be a popular decorative motif. For example, William Morris designed a wallpaper titled *Acanthus* in 1875.[23]

Figure 12.27 **The origin of the Corinthian capital.**[20] Vitruvius records that the Corinthian capital was invented by the Athenian sculptor Callimachus after seeing the grave of a Corinthian maiden.[21] A basket containing offerings, with a tile over the top to protect them, had been placed in the winter over a dormant acanthus plant. In the summer when Callimachus passed by again, the leaves had grown up and around the basket. We shall never know whether this story is apocryphal.

Figure 12.29 The Choragic Monument of Lysicrates. The original in Athens was 34 ft (10.4 m) high. This copy is in the Botanic Gardens, Sydney. A bronze tripod stood on top of the original.

This monument was first detailed in twenty-six plates in the first volume of the *Antiquities of Athens* (1762) by James Stuart (1713–1788) and Nicholas Revett (1720–1804).[24] The first copy was built at Shugborough, Staffordshire, in 1770.[25]

12.4 ROMAN COLUMNS

The power of the Etruscans of west-central Italy grew from the eighth to the sixth century B.C. In 510 B.C. the Romans revolted against their Etruscan king and established a city-republic. Etruscan power then continued to decline while that of Rome grew, until by 273 B.C. Rome controlled all central and southern Italy. Friction grew with the north-African power Carthage, and after three Punic wars between 264 and 146 B.C., Carthage became Roman territory. Roman conquests continued: Macedonia (168 B.C.), Greece (146

B.C.), Spain (218–210 B.C.), Syria (64 B.C.), Gaul (58–49 B.C.), Egypt (c. 30 B.C.), and England (A.D. 43). From about A.D.192, however, Rome declined due to political confusion, internal dissension, and barbarian attack.

Constantine, Emperor between A.D. 324 and 337, recognized Christianity as a religion equal to all others, continued the decentralization of the Empire initiated by Diocletian, and inaugurated the city of Byzantium as his

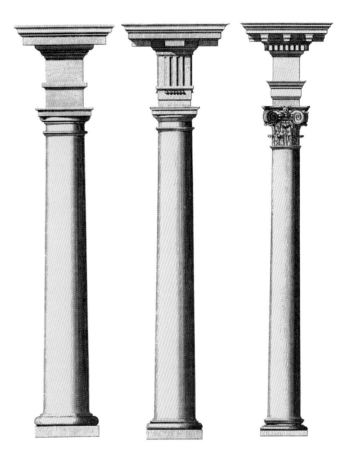

Figure 12.30 The three new orders used in Roman architecture. *Left to right*, the Tuscan, Roman Doric, and Composite.[26] The Romans also retained the Ionic and Corinthian orders.

The Tuscan order derived from an ancient type of Etruscan temple. It is the crudest and most massive of the five Roman orders.

Many forms of Roman Doric have bases similar to that shown here on the Composite order.

The Composite was a combination of the Ionic and Corinthian, and was first used in its final form in the Arch of Titus which was built shortly after A.D. 81 to commemorate the capture of Jerusalem.

In multistory buildings the orders lightened going up in the sequence Tuscan, Doric, Ionic, and Corinthian. The lowest order did not, however, have to be Tuscan (figure 12.34).

capital Constantinople, the City of Constantine. The Roman Empire was first formally partitioned into East and West in A.D. 364; Rome was sacked by the Goths in 410 and 455; and in 476 the last Roman emperor in the West was deposed by the Goths.

Mud brick, wood, and terra cotta were the building materials used by the Romans before Rome became an independent power. Direct exposure to Greek influences, both imported and from the already Hellenized Compagna south of Rome, the exploitation of local tufa and travertine, the importation of foreign marbles, and the development of cement and concrete, were mated with the need for a growing variety of buildings as Rome grew and prospered (figure 12.31).

Greek temple construction was trabeated (based on posts and lintels), and essentially single story. Roman construction also used the post and lintel. In part because of the shortage of wide-spanning stone lintels, the Romans also used the arch, its elongated version the vault, and its rotated version the dome (figures 12.32 and 12.33). Buildings of two, three, and four stories were built (figures 12.31 and 12.34).

The three Greek orders were used, but the proportions of the Roman Doric were more slender than its Greek predecessor, and its detailing was different. Two additional column orders (the Tuscan and the Composite (figure 12.30)) were introduced. The orders (the systems of columns, pedestals, and entablatures) became superimposed on the building structure in many cases rather than being an essential part, but still disciplined the design. On multistory buildings the orders came to be stacked.

Vitruvius had likened his three column types to people. Karl Philipp Moritz was to opine in 1793 that the Tuscan and Doric carried their entablatures, the Ionic exerted a gentle upward force, and the Corinthian characterized upward striving.[27]

A unique result of Roman rule was that there was an unprecedented uniformity in the architectural style of major buildings from the Rhine to the Sahara, from the Atlantic to the Euphrates. The aim of this style was to achieve a demonstrable harmony of parts. Exactly how the style was promulgated through the Empire is unknown because only one Roman text with significant architectural content (Vitruvius) survived.

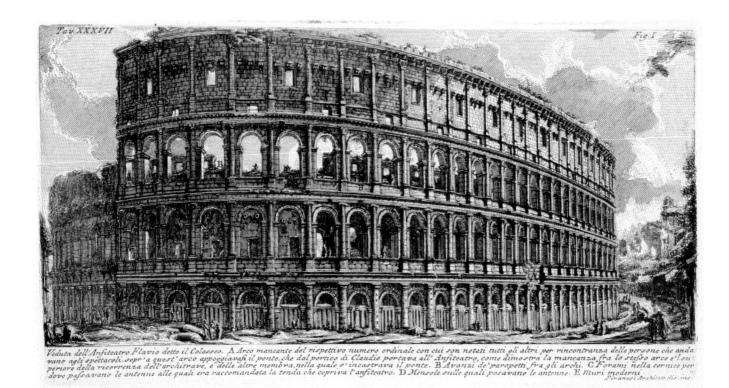

Figure 12.31 The Colosseum (also called the Flavian Amphitheatre), constructed between A.D. 70 and 80 to accommodate 50,000 spectators. This and the next two figures are scanned from engravings by Piranesi.

Figure 12.32 **The Pantheon** was a temple dedicated to "All the Gods". The columns of the octastyle (having eight columns) portico are Corinthian, 46.4 ft (14 m) high, with shaft diameters tapering from 4' 11.5" (1.51 m) to 4' 3.5" (1.31 m). The gap between the two central columns (the intercolumniation) is a little wider than the gaps between the other columns.

Figure 12.33 **The domed interior of the Pantheon,** built between A.D. 118 and 128, spans 142.5 ft (43.4 m). This span was not exceeded until the fifteenth century.

Figure 12.34 **Stacked orders on the 157.5 ft (48 m) high outside of the Colosseum.** Doric columns support Ionic columns, which in turn support Corinthian columns, which support shallow Corinthian pillasters.[28]

12.5 ROMANESQUE AND GOTHIC COLUMNS

The Roman orders continued to be used after the fall of Rome. In some cases Roman columns were reused, in others they were copied, sometimes crudely. Generally through the Romanesque and Gothic periods, in Europe, in Byzantium, and in Islamic architecture:

1. There was an increased variety of column capitals. Many were robustly-carved variations of the Corinthian or the cushion (cubiform) capital (figures 12.35 and 12.36).
2. Shafts were often cylindrical (without entasis or diminution) especially when supporting arches (figure 12.36). Although plain and fluted shafts continued to be produced, ornately carved shafts sometimes complemented the robust carving of the capitals and bases (12.37).
3. Shafts became both squatter and more slender. One or more bands were sometimes added around slender shafts.
4. Shafts were often engaged (partially integrated into walls and piers). Vault ribs were developed, refined, and integrated with the columns so that the column was sometimes so absorbed that it disappeared as an entity, notably in late Gothic cathedral architecture.

Figure 12.35 **Column capitals from St. Peter's church, Northampton, circa 1160.**[29]

Figure 12.36 **Massive columns at Great Malvern, Worcestershire, circa 1100.**[30]

Figure 12.37 Marble columns around the cloister of San Paolo, Rome, thirteenth century.
Some of these shafts were inlaid with small pieces of coloured mosaic called *smalto*.[31]

12.6 THE FORMALIZATION OF THE ORDERS

Buildings with classical features continued to be built in Europe, especially in Italy, after the end of the Western Roman Empire in A.D. 476. In Italy also, the remnants of classical buildings were commonplace, some were largely intact, and some, like the Pantheon (figures 12.32 and 12.33), were in daily use.

The interest in Roman architecture during the Renaissance lead to the formalization of the five Roman orders during the sixteenth century and afterwards. Major architectural handbooks on the orders were published by Serlio, Vignola, Palladio, and Scamozzi. In them, as dictated by Vitruvius, the proportions of columns were expressed in terms of a module. The module selected was usually the maximum shaft radius or diameter. However, the proportions which each author specified were different, and varied according to the accuracy of the measurements made from the extant buildings, the particular buildings chosen, arithmetical competence, and personal preference (figure 12.38).

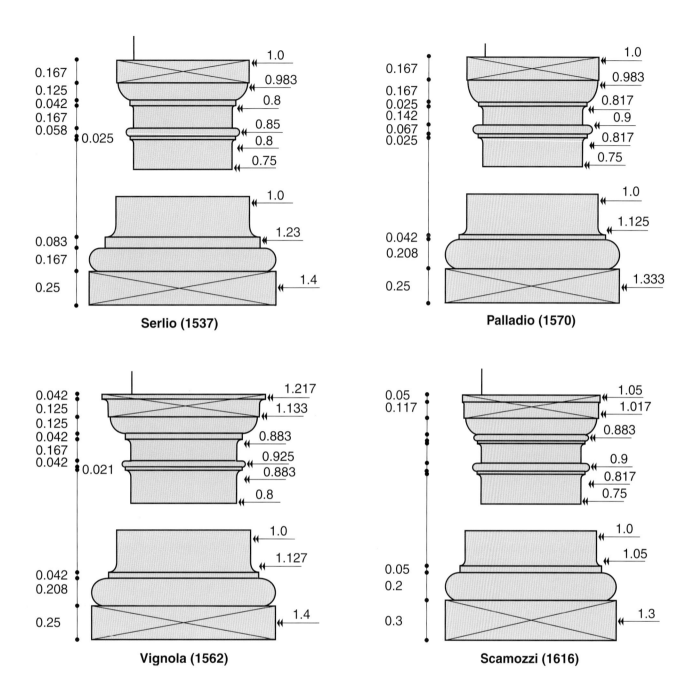

Figure 12.38 The different versions of the Tuscan column recommended in the four most important Renaissance handbooks on the orders.[32] These books were:

1. Sebastiano Serlio (1475–1555), *De Architectura libri quinque* (*The Five Books of Architecture*). The five books were published separately in Venice and Paris between 1537 and 1547. They were first published together in Venice in 1584.
2. Giacomo Barozzi da Vignola (1507–1573), *Regola delli cinque ordini d'architettura*, first published in 1562.
3. Andrea Palladio (1508–1580), *I Quattro Libri dell'Achitettura* (*The Four Books of Architecture*), first published in Venice in 1570.
4. Vincenzo Scamozzi (1548–1616), *L'idea della architettura universale*, first published in 1615.

There has never been a single, universally accepted standard Tuscan column design, or one for any other order. Of the four versions, I prefer Vignola's.

The four architects also recommended different column heights. For the Tuscan they were in multiples of the maximum shaft diameter D: Serlio 6D, Vignola 7D, Palladio 7D, and Scamozzi 7.5D.

12.7 COLUMNS AFTER THE RENAISSANCE

The variety, ornamentation, and decoration of columns multiplied after the Renaissance (figure 12.39). This trend was encouraged by the excavations which began at Herculaneum in 1739, and at Pompei in 1748, and by exploration and conquest, particularly in Asia. Undue restraint in decoration was further discouraged after the confirmation in the early nineteenth century that classical buildings and sculpture had been polychromed. The architectural arrangements and applications in which columns were used also increased; for example, monumental columns which rose through two or more stories were used more often. Woodwork took its lead from architecture, and classical columns were increasingly used to fit-out buildings and in furniture (figures 12.40 and 12.41).

Books on the orders continued to be published along with successively more-accurate measured drawings from a widening range of Roman, and later Greek and Asian extant sources. Particular orders and architectural styles became preferred for particular building uses. In Britain from about 1750, neoclassical design was regarded by the Whigs as desirable because of its association with the grandeur of

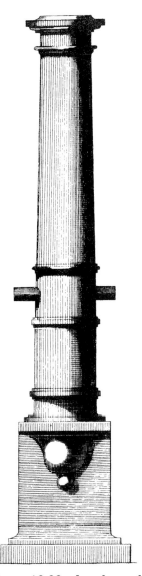

Figure 12.39 **A column in the form of a gun,** pictured in P. Hamelin Bergeron, *Manuel du Tourneur*, volume 1, plate XXX.

Figure 12.40 **Legs turned to resemble Tuscan columns on a walnut drawleaf table, circa 1600.** The columnar leg is aesthetically attractive without needing dramatic waisting which would lessen its stiffness; this form also has desirable classical associations. The candlesticks are also of interest to woodturning designers. Photograph from Huntington Antiques, Ltd., Stow-on-the-Wold, Gloucestershire.

ancient Rome.

The favored uses for Greek Doric columns were mentioned on page 225. Roman Doric columns were also considered to have great gravitas, and were used in the same types of buildings.

From the late eighteenth century the neoclassical styles were challenged by the revival of Gothic styles (figure 12.42). In Britain and northern Europe Gothic styles were promoted as the natural historical styles of the region, they were also promoted as structurally superior to the trabeated classical styles.

By the nineteenth century some believed that the orders had run their course and could not be developed further. Peter Nicholson (1765–1844) in *The Builder and Workman's New Director* (1824) could describe the orders as merely "five pillars of specific character supporting a roof".[33] However they have continued to be used to the present day, and even enjoyed spectacular popularity during the postmodern period.

Figure 12.41 A globe-stand incorporating Roman Doric columns. One of a pair (the other having a celestial globe) made by John Bennett in London between 1760 and 1770. The wood is oak, the height 50 in. (1270 mm), the globe diameter is 28 in. (710 mm).

The globe stands are displayed at Temple Newsam House, Leeds, Yorkshire, and this illustration was provided by the Leeds Museum Resource Center.

Figure 12.42 A neo-Gothic column with a cylindrical shaft in Washington D.C.

12.7.1 TECHNOLOGICAL PROGRESS

Until towards the end of the eighteenth century large columns were mainly carved in wood or stone, or constructed from a combination of brickwork, wood, stucco, and plaster. Only occasionally were large columns cast in metal, for example the four bronze, baroque columns of Bernini's baldachino in St. Peter's, Rome (1624–1633). After the eighteenth century technological developments affected the manufacture and design of classical-style columns, and resulted in an increasing demand for turned wooden column patterns for producing molds for casting.

Figure 12.43 **The Greek Doric columns of the octastyle portico befit the solemn purpose of the War Memorial in Melbourne.**

Figure 12.44 **Slender cast-iron Corinthian columns** at Bowral railway station (1867), New South Wales. The form of the capital has been modified to eliminate any undercutting so that a simple pattern in two longitudinal halves can be used to produce the mold, and the whole column can be cast in one piece.

COADE'S STONE

One of the earliest materials used for the batch casting of column elements was Coade's Artificial Stone. Mrs Eleanor Coade initially operated the firm which flourished between about 1760–1820 in Lambeth, south London. A plain Ionic capital cost thirteen shillings. Products were even exported to Washington and Boston in America.[34]

CAST IRON AND STEEL

The materials most used in the large-scale manufacture of columns have been cast iron, reinforced concrete, and rammed mortar. The last two materials depend on steel reinforcement for their tensile strength, but cast iron has been the most important column material during the last two centuries.

When charcoal was used to smelt (melt and thereby separate the metal from the impurities in the ore) iron, the wood from about one acre (4000 m²) of forest was needed. In 1709 Abraham Darby succeeded in smelting iron using coke—a fuel made by heating high-quality coal in the absence of air. His son, also an Abraham, continued to develop the process and constructed first iron structure, a bridge, over the River Severn at Coalbrookdale in England. It containing 400 tons of cast iron, and was opened on New Year's Day 1781. It advertised that iron was both sufficiently affordable and plentiful to be used for main structural components—until then the use of iron had been largely restricted to fasteners and brackets. From 1828 the smelting of iron was made more efficient by the addition of a heated air blast, a process introduced by James Neilson.

Cast iron contains 5% to 10% of impurities, has high compressive strength, and a low tensile strength which is however much higher than that of stone. The advent of affordable cast iron which was strong in compression not only allowed more slender compression members, but enabled batch production because it could be cast in multiples from one pattern. The growth in its use was slow until Paxton's Great Exhibition building of 1851 proved its potential.

Steel is pure (wrought) iron with a small percentage of carbon, usually between about 0.3% and 1.0%. Steel has great tensile and compressive strengths; it can also be welded. In 1784 the puddling process for the production of steel from cast (pig) iron was introduced into England. With this introduction steel ceased to be a semiprecious material and became merely expensive because puddling furnaces were still labor- and-fuel-intensive. Each puddling furnace could only produce about 1.5 tons of steel per 12 hour shift, and by 1860 there were about 3000 in Britain. There were then two almost simultaneous breakthroughs which enabled the cheap and rapid removal of the embrittling carbon from the cast iron: Henry Bessemer's converter, announced in 1856, but not working satisfactorily until a decade later; and the open hearth furnace invented and developed between 1864 and 1868 by Sir William Siemens and Pierre Émile Martin.

Figure 12.45 **Columns with cylindrical plastic shafts and glued-on annular moldings masquerading as capitals and bases** (see below).

Figure 12.46 **Annular moldings which can be glued onto plastic pipes** to imitate bands, astragals, capitals, and bases.

The reducing cost of steel made it feasible for use in structures. It could also be rolled into structural sections which enabled slender, new structures. An additional spur to the increasing use of steel structures was the collapse of the cast and wrought iron River Tay railway bridge in 1879 with the loss of 78 lives. Other technological advances, such as the railways and engine-powered ships, utilized and depended on cast iron, steel, and other new materials; they also required classical and Gothic columns, if only to supply gravitas, which in turn increased the demand for turned wooden columns and column patterns.

LABOR COSTS
The relative cost of skilled labor has increased rapidly over the last two centuries. Ionic, Corinthian, and Composite capitals carved in wood and stone became increasingly expensive compared to Doric and Tuscan, as did fluted shafts relative to plain shafts. Even when the carved capitals have been used, their designs have often been modified to enable them to be cast or built up from components.

Other materials used in the construction of columns include reinforced and precast concrete, dry-rammed mortar, asbestos cement, plastic, and cardboard. The last three have been used mainly in pipe form for shafts, but their low cost has caused many modern designers to forsake diminution. We are therefore often assaulted by aesthetically-inferior imitations of classical columns (figure 12.45). If turners had any role, it was limited to producing bases, capitals, and sometimes astragals, either from wood or laminated MDF to glue onto the cylindrical shafts. Even this role has now been subsumed by large manufacturers (figure 12.46).

12.8 ASIAN COLUMNS

Egypt, the rest of the Near East, and Europe are not our only sources for turned or turnable column designs (figures 12.47 and 12.48). Column designs from Asia were copied and adapted, notably between 1750 and 1850 when the picturesque style in its various manifestations was in fashion.

Figure 12.48 **An Indian stone column** from the rock-temple of Parasona Rama at Ellora.[35]

Figure 12.47 **Plain round columns with little taper are a feature of this replica Chinese gateway** at Bendigo, Victoria, Australia. The general Chinese word for column is *chu*; then there is *p'ing chu*, a central bay column; and *chiao chu*, a corner column, etc.[36]

One of the West's earliest sources for information on Chinese construction and columns was *Designs of Chinese Buildings, Furniture, Dresses, Machines, etc.*, by William Chambers, first published in London in 1763.

12.9 DESIGNING CLASSICAL COLUMNS

There is a continuing demand for nicely designed classical and classically inspired columns in buildings, furniture, and treen. As woodturning designers we are unlikely to be asked to design classical buildings, but we can legitimately use the orders as a child's box of bricks, picking out parts that we want and using them with little understanding. You can also mix classical and nonclassical column elements; or originate your own column designs. However, the deeper our understanding of the orders, of, as Sir John Summerson puts it, "their variety within unity", the better we will serve our design intentions.[37]

During stage 1 of the design process you will usually have defined: the exact or approximate overall height; whether the column is on a pedestal; and, if the column is a component, how it integrates with the rest of the object. If you intend a column to conform at least fairly closely to an order or other known column style, you should have sufficient information to start the detailed design. It is then a process of refinement requiring some or all of the following steps, although the sequence is not necessarily as linear as set out below:

1. If not finalized in stage 1, finalize the column's total height, and the details of its surroundings. Columns should usually be designed wholistically to integrate visually and structurally with any surrounding structure.

    Columns are often grouped, usually in rows to support (even if only visually) walls, beams, arches, vaults or domes (figures 12.59 and 12.60). Isolated columns such the 115 ft (35 m) Trajan's Column in Rome and Nelson's in Trafalgar Square, built 1700 years later, are architectural rarities, but smaller versions are often used as pedestals to support statuary or vases (figures 12.49–12.52). Columnar pedestals usually have squatter proportions and enlarged capitals and bases. Another pedestal design which provides a large flat top is shown in figure 12.52.

2. Another design step which is properly part of stage 1 is to decide whether the column should be on a pedestal or not. Although different writers specify different relative pedestal heights, a typical ratio of column height to pedestal height is 10:3 irrespective of the order. This pedestal height is thus 23% of the combined height of the pedestal and the column. I have not detailed the designing of classical pedestals as full information is given in all the major texts on the orders.

3. Choose the ratio of height to maximum shaft diameter. The ratios specified in the usual references apply to stone columns incorporated into classically-styled buildings. Typical ratios for stone columns are listed in table 12.1. You can make columns far more slender when

they are wood or the turning is a pattern for columns which will be cast in metal, reinforced concrete, or another material or composite which has a significant tensile strength and thus resistance to buckling. Another factor which will influence the slenderness of columns is how far apart they are, and whether they are grouped. The spacing of columns is termed intercolumniation, and is discussed on pages 245 to 247.

The typical classical ratios of column height to maximum shaft diameter cannot be applied unthinkingly. The dimensions of the available solid wood or other constraints you may cause you to opt for greater slenderness rather than conglutinate the shafts (page 256). If the height to diameter ratio becomes visually too large, you may prefer to put a pedestal below rather than thicken the column. There is a good deal of aesthetic judgement in successful column design.

4. Calculate the maximum shaft diameter (the module).
5. Decide the column taper, the ratio of the shaft diameter under the capital to the maximum shaft diameter—0.85 is a typical but not compulsory value.
6. If you intend your column to accord to an established order, decide on which one, and which variant. If you want to avoid carved capitals, you are restricted to three classical types: the Greek and Roman Dorics and the Tuscan. The cushion capital is also turnable (page 137).
7. Design the base and capital, also any astragal and fillets. You can consider eliminating the astragal and its adjacent fillet and congee on a stumpy, strongly-tapering shaft (figures 12.50 and 12.51). Depending on the construction of the column and the likelihood of damage, you may decide not to use congees and fillets at the shaft's ends.
8. Knowing the thickness of the capital and base, and the height of any pedestal, calculate the net shaft length.
9. Calculate the diminution, the tapering profile of the shaft. This is detailed on pages 248 to 254.

    On slender columns a length at the bottom of the shaft is often, but does not have to be, left cylindrical (page 12.65). The stumpier and more tapered a column is, the shorter this cylindrical section should be.

10. Decide position and design of any astragal, sinkage, etc.
11. Review the design. I find it useful to draw the column and its surroundings to scale, invite reactions from others, especially clients, and allow time for incubation and fresh assessments. Make any design adjustments resulting from the review.
12. Decide whether the shaft will be molded, and if so decide on the number, and details of the flutes, reeds, fillets, or cables. Decide whether there will be any other features such as rustication.
13. Design the construction of the finished column. If it will be made in pieces, design how the components will fit together, any installation procedure, and any fixings (figure 12.56).

Figure 12.49 **A pedestal based on a Greek Doric column at Paestum.** The shaft is turned from an old tallowwood (*Eucalyptus microcorys*) power pole (figure 12.77). The capital is MDF which has been laminated, turned, and lacquered. The three other pedestals on this page were made in the same way.

Figure 12.51 **A Roman Doric pedestal.** As in the column in figure 12.50, the astragal has been omitted.

Figure 12.50 **A Doric-style pedestal with a shaft with strong diminution.** This pedestal and that in figure 12.51 have been designed to have large-diameter abacuses. Collection of Robyn Hawkins.

Figure 12.52 **A broken-shaft pedestal with a Roman Doric base.** The tallowwood shaft has an integral congee.

Writer	Tuscan	Doric	Ionic	Corinthian	Composite
Vitruvius	—	7	9	9.5	—
Serlio	6	7	8	9	10
Vignola	7	8	9	10	10
Palladio	7	8.7	9	9.5	10
Scamozzi	7.5	8.5	8.8	10	9.7
Perrault	7.4	8	8.7	9.7	10
Gibbs	7	8	9	10	10
Chambers	7	—	9	—	10

Table 12.1 The column heights recommended by various writers on the Roman orders expressed in multiples of the maximum shaft diameter.[38]

Figure 12.53 Columns and pedestals made for interior design exhibitions. The red column capitals are Greek Doric, the bases are Roman Doric. As tallowwood is a dense wood, the shafts are in two parts so that they can be carried without too much difficulty. There are no projecting congees and fillets at the tops and bottoms of the shafts which could be broken off during movings.

Figure 12.54 **Column diameters limited by material dimensions.** Each column is turned in one piece from an old power pole, and is a stretched Tuscan.

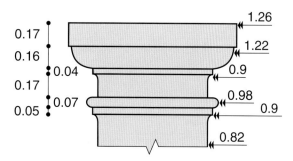

Tuscan/Roman Doric Capital

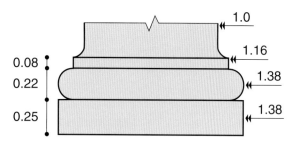

Tuscan Base

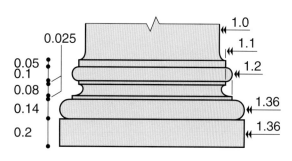

Roman Doric Base

Figure 12.55 Tuscan and Roman Doric column proportions for small wooden columns. The multipliers are in decimals of the maximum shaft diameter.

These column proportions are more exaggerated than recommended in architectural texts on the orders because the wooden columns most readers might design will be shorter than typical architectural stone columns. However there are no fixed or ideal proportions, and readers should select multipliers which best satisfy their intentions.

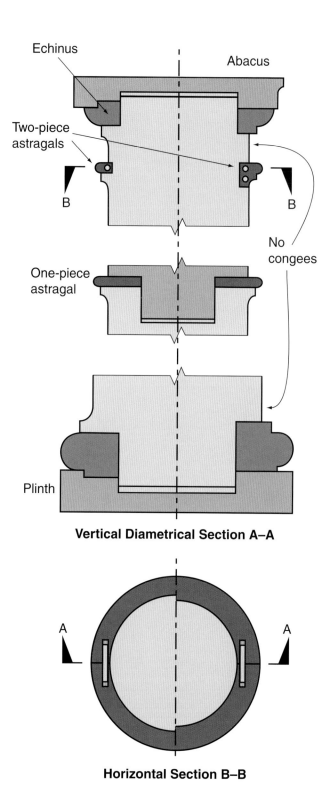

Vertical Diametrical Section A–A

Horizontal Section B–B

Figure 12.56 Common column constructions. You can usually reduce the overall cost by constructing a large column from components. This figure shows various alternatives.

When a column is to be installed between an existing floor and entablature, it is usually best to design the plinth or abacus so that it can be slid in after the rest of the column has been erected in its final position.

The most common method of column construction requires a pin to be turned on each end of the shaft. These pins house in holes or recesses in the capital and base. The astragal can be turned with the shaft; be a split ring let into a channel in the shaft; or be a one-piece ring which is sandwiched between two lengths of the shaft.

14. Decide the turning procedure and how to cut any flutes, reeds, or cabling. If the column is to be engaged or to be a pattern for casting, decide whether to conglutinate it before the turning with a paper joint (*Woodturning Techniques*, pages 13 to 17), or whether to saw along the turned column to separate it into the usually two pieces.
15. Decide the finishing.

12.9.1 INTERCOLUMNIATION

The intercolumniation (spacing of columns) in stone-based *trabeated* (post and lintel) construction was limited by the bending strength and feasible length of the stone lintels; it was also influenced by the character that the architect wished the spacing to communicate. The Greeks and Romans realized the importance of intercolumniation in determining tempo and expressiveness: close spacing yields a sombre, claustrophobic effect; very wide spacings may suggest imminent collapse. Vesuvius dwelt on this topic, and gave names to the spacings he specified (figure 12.57). There are also terms which signify the number of columns along the front of a portico or other structure (figure 12.58).

Columns need not, in some cases cannot, be arranged at equal spacings or in straight lines:

1. Vitruvius recommended that the central entrance pair of an even-numbered eustyle row of portico columns should be *diastyle* (figure 12.32).
2. Columns can be clustered in pairs, threes, or fours. The spacings between the clusters can then be wider than the spacings would be between single columns, and still look appropriate.
3. Colonnades and arcades can be curved in plan (figure 12.59).

Column spacings are also restricted by the desirability of harmony between the columns and any features on any entablature or the surrounding structure (figures 12.60 to 12.62). Column spacings may also influence the choice of column slenderness. For example, doubled columns can be individually slenderer than single columns used in the same situations.

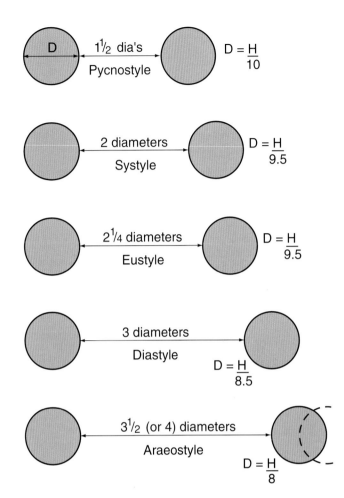

Figure 12.57 Intercolumniations measured in multiples of the maximum shaft diameter as discussed by Vitruvius.[39] In the terms used to describe column spacings, the first syllable signifies the length of the spacing in column diameters, and "style" is from the Greek *stylos* for column.

Vitruvius advises that the diastyle "involves the danger that the architraves may break on account of the great width of the intervals", and that the span of araeostyle is too great for stone lintels and requires "a series of wooden beams laid upon". Eustyle was the favored spacing, having its "intervals apportioned just right".

Vitruvius also stated that the "thickness of the shafts must be enlarged in proportion to the increase of the distance between the columns". If the ratio of column height to maximum shaft diameter was say 10:1 for the narrow pycnostyle spacing, then if the intercolumniation was increased, the columns diameters should also be increased—the appropriate diameters as a proportion of the column height recommended by Vitruvius are shown adjacent to each right-hand column plan.

Figure 12.58 A hexastyle portico, here on the Greek revival Schauspielhaus (Berlin Theatre) (1819–21) designed by Karl Friedrich Schinkel.[40]

Porticos and temples are called according to the number of columns along the front. This number is always even. *Tetrastyle, hexastyle, octastyle, decastyle,* and *dodecastyle,* mean having four, six, eight, ten, and twelve columns respectively.

Figure 12.59 A *monopteral* structure, *Selene II*, by Dewey Garrett of Livermore, California. A "monopteral" structure is a roofed ring of columns. In a *peripteral* temple, the circular colonnade is not just roofed, it also encloses a *cella,* a sanctuary chamber containing the statue of a god. In Greek temples the god was usually Hestia, the goddess of the hearth; she was called Vesta during the Roman civilization

The brightest minor planet is named Vesta. The name was also given to a short type of match originating in about 1839.

Also associated with Vesta are the Vestal virgins, made famous by the rock group Procol Harum. In Roman religion, these were six priestesses who tended the state cult of Vesta. One of their duties was to tend the perpetual fire in the Temple of Vesta. Chosen between the ages of six and ten, they served in ancient times for five years, in historical times for thirty. During their service they had to remain virgins—they were buried alive if they violated this rule. After their service they were free to marry, but few did as it was thought unlucky.

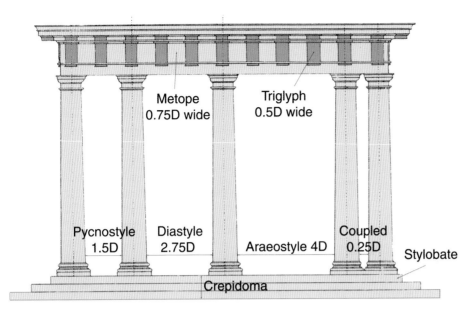

Metope
0.75D wide

Triglyph
0.5D wide

Pycnostyle
1.5D

Diastyle
2.75D

Araeostyle 4D

Coupled
0.25D

Stylobate

Crepidoma

Figure 12.60 The intercolumniation of Roman Doric columns.[42] The column center lines should pass through the centers of any triglyphs on the frieze above (figure 12.61 below). (John Ruskin said of triglyphs, "Do you seriously imagine . . . that any living soul in London likes triglyphs?"[43] Column spacings are less restricted with other entablatures:

1. The entablature of the Tuscan has no vertical features to restrict column spacings.
2. The Ionic entablature has dentils which are very small and closely spaced, and therefore barely restrict column spacings (figure 12.62).
3. The Corinthian and Composite entablatures have both dentils and horizontal brackets or consoles called modillions (figure 12.62). As the length between the centers of modillions is typically four times larger than that between the dentils, the modillions should govern these columns' spacings.

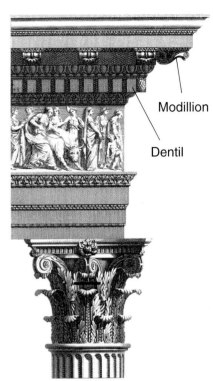

Modillion

Dentil

Figure 12.62 A Corinthian capital and entablature.[45]

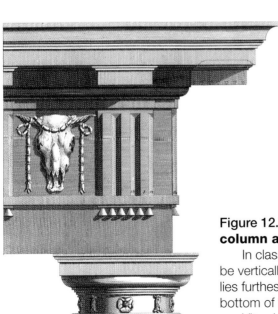

Figure 12.61 The alignment of a Roman Doric column and its entablature.[44]

In classical architecture, the neck of the shaft should be vertically in line with the plane in the entablature which lies furthest back—this plane is typically, as here, at the bottom of the architrave.

Vitruvius also suggested that because corner columns are isolated, they should be 2% thicker than the internal columns.

12.9.2 ENTASIS AND DIMINUTION

Column shafts look pleasing if they taper from bottom to top; and more pleasing if the taper is not uniform, but accelerates towards the top, and in some cases the bottom (figures 12.63 to 12.65). This tapering of the shaft is often termed *entasis*, from the Greek *enteino*, to stretch. The term's use is due to Vitruvius who referred to it as the "enlargement made at the middle of columns".[46] However the 1755 Leoni, English edition of the first Renaissance text on the orders by Alberti uses the term *diminution* to describe bellied columns which have their maximum diameter some way up the shaft. "Diminution" has also been used to refer to columns with shafts with single tapers by Isaac Ware on page 12 of his 1738 translation of Andrea Palladio's *The Four Books of Architecture*, by William Chambers, and by Robert Peake in his 1611 English translation of Serlio. Entasis or diminution? Gwilt,[47] and more recently Chitham,[48] suggest that "diminution" should be preferred for tapering columns, and that "entasis" should be reserved for bellied columns. I will follow this sensible solution.

To determine the diminution or entasis of a column shaft you must decide the maximum and minimum shaft diameters, and the shaft profile. For architectural columns, the shaft diameter at the top, d, is usually 5/6 (83.33%, or usually rounded to 85%) of the maximum shaft diameter, D. This is not a fixed proportion, and you should vary it according to the visual effects you intend to create. A visual effect which is restricted to large architectural columns is the apparently-greater diminution perceived by viewers in longer columns. To counter this Vitruvius had recommended that the upper minimum diameter, d, be increased from 5/6D for columns with a height of less than 15 feet (4.6 m) to 7/8D for column heights between 40 and 50 feet (12.2 and 15.2 m). Claude Perrault was the first to deny the validity of the need for this now defunct practice of optical correction on the ground that although the eye saw apparently greater diminution in taller columns, the mind was not fooled. Other factors which may influence the total diminution you choose for a column are: the situation in which the column will be installed; the spacing if the column is arranged with others; and the ratio of the column height to its maximum diameter.

When determining the diminution or entasis I suggest that you adopt the vertical distance between top of the column base and the bottom of the capital as the shaft length, H. When there is an astragal on the shaft a short distance below the capital, as in the Tuscan and Roman Doric, assume that the shaft runs through the astragal. When there are congees and fillets at the top and/or bottom of the shaft, include them in the shaft length.

After deciding on the magnitude of the taper as a proportion of the maximum shaft diameter, you can to determine the detailed shaft profile by drawing, by calculation, or from a table. These methods are described in figures 12.64 to 12.67, 12.69, and 12.70, and in Table 12.2.

Each method gives a unique shaft outline, although the differences in shaft profile between those given by the various methods for shafts with the same parameters are minor.

The proportions of classical columns, both actual and "ideal" are given in many texts. Most texts express their recommended proportions in terms of a *module*, usually the lower shaft diameter or radius. In older texts the module is usually divided into 30 *minutes* or *partes*, and the detailed dimensions are expressed in these minutes or partes. Robert Chitham in his *The Classical Orders of Architecture* (1985) rightly states that such systems are inconvenient in this age of the inexpensive electronic calculator, and sensibly expresses detailed proportions in his book as decimals of the maximum shaft diameter, D. Decimal-based calculation is also quicker and more precise than drawing for defining diminution, although for small columns you can often "eye" the diminution with sufficient accuracy (figure 12.72).

Figure 12.63 Entasis is not just used in classical columns, *Shogun* (1985–1986), by Mark Lindquist of Quincy, Florida; black walnut; 67 in. (1700 mm) high. Photograph by Paul Avis

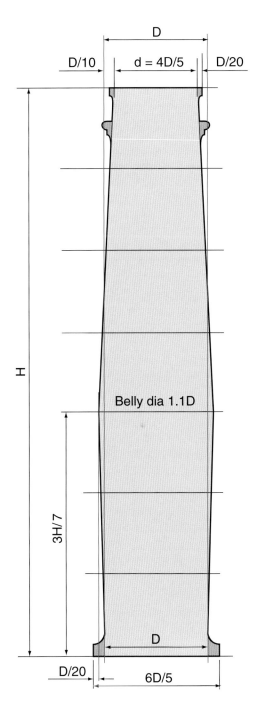

Figure 12.64 Alberti's method for determining column diminution shown in plate 20 of *The Ten Books of Architecture*. The explanatory text for plate 20 printed on p. 131 of Leoni's 1755 edition does not agree with the method shown in the plate. Note that here *D* is used for the shaft diameter at the bottom, not the maximum shaft diameter which is at the belly.

Chambers prefers diminution to entasis, and calls the bellying promoted by Alberti an "absurd excess . . . neither natural, reasonable, nor beautiful".

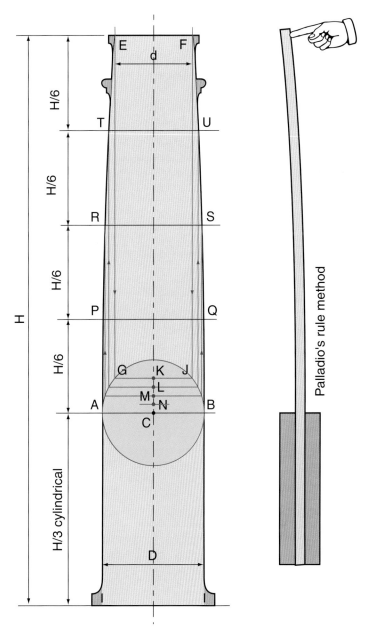

Figure 12.65 The methods for drawing the diminution of Roman columns advocated by Serlio and Palladio.[49]

The bottom third of the shaft is left cylindrical, the rest of the shaft is divided into, say, four drums of equal height.

ACB = D, and is the diameter of a circle drawn about *C*. *GK,J* is a horizontal chord of the circle of length *d*. *KC* is divided by *L*, *M*, and *N* into four equal parts. Horizontals are projected to the left and right from *L*, *M*, and *N* until they meet the circle of diameter *D*. Vertical lines are then projected upwards from these meetings. These lines cross the respective horizontal drum boundaries at points on the outline of the shaft.

Palladio holds a flexible rule of uniform cross section in line with the outline of the cylinder below *ACB*, and pushes the free end across until it comes to *F*. The entasis can then be drawn along the rule.

Figure 12.66 Drawing shaft diminution using Vignola's method.

1. Draw the shaft center line GC.
2. Mark E at the top of the shaft where EG = 0.5d
3. Mark O on the horizontal projection through C — there are two methods, the second being more accurate:
   i.   From E draw an arc of radius 0.5D to intersect the column center line at J. Through E and J project a line to intersect the horizontal line projected through C at O. I term the angle EOA the *diminution angle*. Its value depends on the ratio d/D; values are given in table 12.2.
   ii. EG and EJ are relatively short so that the resulting position of O may not be accurate. A superior alternative is to multiply d by any suitable constant y to give length EG'. Set EG' along EG projected. Drop a vertical from G'. Draw an arc of radius yD about E to intersect the vertical from G' at J'. Project EJ' to intersect the horizontal projection through C at O.

4. Divide the height of the shaft H along the center line as many times and at whatever spacings, regular or irregular, as you need to yield sufficient spots to draw the column outline. These spots are represented by K, M, and P.
5. Project lines from O through the points K, M, P, and C on the center line.
6. Using compasses, swing arcs of radius EJ (= D/2) about K, M, P, and C.
7. Draw the side of the outline through E, L, N, Q, and A.
8. If required, draw the other side of the outline through F and B.
9. Measure the shaft radii or diameters at the heights required.
10. Draw the capital, base, and any astragal, congees, or fillets on the shaft.

The next figure shows an instrument which mimicks Vignola's method, and which can be used to drawing a column outline automatically.

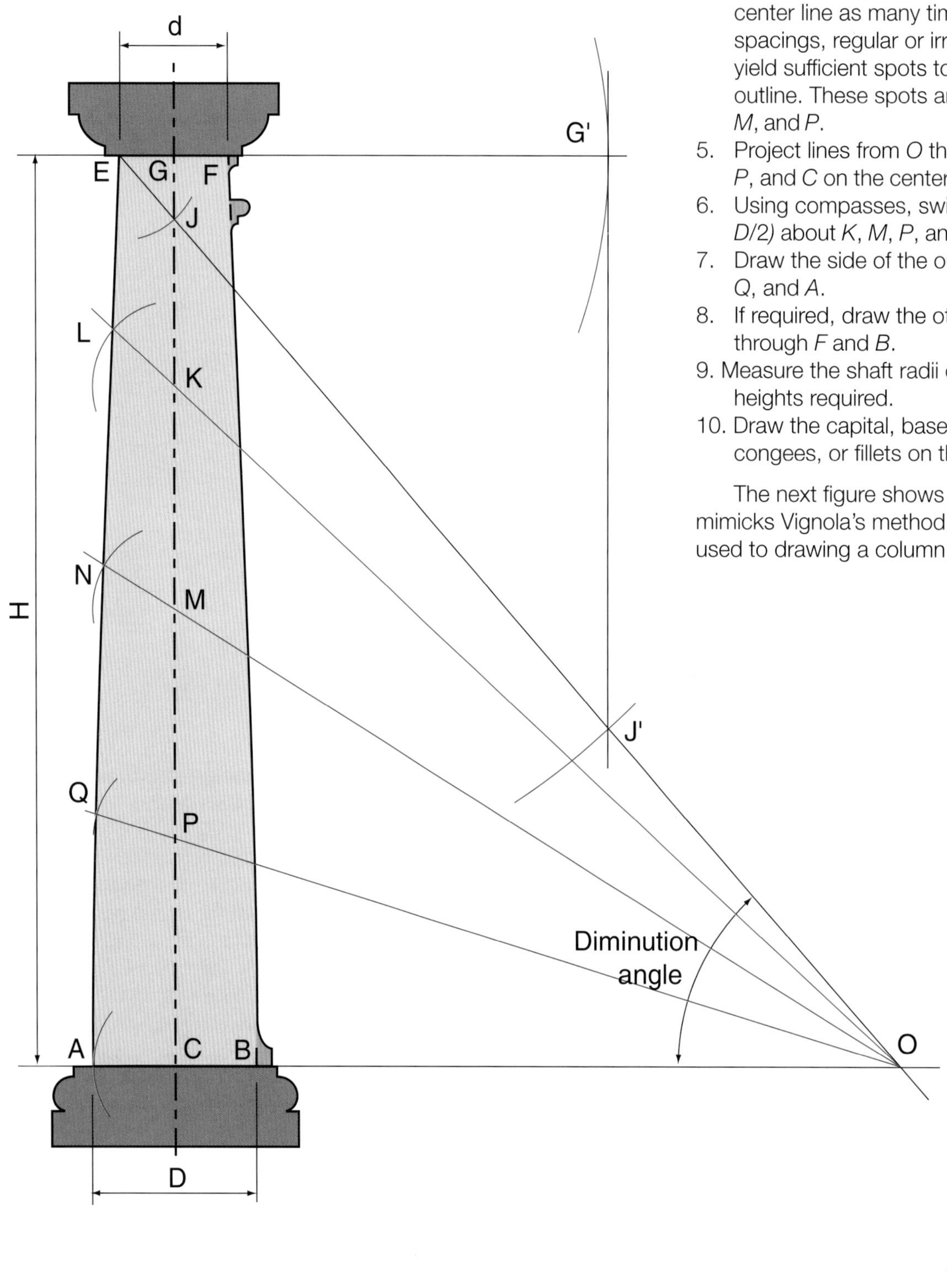

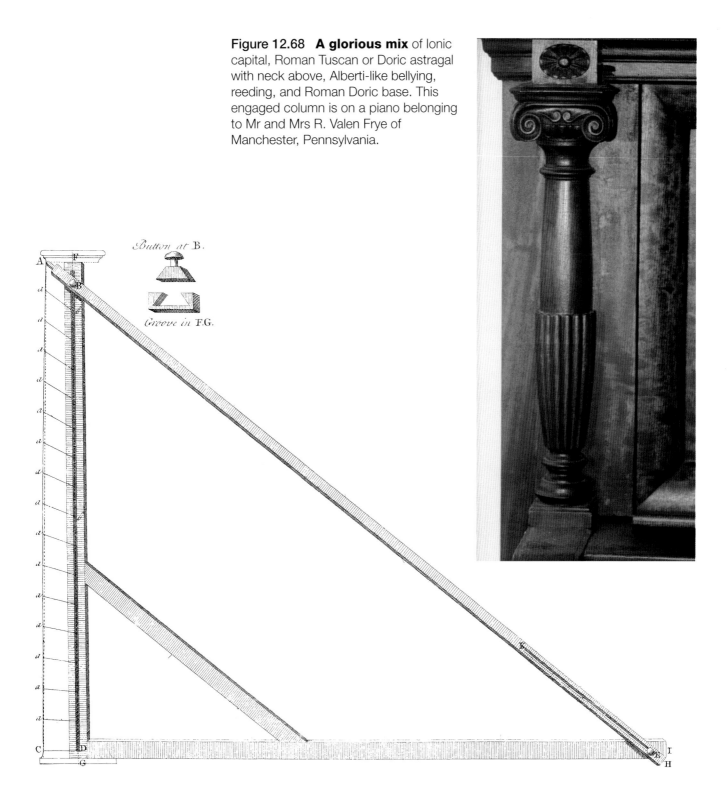

Figure 12.68 A glorious mix of Ionic capital, Roman Tuscan or Doric astragal with neck above, Alberti-like bellying, reeding, and Roman Doric base. This engaged column is on a piano belonging to Mr and Mrs R. Valen Frye of Manchester, Pennsylvania.

Figure 12.67 An instrument for drawing a column outline by Vignola's method, invented by Nicomedes.[50] It was recommended for drawing the diminution of a column shaft by the French architect Blondel in his *Resolution des quatre principaux Problemes d'Architecture*.[x] A unique variation of this instrument must be constructed for each combination of *d*, *D*, and *H*.

Jacques-Francois Blondel (1705–1774) was a French architect and teacher. He wrote *Cours d'Architecture*, the first architecture textbook for the students of the Academie Royale d'Architecture in Paris. He was more conservative than his contemporary Claude Perrault.

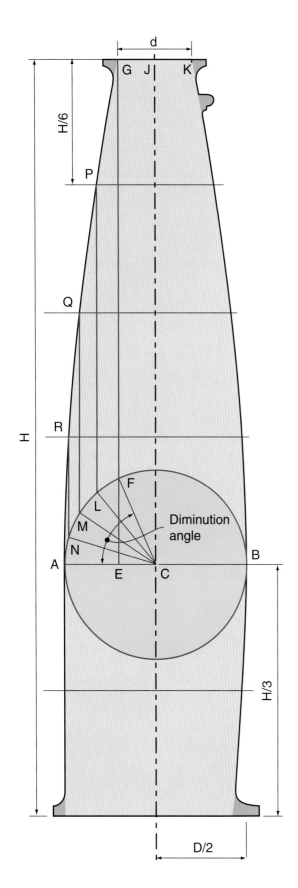

Figure 12.69 Another method for determining column diminution (or entasis) by drawing and by calculation.

When the diminution is small or moderate and the shaft not stumpy, you can adopt the convention that the bottom third or less of the shaft is cylindrical as shown on the left-hand side of the drawing. If the shaft is bellied, the maximum shaft diameter *D* should be measured at the center of the belly.

The steps below illustrate the method through showing how to derive and draw the diminution of a shaft:

1. Draw the vertical column center line.
2. Draw *AB* and *GK* which are the maximum and minimum diameters of the shaft respectively. Draw a circle of radius *D*/2 about *C*.
3. Mark *E* on *AC*, distance 0.5*d* to the left of *C*.
4. Draw the vertical line *EG*. This line crosses the circle at *F*.
5. Divide angle *FCA* into four (the number of drums above *AB*) equal angles, or arc *AF* into four equal arcs, and mark *L*, *M*, and *N*.
6. Through points *L*, *M*, and *N* project vertical lines to intersect with the horizontal tops of the three lowest drums at *P*, *Q*, and *R* respectively.
7. Draw the profile of the column diminution through points *A*, *R*, *Q*, *P*, and *G*.

This method also lends itself to the ready calculation of shaft diameters.

1. *EC*:*AC* = *d*:*D*.
2. To find *L*, *M*, and *N*, angle *ACF* has to be divided into four equal angles.
3. Cos *ACF* = *EC*/*CF* = *d*/*D*. This allows you to look up the magnitude of angle *ACF*, the diminution angle.
4. Divide the diminution angle *ACF* into four (the number of drums) equal angles, each of magnitude X. In this example the diminution angle therefore equals 4X.
5. Calculate the column diameters along the shaft as follows:

Diameter at *R* = *D*cosX
Diameter at *Q* = *D*cos2X
Diameter at *P* = *D*cos3X

EXAMPLE
For a column with *D* = 240 mm and *d* = 201 mm, the cosine of the diminution angle = (*d*/*D*) = (201/240) = 0.8375
Therefore the diminution angle = 33° 6' and X = 8° 16.5'
Therefore the shaft diameter at *P*
= 240 x cos (3 x [8° 16.5'])
= 240 x 0.9076 = 218 mm

Table 12.2 enables you to more easily calculate diminutions using this method for a range of ratios of *d*/*D*.

Table 12.2 Column shaft diameter coefficients for ratios of d/D between 0.85 and 0.75, derived using the method described in figure 12.69.

d/D	Diminution angle	d_1/D	d_2/D	d_3/D	d_4/D	d_5/D	d_6/D	d_7/D	d/D
0.85	31° 48'	0.9976	0.9903	0.9784	0.9617	0.9405	0.9147	0.8843	0.8500
0.84	32° 52'	0.9974	0.9898	0.9769	0.9591	0.9373	0.9088	0.8765	0.8400
0.83	33° 54'	0.9973	0.9891	0.9754	0.9566	0.9324	0.9031	0.8689	0.8300
0.82	34° 55'	0.9971	0.9884	0.9740	0.9539	0.9283	0.8973	0.8610	0.8200
0.81	35° 54'	0.9969	0.9878	0.9725	0.9513	0.9243	0.8917	0.8536	0.8100
0.80	36° 52'	0.9968	0.9871	0.9710	0.9487	0.9202	0.8858	0.8457	0.8000
0.79	37° 49	0.9966	0.9864	0.9695	0.9460	0.9160	0.8799	0.8475	0.7900
0.78	38° 44	0.9964	0.9857	0.9634	0.9434	0.9048	0.8567	0.8201	0.7800
0.77	39° 38'	0.9962	0.9851	0.9666	0.9408	0.9080	0.8684	0.8223	0.7700
0.76	40° 32	0.9960	0.9844	0.9650	0.9377	0.9038	0.8625	0.8144	0.7600
0.75	41° 24'	0.9960	0.9838	0.9634	0.9354	0.8998	0.8568	0.8068	0.7500

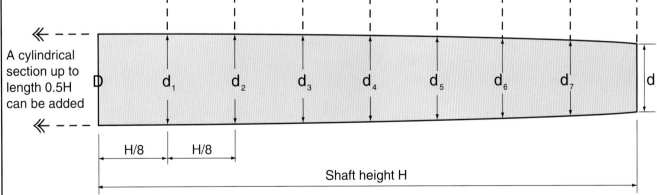

USING TABLE 12.2

As an example, consider a shaft 1000 mm tall without a cylindrical section and with a maximum diameter of 120 mm. You have chosen d/D as 0.80. Therefore d = 0.80 x 120 = 96 mm.

The diameter d_5 at the top of the fifth drum, $5H/8$ or 625 mm above the base of the shaft = 120 x 0.9202
= 110.4 mm

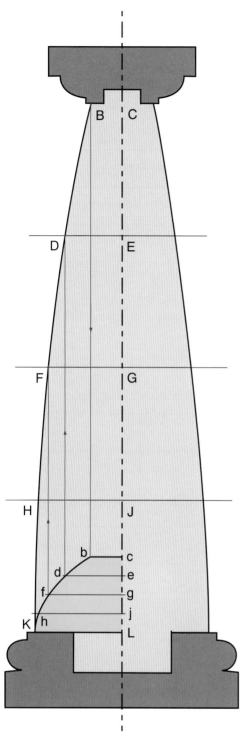

Figure 12.70 Drawing diminution by scaling. To accurately draw the shaft profile of a building column full-sized is a major task. If you greatly compress the vertical scale, and draw a likely smooth curve such as *K*, *h*, *f*, *d*, *b*, you can then measure intermediate shaft radii such as *hj*, *fg*, and *de* accurately. To see the resulting shaft profile, project up from *h*, *f*, and *d* to the tops of the drums to find *H*, *F*, and *D* respectively. This method can be used with the shaft drawn full-sized, or to a reduced scale.

Figure 12.71 Diminution by eye. You do not usually need to calculate or precisely draw the shaft profiles of small columns. Here the top and bottom shaft diameters were calipered, the diminution was "eyed". These columns are components of the *Woznot* pictured in figure 7.47, page 170.

12.9.3 POSITIONING ASTRAGALS

Although it is a physically small feature, the design and placement of the astragal on Roman Tuscan and Doric shafts can significantly affect the aesthetic success of a column as shown in figures 12.72 to 12.74.

Figure 12.72 An unduly low astragal on Roman Doric columns in Colmore Row, Birmingham, England.

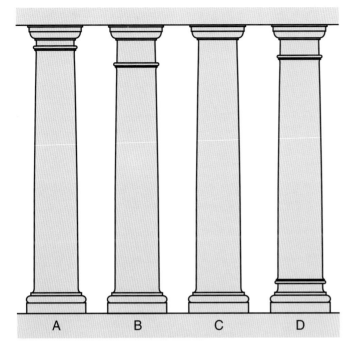

Figure 12.73 **The role and placement of astragals on Tuscan (and Roman Doric) columns.**

A is a typical Tuscan column with the astragal in its usual position. Perhaps the astragal acts as a transitional detail so that the change from shaft to capital is not too sudden.

In *B* the astragal has been lowered, has lost its connection with the capital, and has become an isolated and illogical distraction on the shaft.

With the astragal removed, column *C* looks bare. Is this though because we are used to seeing astragals? The Roman columns without separated astragals (the Ionic, Corinthian and Composite) have much deeper capitals.

In *D* the upper astragal is midway between its position in *A* and *B*, and midway in its effect. Adding an astragal just above the base makes the lower part of the column shaft perhaps too detailed, but if it was lowered a little more it would combine with the large bead of the Tuscan base, to create a Roman Doric base.

Figure 12.74 **Low astragals and poor diminution on shafts in the portico of Berrima Goal,** New South Wales. It is perhaps unreasonable to expect sophisticated shaft design in columns carved between 1834 and 1839 by convict labor.

12.9.4 FLUTE GEOMETRY

Although not all classical column shafts have flutes, when flutes are present they are always even in number. The numbers of flutes for the six column types are:

Greek Doric	Typically 20, also 12, 16, 18, or 24
Tuscan	No flutes
Roman Doric	20
Ionic	Typically 24, early Greek examples had 40, 44, or 48
Corinthian, and Composite	24

Flutes and/or reeds usually run axially. They can also run helically, or in circles around a shaft.

The flutes on a shaft are typically identical, but need not be—the portico of the Temple of Apollo in Rome, built circa 431 B.C., had shafts with sixteen wide and sixteen narrow flutes which alternated with wide fillets between. Typical flute geometries are detailed in figure 12.75.

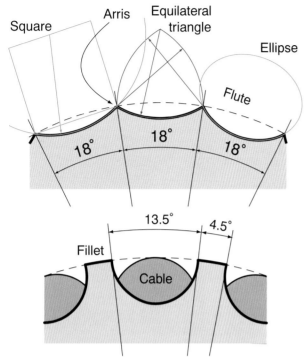

Figure 12.75 Greek Doric and Roman flute cross sections.

Upper drawing. The flutes of the Greek Doric are not separated by fillets, and are shallow so that the arris retains sufficient durability.

Lower drawing. Serlio, Chambers, and Chitham suggest that flutes be semicircular when separated by fillets, with the fillets a third of the flute diameter in width.

Flute, fillet, reed, and cable cross sections should remain constant in their form but not in their size along a diminishing column shaft. This requirement cannot be strictly met when running a molding with a single fixed or fast-rotating cutter.

12.10 THE MANUFACTURE OF COLUMNS

To save wood and often also turning time, the capitals and bases of architectural columns are usually faceplate-turned separately. The grain in column shafts is always axial because the turning is easier and because the shaft length will not change with changes in relative humidity. For large column shafts you can:

1. Laminate planks face to face. Cracking is less likely if you leave a hollow core.
2. Use stave conglutination as shown in figure 12.76 and described on pages 8 to 10 of *Woodturning Techniques*. You should use loose splines to locate the staves. The number and dimensions of the staves and the placement of the splines need to be carefully considered.

3. Turn the shaft from one piece of wood. There may be cheap sources if you need large sizes (figure 12.77). However, surface cracking is likely to develop over time if the pith remains within.

Obviously you need a lathe and handling equipment appropriate to the size and weight of columns you intend to turn (figure 12.78). There are though no special difficulties in the turning process for forms which continue to be relevant despite being ancient (12.79).

Figure 12.76 Column shafts conglutinated from staves. These staves are located with biscuits.

Figure 12.77 **Not roadside power poles but potential classical column shafts.** Old power poles when removed are partially seasoned, and, unlike these new green colored replacement poles, were not chemically treated and are therefore safe to turn.

Figure 12.79 **The classical column continues to be relevant in contemporary design.**
Postmodern designers such as Michael Graves and Thomas Gordon Smith "rediscovered" classical columns, modifying their forms and applying color. From 1980 I pioneered the turning of power pole columns using waste *Eucalyptus* power poles to provide an affordable source of shaft raw material. In the process I created an Australian vernacular. These columns were produced in heights from 20 ft (6.1 m), down to 16 in. (400 mm) for table legs.

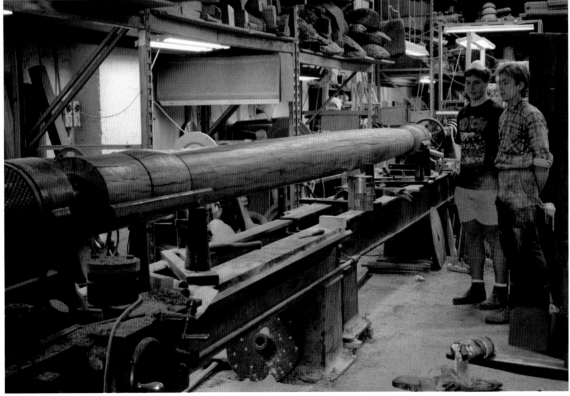

Figure 12.78 **Turning the pole-house column shown earlier in figure 7.17, page 156.**

12.11 BALUSTERS

The baluster is a short bulbous shaft or column supporting a handrail. Although possibly derived from the colonnade, balusters were not used in ancient Greek or Roman buildings. According to Parker,[51] balusters were first used in eleventh-century Romanesque buildings, and were crudely turned in wood (figure 12.80). Balusters did not become significant design elements until they were co-opted into the revived classical architecture of the Renaissance (figure 12.81). The derivation of the name "baluster" is explored in figure 12.82.

The role of the baluster form as a short column supporting a handrail was later miniaturized in galleries (figures 12.84 and 12.85), but the baluster form was not subsumed in its main role by stubby, classical-column forms. However the classical column and baluster were later combined, the long, gently diminishing column shaft being contrasted against the curvaceous and detailed baluster part-group in legs, stair balusters (figure 12.83), stems (figure 12.86), and newel, verandah, and bedposts.

Figure 12.82 Immature pomegranates, the fruit of the tree *Punica granatum*. The English term baluster comes from the French balustre, which was in turn derived from the Latin (balaustium) and Greek names for the blossom of the wild pomegranate. In my view the immature fruit pictured above rather than the calyx (bud) is more likely to be the inspiration for the name. A book of 1526 by a Spanish priest Diego de Sagredo virtually gives the baluster the status of a separate order, and notes its derivation from the pomegranate, a name derived from the Spanish city of Granada.[53]

The term baluster is applied to both the bulbous shaft which supports handrails (or banisters), and to the shape of a bulb with a cylindrical neck or a flared top above the neck which is used in many types of spindles and vessels. A balustrade is the assemblage of a row of balusters and the bottom rail and handrail.

Figure 12.80 A Romanesque turned wooden baluster from St. Alban's.[51]

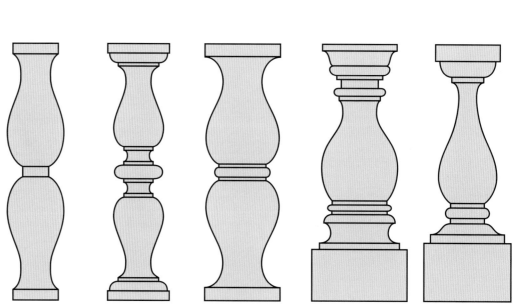

Figure 12.81 Renaissance baluster designs originally turned in stone. The three on the left are of the earlier form in stone, and have two matching bulbs, the lower ones inverted. The two balusters on the right are of the later, one-bulb type. [52]

Figure 12.83 **A stair baluster design using a Roman Doric column above a baluster.** These stair balusters are at No. 44 Great Ormond Street, London, built in 1709. Illustration scanned from Tunstall Small and Christopher Woodbridge, *Houses of the Wren & Early Georgian Periods* (London: The Architectural Press, 1928), page 138.

Figure 12.84 **A bottle coaster with a miniature balustrade or gallery.**

Figure 12.85 **Balusters in the spindle gallery of a mahogany and oak urn stand.** Height 25 in. (640 mm). This and the stand below are displayed at Temple Newsam House, Leeds, Yorkshire; and the illustrations were provided by The Leeds Museum Resource Centre.

Figure 12.86 **A column and baluster combined** in the stem of this mahogany teakettle stand, circa 1755. Height 21.5 in. (540 mm), diameter 14.3 in. (360 mm).

12.12 ENDNOTES

1. Charles Freeman, *Egypt, Greece and Rome* (Oxford University Press, 1996), p. 1.

2. Hanno-Walter Kruft, *A History of Architectural Theory from Vitruvius to the Present* (Princeton Architectural Press, 1994), p. 278.

3. Alfred W. S. Cross, *History of Architecture* (London: International Correspondence School, no date), fig. 15.

4. G. Perrot and C. Chipiez, *Histoire de l'Art Egyptien*.

5. Ibid.

6. Ibid.

7. Ibid.

8. James Fergusson, *A History of Architecture in All Countries*, Vol I (London: John Murray, 1874), pp. 110–111. Fluted columns and reeded columns are also used internally at Beni-Hasan.

9. R. Phené Spiers, *Egypt. A Series of Thirty-six Views of Ancient and Modern Egypt* (London: B. T. Batsford, 1887).

10. D. S. Robertson, *Greek and Roman Architecture*, 2nd ed (Cambridge University Press, 1945), pp. 16–19.

11. A. Rosengarten, *Architectural Styles* (London, Chatto And Windus, 1878), p. 52.

12. Henri Stierlin, *Greece from Mycenae to the Parthenon* (Cologne: Taschen GmgH, 2001), p. 72.

13. William Wilkins was the architect for the first Grecian portico in Britain, built at Osberton House, Nottinghamshire. James Stevens Curl, *Georgian Architecture* (Newton Abbot, Devon: David & Charles, 1993), p. 84.

14. R. Phené Spiers, *The Orders of Architecture*, 5th ed. (London: B. T. Batsford, 1926), plate II.

15. Charles Normand, *A Parallel of the Orders of Architecture* (London: John Tiranti, 1942), plates 6, 8, 9.

16. F. M. Simpson, *A History of Architectural Development*, vol. I (London: Longmans, Green, 1921), p. 63.

17. Simpson, p. 63; Norman, plates 21 and 22.

18. Normand, plate 34.

19. Spiers, *The Orders of Architecture*, plate XII.

20. Chambers, William. *A Treatise on the Decorative Part of Civil Architecture* (1759; reprint, New York: Benjamin Blom, 1968), opp. p. 26.

21. Vitruvius, *The Ten Books on Architecture*, trans. Morris Hickey Morgan (1914; reprint, New York: Dover Publications, 1969), pp. 104, 106.

22. H.C.D. de Wit, *Plants of the World*, Vol II, (London: Thames & Hudson, 1967), p. 180.

23. *William Morris by Himself*, ed. Gillian Naylor (London: Little, Brown, 1994), pp. 158–9.

24. Kruft, p. 212.

25. Curl, p. 79.

26. Chambers, opp. p. 42.

27. Kruft, p. 190.

28. Rosengarten, p. 123.

29. John Henry Parker, *A Glossary of Terms Used in Grecian, Roman, and Gothic Architecture* (London: David Bogue, 1845), plate 28.

30. Parker, *A Glossary*, plate 9.

31. Rosengarten, p. 256.

32. The proportions were abstracted from Normand, plates 1–4.

33. Kruft, p. 326.

34. George Savage, *Dictionary of Antiques* (London: Book Club Associates, 1973), pp. 99–100.

35. Rosengarten, p. 6.

36. Ed. Cyril M. Harris, *Illustrated Dictionary of Historic Architecture*, (New York: Dover Publications, 1983), p. 114.

37. John Summerson, "Classical Architecture," *New Classicism*, ed. Andreas Papadakis and Harriet Watson (New York: Rizzoli, 1990), pp. 16–17.

38. Robert Chitham, *The Classical Orders of Architecture* (London: Architectural Press, 1985), pp. 28–41.

39. Vitruvius, Morgan, pp. 78–86.

40. Rosengarten, p. 472.

41. Rosengarten, p. 69.

42. Chambers, opp. p. 91.

43. John Ruskin, *The Stones of Venice* (1851, 1853; reprint, London: Penguin Books, 1960), p. 36.

44. Chambers, opp. p. 46.

45. Chambers, opp. p. 61.

46. Vitruvius, Morgan, p. 86.

47. Joseph Gwilt, *The Encyclopedia of Architecture* (1867; reprint, New York: Bonanza Books, 1982), p. 809.

48. Chitham, p. 99.

49. Serlio, fourth book, fifth chapter, fol. 4; Palladio, first book, pp. 12–13.

50. Chambers, opp. p. 27.

51. J. Henry Parker, *Classic Dictionary of Architecture* (1846; reprint, Poole, Dorset: New Orchard Editions, 1986), p. 27.

52. Based on balusters illustrated in Rudolf Wittkower, *Palladio and English Palladianism* (London: Thames and Hudson, 1974), pp. 44, 45, 47, 48.

53. Kruft, p. 219.

Chapter Thirteen

WHERE NEXT?

This final chapter discusses "where next?" for woodturning, and for the series of books of which this is the fourth, but not the last.

13.1 WHERE NEXT FOR WOODTURNING?

Woodturning is a popular hobby in many Western countries, although its popularity varies widely between and within them. National popularities are influenced by wealth, culture, environment, and population density. National and local variations in woodturning's popularity are also influenced by the presence or absence of individuals who are committed to enthusing others. In these same countries the number of professional turners declined through the twentieth century, but has now probably stabilized, albeit at a level close to extinction. The types of work that professionals do continue to change, as does the mix. Several questions arise:

1. Why has there been the fall in the numbers of professional turners? and has the decline been stemmed?
2. Why has there been a rise in amateur turning? and will the numbers be sustained, increase, or decline in the future?
3. Is it desirable that the number of amateur turners does not decline?
4. Where should woodturners attempt to take woodturning in the future?

13.1.1 WOODTURNING PAST AND PRESENT

Woodturning was probably invented around 1000 B.C. It continues into the twenty-first century because it enables:

1. Rapid hollowing and boring.
2. The quick and accurate production of round and annular cross sections about straight turning-axes, and the ready profiling and ornamentation of the resulting forms.
3. The cutting of circular spigots to fit into drilled holes.
4. The efficient production of turnings, both singly and in batches.

However, the woodturning techniques used in these four areas remain essentially unchanged, as does the main working material, solid wood.

WOOD
Wood is a natural material which cannot be synthesized but can be replaced over a few or many decades depending on species and growing conditions. It is tough, but has an easily scarred surface. Seasoned wood is "warm" and inviting (being a good insulator), and the pattern on any surface is unique due to wood's natural variations in structure and colors. Before man started moving tree species, each was specific to a region, although the sizes of the regions differed considerably.

Wood's properties are not universally regarded as positive: wood is naturally variable, dimensionally unstable, is not isotropic, and has planes of weakness. It cannot be cast, molded, drawn, or welded, and is therefore poorly suited to industrial manufacturing. Also, supply is deteriorating. There is a continuing reduction in the species and sizes available, and the price of wood is increasing faster than those of competing materials.

Solid wood has decreased in relative importance as a working material since the Industrial Revolution, although this has been masked by increasing demand caused by the rapid increase in the world's population and wealth. Solid wood has largely been replaced by metals, stones, plastics, glass and ceramics. The lower costs and advantageous physical properties of these solid-wood-replacing materials has been extensively promoted. Plastic is becoming a luxury and desirable material. Solid wood is also being displaced by manufactured sheet materials such as plywood and MDF which enable large and stable faceplate turnings to be produced. These manufactured materials are often unpleasant to turn.

PROFESSIONAL TURNERS
The development of manufactured materials which can replace solid wood has been accompanied by an increasing proficiency in shaping them. Consider tool handles. Until the late nineteenth century they were turned individually by hand from solid wood. Automatic lathes then took over until about the 1960s. Now tool handles are usually molded from plastic, and are cheaper and more durable than their wooden equivalents.

The erosion of repetitive professional hand turning is not entirely a bad thing—turning tool handles throughout your working life is not attractive to many. Production hand woodturning is now restricted to jobbing, and small runs. The declining numbers of large runs are increasingly done on automatic lathes in low labor-cost countries, particularly in those which have plantation timber or still have native forest.

Another factor influencing the viability of production turning is fashion—as has been described, a euphemism for commercial manipulation. The decline in commercial woodturning was arrested, even reversed, during the periods when the arts & crafts, postmodern, and colonial/country/manorial styles were popular. However, with the new millennium, manufacturers' and designers' continued pressure has resulted in the belated acceptance of a softened modernism which is adversely affecting the demand for commercial woodturning.

Fortunately, as the demand for turned building and furniture components and woodware has declined, three new employment opportunities for professional turners have grown: souvenirs based on species' regional specificities and nostalgia for hand craftsmanship, the art/gallery/collectors market, and servicing the increasing numbers of amateur turners.

ART/GALLERY/COLLECTORS MARKETS

I fully support turners developing and serving the art/gallery/collectors markets. The growth of these markets has:

1. Increased the range of items turned through rewarding creative competition and aesthetic exploration.
2. Promoted an increase in the vocabulary of techniques associated with turning, and in the range of special-purpose equipment.
3. Enabled a few turners to achieve the status and incomes of successful artists.
4. Encouraged into turning many who would not have been attracted by traditional production turning.
5. Promoted woodturning generally, and given it a new glamor which has attracted new buyers of woodturnings.

AMATEUR TURNERS

Peoples of the developed world now live longer. Many can afford to retire with possibly decades of active life ahead of them. Turning has become a popular hobby because:

1. You can turn in isolation: you can enjoy the companionship of being in a woodturning club or association. Such bodies also provide opportunities for those who like to be involved in administration, teaching, leadership, etc.
2. It is not too expensive, nor too demanding of skill or space.
3. It offers variety. Being at the junction of art, craft, and manufacturing, turners can concentrate on any of a large number of particular aspects.
4. It uses a natural material which in the case of "found wood" is widely and often freely available.
5. Finished items can be produced relatively quickly.
6. You produce something "concrete" which can be useful or nonfunctional.
7. You can keep, give away, or sell your turnings. There are opportunities to earn income, although they tend to be overrated.

However, there are signs that the rapid growth of amateur woodturning in some developed countries has slowed. This is to be expected—it is unreasonable to expect everyone to become an enthusiastic woodturner, but it should cause us to question the future.

13.1.2   THE FUTURE

If woodturning were to stagnate or decline, there would be an accompanying decline in the services and opportunities which woodturners have come to expect. These include the availability of: a wide range of equipment, a specialist media, specialist suppliers, tuition, clubs and other organizations, facilities to sell and exhibit, and public awareness and support. This decline would not be desirable for the remaining turners who would in turn be more likely to cease turning. The decline would thus tend to accelerate.

MANUFACTURERS AND SUPPLIERS

Woodturners are not held back by an absence of suitable and affordable equipment. Woodturning equipment does not rapidly become obsolete, and should not wear out quickly. Manufacturers' responses to the resulting plateauing of equipment sales have in some cases been to:

1. Lower specifications.
2. Proliferate gimmicks.
3. Promote signature lines, some of doubtful merit.

A lack of overt criticism has fostered these trends, and some manufacturers have undermined long-term growth by short-term strategies. For example, the purchase of unsuitable equipment contributes to turners giving up prematurely. Perhaps the answers to sluggish equipment sales include:

1. Shift the focus of woodturning promotion to non-woodworkers.
2. Manufacture and promote more responsibly within woodturning so that turners are encouraged to become more committed and more selective.

THE FUTURE OF WOOD

Although wood and woodturning are declining in importance in mass manufacturing, many of the shaping processes for the competing, alternative materials are unsuited to the home workshop. If home-based and small-scale manufacture are to continue, wood and woodturning should have a future, but it will not be a future based upon a conformance to the dictates of mass manufacture. Woodturners must promote wood as:

1. Warm and variable in contrast to the sterile, cold, nonporous manufactured materials.
2. Costly and increasingly rare in large sizes, knot-free straight-grained sections, and non-plantation species. Even found wood is expensive if the all the costs

associated with preparing it for turning are costed at appropriate rates.

3. Regionally specific.
4. Needing to be working in labour-intensive and skill-demanding ways.

But the promotion must be responsible. Wood doesn't like dishwashers.

Wood and woodturning can compete successfully with mass manufacturing as has already been shown by the wooden-bodied pen. It works no better than one with a plastic body, but a proportion of the public is prepared to pay a premium for the little extra pleasure it expects to receive from handling a natural material which has been hand worked, in some cases by an identifiable person. However, the number of wooden-bodied pens produced, although considerable, is minute when compared with the number produced in plastic.

AMATEUR TURNERS

Why not in the twenty-first century spend all your leisure time watching television, on the Internet, playing golf, and enjoying café society? Why not indeed? particularly if your secondary education did not include an introduction to handskills with wood and metal, and/or if you have had little contact with them in the years after school. One reason "why not" is if you have an urge to make "concrete" things. Even if that urge has been repressed, the seven factors listed on the preceding page should attract you to turning.

With the urge to make comes the human need to strive. One's striving appetites and capabilities may decline with age, but they remain strong within many, and produce a need for mental and physical involvement which woodturning can satisfy.

My contacts with amateur turners suggest that few turn as well as they could. There are two causes: poor teaching, and lack of commitment. I have discussed poor teaching on pages 6 and 7 of *The Fundamentals of Woodturning*. Your level of commitment is essentially your choice. While I fully support people's right to treat turning casually, the likely result is that they will not clear the hurdle of frustration due to poor technique, and are therefore denied access to the lush meadows beyond.

If you are an amateur the important thing is that you get lots from your turning; lots of fun, companionship, profit, challenge, and satisfaction. Many amateurs believe that the route to these maxima lies mainly through bowl, hollow, and art turnings. This view is reinforced by the media exposure of turners who specialize in these areas and the high prices they can supposedly demand.

THE TURNED OBJECT

A characteristic of the art/gallery/collectors market is that the umbrella of turning has become a convenience for works which even when excellent are not yet acceptable to those who control the fine arts and sculpture markets. The result

has been a dilution in the turning content of turnings for this market. Why? I suggest because turning is:

1. Regarded as tainted by its associations with craft and manufacturing by some practitioners and buyers.
2. Seen as too restrictive by some creative minds. While turning is restricted in its ability to shape, that restriction should be our challenge. Rather than accept the challenge, some turners duck it in favor of non-turning techniques which give a greater superficial impact. The success of this approach in the market when compared with a more purist one confirms that ignorance and a lack of connoisseurship is common among both practitioners and buyers.

This lack of connoisseurship is related to a lack of open criticism and debate, discouraged because the market is seen as fickle and vulnerable by some of those who seek to serve and exploit it. Those who see collecting turnings as a cheaper path to self-glory than, say, collecting impressionist paintings, must not be scared off. Values must not implode. The downside is that this lack of criticism has encouraged dross and gimmickry, and a continued ad nauseam replication of art turnings with proven market acceptance.

The lack of connoisseurship is also reflected in the poor image of functional turnings. They are often portrayed as being mere replicas of antique forms. Thus a poor functional design in a recent style is preferred to a superbly functional and aesthetically beautiful design in an antique style. Surely the only difference between a turning in a recent style and one in an antique style is that one style is older—both styles are still secondhand.

Works of art are supposedly superior to functional works because they manifest concept and expressiveness. There is not a clear difference in the quality and quantity of either factor between art and functional objects. Even if there were, it could be argued that the value system which places such a high premium on concept and expressiveness is as grossly distorted as that which rewards film and sport stars with incomes many times greater than those of nurses and postmen.

There is also an ignorance of the importance of restraints. In art turning there are essentially few design restraints. In contrast, functionality is a design restraint which demands design effort to satisfy it. That effort is largely ignored, and good functional design is undervalued in comparison with art design. Another factor which contributes to the stupid exclusion of functional turnings from the collectors market is that art and function are supposedly mutually exclusive.

Woodturners who do not have a vested interest in disparaging functional turnings have to be more effective in promoting them. It should not be too difficult to show that something you use does not have to be inferior in status and value to something which supposedly deserves to be in a display case. The bar is that conspicuous consumption on things which you don't need confirms wealth, and because of their unfortunate nexus, status. Thus art's overt rejection of function and high price are the attractions to status-seaking buyers.

13.1.3 SUMMARY

Woodturners apply ancient methods to an even more ancient and increasingly obsolete material. I believe that woodturning will surely fade away, even as a therapy, unless its products are sought in the twenty-first century. What is needed now is a four-pronged approach:

1. Better teaching to help amateurs over the technique hurdle so that they can then focus on what to turn and on design.
2. The encouragement of criticism and debate (alas, discouraged by the establishments of some national woodturners associations).
3. Continued innovation in art turning.
4. A new emphasis on functional domestic woodware. The new designs should not imitate those of modern mass-manufactured equivalents or merely replicate earlier or antique designs. There should not be a single mandatory style. The aim should be to design useful and delightful turned objects which accept the limitations and display the benefits of our chosen material for twenty-first-century consumers.

13.2 WHERE NEXT FOR THIS SERIES?

The three earlier books in this series have covered woodturning's basic and special techniques, this book has tackled design. If you have read and absorbed all four you should be well equipped to tackle any woodturning project.

Many woodturners seek detailed project advice, others seek a trigger which they can develop into a project. I hope to please both with my next woodturning book which will probably feature functional projects.

I am sometimes asked how many books there will be in this series. Only time will tell, but between six and eight.

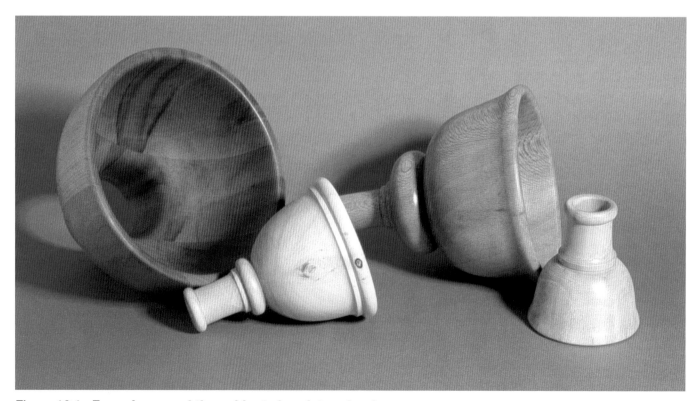

Figure 13.1 **Funnels, one of the subjects in a future book.**

INDEX